Zaner-Bloser

Resource Book
for the
Kindergarten
Teacher

Compiled by
VIRGINIA H. LUCAS, Ph.D.
Associate Professor of Education
Wittenberg University

Under the editorial direction of
WALTER B. BARBE, Ph.D.
Editor-in-Chief,
Highlights for Children

Zaner-Bloser, Inc., Columbus, Ohio

Designer

Thomas M. Wasylyk

Contributing Artists

Peter C. Hulse, Jeffrey E. George,

Timothy J. Gillner, Sidney Quinn,

Jerome Weisman, Anthony Rao

Editorial Assistance

Kevin O'Hara

©1980, Zaner-Bloser, Inc.
P.O. Box 16764
Columbus, Ohio 43216-6764

ACKNOWLEDGMENTS

Zaner-Bloser wishes especially to thank its parent company, Highlights for Children, Inc. for permission to reprint their material that appears in this book.

Grateful acknowledgment is also made to the following publishers and authors for permission to use their material:

POETRY

"Adventure Calls" from "Happy Moments" by Vera Ramsdell Hardman, copyrighted 1972 by Vera Ramsdell Hardman, published by Dorrance and Company.

"First Day of School" from *I Wonder How, I Wonder Why*, Abelard Schuman, New York, 1962. Reprinted by permission of Aileen Fisher.

"Furry Bear" from NOW WE ARE SIX by A.A. Milne. Copyright, 1927, by E.P. Dutton and Co., Inc. Copyright renewal, 1955 by A.A. Milne. Reprinted by permission of the publisher, E.P. Dutton.

"Galoshes" from *Stories to Begin On* by Rhoda W. Bacmeister. Copyright 1940 by E.P. Dutton & Co., Inc. Copyright renewal, ©, 1968 by Rhoda W. Bacmeister. Reprinted by permission of E.P. Dutton.

"I Meant to Do My Work Today" reprinted by permission of DODD, MEAD & COMPANY, INC. from THE LONELY DANCER by Richard LeGalienne. Copyright 1913 by Dodd, Mead & Company. Copyright renewed 1941 by Richard LeGalienne.

"Icicles" from THAT'S WHY, Thomas Nelson & Sons, New York, 1946. Reprinted by permission of Aileen Fisher.

"If I Were Otherwise" from The Christian Science Monitor. Reprinted by permission.

"Jonathan Bing Visits the King" (formerly called "Jonathan King") from JONATHAN BING by Beatrice Curtis Brown. Copyright 1936 by Oxford University Press; copyright renewed 1964 by Beatrice Curtis Brown. By permission of Lothrop, Lee & Shepard Co. (A Division of William Morrow & Co.)

"Merry-Go-Round" reprinted with permission of Macmillan Publishing Co., Inc. from *Poems* by Rachel Field. Copyright 1924, 1930 by Macmillan Publishing Co., Inc.

"Mice" from the book FIFTY-ONE NEW NURSERY RHYMES by Rose Fyleman. Copyright 1931, 1932 by Doubleday and Company, Inc. Used by permission of the publisher.

"My Legs and I" from IS SOMEWHERE ALWAYS FAR AWAY? by Leland B. Jacobs. Copyright © 1967 by Leland B. Jacobs. Reprinted by permission of Holt, Rinehart and Winston, Publishers.

"Roads" reprinted with permission of Macmillan Publishing Co., Inc. from *The Pointed People* by Rachel Field. Copyright 1924, 1930 by Macmillan Publishing Co., Inc.

"School is over . . ." from UNDER THE WINDOW by Kate Greenaway. Copyright © F. Warne & Co. Reprinted with permission of the Publisher.

(continued on **page xiv**)

Contents

INTRODUCTION

The purpose of the Zaner-Bloser Kindergarten Resource Book is to provide teachers with a large collection of productive activities for use in the classroom. These activities were selected to encourage the kindergarten child to think, to communicate, to participate, and to grow. The materials, which call for a broad spectrum of responses from the child, include worksheets, fingerplays, stories, poetry, reasoning exercises, music, crafts, and movement activities. Many of the projects were compiled from the renowned and award-winning magazine, *Highlights For Children.* In its over three decades of existence, *Highlights'* motto has always been "Fun with a Purpose." Such an attitude also reflects the goal of this book. Even the new material especially created for the Resource Book has attempted to communicate to the child the joy of learning, along with the actual substance of learning.

The book is designed to be used by the teacher as he or she sees fit. It is meant to supplement any program or activities already in use, supporting, bolstering or reinforcing the present method of teaching. No rigid structure or dictated, unchangeable time sequence limits the utilization of the material. Instead, the Resource Book allows the teacher's creativity and individual needs to dictate how it is used to fulfill personal teaching goals.

Yet the book is not without a framework. The materials included here have been organized to take advantage of the natural curiosity of kindergarten children. It is the author's belief that if children are to learn, curiosity and exploration must be encouraged. In satisfying that curiosity, children begin to attend, discriminate, and respond, thus developing the needed skills for their future learning.

Kindergarten teachers often differ in their view of the educational function of kindergarten. Some believe it exists basically as a period to develop the social orientation of the child, while others stress an academic role. Within this book, there are materials and activities reflecting both approaches. Social, linguistic and cognitive aspects of a child's growth are all extremely important and heavily intertwined. Many activities here touch more than one area of the child's needs in an attempt to prepare the child fully for future schooling.

It should be remembered that not all children learn in the same way. Each person receives and processes information through sensory channels, often favoring one channel over the others. The important sensory modalities in education are the visual, auditory and kinesthetic. There are activities for all three modes throughout this book, and when seeking to reinforce learning, the teacher should attempt to match a child to the activities best suited to him or her. For further guidance in assessing modality strengths and meeting them, see the article "Modality and the Kindergarten Child" by Dr. Michael Milone, on page xii of this book.

FORMAT

This book is divided into three parts.
Theme units
Seasonal units
Pre-academic skills units

The first part, theme units, contains seven sections, each concentrating on one aspect of the kindergarten child's universe. In each, a set of related concepts about a single topic is presented to focus the child's attention, increase his enthusiasm and expand his understanding. The theme units follow a logical progression beginning with "At School" and moving on to "All About Me," "How I Learn," "Exploring My World," "Moving About in My World," and "Work To Do," before ending with "Fun and Play." These units are identical to those in *Foundations for Formal Learning,* Zaner-Bloser's kindergarten pupil's book, although the activities within them are different. An optional teaching plan to aid in guiding the development of the concept in each unit is included at the beginning of the unit. This is the only section of the book containing teaching plans.

The four seasonal units constitute the second part of the Resource Book: fall, winter, spring and summer. Each one contains a variety of activities and crafts to broaden and bolster the child's concept of that season. The activities are grouped by similarity in the type of material. Also contained within each of these units is material relating to the major holidays that occur during that season, such as Halloween and Valentine's Day.

The last part of the Resource Book is devoted to pre-academic readiness skills—the body of fundamental skills and accomplishments necessary for a pupil to proceed successfully with academic instruction in the areas of reading, writing and arithmetic. These skills prepare the child to handle what will come when formal learning begins. In this book, the skills are grouped into six units:

Matching and Classifying

Directionality and Relationships

Shapes and Strokes

Colors

Numbers

Letters

Within all the units of this book, there are four distinct types of pages. One type comprises black-line masters for the teacher to duplicate, creating worksheets for the pupils.

Examples of such pages are shown here.

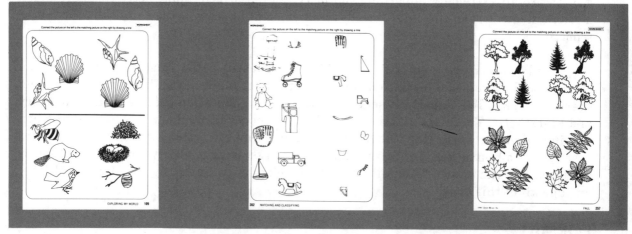

The pages with horizontal midlines can be cut in half to make two worksheets. Each black-line master page is marked with a label to indicate that it is for duplication. Retain these pages for future use after they have been removed from the book.

Another type of page has been designed for the teacher to use with the class by showing it to the children.

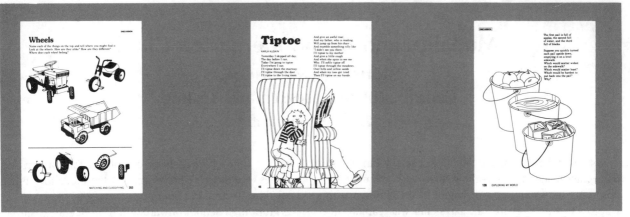

These pages are primarily for the development of language and ideas and have large illustrations. Such activities as pictures depicting size relationships, poems with relevant pictures, and likeness and difference comparisons will be found on these pages. They are marked with labels to show that teacher guidance is required for their presentation.

A third type of page contains material for the teacher to share by reading to the class.

Some of these pages consist of stories and poems for listening by the children, while others are devoted to thinking and reasoning activities.

The fourth type of page contains instructions for the teacher's use, though it may be shared with the class.

Rules for games and activities are included here, as are instructions for crafts and music. It should be noted that not all the crafts can be made by kindergarten children. Some are for the teacher's use as classroom decorations or illustrations.

In addition to the units, this book also contains a Check List of Kindergarten Skills on page xv to assist in evaluating pupil progress throughout the term. A professional bibliography and a story bibliography are also included, on pages 521 and 522.

Modality and the Kindergarten Child

MICHAEL N. MILONE, JR.
Coordinator of Research and Testing
Zaner-Bloser, Inc.

Just after the turn of the twentieth century, an Italian physician made a far-reaching discovery. Simply by observing the spontaneous behavior of the children with whom she was working, the physician was gaining insight as to how they learned best. Maria Montessori used these insights to develop a system that revolutionized the education of young children.

Maria Montessori recognized two things: children have obvious preferences or strengths when it comes to how they learn; and if you can capitalize upon these preferences and strengths, learning ceases being a chore and becomes an exciting and wondrous adventure.

Among the most important preferences and strengths a child exhibits are those that relate to perception. Educators refer to the perceptual channels as the modalities. A modality strength describes the channels that are most efficient. A child may have a strength in a single channel, or a combination of two or more channels may be the most efficient. When the latter is the case, a mixed modality strength is evident.

The educationally relevant modalities are vision, audition, and kinesthesia. It is through these three channels that the vast majority of information is received, particularly that contributing to educational success.

It is not surprising to learn that the modality characteristics of kindergarten children as a group differ from those of younger and older children. Like many other human attributes, modality characteristics change with age.

The newborn child's strongest modality is the kinesthetic. During the time the child was growing in the mother's womb, movement, vibrations, and the changes in the mother's body were being sensed by the unborn child. The kinesthetic modality, therefore, had been stimulated, whereas vision and audition remained unused.

From birth onward, visual and particularly auditory cues dominate the child's world. Infants interact with the significant others in their lives primarily through the auditory mode. Preschool children relate with both peers, older children, and adults auditorily. Consequently, the auditory modality of kindergarten children is often the strongest, simply because they have had more practice and reinforcement in the aural/oral mode.

After kindergarten, auditory interaction plays a less important part in the child's life, especially at school. When formal reading and writing activities occupy the majority of the school day, it is no wonder that the visual and kinesthetic modalities become more important.

By the time children have completed the intermediate grades, the order of precedence of the modalities is visual, kinesthetic, and auditory.

From high school onward, audition begins to surpass kinesthesia. Vision remains the most important modality for most adults, with audition running a strong second.

We have noted that the kindergarten child's modalities can be ordered in the following way: audition, vision, and kinesthesia. A second feature is also characteristic of the kindergarten child's modalities: they are not so well integrated as those of older children and adults.

Modality integration describes the process whereby information from two or more modalities is interpreted simultaneously. For example, the printed word *cat* comprises a visual image (the letters themselves or the image of a cat), an auditory image (the sound of the word or the purr of a cat), and a kinesthetic image (writing the word or petting a cat). Most adults would have no difficulty generating all three images when the single visual stimulus *cat* is presented. Through their experiences and education, adults have learned to integrate their modalities.

Kindergarten children have not had the education or experience of older children or adults, so their modalities are more discrete. It is relatively difficult for the kindergarten child to transfer information from one perceptual channel to another.

The predominance of audition and the lack of modality integration are attributes of kindergarten children in general. Without assessment or observation, however, statements can not be made about the modality characteristics of an individual pupil. An introductory discussion of modality assessment and other aspects of modality-based instruction can be found in the January, 1980 issue of *Instructor* magazine.

In any consideration of kindergarten children, it is always advisable to recall that because chronological age varies so greatly within this group, characteristics that are associated with chronological age can also vary greatly. In the same kindergarten, it is not uncommon for two children to have been born ten months apart. This is the equivalent of over one-sixth of the child's life span to that point. Thus, discrepancies as great as one-sixth of expected development may be attributable solely to differences in chronological age.

With this in mind, it is necessary to caution the kindergarten teacher that not all children in a class will exhibit the same modality characteristics. Some may manifest accelerated development, and be more visual or have mixed modality strengths. Others may be lagging slightly, and be more kinesthetic. In any case, there is no need for alarm. Children in a class may vary inexplicably simply because of individual differences.

As is the case with many other qualities, the determinants of an individual child's modality strengths are not clear-cut. There is evidence to suggest that some aspects of modality are inherited and have a physiological basis. Equally persuasive evidence implies that other aspects are learned, sometimes as early as the first few months of life. Perhaps the best path to choose in describing the development of modality strengths is to say that nature and nurture interact to the same extent in forming this characteristic.

Assume now that your kindergarten class is typical. Your pupils as a whole favor the auditory modality, and their modalities are relatively distinct. Assume further that through observation or assessment, you have identified the modality strengths of each pupil in your class. What next?

For starters, do not forget your own modality strength. It appears that we teach not as we were taught, but how we learn best. Your teaching style will reflect your own modality strength. This is not a shortcoming to be remedied, but a fact of educational life. Because you are most familiar and comfortable with your own modality style, when your teaching is consistent with this style, it is probably most effective. And, it is always good advice not to tamper with success.

Conduct your initial instruction in the way in which you are most comfortable. If you notice one or more children are having difficulty with a lesson, try another approach with these children. This is called the *point of intervention*. At this point, you provide supplemental instruction, either individually or in small groups, that is consistent with the modality strengths of the children involved. Modality specific instruction at the point of intervention is a second aspect of modality based instruction.

The following example will illustrate these points. Ms. Smith, a kindergarten teacher for seven years, has known for some time that she is a very visual teacher. Her walls are covered with posters, charts, and examples of her pupils' work. She reads to her class using books with many pictures, and spends as much time showing the pictures to her class and eliciting responses as she does reading the text. Her principal has joked with her about being the only teacher in the county who can teach a phonics lesson visually.

When Ms. Smith teaches cardinal association (matching sets of objects with the corresponding numeral), she relies heavily upon the chalkboard, large numerals cut from construction paper, and the flannel board. She presents a great lesson, but notices that several pupils seem to be unsure of themselves about the concept. After she concludes the group lesson, she allows the majority of the class to go to their next work stations. She then takes the four children aside who failed to grasp the lesson. She knows that Sally, John, and Peter are very auditory, and that Marsha is kinesthetic. Marsha, by the way, has the shortest pencil in the class. She presses quite hard with it, and is always up and down sharpening it. Kinesthetic children just seem to have a way of making the school day conform to their strength.

Teaching Marsha to match the numeral *3* with three objects is easy. Ms. Smith asks her to walk to the front of the room and pick up the big red number, and on the way back, to pick up an eraser, the book on her desk, and the basketball. Marsha has a terrible time carrying all of those things, but finally succeeds, and is very proud of herself. Ms. Smith congratulates her on being able to carry the numeral *3* and three things. You can almost see the light come on in Marsha's head . . . the numeral *3* and three objects. She turns to Sally, John, and Peter and says, "There are three of you! And you are sitting in three chairs." Ms. Smith then sends Marsha to the work station that is Marsha's favorite, pegboard letters.

Sally, John and Peter require a different approach. Ms. Smith explains that they are going to play a special kind of "Simon Says." They will follow her commands only when she says them three times. The game begins, and before long, the group can discriminate three sounds very easily.

Ms. Smith allows the three to go to their work stations. She knows that the job is not finished for Marsha, John, Sally, and Peter. Even though they have learned cardinal correspondence in their preferred modality, they still must learn to generalize the skill to other modalities. She is already planning the next lessons to do just that.

Kindergarten teachers face two major issues relating to the modality strengths of their pupils: teaching relevant skills through the strongest modality, and preparing the child for the coming years. The latter task is based on the expected shift toward the visual and the integration of the modalities.

Although the deficit-strength issue remains open, many teachers find themselves favoring the concept of capitalizing upon pupils' strengths. This practice has great logical appeal, and brings about a higher rate of skill acquisition than does remediating weaknesses.

The most important outcome of the kindergarten year should be the attainment of the skills necessary for a child to succeed in the later grades. Teaching to strengths, particularly modality strengths, is the best way to bring about this outcome. Once relevant skills have been acquired, the secondary purpose of strengthening areas of deficit can be considered.

The second issue, preparing the child for the modality shifts that are a consequence of maturation, is not so readily resolved. The issue has spawned two major schools of thought: a *laissez-faire* approach, and active intervention.

The *laissez-faire* approach is based on the belief that naturally occurring events will promote appropriate growth and development. This natural unfolding occurs for some children under some circumstances to be sure, but it is not universal. The environments in which children are raised must be presumed to be ideal if natural development is to take its course. Since few children are raised in an ideal environment, the *laissez-faire* approach is of only limited utility.

We advocate an active intervention strategy when it comes to the development of modality strengths in kindergarten children. The first consideration is, of course, to teach necessary pre-academic skills through the most effective means. Once this has been accomplished, it is important to structure the kindergarten environment so that kinesthetic and visual skills have a chance to emerge, and modality integration is enhanced.

This recommendation should not be misinterpreted. We are not suggesting that all children be forced into a single model of development. No useful purpose would be served by this. Instead, try to provide your pupils with the opportunity to acquire and refine visual and kinesthetic skills to the same degree as the non-school environment promotes auditory development. In addition, make it clear to your pupils that objects and events often comprise multiple sensations.

Reading, the most critical adademic skill, is a process that can not be learned unless modality integration is present. Fostering modality integration in kindergarten children through motivating and enjoyable activities is an important step in learning to read. It is also a pre-reading skill that is highly appropriate for the kindergarten.

The modality notion has been well received by kindergarten teachers. Parents have also responded favorably to it, for they find the concepts of identifying strengths and capitalizing upon them very understandable. Modality, then, is a credible construct.

To the lay audience with whom the kindergarten teacher must interact, credibility is not to be minimized. Parents of young children have great expectations about the educational process, and want to believe in its potential. An approach so comprehensible as modality based instruction fosters credibility, bringing about greater cooperation from parents. Such cooperation increases the probability that the kindergarten experience will be successful for the young child.

Applying the principles of modality based instruction in the kindergarten is to be strongly encouraged. It is an effective method, for it results in the skill attainment that is the primary goal of kindergarten. And, it does so in a way that is understandable to both teachers and parents. When modality strengths are an important consideration in the development of kindergarten curricula, the young child is the greatest beneficiary.

Zaner-Bloser KINDERGARTEN CHECK LISTS

FOUNDATION SKILLS

I. Pre-Reading

A. Matching
1. Matches familiar objects
2. Matches basic colors: red, yellow, blue, green, orange, purple, black, brown
3. Matches basic shapes: square, circle, triangle, rectangle
4. Matches objects by other features: taste, size, smell, texture, etc.

B. Labeling
1. Names familiar objects
2. Names basic colors
3. Names basic shapes

C. Classification
1. Classifies objects by color
2. Classifies objects by shape
3. Classifies objects by other characteristics

D. Sequencing
1. Sequences objects by size
2. Sequences four pictures to make a story

E. Symbolic ability
1. Recognizes own name in print
2. Names upper-case letters
3. Names lower-case letters
4. Matches upper-case and lower-case letters
5. Associates printed words with objects
6. Groups spoken words by final sounds
7. Groups spoken words by initial sounds
8. Recognizes final sounds in spoken words
9. Recognizes initial sounds in spoken words
10. Associates letters with their most frequent sounds

F. Closure
1. Completes a picture in which a part is missing
2. Completes a spoken sentence in which a familiar word is missing

G. Comprehension
1. Follows directions involving spatial relationship words: under, over, in, out, near, far, up, down, left, right, front, back, top, bottom, above, below, inside, outside, beginning, end, on, off, before, after
2. Understands opposites: (see words above)
3. Recalls main idea and main characters from a short story or a picture
4. Recalls details from a short story or picture
5. Identifies cause and effect relationship in stories, events, or pictures
6. Predicts outcomes in stories, events, or pictures
7. Draws inferences from stories, events, or pictures
8. Distinguishes reality from fantasy
9. Creates stories based on a described or pictured situation

II. Pre-Writing

A. Distinguishes top from bottom
B. Follows top-to-bottom progression
C. Distinguishes left from right
D. Follows left-to-right progression
E. Recognizes basic shapes in an object or picture
F. Names basic writing strokes: top-to-bottom, left-to-right, slant left, slant right, backward circle, forward circle
G. Recognizes basic writing strokes in an object or picture
H. Traces and writes basic strokes
I. Traces upper and lower-case letters and numerals 0-10
J. Writes name beginning with inital upper-case letter

III. Pre-Arithmetic

A. Matching
1. Matches sets containing same number of objects (*1-10*)
2. Matches like coins: penny, nickel, dime, quarter

B. Identification
1. Identifies larger of two groups containing unequal numbers of objects (*1-10*)
2. Associates numeral with corresponding group of objects (*1-10*)
3. Associates numeral *0* with an empty set
4. Names coins: penny, nickel, dime, quarter

C. Sequencing
1. Counts from *1* to *10*
2. Sequences numerals *1* to *10*
3. Sequences objects using: first, last, next, middle
4. Sequences objects using ordinal numbers
5. Follows numbered directions to complete a task

COMPANION SKILLS

I. Task Orientation

A. Attention span is adequate for age appropriate assigned tasks
B. Follows directions
C. Makes decisions
D. Marks responses
E. Works independently
F. Works cooperatively
G. Interacts appropriately with peers and adults
H. Asks help of an adult when appropriate

II. Affect

A. Expression
1. Interprets feelings given pictures or facial expressions
2. Expresses emotions appropriately
3. Expresses self spontaneously
4. Shares personal experiences

B. Attitudes
1. Respects others
2. Has a positive attitude toward self
3. Has a positive attitude toward school and learning

III. General Readiness

A. Perceptual and motor skills
1. Gross and fine motor skills are adequate for age appropriate tasks
2. Recognizes familiar textures, tastes, etc.
3. Locates sounds
4. Follows moving stimuli
5. Recognizes that objects and events have characteristics in more than one modality

B. Self Awareness
1. Identifies body parts: head, arms, hands, legs, ears, nose, mouth, feet, eyes, fingers, toes
2. Matches body parts with their function

C. Memory
1. Long and short term memory are adequate for age appropriate assigned tasks
2. Gives name and address upon request

D. Cognition
1. Identifies the disparity in a set in which only one element is different: B B A B
2. Progresses from concrete to abstract
3. Understands part to whole relationship
4. Seeks new information
5. Grasps fundamentals of conservation of mass and number

E. Time concepts
1. Understands morning, afternoon, day, night
2. Understands the seasons and their weather
3. Associates time with events: in the morning, you go to school

F. Language
1. Auditory
   a. Is interested in spoken language
   b. Enjoys being read to
   c. Reproduces pronounced familiar words
   d. Communicates using sentences
   e. Recognizes minimal differences in spoken words
   f. Differentiates between spoken words on the basis of length
   g. Reproduces a spoken sentence consisting of five familiar words
   h. Retells a story in own words
2. Visual
   a. Is interested in written language
   b. Knows that the purpose of written language is to communicate
   c. Recognizes word boundaries
   d. Paces dictation to the writing speed of the person recording
   e. Has book awareness skills
      1. Distinguishes top of book from bottom
      2. Distinguishes front of book from back
      3. Holds book with right side up and cover facing front
      4. Distinguishes among pictures, letters, numerals, and words

Section 1

Themes

At School

Introduction

Kindergarten is the beginning of school for most children. Such beginnings, though they can be quite stimulating for a child, can, nevertheless, fill the child with anxiety. Even if the child has attended pre-school programs, he or she is still likely to consider kindergarten as his or her first "real" school. For most children, school is identified directly with the place that houses the elementary grades, and a child sees attending that place as a major step in his or her life. Thus, this first unit seeks to assuage the child's anxiety at starting school and to make him or her feel comfortable in his or her new world.

To do so, the emphasis throughout is placed upon the inherent likenesses the children possess, their sharing of this school, this classroom, this teacher. It is sought to expand the child's view of himself or herself from one of isolation to one of involvement in a larger community. This transition is accomplished by exposing the child to the conception of school as a place filled with new and exciting ideas and skills.

It is essential that children develop positive concepts of school early in life. The fun and play involved, the joy of learning, the pleasure of new friends, all make school rewarding for children while, in turn, making them feel important for being part of it. They will also discover the necessity of working together and how this requires order, rules, cooperation, caring.

Though a child should continue to see his or her position in school as central, by acquainting himself or herself with the roles of others in the school community, such as the principal, custodian and teacher's aides, he or she can develop an awareness of the interdependence of many people in making a school operate successfully. Often, the sheer size and complex layout of the school premises appear overwhelming and bewildering to a kindergarten child. But clarifying the relationship of school personnel with their corresponding areas of the school building helps to reduce this impression to a manageable size for the child and, consequently, remove some of the apprehension from his or her school beginning.

A teacher's goal is to engross the child from the start in the alive and exciting world of school and the many benefits of learning. Then, the positive attitudes formed today will echo through the classroom performance of the future.

Concepts To Be Taught

I   All the children in the kindergarten class have likenesses.

II Children can learn many things in school.

III Children can share ideas, materials, toys and a teacher.

IV Children will be safer in school when they follow the rules.

V   Children have many new friends at school.

VI The school building is made up of many areas.

Information for Teaching Concepts

I. All children in the kindergarten class have likenesses.

Introduce the unit by saying, "I am   (Ms. Hill) . I teach kindergarten. In my kindergarten class there are (twenty-five)   children. They are all alike. Can you guess how they are all alike?" Encourage various responses. Explain that they are alike because they each go to   (Monroe)   School, they are in kindergarten, and they are in   (Ms. Hill's)   class. Explain that many children are going to kindergartens in many different places. Have the children say, "I am   (John) . I go to kindergarten at   (Monroe)   School."

Demonstrate various activities the children will be sharing in kindergarten and show the locations where they will engage in those activities.

Examples are:

| painting | singing | movement exercises | playing |
| listening | drawing | modeling clay | reading |

Have a bag containing a paint brush, a block, a record, crayons, a toy, clay and a book. Pull out one object at a time and ask the children to tell you what can be done with the object and where it would be found in the classroom.

II. Children can learn many things in school.

Tell the children you have something very interesting to show them. They are to listen and watch carefully so they will learn something new. Recite and demonstrate the finger play, "Little Schoolhouse", page 16. Next, have the children say it as you again demonstrate the movements. Then, step-by-step show the children how to do the finger play themselves.

Ask the children what they have learned so far in school. Examples are:

name of the school	objects in the classroom
locations of special areas	activities they will do
teacher's name	a new finger play
friend's name	

Tell the children there are so many additional things to discover. Ask them how they might learn more about the world. Encourage creative thinking and be willing to wait for the children to respond. Explain some of the things they will be discovering as they attend kindergarten. Examples are:

arts and crafts	colors	songs	letters
poems	numbers	games	words

Talk about the topics that they will be learning more about during the school year. Examples are:

animals	homes	their senses	transportation

III. Children can share ideas, materials, toys and a teacher.

Read the story, "No Pets Allowed", page 10. Ask the children the following questions:
What was Cory's pet?   How did Cory share?   Did each child have a tree?

Discuss how Cory changed from sad to happy and how sharing makes us feel good while we also make others happy. Ask what things the children share in their classroom. If necessary, point out that they share toys, paints, books, plants, light, smiles and *a teacher*.

Explain that when you share you must be concerned that others get equal parts of time, attention, experiences and participation. Ask the group to think about how a classroom teacher can give equal time and attention to all the children in a class. Point out the importance of taking turns, listening in a group, and being responsible to complete jobs and put away supplies. These actions provide the time for the teacher to attend to all the children.

Role-play situations to demonstrate sharing. Examples are:
1) One child is listening to a record and another child would like to listen also.
2) The blocks are in the middle of the floor and Kelly is building a barn. Jamie would also like to play with the blocks.
3) There is only one rope, but three children who want to jump rope.
4) Five children have important stories to tell about their pets.

IV. Children will be safer in school when they follow the rules.

Discuss with the class the school safety patrol. Ask the students to think about the words *safety patrol*. What does *safety* mean? (freedom from dangers, risk or harm) What does *patrol* mean? (people who move about to keep an area secure and free from dangers) Now ask the children to describe the safety patrol. Ask where they find the safety patrol. Ask if there are areas in or around the school where danger could occur, but where there is no safety patrol. Examples are: classroom, hallways, cafeteria, playground, restrooms.

Tell the children that school should be a safe place, so it is important that they think about how to keep it safe. Discuss the need for order and safety rules in a school. More specifically, talk about safety rules to be used in this classroom. Establish only a few rules and keep them brief. Examples are:

Walk while in the classroom.	Keep hands to self.	Clean up after an activity.

Repeat this type of discussion on other days, designing and role-playing rules for:

playground safety	drinking fountain/restroom safety
fire drill	safety in opening doors

V. Children have many new friends at school.

Read, "Timothy Turtle Is On Time", page 13, to the children. After the story ask the children:

> What was Timothy's problem?
> Why was Timothy late?
> Did Timothy have friends?
> How do you know he had friends?
> What is a friend?

Ask the children to tell how they are a friend to someone. Emphasize that we enjoy being with our friends. Encourage children to think about why having a friend is so much fun.

Build a chart showing the best ways to have friends. Use pictures to emphasize the points. Examples are:

share time and toys	be polite
smile	follow the rules

VI. The school building is made up of many areas.

Draw a simple map of the school and color it by areas. Cut the map apart by colors. Place puzzle parts in an envelope and write label cards for the areas.

Tell the children that you have ___(Monroe)___ school in this envelope (hold up the puzzle envelope). "Let me show you our school." On a large sheet of paper, paste the puzzle pieces and tell the children the name of each piece (i.e. gymnasium, classrooms, office, library). Also, paste labels next to each area and repeat the name for the class. Use this map to have children identify:

1) how they come to their classroom.
2) where each area is located.
3) how to go to the principal's office.
4) where specific school workers are found.

Visit various areas of the school with the class. Upon returning to the classroom, review the details of *who, what,* and *where* as related to the children's outing. Discuss why a school would need so many areas. Focus on the types of activities that occur in each area.

Encourage the children to understand that school is both a building and people. The structure itself has a purpose (a place for instruction), but without children, who come there to learn, there would be no school. Emphasize the importance of coming to school, as well as the importance of having a building where they can be with friends, working and playing together.

Thinking and Reasoning

Ask your children these questions:

Do boys and girls go to school in the evening or in the morning?

Tell how you would feel if you had just entered a school where all the children in your classroom spoke a language you could not speak or understand.

Suppose the electricity went off while you were at school. What problems would this cause?

Willard is fourteen and his little brother is six. If they walk to school together which boy will take more steps on the way?

How many days each week do you go to school?

Why do most schools have a vision test?

Would you like to be in the same classroom as the sixth graders? Why?

Do children bring their own desks to school?

Can you write and draw with spoons?

What would you do if your teacher didn't come to school one day?

Can you learn things when you are not in school?

Are there more children in your family, or in your class at school?

Why is it not a good idea to bring a frog to school?

How do you suppose blind children learn to read?

Would you like to go to school in the summer?

Are there any beds in your classroom?

Do dogs go to school? Why?

Which are there more of in your classroom, teachers or children?

Name some of the things you learned to do while you were in school.

Why is it important to be quiet while your teacher is talking?

Do you go to school for a full day or a half day?

Did you learn to talk and walk at school? Where did you learn to do these things? What else can you learn at home?

Why do you sometimes stay home from school on a very snowy day?

How many things are you able to draw with?

Why do we sometimes use book covers?

Why do pencils have erasers?

When your teacher reads a story to the class, do you read with her, or do you listen?

Sarah walks to school on nice days. One day she looked out of the classroom window and said, "My father will pick me up in the car today." How did she know this?

If four children all want to play with blocks at the same time, how might they do this? Are you older or younger than your teacher? Are you bigger or smaller?

Do you bring your lunch to school?

Which do you do first in the morning, eat breakfast or go to school?

Why is it important to get to school on time?

Is your mother in your class at school?

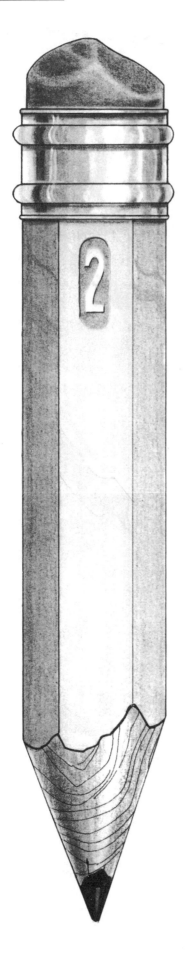

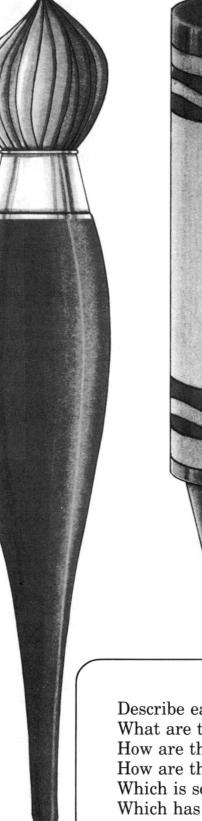

Describe each of these.
What are they used for?
How are they alike?
How are they different?
Which is softest?
Which has to be sharpened?

Connect the picture on the left to the matching picture on the right by drawing a line.

Can you find the hidden dragonfly, rooster, heron, teddy bear, duck's head, and whale in this picture?

Table or Child?

Which has the most legs?
Which has the fewest?
How are the table legs different from the child's legs?
Which legs will grow longer?
Do table legs ever fold?
What other things have legs?

No Pets Allowed

EILEEN BAILEY

On Cory's first day in school his teacher, Mrs. Snow, asked the children to tell about their homes.

Patty, with the pink dress, raised her hand. "My house is green with white shutters," she said proudly. "I live there with Mom and Dad and Gran. And I have a cat named Marmalade who sleeps behind the kitchen stove."

Richard, with the red hair, called out, "I live in a house by the river with my father and sister and a dog named Daisy."

When it was Cory's turn, he was sad for the first time that day. "I don't live in a house," he said. "I live in an apartment with my mom and dad. But no pets are allowed."

"What is a pet?" someone asked.

Mrs. Snow smiled and said, "A pet is something that you love and take care of."

Patty asked, "Why aren't pets allowed in your apartment, Cory?"

"I don't know," said Cory.

Mrs. Snow explained to the class that apartments are for people, not for pets, because there are no backyards for dogs or cats to play in.

"No pets allowed," the children said. And they all sighed at once. "Poor Cory!"

Cory was very sad. He wanted a pet more than anything else in the world.

"I want something to love and take care of, too," Cory said to his mom after school that day.

Mom smiled. The next day, when she came home from work, she brought something for Cory. It was tiny and green and growing in a pot. "A baby tree," Mom said. "A tree is something to love and to take care of."

Cory hugged his mom. "Does that mean a tree is a pet?" he asked.

Mom smiled again. "A tree is anything you want it to be," she said.

Cory was happy now. At last he had something he could love and take care of. At last he had a pet. He named his tree Ralph and kept him on the windowsill, where it was sunny and warm. Every day after school, Cory would run home and give Ralph a drink of water. And in return, Ralph would fill Cory's room with the wonderful smell of green things.

After a while, Ralph began to grow. First he had five leaves, and then one day Cory counted six. Soon Ralph had sprouted seven, eight, nine leaves in all. Cory was very proud. He was taking good care of his pet.

Ralph grew so big that one day Cory's dad said, "I think you will have to plant him in the ground now."

Cory thought for a long time about where he could plant Ralph. Then finally he decided. School was the place for his pet.

There was a rule that no dogs and cats were allowed in school, but Cory didn't think Mrs. Snow would mind about Ralph. There was a beautiful spot of ground by the playground fence that would be just right for Ralph.

"It's the most beautiful tree I have ever seen," said Mrs. Snow, when Cory brought Ralph to school. "I can see that you have loved and taken good care of him."

She dug a deep hole in the ground by the fence and everyone watched while Cory planted his tree in it. He knew Ralph would be happy there, and Cory would still be able to see him every day.

Now Cory's tree was the only pet allowed at school. And everyone agreed it was a very special pet.

Billy Rainbow's Special Friend

BONNIE HIGHSMITH

Billy Rainbow skipped happily across the prairie toward the little schoolhouse. As he ran, he whistled a merry tune.

Yesterday had been his first day at school, and he had found many new friends. But one friend was better than all the others. One was very special.

That was why he was hurrying so. He could hardly wait to see his special friend again.

"Stop, Billy Rainbow," called Granny Mae from the door of her hogan. "Stop and have some hot corn bread."

"No, thank you, Granny. Not this morning," Billy answered. "I'm on my way to school to see my special friend."

His sneakers kicked up dust as he raced on.

When he reached the sheep pen, Little Luke was sitting on the top rail. Little Luke was not old enough to go to school.

"Stop, Billy Rainbow," he called. "Stop and see my new lamb. Father said I could have it for my very own."

Billy smiled and shouted, "No, thank you, Little Luke. I can't stop now. I must hurry to school to see my special friend."

He ran faster and faster, his black hair waving in the wind.

On the long front porch of the leather shop stood Mr. Perkins.

"Stop, Billy Rainbow," he called. "Stop and see the fine new saddles that just arrived."

"No, thank you, Mr. Perkins. Some other time," Billy hollered. "I am rushing to school to see my special friend."

On he flew. Along the river bank. Through the willow grove. Over the sand dunes.

"I'm going to see my special friend. I'm going to see my special friend," he sang merrily.

At last Billy reached the school. The teacher and the other children were on the playground.

"Good morning, Billy Rainbow," they called. "Come and play with us."

"In a little while," cried Billy. "First I must see my special friend."

He darted past the children and into the schoolhouse. He opened his desk and took out—a shiny new book.

"Good morning, my special friend," said Billy Rainbow.

No Dogs at School

LOTTIE TRESNER NORTON

Wally walked along the path to school, his dog following right behind.

"Here, Prize," Wally said. "We have to go to school today. Mother says so. She says when a boy gets to be six, then he's big enough to go to school. So come on. I've been six for a while now, and this is the first day of school."

Prize barked and wagged his tail. You'd think he knew what Wally was saying. Wally had won him as a prize when he was just a tiny puppy, so he had named him Prize. And since that day they had always been together.

Wally saw many boys and girls going into the schoolhouse. But he didn't see any dogs at all.

"Come on, Prize," he said. "Let's go in and see what we have to do."

"Oh," someone said. "You can't bring your dog to school!"

Wally looked at the bigger boy. "Why can't I?" he asked.

"They don't allow dogs at school. School is just for children."

Wally couldn't believe his ears. "Wait here," he said to Prize as he walked up to the teacher's desk.

"Teacher," he said, "will you please tell me if dogs are allowed at school? If they aren't, I'm afraid I can't come."

The teacher looked up from her papers and smiled at him.

"You are Walter Evans, aren't you?" she said. "No. Walter, I'm afraid dogs aren't allowed in the schoolroom, but your dog may wait outside for you."

"But Prize always stays with me. I guess I'll have to go back home then. And I'm Wally, not Walter, please."

"Well, Wally, let me see this fine dog of yours." The teacher went to the door with Wally.

"He isn't a real fine dog, but he's nice. And he wants to be with me."

"I think he's a nice dog, too, Wally. And you're a fine boy, too. Your dog is proud to have you as his owner, don't you think?"

"I think he likes me."

"Do you think he'd be proud of a big boy who couldn't read or write?"

"No, I guess not."

"How can you learn if you don't come to school?"

Wally thought and thought. Then he knelt down beside Prize. "Prize, you're going to have to get along by yourself while I learn some things. You be here when I get out of school, and we'll have fun." Then he got up and looked at the teacher. "All right, show me how to read and write, please," he said to her.

"It's going to take a long time, Wally."

"Well, I want to be a boy Prize can be proud of. He'll wait for me. It's all right if it takes a while."

The teacher smiled and showed him where to sit. Wally looked around at all the boys and girls. After school he called Prize, and they started home.

"You know, Prize," he said, "I'm going to like it at school. Of course, I'll miss you, but I think it will be fun to get to know all those boys and girls and learn with them."

Timothy Turtle Is on Time

WILMA K. RICH

"Timothy Turtle, you're tardy," scolded Mrs. Owl.

Timothy looked up at Mrs. Owl with big, sad eyes. "What does that mean, Mrs. Owl?"

"It means you're late—fifteen minutes late for school this morning. Why?"

"I just can't seem to get here on time. I don't know why." Timothy spoke slowly. "I get up early and I really do try to hurry."

The rest of the students in Mrs. Owl's Forest School all nodded.

"That's right, Mrs. Owl," Barnaby Bear rumbled. "Timothy starts to school before I do."

Suzanna Snake hissed softly, "Mrs. Owl, I think Timothy has too far to travel. He can't move very fast, you know."

Mrs. Owl spoke sternly. "Timothy will have to get here on time, or I'll have to send a note to his mother."

After school the animals met under the big beech tree to talk.

"What can we do to help Timothy?" Sally Squirrel chattered.

"There must be some way we can help him," Ronald Rabbit said.

"Let's all put on our thinking caps," Freddy Fox suggested, waving his beautiful, bushy tail back and forth.

For a while it was very quiet under the beech tree. Then Barnaby Bear stood up on his hind legs and waved his front paws.

"I know what we can do. Everybody meet in front of Timothy's house tomorrow morning early!"

"What are we going to do, Barnaby?" Suzanna Snake hissed.

But Barnaby wouldn't tell. He just smiled and looked mysterious.

Next morning the students met in front of Timothy Turtle's house. Soon Barnaby Bear came walking down the forest trail, pulling a wagon behind him. At least, once upon a time it had been a wagon. Almost all the paint was worn off and there were no sides. But there were four wheels and a long handle.

"Where did you find it, Barnaby?" Freddy Fox asked, shaking his head.

"Down by Troll Creek," Barnaby replied. "Someone must have thrown it away."

Everybody helped to push Timothy up onto the wagon. It was just the right size.

"I'm biggest. I'll pull," Barnaby said.

"I'll push," added Freddy Fox.

"I'll stay on this side of the wagon to see that Timothy doesn't slide off," said Sally Squirrel.

Ronald Rabbit hopped over to take his place on the other side of the wagon.

Suzanna Snake hissed, "I'll come along behind, to be sure everything is all right."

With everybody helping, they reached the Forest School in no time.

"You're on time, Timothy Turtle," hooted Mrs. Owl, and she smiled.

All of her students smiled. And Timothy Turtle said proudly, "Mrs. Owl, I'm the luckiest turtle in the world. I have good friends."

First Day of School

AILEEN FISHER

I wonder
if my drawing
will be as good as theirs.

I wonder
if they'll like me
or just be full of stares.

I wonder
if my teacher
will look like Mom or Gram.

I wonder
if my puppy
will wonder
where I am.

Poems

Look in a Book

IVY O. EASTWICK

Look
in a book
and you will see
words
and magic
and mystery.

Look
in a book
and you will find
sense
and nonsense
of every kind.

Look
in a book
and you will know
all
the things
that can help you grow.

A Great Day

ALICE W. NORTON

Clatter, clatter, down the street
Comes the sound of children's feet,
Each one with a book and rule
Heading merrily to school.

Hello Judy! Hello Clair!
Merry greetings fill the air,
Hello Victor! Hello Jane!
Aren't you glad we're back again?

Everybody's on the run,
Everybody's having fun,
What's the use of book and rule
On the first day back to school?

The Library

BARBARA A. HUFF

It looks like any building
When you pass it on the street,
Made of stone and glass and marble,
Made of iron and concrete.
But once inside you can ride
A camel or a train,
Visit Rome, Siam, or Nome,
Feel a hurricane,
Meet a king, learn to sing,
How to bake a pie,
Go to sea, plant a tree,
Find how airplanes fly,
Train a horse, and of course
Have all the dogs you'd like,
See the moon, a sandy dune,
Or catch a whopping pike.
Everything that books can bring
You'll find inside those walls.
A world is there for you to share
When adventure calls.

You cannot tell its magic
By the way the building looks,
But there's wonderment within it,
The wonderment of books.

Mary Had a Little Lamb

Mary had a little lamb,
Its fleece was white as snow;
And everywhere that Mary went
The lamb was sure to go.

It followed her to school one day,
Which was against the rule;
It made the children laugh and play
To see a lamb at school.

Fun With Fingers

ELLEN BRIGGS

Here's the little schoolhouse
Where I'll go today.

Here are many children
Marching on their way.

Here's my little desk
Where I'll sit up tall.

Here are flowers hanging
In a vase up on the wall.

Here's a sheet of paper. Neat and clean and white.
Here's my pretty pencil Which I'll use to write.

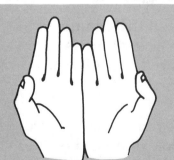

Here's the book I'll open
When I learn to read.

Here's the teacher, saying,
"Very good, indeed!"

Book Covers

Begin the school year by protecting your books with special book covers. Here are some fun ones that you can make.

Your teacher may want to write your name and school on the book covers.

Cat or Dog Cover

Cut cat or dog pictures from scrap magazines. Glue the pictures on lightweight cardboard.

Cutout Cover

Cut interestingly shaped holes in a sheet of colored paper. Glue this sheet to a sheet of different colored paper. Turn cover over.

Checkerboard Cover

Glue patches of scrap fabric in a checkerboard pattern to colored paper or lightweight cardboard.

How To Cover a Book

To make a good-fitting book cover, follow these steps:

1. Select a strong piece of paper or lightweight cardboard for your cover.

2. Cut it so that it is about four inches longer and wider than the book (when opened out).

3. Fold the top and bottom edges so that the cover becomes the same height as the book.

4. Center the open book on the cover.

5. Fold the right-hand side of your cover snugly over the back cover of the book.

6. Close the book.

7. While the book is closed, fold in the other side of the cover.

8. Slip edges of book into the cover.

For Your Books

Handy Bookmark

Cut one of the corners from an envelope so that you have a good sized triangle. It will be double with one open side. The open side can be slipped over the corner of your book page when you finish reading.

A bookmark can become a very gay and colorful thing. Use crayons, paints, pictures, or colored thread for a border.

Each member of your family could use one. Bookmarks make appropriate gifts.

Book Bag

A trip to school or the library can be easier when you carry your books in your own book bag made from a plastic shopping bag.

Cover any unwanted lettering on the bag with shapes cut from contact paper. These shapes can be geometric figures or objects that you like such as horses, cars, or flowers.

Leave your initials showing if the lettering on the bag includes them, or cut contact letters and stick your initials or name on the bag.

Bookmark Verse

Use this marker
In your book
To help it keep
A nice new look.

When it's raining
Grab a book,
Settle down,
And take a look.

Books are magic.
Books are fun.
This will mark
Your favorite one.

When yawns are spread
Across your face,
Let this marker
Keep your place.

For Your Desk

Coupon or Stamp Holder

You will need two plastic-foam meat trays of equal size. Cut one in half.

Thread yarn through a large needle and whipstitch the cut edge of one half.

Glue the stitched half to the whole tray. Beginning at center top, whipstitch around the holder. Tie ends of yarn into a bow at center top.

Cut pictures from wrapping paper or paper napkins and glue to front.

Write "coupons" or "stamps" on the front. Keep coupons or trading stamps in the pocket.

Pencil Pets

Here is an easy way to decorate pencils for yourself or to use as gifts. These little "pets" are planned to use the pencil as part of themselves. The crow is made of black construction paper, with yellow feet and a red and white eye. The pencil makes his beak. The mouse is made of two triangles of brown construction paper, with a pencil for a tail. The pencil serves as a bill for the swordfish. Make all body shapes double and glue only at the sides and top, so the eraser end of the pencil can slip in and out. In that way, the eraser can be used whenever needed. Add details to all the pencil pals with cut paper or felt-tipped marker.

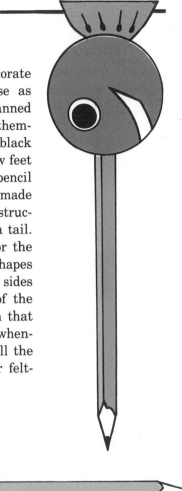

Toadstool Pencil Holder

Choose a small paper bag about 7 inches high for your toadstool pencil holder. Carefully turn the open end of the bag until about 2 inches of it hangs over all around the outside of the bag. This will form the top for the toadstool. The opening in the top will provide room for pencils.

Paint the turned-out part of bag yellow. After the paint is dry, make large white circle decorations all around the border of the bag. Paint the bottom part of the toadstool blue. After this is dry, make white lines up and down the bag for decorations.

Off To School

Czech Folk Song

Brightly, with spirit

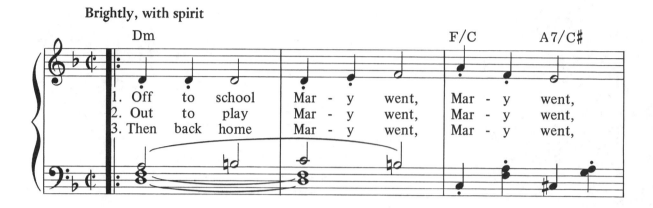

1. Off to school Mar - y went, Mar - y went,
2. Out to play Mar - y went, Mar - y went,
3. Then back home Mar - y went, Mar - y went,

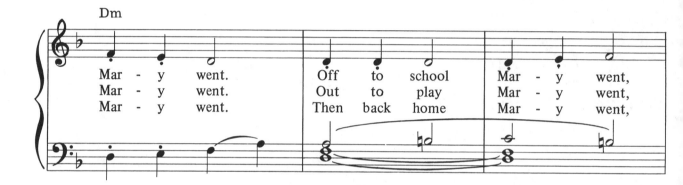

Mar - y went. Off to school Mar - y went,
Mar - y went. Out to school Mar - y went,
Mar - y went. Then back home Mar - y went,

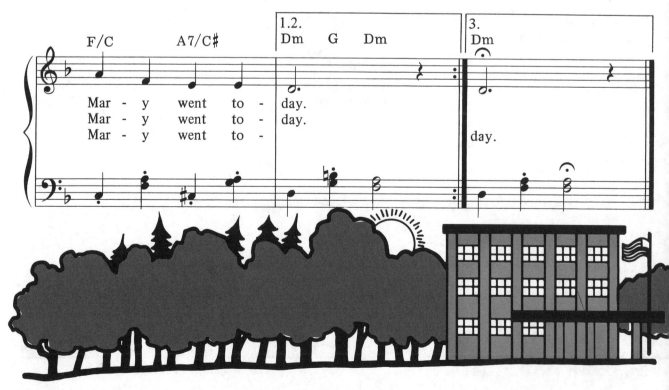

Mar - y went to - day.
Mar - y went to - day.
Mar - y went to - day.

day.

Busy Children

Words by
JOHN HALL

Music: Traditional

Lightly

C6   G7

1. In our | class-room we are singing, we are singing, we are
(2. In our) school-bus we are rid-ing, we are rid-ing, we are
(3. In our) play-ground we are play-ing, we are play-ing, we are

mf

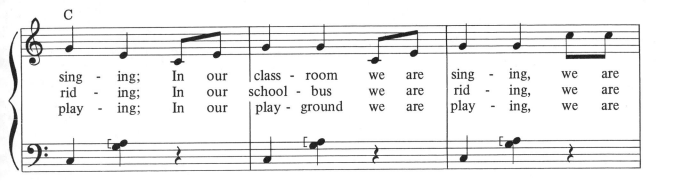

C

sing-ing; In our | class-room we are sing-ing, we are
rid-ing; In our school-bus we are rid-ing, we are
play-ing; In our play-ground we are play-ing, we are

G7   1.2. C   3. C

sing-ing to-day.   2. In our
rid-ing to-day.   3. In our
play-ing to-   day.

AT SCHOOL   **21**

All About Me

Introduction

In the first unit, "At School," an attempt was made to have the child understand and appreciate the things she or he had in common with the other members of the class. Stressing group identity eases the child's entrance into the school world. But the child is more than just a member of a group and this, too, must be made clear. Therefore, in this unit, the focus is shifted from likeness to uniqueness, the individuality of each child.

For a five-year-old the question of who and what she or he is holds vast interest. The child is exploring daily what she or he can and cannot do, how she or he works. The desire for an answer to "Who am I?" should extend beyond the obvious "You are our daughter," "You are our son," or "You are a kindergarten pupil." This curiosity on the child's part offers an excellent opportunity to the teacher to reinforce the child's feelings of self-worth, to make her or him proud of being an individual.

Differences need not be avoided. The child will quickly observe that there are some things she or he does not do as well as other children in the class and some she or he does better. This unit attempts to stress that no two people are alike; we are the sum of the many traits we have. Our differences are positive; they make us more interesting, more identifiable, and more pleasurable.

Activities in this section are used to acquaint the child with the workings of the body and its ability to perform, for these are part of the child's uniqueness as much as her or his thumbprint or description or name and address. The child who begins to understand and accept her or his individuality will greatly increase her or his chance of productive performance in the future.

Concepts To Be Taught

I. No two people are exactly alike.

II. Each individual's thoughts or ideas have value.

III. A child's feelings change and so do the feelings of others.

IV. The human body can move in many wonderful ways. Everybody can do some things easily and others not so easily.

V. The children are growing.

Information for Teaching Concepts

I.   No two people are exactly alike.

Introduce this unit by asking the children, "Who are you?" Accept every response. Next ask, "Are you special?" Then explain, "You are special because you are the only person exactly like you in the world." Remind the children of the ways they are alike (as discussed in the unit, "At School"). Tell them that now they are going to learn that each of them is special in some way.

Explain to the class that today each is going to make something that only she or he (individually) can make. On an overhead projector or on the chalkboard demonstrate Thumb Fun, page 54. Tell the children that each of their drawings will be different because nobody has a thumbprint just like anyone else's. While the children are engaged in this activity, collect a copy of each child's thumbprint on separate index cards. Label the reverse side of index card with the child's name and address. Write an envelope for each child with her or his name and address on it. Hold up a thumbprint card and let the children guess whose thumbprint it is. Then show the name and address and have the child with the matching envelope come and get the card. Use the cards and envelopes for a learning center activity, such as matching or post office.

Ask the children how the mail carrier knows where to deliver the mail. Ask them to think about why it is important for each of them to know her or his name and address. Role play situations where children are to give names and addresses.

Examples for the children to consider are:
1)   Mary has won a prize which will be delivered to her home.
2)   Harry's dog is lost and he is going to place an ad in the newspaper.
3)   Mark sprains his ankle at the park and somebody is going to take him home.
4)   Linda's painting is going on display in an art show and she wants it returned to her after the show is over.

Also, ask the children to think what the kindergarten class would be like if they all had the same name. Have them think about some of the problems that might occur.

Pass a mirror around the class and ask each child to tell what she or he sees in the mirror. Then take the mirror and hold it at an angle, as if to catch a reflection from the class. Say, "I look into the mirror and guess who I can see?" Describe a child and have the child who is being described say, "Is it I?" Next, have the children take turns looking in the mirror and describing a child.

Have each child give a description of herself or himself as each role plays a lost child. Help the children to use descriptive adjectives for size, color of eyes and hair, and design of clothing.

Again, have them think about what the class would be like if everyone looked exactly the same. Emphasize the positive aspects of being different.

II. Each individual's thoughts or ideas have value.

As the children come into the classroom, ask each one to tell you her or his favorite color. Tally the score for the class's favorite color. Talk about differences people display in preferences for food, television programs, colors, places, and games. Encourage the class to be aware that each of them is special and part of that specialness is thinking differently. Explain that ideas are sometimes called opinions. Stress the importance of respecting other's rights to have an opinion. Have the class think about times when it might be important. Examples are:

1) Planning a trip with others.
2) Selecting clothes for a special occasion.
3) Seeking help to train a puppy.
4) Deciding what materials to use in an art project.
5) Selecting a book for the teacher to read.

Arrange 'opinion poll' sessions about issues in the kindergarten class. Review with the class the rules for a class discussion. Examples are:

1) Only one person is to speak at a time.
2) Everyone is to have an opportunity to speak.
3) State your idea. Do not argue that another person's idea is wrong.
4) Be a good listener.

There are many social issues that are important for the class to discuss. By having the opportunity to think about and express an idea without being judged, a child learns to value himself.

III. A child's feelings change and so do the feelings of others.

Draw facial expressions on the chalkboard or use pictures that illustrate happiness, sadness, fear, worry, surprise. See page 32.

Ask the children, "Are these faces alike or different? What makes each different? How do you think the person in the picture feels?" Elicit responses that use the adjectives describing feelings. Continue by having the children identify what makes them feel happy, sad, frightened, worried or surprised.

Read the story, "What the Little Elephant Found Out," on page 38. Ask the children to think about the story and to identify when the little elephant was sad and when he was happy. Also, have them think about when the elephant was worried and frightened. Have the children show a facial expression to demonstrate each of these feelings as you review specific parts of the story. Examples are:

1) He thought none of the animals liked him.
2) The squirrels were worried that the nuts had all blown off the trees.
3) The little elephant felt the net getting tighter.
4) The elephant found that the animals didn't think his nose was ugly. They were his friends.

Discuss how the elephant's feelings changed. Ask the children if their feelings also change. Emphasize that all of us have feelings and that these feelings change. Encourage them to think about people and events that change their feelings. Talk about the importance of having friends and of being a friend who understands about other's feelings.

IV. The human body can move in many wonderful ways. Everybody can do some things easily and others not so easily.

Tell the children that their bodies are wonderful machines. Relate that the body has many movable parts that can work to lift, haul, push, pull, and so on. Ask the children to listen while you recite the "Action Rhyme" on page 50.

Have the children repeat the rhyme with you and then demonstrate the actions. Encourage the children to think how their bodies feel as they move different parts.

Hold out your hand and look at it carefully. Talk about the idea of a hinge (use a hinge for demonstration if available). Ask the children to each hold up one hand and see if they can move their fingers as if they were hinged. Read "Tired and Sleepy", on page 51.

Discuss why thumbs are important. Ask the children to think about what they do when they use their thumbs. Do the activity on thumbs, page 52. Now ask, "How important are your thumbs?"

Explain to the children the wonders of the human machine. Tell them that a machine is something that can do work and since human beings can do work their bodies are also machines. Read "How A Body Does," page 38.

V. The Children are growing.

Ask the children to describe how each of them is a machine. Then explain that the machines they buy do not grow or keep changing, but the human machine is always changing. Have the children describe how they have changed since they were born. Encourage them to think about the changes they have experienced since beginning kindergarten, such as new friends, skills learned. Ask them to think about:

The needs of a growing plant. Examples are:

water	sun	removing weeds

The needs of a growing puppy. Examples are:

food	shelter	care	love	water

The needs of a growing child. Examples are:

food	care	shelter	opportunities to learn
water	protection	love	exercise

Help the children to identify the things that they have learned. You might want to create booklets on "Things I Have Learned" or make collages. This will reinforce for children the concept that growing is more than just getting taller. Growing requires taking care of their minds and their bodies in order to increase in knowledge.

Thinking and Reasoning

Ask your children these questions:

Do you scratch with your feet or your fingers?

Which is longer, your big toe or your thumb?

Is a child who is old enough to cry also old enough to sing?

You have a pair of feet. What other parts of your body are in pairs?

Do you go faster when you run or when you walk?

Which knows more, you or a dog?

What is the difference between a paw and a hand?

What do you want to do when you are thirsty?

When you jump, do you use your feet or your hands?

Tell what you can do that a puppy cannot do.

Can you see when you are asleep?

Which is bigger around, your arm or your leg? Your head or your fist?

How can you see the back of your head?

Can you dig in the ground with your bare hands as well as a puppy can?

If you had two more eyes, where would they be most useful to you, do you suppose?

Do all children have curly hair?

Do you ever sleep while you are running?

Is your skin on the outside of your body or on the inside?

Is it easier to walk on a clean dry path, or an icy path?

Which takes more years to grow up, a boy or a puppy?

Can you walk on your tiptoes?

Do you breathe when you are asleep?

Why do you never see footprints on the ceiling?

When you talk or eat, does your upper jaw move?

How may you know when you are catching cold?

Could you drink a whole pail of water at one time? Could a horse?

Do you go to bed with your shoes on?

Are your toes on the front of your feet or on the back of them?

Do you have teeth in your stomach?

Which is easier to move, your big toe or your little toe?

Can you run as fast as a dog?

Which are longer, your fingers or your toes?

Where is the skin softer, on the back of your hand or on the palm of your hand?

When you are sitting, is your head nearer the sky or farther from the sky than when you are standing?

Are your knees below your feet or above your feet? Below or above your stomach?

Who needs more sleep, a baby or its mother?

When you stand up, is it easier to see the heel of your shoe or the toe of your shoe?

What is your house number?

Do you fall more often when you run or when you walk?

Which are using their hands more? Their feet more?
Name some other things you do with your hands.
Name some other things you do with your feet.
What are some of the differences between your hands and your feet?

ALL ABOUT ME

Connect the picture on the left to the matching picture on the right by drawing a line.

Can you find the hidden horse's head, cup, house, fish, hot dog, and football in this picture?

Thinking Questions

Do you stand, walk or sit when:

you throw a ball?
you read a book for fun?
you push a wheelbarrow?
you shell peas?
you wash dishes?
you type on a typewriter?
you hang clothes on a line to dry?
Name some other things you usually do sitting. Some you do standing. Some you do walking.

Do you use your fingers more when:

you play a piano or beat a drum?

you strike a ball with a bat or write on a typewriter?

you thread a needle or clap your hands?

you turn the pages of a book or close a door?

you pick up an orange or sew a button on your coat?

you play a violin or when you go up in a swing?

you throw a ball or when you wind yarn on a ball?

Tell what you do when:

you drink water
you cry
you laugh
you smile
you shout
you sing
you whisper
you ride a tricycle
you make a fist

Answer these questions about yourself.

When and where were you born?
How many brothers and sisters do you have?
What are some things you are good at?
What do you like best to do?
What one thing would you like most to do if you had the chance?

Photo Necklace

KATHY ROSS

Paint a bottle cap a pretty color on the outside. When the paint is dry, glue on a tiny flower or other picture cut from a magazine or greeting card.

Paint over the entire outside of the bottle cap, including the picture, with white glue. Tie a long piece of yarn or string around the gluey sides of the cap; then tie the ends together to make a necklace.

When the glue is dry, turn the cap over. Find a photo of yourself or someone else and cut around the picture until it just fits inside the bottle cap. Glue it inside the cap.

Cut a circle from stiff, clear plastic (found on stationery boxes and so on). Glue it over the open side of the cap to form a protective window.

ALL ABOUT ME   **31**

Can you tell which child is scared?
Which is laughing?
Which is very angry?
Which is crying?
What do you think caused each of them to feel that way?

Connect the picture on the left to the matching picture on the right by drawing a line.

Connect the picture on the left to the matching picture on the right by drawing a line.

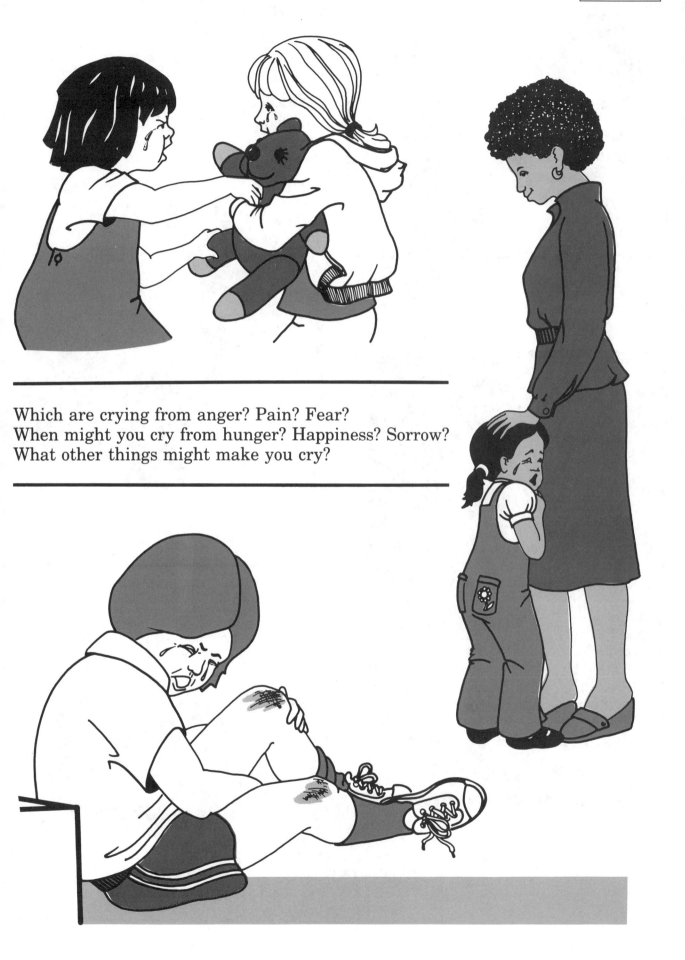

Which are crying from anger? Pain? Fear?
When might you cry from hunger? Happiness? Sorrow?
What other things might make you cry?

Which children are happy?
Which are sad?

The Package You Live In

NANCY MADDUX THORNTON

You live in the most perfect package that has ever been made. No matter how big you grow, it will never be too small. When you reach or bend it stretches with you. It makes you cooler when the weather is hot. It helps keep you warm when the weather is cold. If it is torn or cut, it mends itself.

Many manufacturers wish they could make a covering that is as good as your skin.

Did you know that a little of your skin rubs off each day? You usually don't notice because it is such a tiny amount. Sometimes you can see it, though. If you leave a dirty ring around the bathtub, some of that stain is your lost skin. After you get sunburned, the dry, flaky stuff that peels off is your old skin.

It doesn't hurt when you lose this skin. Why? It's dead! You are covered by a layer of dead tissue. Underneath, of course, your skin is alive and growing. Your dead outside layer of skin is always replaced. Your skin will keep growing even after you stop growing up.

You are covered with more than just one layer of protection. Your skin is made of two layers. The outer skin is called the epidermis. The epidermis is quite thin. Part of it is made up of the dead layer of skin. Underneath the epidermis lies the dermis. It is thicker and tougher.

Your skin helps cool you. Feel your skin some time when the weather is hot. Probably it feels absolutely cool, although you, inside your skin, may not. At such times, your skin also may feel sticky. Sweat glands are working. Buried within the skin, they release moisture which evaporates and cools like an air conditioner.

What color are you? The color of your skin depends upon three things.

Most of your skin's color lies in the deep dermis. Your dermis has little blobs of brown within it. If you are light-colored, you have very few brown specks in your dermis. If you are dark, you have many. When you get tan in the summertime, it's because you are increasing the brown specks in your skin by the sun's rays.

A second cause of skin color is due to your blood which, of course, is red. If your skin is very dark, it will hide the color of your blood. The pinkness of blood shows only if the dermis is light-colored. You may have noticed that the color of your skin sometimes changes. Dark skinned people may get pink. These changes are due to increased blood next to the skin.

The third cause of your skin's color comes from the epidermis, which is a little yellowish, like the substance of your fingernails.

Your skin is one of the most important parts of your body. It keeps out germs and harmful chemicals. It keeps in body fluids. Without skin, your body would dry up.

Since you are not covered by feathers or fur or scales, your skin is especially likely to be hurt. Clothes help your skin do its job by adding warmth and protection. It is unlikely, though, that anyone will ever make a suit of clothes that is half as good as your own skin.

How A Body Does
MARCUS O'BRIEN

Your body is a very special machine, just as a clock or a washing machine, or a steam engine is a machine. It can do work, it needs something to make it go, and sometimes it needs to be fixed.

And you don't have to pretend that you are a washing machine or automobile. Anything that can do work is a machine. And since you can do work you are one without pretending or being a bit different from what you are. You can carry things just as a car can, and you can wash clothes just as well as the washing machine can.

You are a very special machine. You can see like a camera, and talk like a radio, and hear like a telephone. No one ever invented any machine that can do all that you can do. You are a person and that is more than any machine.

Your body isn't built with gears and wheels but it has muscles and bones that do the moving kind of work. The bones of your arms and legs are put together like levers and your muscles pull the levers.

Put your hand over the muscle on the front of your other arm between your shoulder and your elbow. Now let your elbow be a hinge and raise your forearm. You can feel the muscle get short and fat. This is how a muscle works. It is made of a lot of little fibers like the threads in a rope. The fibers can make themselves shorter. When they do, the muscle pulls.

You have 374 muscles all over your body. They work your legs and toes and fingers in very much the same way that they work your arms. There are muscles in your chest that make you breathe, and muscles in your heart that make it beat and pump blood, and little muscles that turn your eyes so that you can look wherever you want.

That is one of the amazing things about our bodies. We may be big or little or thin or fat, but we are all built with the same kind of machinery.

What the Little Elephant Found Out

MARGARET BUELL ALLEN

The little elephant was sad. He was so big and clumsy that he thought none of the other animals liked him. And that funny long nose! None of the other animals had noses like that.

So most of the time he hid in a corner of the jungle with his long nose curled up and his head down, hoping nobody would notice him.

One day the myna bird was chirping loudly, and the little elephant saw that her baby bird had fallen out of the nest.

The little elephant knew what to do. With his funny long nose he gently picked up the baby bird and lifted it into the nest. After that, the mother bird was his very good friend.

The brown bear was eating honey in the bee tree one day when the bees came home and began to sting him. The little elephant heard him crash through the jungle, roaring in pain.

The little elephant knew what to do. He ran to the river and sucked up water in his long nose and gave those angry bees a surprise shower.

They didn't like this and flew away. After that, the brown bear was the little elephant's very good friend.

A terrible storm hit the jungle one day. The wind blew and the rain came down and the lightning flashed. When it was over, everything was in a mess.

The squirrels were chattering that the nuts had all blown off the trees.

They worried about finding them with all that trash on the ground.

The little elephant knew what to do. He picked up the branches with his funny long nose and took them away.

Then the squirrels could find the nuts. And the squirrels were his very good friends, too.

Then the elephant heard a terrible roar and knew it was the lion. Everyone was afraid of the lion, but the little elephant went to find out what the trouble was. A big rock had fallen down the hillside in the storm and was stuck in the mouth of his den, and the lion couldn't get out.

The little elephant knew what to do. He pushed the rock with his big feet and poked the dirt loose with his tusks and at last he rolled the rock away with his funny long nose. After that, even the lion was his very good friend.

But one day hunters came into the jungle with a big net. They hung it between two trees where the little elephant often walked. Then they went away. They wanted to catch him and take him out of the jungle.

Sure enough, the little elephant did walk into the net and was caught. This time he did not know what to do. The harder he tried to get loose, the tighter the net became.

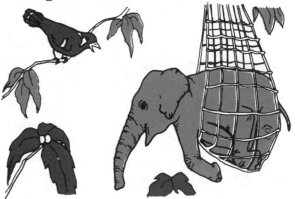

The myna bird saw what had happened. She called the bear and the lion and said, "Bear, you go to the path on this side and growl. Lion, you go to the path on the other side and roar so the hunters will be afraid to come after the little elephant."

Then she flew off to call the squirrels. The myna bird said, "Squirrels, the elephant is your friend. You have sharp teeth. Now get busy and chew the ropes of the net and help your friend."

The squirrels chewed as hard as they could. They chewed all night, and the bear growled, and the lion roared. At last the net was all chewed, and the little elephant was free.

My, he was happy! Not only because he was free, but because he knew he had so many good friends. They didn't think his funny long nose was queer after all. He was so happy that he swung his long nose back and forth and said, "Thank you, friends. Thanks a lot!"

Friends Can Be Different

G. M. HALVERSON

In a country far, far away, there once lived a giraffe and a mouse who were very good friends.

Now the giraffe was very, very tall; and the mouse was very, very small.

The giraffe had a very long neck, and the mouse had a very long tail.

The giraffe was very proud of his great long neck, and the mouse was very proud of his nice long tail.

One warm day the two friends went out into the country for a walk and to talk as friends like to do.

As they went along, the giraffe said, "The best thing in the world is to be tall."

The mouse with the long tail answered, "That is not so. The best thing in the world is to be short."

The giraffe said, "Follow me, and I will show you why it is better to be tall than short. If I do not, I will give you my long neck."

The mouse said, "I will go, but I shall soon show you why it is better to be short than tall. If I do not, I will give you my nice long tail."

"Very well," said the giraffe.

On down the road they went. It was not long before they came to an apple orchard with a low wall around it.

The giraffe said, "Now, mouse, just watch me."

The giraffe was so tall that he put his head over the wall and ate all the apples he wanted.

He said, "I have had a good dinner, but you will have nothing, little mouse, because you are so small."

"My turn will come, friend giraffe; my turn will come. Just wait," answered the mouse.

A little way down the road they came to a garden with a very high wall around it, but near the ground there was a small hole in the wall.

In ran the little mouse and ate everything he could find.

When the mouse came out of the garden, he said, "Now, friend giraffe, is it better to be tall or short?"

"Well," answered the giraffe, "sometimes it is better to be tall. Sometimes it is better to be short."

"So it is," said the mouse. "You may keep your long neck, my friend, and I will keep my long tail."

So both friends went home as happy as happy could be.

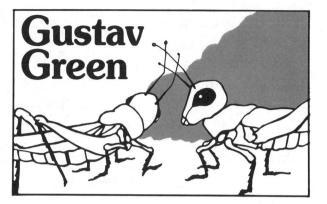

Gustav Green

ANN DEVENDORF

Once upon a time, there lived a grasshopper by the name of Gustav Green.

"Hop!" said his cousin, Jumping Jack.

"Hop!" said his cousin, Leaping Lena.

Gustav tried to hop. He could not.

"Like this," said Leaping Lena. And she hopped three feet, six inches.

"Like this," said Jumping Jack. And he hopped three feet, six inches.

"I can't get myself off the ground," said Gustav.

"Yes, you can," said Jumping Jack. "Water skippers skip. Butterflies fly. Grasshoppers hop."

"I can't," said Gustav. "I will have to walk through life—step, step, step!"

"Let's walk up to the top of this pile of hay," said Leaping Lena. "Then we'll hop off—one, two, three."

"All right," said Gustav.

The three grasshoppers walked up to the top of the pile of hay. Leaping Lena took a fine leap off the hay. Jumping Jack took a big jump off the hay. Gustav tried with all his might, but he just tumbled horns over heels off the pile of hay.

"Are you all right?" asked Leaping Lena.

"Yes," said Gustav. "But I am not going to try *that* again!"

"Let's try something else," said Leaping Lena.

"Yes," said Jumping Jack. "I will boost your left side. Leaping Lena will boost your right side. Then, you will hop."

"All right," said Gustav.

Leaping Lena boosted. Jumping Jack boosted. Gustav stretched and stretched. He raised his head higher and higher and higher. He lost his balance. PLOP! The three grasshoppers tumbled down in a pile!

"It's no use," cried Gustav. "I'll be a walker."

"No, no!" said Jumping Jack. "Try again."

Gustav tried. He got his right jumping foot off the ground.

"Get your left jumping foot off the ground, too," said Jumping Jack.

Gustav got his left foot off the ground but his right foot came down. Gustav gave a little hop on his right foot. His left foot came down. He gave a little hop on his left foot. His right foot came down. He gave a little hop.

"I'm skipping! I'm skipping!" called Gustav. "Look at me! Look at me!"

Gustav skipped around and around.

"A skipping grasshopper!" said Jumping Jack with a frown. "I've never seen a skipping grasshopper."

"Call me a grass-skipper," said Gustav with a smile.

"Yes," said Leaping Lena. "That's what you are—a grass-skipper. And do you know what?"

"What?" asked Gustav.

"It's nice to have a grass-skipper in the family," said Lena. "It's nice to have someone different around."

"Yes," said Jumping Jack. "It is."

Gustav grinned in happiness and skipped across the grass.

), Zaner-Bloser, Inc.

Charlie Chicken

CAROLYN NYSTROM

"I don't think I like the way I look," Charlie Chicken said as he gazed in the hen-house mirror.

"My feathers are black and white splotchy. My tail is pointy. And my toes are too long."

No other chicken in the barnyard looked quite like Charlie. He wondered if they all thought he looked strange.

Polly Pullet, for example, had lovely brown and reddish feathers, and he noticed that her toes looked just right.

"Hello, Polly," Charlie said. "I have just decided that I don't like the way I look. My feathers are black and white splotchy. My tail is pointy. And my toes are too long. Do you think that I look strange?"

"Well, Charlie," Polly replied carefully, "you are the only chicken in our barnyard who is black and white splotchy. But I never noticed it until now. Maybe black and white splotchy *is* a little strange."

Charlie Chicken lowered his head and walked slowly away. Next he saw Chick Chester picking at bugs near the fence. Chester was big and white and his tail curved beautifully.

"Hello," Charlie whispered.

"Why are you whispering?" asked Chester.

"Because I don't want anyone to see me," Charlie continued to whisper. "I look terrible!"

Chick Chester stopped and looked up. "I guess your tail is a little pointy. I'm glad that mine is nice and

curved." And with that Chester returned to his bugs.

Charlie couldn't change his feathers to brown or white, and he couldn't make his tail grow curved instead of pointy, and he certainly couldn't cut off his toes.

He thought, "I'll talk to just one other person." Hattie Hen was near the feeding trough.

"Hattie Hen," he cried, "I must talk to you."

"Well then, talk fast," she told him. "My baby chickens need their lunch."

Charlie Chicken blurted, "I don't like myself."

"Why on earth not?" clucked Hattie.

Charlie began again. "My feathers are black and white splotchy. My tail is pointy. And my toes are too long."

Hattie Hen looked thoughtful and was about to reply. But she didn't get a chance.

Mean old Russell Rooster rushed to the feeding trough. He pushed Hattie Hen's baby chickens. He even stepped on some of them. They peeped and chirped and tried to reach their food, but Russell would not let them near the trough.

Charlie Chicken was so angry that he forgot all about being afraid of the mean old rooster. He even forgot about not liking himself.

He ruffled up his black and white splotchy feathers, stuck his pointy tail up in the air, planted his long toes firmly on the ground, and shouted in his loudest voice, "You stop this minute, Russell Rooster." Charlie came closer and closer to the rooster.

Russell Rooster ever so slowly backed away and tried to pretend that what he really wanted was a drink of water.

Hattie Hen gathered her scattered babies. When they began to eat, she told Charlie, "You *are* different from any other chicken in the barnyard. Your black and white splotchy feathers, pointy tail, and long toes frightened Russell Rooster away. But most of all it was your inside strength. I'm glad you are you."

Charlie settled his feathers and chuckled. "I'm glad I'm me, too. There's no other me in the barnyard."

Detective Dog

One morning all the animals with fur coats woke up to find their fur coats missing. Only Lion's and Tiger's weren't stolen. "Help," the animals cried. "Our coats are missing."

The zoo keepers called the police. The police sent Daisy, The Detective Dog, to find out who stole the fur coats.

Daisy came to Lion's cage. "Your coat wasn't stolen. Maybe the robber will come tonight. I will set up a trap," said Daisy to Lion.

All that day Daisy set up the trap. She put a net on the ceiling of Lion's cage. She tied a rope to the net. Daisy said, "I will hide by the cage. When the robber comes, I will pull the rope, and the net will fall on him."

That night Daisy hid by the cage. Late at night the robber came. He stole the coat. Daisy didn't pull the rope. She had fallen asleep. She woke up just in time to see the robber run away. It was dark and Daisy only saw the robber's long tail.

"Wake up, Lion," said Daisy. The Lion woke up. "I didn't catch the robber, but I saw he had a long tail. Which animals have long tails? One of them must be the robber."

They thought about animals with long tails. Daisy said it could be a fox or a raccoon or a monkey. Lion said it could be a kangaroo, too.

Daisy came to Tiger's cage. His coat wasn't stolen yet. She put the same trap in his cage.

Later in the afternoon, Daisy went to Owl's cage. Daisy said to Owl, "Owl, you do not sleep in the dark. At night, hide with me by Tiger's cage. When the robber comes, you will wake me, and I will catch him in the net."

That night Owl and Daisy hid by the cage. Soon Daisy fell asleep. Later the robber came. Owl woke Daisy. Daisy pulled the rope, and the net fell on the robber.

"Alligator is the robber!" cried Daisy. "Why did you steal the coats?"

"I think green skin is ugly," said Alligator. "I wanted a fur coat like you. I stole a lot so my children could have some."

"A fur coat would look silly on an alligator," said Daisy. "Green skin is *special* on an alligator."

"Now I think you are right. I will give back the coats. Now I think my green skin is better."

So he gave back the coats, and everyone in the zoo was happy.

NEAL BYLUS, Age 11

Little Pete and the Wise Old Owl

RUTH HOLT CROWLEY

Little Pete sprang from his bed and dressed himself quickly. He was eager to get out and play with the beautiful new spotted dog and the fluffy yellow cat Grandfather had given him for his birthday.

He ate every bit of his cereal and drank all of his warm milk. Then, out he went into the bright sunshiny day. He skipped over to the big barn.

"Come, Doggie. Here, Kitty. Let's romp and run in the meadow!" cried Little Pete as he snapped his fingers and clapped his hands. But the little spotted dog just looked at him sadly and turned over for another snooze. The fluffy yellow cat twitched her pink nose, switched her tail on the barn floor, curled up in her corner of the barn with her back turned rudely to Little Pete. She looked very much as if she were very angry.

"Oh dear!" thought Little Pete, "my new spotted dog and my fluffy yellow cat don't like me. They won't romp and run in the meadow."

Once more Little Pete called and snapped his fingers and clapped his hands but the spotted dog still looked sad and the fluffy cat still looked mad and neither one would move.

Poor Little Pete sat down on an old tree stump and before he knew it, he was crying. Mother Robin perched on the fence right behind him.

"What's the matter, Little Pete?" chirped Mother Robin. She liked Little Pete because he always put out crumbs and little pieces of fat for her and her friends when she came back too soon in the spring and the snow was still on the ground.

"I have a new spotted dog and a new fluffy cat. I wanted them to run and romp in the meadow but they won't pay any attention to me at all," sobbed Little Pete.

"How do you call them? What are their names?" asked Mother Robin.

"Names?" questioned Little Pete, "Why, I don't know. I just call them 'Doggie' and 'Kitty' and clap my hands. Do you think that is why they won't come to me? Because I don't know their names?"

"Why, of course!" chirped Mother Robin happily, "everyone wants to have a name. Your spotted dog and fluffy cat probably feel very, very hurt because you haven't called them by name. They don't want to be just any dog and cat. They want to be their very own selves. You call them by their names and watch them come."

"But Mother Robin, I don't know their names. Do you?" asked Little Pete anxiously.

"No, Little Pete, I don't. But why don't you ask Brother Red Fox? He's sharp about so many things, maybe he'll know the names of your new spotted dog and fluffy yellow cat." And as it was getting late for Mother Robin to be away from her babies up in the nest, she flew away.

Little Pete went into the meadow and walked to the old fallen log where he knew he would find Brother Red Fox sunning his lazy old self. Sure enough, there was Brother Red Fox pretending to be asleep, but anybody could see his bright little eyes peering out beneath his half-closed lids.

"Brother Red Fox, my spotted dog and fluffy yellow cat won't run and romp with me because I don't know their names. Could you tell me their names?" asked Little Pete, keeping his distance from Brother Red Fox. (You never can be sure about a fox.)

"Sorry, Little Pete, I don't know the names of your dog and cat and I wish you wouldn't bother me," said Brother Red Fox impolitely. Then feeling ashamed, he added, "Mrs. Wise Old Owl lives up in the big tree near the pond. You ask her. She's very wise and clever. She'll know."

Little Pete ran the length of the meadow very quickly. When he came to the big tree near the pond he looked up. There was Mrs. Owl.

"Oh, Mrs. Owl, please help me. I have a new spotted dog and a fluffy yellow cat but neither one will run and romp with me because I don't know their names. Can you tell me what their names are?" pleaded Little Pete.

"Humph, humph," said Mrs. Owl in a deep voice as she ruffled up her

feathers and looked down at Little Pete with her great eyes. "I'll see what I can do for you, Little Pete."

Mrs. Owl then turned her back to Little Pete and peered into the hollow of the tree where she lived.

"I'll have to look it up in the Animal Book, Little Pete," said Mrs. Wise Old Owl in a very stern voice.

Little Pete was more than a bit frightened but he stood and waited.

"Now, you say the dog is a spotted dog?" asked Mrs. Wise Old Owl.

"Yes, oh yes. He's white with black spots all over," said Little Pete excitedly.

"Yes sir! Here it is—Little Pete's spotted dog. His name is SPOT or SPOTTY!" shouted the owl triumphantly.

"Oh, Mrs. Owl, you're so wise and good. Spot or Spotty, isn't that nice? And the cat, what about the cat?" cried Little Pete.

"Humph, humph," said Mrs. Owl, "Now let's see. Here it is—Little Pete's cat. Her name is FLUFF or FLUFFY!" hooted the owl as she shook out her feathers once again in triumph.

"Oh, Mrs. Owl, you are wise. Spot and Fluff! Thank you very, very much," shouted Little Pete as he raced back to the barnyard.

"Here, Spot! Here, Fluff!" cried Little Pete as he came to the barn. But before he ever got there, out scampered Spot, jumping and wagging his happy tail. And Fluff followed behind, more slowly, to be sure, for that is the way with dignified little lady cats.

Who can tell how Mrs. Owl knew the names of Little Pete's spotted dog and fluffy yellow cat?

Tiptoe

KARLA KUSKIN

Yesterday I skipped all day,
The day before I ran,
Today I'm going to tiptoe
Everywhere I can.
I'll tiptoe down the stairway.
I'll tiptoe through the door.
I'll tiptoe to the living room

And give an awful roar,
And my father, who is reading,
Will jump up from his chair
And mumble something silly like
"I didn't see you there."
I'll tiptoe to my mother
And give a little cough
And when she spins to see me
Why, I'll softly tiptoe off.
I'll tiptoe through the meadows,
Over hills and yellow sands
And when my toes get tired
Then I'll tiptoe on my hands.

46

Poems

Jonathan Bing

B. CURTIS BROWN

Poor old Jonathan Bing
Went out in his carriage to visit the King,
But everyone pointed and said, "Look at that!
Jonathan Bing has forgotten his hat!"
(He'd forgotten his hat!)

Poor old Jonathan Bing
Went home and put on a new hat for the King,
But up by the palace a soldier said, "Hi!
You can't see the King; you've forgotten your tie!"
(He'd forgotten his tie!)

Poor old Jonathan Bing
He put on a beautiful tie for the King,
But when he arrived an Archbishop said, "Ho!
You can't come to court in pyjamas, you know!"

Poor old Jonathan Bing
Went home and addressed a short note to the King:
"If you please will excuse me I won't come to tea,
For home's the best place for all people like me!"

Walking

GRACE ELLEN GLAUBITZ

When Daddy
Walks
With Jean and me,
We have a
Lot of fun
'Cause we can't
Walk as fast
As he,
Unless we
Skip and
Run!
I stretch
And stretch
My legs so far,
I nearly slip
And fall—
But how
Does Daddy
Take such steps?
He doesn't stretch
At all!

My Legs and I

LELAND B. JACOBS

I say to my legs,
"Legs," I say,
"Let's go out
To run and play."

So off we go
My legs and I
Skipping, romping
Jumping high.

Then I say to my legs,
"Legs," I say,
"I'm much too tired
To run and play."

So legs and I
Toward home we go,
Walking and walking,
Slow, slow, slow.

), Zaner-Bloser, Inc.

Friends

Friends can be short or tall,
Big or small,
Wide or slim,
Her or him.
No matter what, they are the best
of all.

LORI HINTZ, Age 10

Speedy

I am speedy up the stairs.
I am speedy down the stairs.

I am speedy here and there.
I am speedy everywhere.

DOUGLAS PEARSON, Age 4

My Shadow

He eats when I eat.
He writes when I write.
Shadow, you're such a copycat.

STEVEN ALMANY, Age 8

Friends

Friends are like an umbrella
On a rainy day.
Even if they leave,
Their friendship will stay.

Friends are like a pool
When it's very hot.
Even if you are little,
Your friendship can be a lot.

Friends are like a song
When you are feeling sad.
But when a friend comes,
It makes you glad.

PRINCE CAMPBELL, Age 9

I Think I'd Like To Be

I think I'd like to be a snake
Or maybe a chocolate foamy cake
Or maybe a camel that can walk
Or maybe a huge beanstalk.
Or maybe, really, I should be
Just plain, ordinary me.

BRET NICHOLAUS, Age 7

How Things Can Shine

The sun is as yellow
As yellow can be,
As bright as my smile.
There's sunshine in me.

EDWARD PUSZ, Age 7

The Two Of Us

KEVIN O'HARA

I am me and you are you,
Together we add up to two.
Our color's different, so's our name,
But we can be friends just the same.

Wanting

When it is hot,
We want it cold.
When it is cold,
We want it hot.
Always wanting
What is not.

AMIR ATTARAN, Age 8

The Sun Song

It's sunning on the sidewalk,
   It's sunning on the trees,
I'll go and put my sun suit on
   And let it sun on me.

JIMMY TUOZZOLO, Age 6

Fun with Fingers

ELLEN MILLER BRIGGS

I'll touch my chin,

my cheek,

my chair.

I'll touch my head,

my heels,

my hair.

I'll touch my knees,

my neck,

my nose.

Then I'll dip down and touch my toes.

Action Rhyme

BETTY WHITE

Choose a ball,
Large or small,
Round as it can be.
(hands form circle)

Toss a ball,
(upward throwing motion)

Watch it fall,
(eyes follow downward)

Bounce it: 1, 2, 3!
(bouncing motion
three times)

Roll a ball,
(bend down and make
rolling motion)

Kick a ball,
(kick with left foot)

Right, left, right.
(three kicking motions,
right foot first)

Catch a ball,
(catching motion)

Bat a ball,
(batting stance)

Swing with all your might.
(full swing around)

Things To Do

Tired and Sleepy   A Finger Play
LUCILLE D. WRIGHT

1. Tired and sleepy, the thumb went to bed.
    (fold thumb down on palm)

2. The pointer, so straight, fell down on his head.
    (fold index finger down on palm)

3. The tall man said he would cuddle up tight.
    (fold middle finger down on palm)

4. The ring finger curled himself out of sight.
    (fold ring finger down on palm)

5. Last of all, weary and lonesome, too,
   The little one hid, and he cried, "Boohoo."
    (fold little finger down on palm)

Body Teasers

KATHY PATTAK

Stand with your back and heels against a wall, legs together. Put a penny on the floor in front of your toes. Now try to pick it up without moving your feet or bending your knees.

Rub your stomach with one hand in a circular motion and pat the top of your head with the other hand.

Try These Tricks

How Important Are Your Thumbs?

Do you know how important your thumbs are? Have you ever thought about what it would mean if you didn't have any? Maybe you don't know the answer.

Here are some experiments you can do to find out just how much you really need your thumbs. Before you begin, tape your thumbs to the palms of your hands with some adhesive tape. (It will be easy to tape the first hand, but it will be difficult to tape the second hand.)

Now you are ready to start:

Try writing your name with a pencil or coloring a picture with a crayon.

Hold a small ball with one hand. If you succeed, then try to throw the ball.

Have someone spread out a few raisins on a plate. Try to pick up one raisin at a time.

Tie your shoes.

Button a coat, a blouse, or a shirt.

Open a car door.

Open a door with a doorknob.

Snap closed some snaps on a piece of clothing.

Zip up a zipper.

Get someone to take the adhesive tape off your tired hands.

When you have those wonderful thumbs free again, wiggle them and look at them. Now ask yourself the question, "How important are my thumbs?" You will find it an easy question to answer.

Leg Lift

Ask a friend to stand next to a wall so that the right side of his right shoe is flush against the wall. Now ask him to lift his left leg and keep it up for a few seconds. He won't be able to do it because, when standing against the wall, he can't shift his weight. The wall prevents him from moving his shoulder to the right in order to maintain his balance.

Lifting Ice

Place an ice cube in a glass about three-quarters full of water. Set it on a table, with a salt-shaker nearby. Ask your friends to try removing the ice cubes with a loop of string. When they fail, show them how. Rest the loop on the cube and shake salt over both. The salt will cause the string to freeze to the cube, and you can lift it easily.

Body Stunts

Try walking like a bear. Keep your arms and legs straight, and move your arms and legs straight. Move the arm and leg on each side at the same time, so that when the right arm goes forward, the right leg goes forward, too. Now if you walk like Bruin, you must move your head from side to side with a growl as you walk. Comical?

Nickel On The Nose

Ask a friend to lie flat on her back on the floor. Balance a nickel on the tip of her nose. Ask her to remove the nickel by moving her nose without moving her head or using her hands. She can't.

Games and Crafts

Description Game

Have a group of children stand in front of the class. One child volunteers to stand in front of the group, facing them. The other members of the group, in turn, then describe the volunteer, one feature at a time. As each feature is mentioned, the persons in the group who do not match that description sit down. Eventually, only the child who is being described is left. For example:

"He is a boy."
(All the girls sit.)
"He has red hair."
(All the boys with hair that is not red sit.)
"He is wearing a blue shirt."
(All the boys wearing another color shirt sit.)
"He has a bandage on his knee."

Play the game with several volunteers. Point out that each child is special, individual in his or her own way. No two are alike.

With movements of their fingers and hands, have the children show how they:

throw	pull	shake
twist	stroke	push
catch	squeeze	pat
hit	wave	tap
scratch	lift	
tickle	point	

You Can See Your Heartbeat

Bend a paper clip as shown, and slip a soda straw over the bent end. Then tape the paper clip to your wrist about in the position shown.

Sit down and rest your arm on a table in order to keep it as steady as possible. If you have taped the paper clip in just the right place, the straw will move back and forth. It will twitch regularly, a little oftener than once a second. It is counting your heartbeat.

If the experiment does not work the first time, don't give up. Try putting the paper clip in different positions. Usually the best place is just below the thick part of your thumb as shown in the illustration. The paper clip must be held down tightly with tape. Or sometimes a rubber band slipped over your hand will hold it tighter and work better. Sometimes it will work better if the hand is bent backward over a milk bottle or a drinking glass.

If you have a watch you can time your heartbeat. How many times does the straw twitch in one minute?

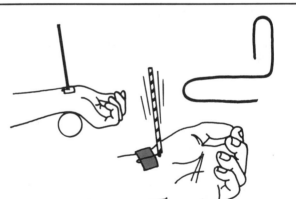

How It Works

How can you count your heartbeat way out on your wrist? Each time your heart pumps blood out into the arteries (the little pipes) in your body, the walls of the arteries stretch. Most of your arteries are down deep inside, but in your wrist there is one close to the surface. It is so close that its stretching makes your skin move in and out slightly every time your heart beats. This is called your pulse.

The straw taped onto your arm is long so that a very slight tilting motion of the paper clip makes the end of the straw move enough to let you see your heartbeat clearly.

Art Projects

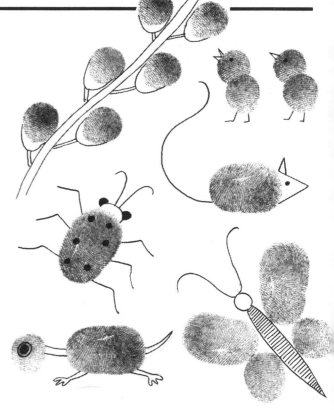

Thumb Fun

Twiddle your fingers and stamp with your thumbs. Imagine things with all your might. Giggle a little or a lot inside, and you're ready for fingerprint pictures.

No one in the wide world can do this art just the way you can, though, and why is that?

Because no one in the wide world has fingerprints exactly like yours. Your fingerprints always say: "Me. Me. Me."

Before you start, cover your work space with newspapers to work on. Keep some paper towels handy, and some soap and water to clean your hands later.

The first step is to press your thumb down on an inked stamp pad. (One that is soaked with ink that will wash off your fingers.) Next press your inked thumb on a piece of paper.

Now what can you do with a thumb print?

Well, practice printing on some paper scraps until you get some good prints. Then take a pen or pencil and add a little of this and a little of that and discover.

A mouse; a ladybird beetle whose house is on fire; a fuzzy, buzzy bumblebee.

Fingertip prints are a quick way to personalize stationery and greeting cards or to make small pictures to frame and hang on the wall.

Funny People

The players sit in a circle. Each one is given a strip of paper. Three inches by twelve inches, is a good size. Fold the paper in quarters, then open it flat again. Each player must draw a head in the top quarter bringing the lines of the neck down into the second quarter. Heads should be like cartoons, the funnier the better. Each player folds the head section back and passes the paper to the neighbor on the left who is honor bound not to peek at the drawing. The neighbor starts with the neck lines and draws the body including the arms down to the waist. He draws the waist lines on to the third section. After folding his drawing under, he passes the paper to the player on the left. Each player draws the legs from the waist to the knees on the third section with lines showing where the legs belong on the fourth section. The fourth player finishes the legs and feet. He passes it to his neighbor on the left, who writes a name on it and tosses it into the center of the group. Someone unfolds the pictures and lays them out like an art exhibit. The names won't fit the pictures, but they add to the fun.

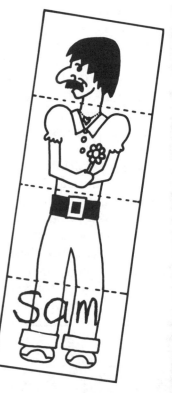

Crafts

Initial Shields

Cut a piece of oak tag, cardboard, or white construction paper in the shape of a shield, about 18 inches high. Divide the shield into three sections as illustrated. In the largest section a picture or design can be created by pasting down a variety of scrap material, circles, or strips. In the upper smaller section a picture can be colored or painted. In the lower section paste your initials, cut out of black construction paper. The finished product can be quite colorful and unique.

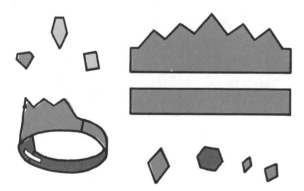

Make A King's Crown

King Midas touched objects and they turned to gold. King Cole was a merry old soul and had three fiddlers to play for him all the while.

You may not be such a king, but you can have a crown just the same.

From yellow construction paper cut two pieces, one 4 inches by 12 inches and one 2 inches by 12 inches. If you don't have construction paper you may use heavy white paper, which you color. The narrower piece will be the back of the crown. The wide piece will be cut into points as in the illustration.

Put dots on the wide piece of paper where you

"Me" Mobile

Sign your name on a sheet of colored paper. Cut around the outline of your name.

Cut your initials from foil. Paste them to another piece of paper. On a third piece of paper, draw a picture of yourself or glue on a snapshot.

Make a small hole at the top of each of the papers and tie a length of yarn through each hole. Use the yarn to attach the items to a hanger.

Attach another piece of yarn to the hanger. Tie a small paper clip to the end of the yarn. Use the paper clip to hang a good school paper, a postcard from a friend, a clipping from the newspaper about your favorite sport, or whatever *you* are interested in.

think the points should come. The first dot will be at the center—6 inches from either end. Look at the illustration and figure where the others should come. Draw the five points so that they look right. Cut on these lines.

To make "jewels" for your crown, you can cut diamond-shaped pieces out of colored construction paper and paste them on, or you can draw the diamonds with colored crayons. Measure your head to see what size the crown should be. With paste or Scotch tape fasten the front and back pieces together. See if it fits your head.

Who said you weren't a king?

Things to Make

Hand Picture

Trace your hand on four different colors of construction paper. Cut the shapes out and arrange on a piece of construction paper of still another color. Glue in place.

This same idea can be used with your footprint.

Necklace of Spools

Materials: twelve empty spools, pure-food coloring, paper toweling, string

Dip the spools in the pure-food coloring, let them dry on a piece of paper toweling. Run a long piece of heavy string through the spools. Tie together, leaving a free space on each side.

Mix and Match Wheel

From heavy black construction paper, cut one 9-inch circle and one 6-inch circle. From old magazines, cut out two people and two animals. Arrange them on the 6-inch circle as shown; then paste the bodies only, with the necks at the edge and the heads extending, unpasted.

Center the small circle on the large one. Fasten them together at the exact center with a large metal dress snap, half of it on the bottom circle and half on the top circle. Cut off the heads one at a time and paste them to the large circle. Be sure that each head fits over the body before cutting and pasting the next one.

Now swing the small circle around, matching bodies and heads. You will come up with some very funny combinations.

Rock Necklaces

Paint a picture or design on a small smooth rock (about the size of a half-dollar). If you use tempera, make the design permanent by covering with varnish or clear nail polish. Squeeze white glue around the edge of the rock. Press yarn onto this for an edging. Glue a yarn loop to the back. Use a piece of yarn for a chain. For the owl, glue a small twig to the bottom. Use two rocks to make the fish.

Cut out the body parts and paste them together.

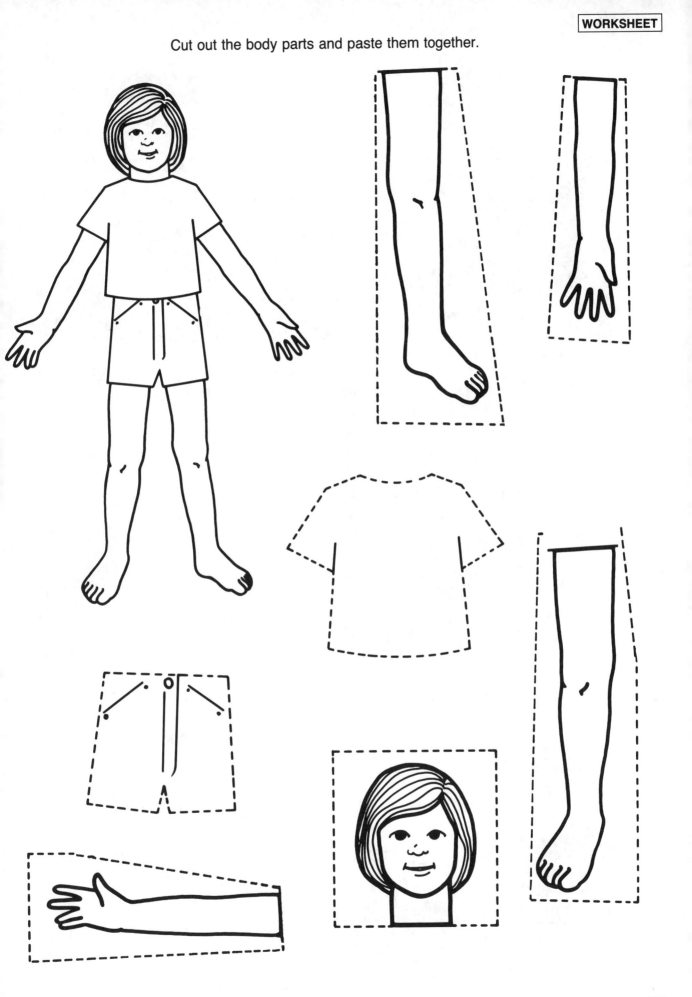

Point to the actions you are able to do.
Which are hard?
Which are easy?
Which do you like best?
Name some other things you would like to be able to do.

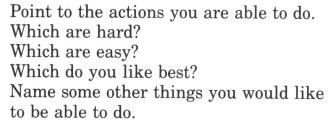

Where Is Thumbkin?

Traditional

Cheerfully

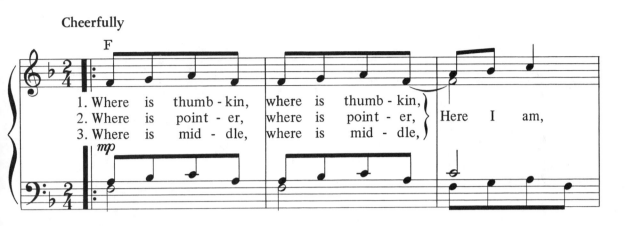

1. Where is thumb-kin, where is thumb-kin, Here I am,
2. Where is point-er, where is point-er,
3. Where is mid-dle, where is mid-dle,

Here I am. How are you this morn-ing? Ver-y well, I thank you.

after last verse repeat and fade

Run a-way, run a-way. Run a-way, run a-way.

(continue similarly)
4. Where is ringer?
5. Where is pinky?

I See A Girl

German Folk Song

Happily

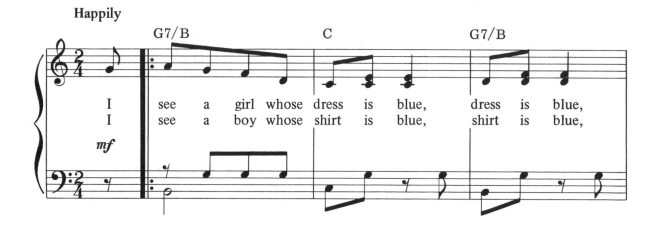

I see a girl whose dress is blue, dress is blue,
I see a boy whose shirt is blue, shirt is blue,

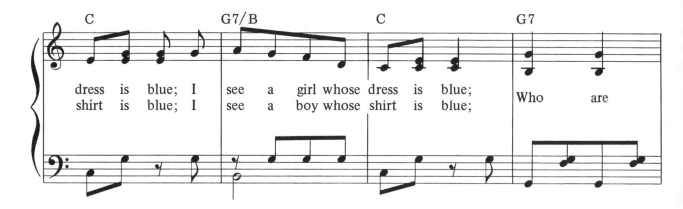

dress is blue; I see a girl whose dress is blue;
shirt is blue; I see a boy whose shirt is blue;

Who are

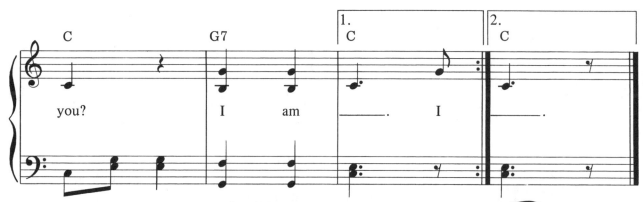

you?

1.
I am _____ . I

2.
_____ .

How I Learn

Introduction

Every day a child's mind records many new impressions. The information gathered comes through one or more of his or her sensory modality channels. These modalities permit the child to receive impressions by seeing, hearing, feeling, smelling and/or tasting.

The learning process is dependent upon a child's ability to receive and interpret messages from the senses. Throughout this unit, the children will be asked to think about how they use their various senses. At the same time, by close observation, the teacher will have the chance to become aware of the unique modality strengths and weaknesses of the individual child. The ways the children approach the variety of activities they engage in should demonstrate clearly to the teacher the differing senses children use to learn about the world.

It is hoped that during this process each child will become more aware of how he or she learns. Individual perceptual modes affect the way each child handles information. As a child receives a stimulus, the brain not only interprets it but stores the resulting information for future use. The teacher's job is to expand and reinforce this process by providing the child with extensive language experience to underscore the relationship between impressions and words. This language experience gives the child greater efficiency in his or her mental sorting, storing and retrieving processes which, to a large degree, determine academic success.

The "How I Learn" unit aims to put the child in closer contact with his or her own senses by showing how each sense works in its own way. With this increased awareness the child begins to develop a fuller understanding of the world.

Concepts To Be Taught

I. **A person learns through his or her five senses.**

II. **Since individuals are different, they are also different in the ways in which they learn.**

III. **Special body parts are used for receiving information.**

IV. The body parts that help the children learn should be protected from harm.

V. A person has *feelings* about the things he or she learns.

Information for Teaching Concepts

I. A person learns through his or her five senses.

Ask the children if they have ever received a present wrapped in special paper. Then ask, "Did you wonder what was inside? How could you find out what was inside?" Encourage a variety of responses that cover the five senses. Examples are:

1) unwrap the gift
2) shake the box
3) look at the size and shape of the package
4) listen for any sounds
5) feel the package
6) smell

Have a surprise package wrapped for the children. Then have them use their senses to determine what is inside. Raisins or popcorn make good contents. Be sure to encourage the children to talk about how they can determine the contents.

Write the five senses on a chart with a rebus figure beside each.

Discuss with the children how they learn by using different body parts. Place a piece of popcorn and a raisin in view of the class. Ask, "Are these two objects the same?" The response should be, "No, they are *different*." Then ask, "How are they different?" Encourage responses that describe size, shape, and color. Ask the children how they were able to tell the differences. Point out that most people use their eyes to see the differences between a raisin and a piece of popcorn.

Blindfold a child and place a raisin on one hand and a piece of popcorn in the other. Ask the children to identify which object is in which hand. Talk about how the children use their sense of touch for learning.

Repeat this activity with other blindfolded children, using taste and smell to determine the object.

Out of view of the class, place a raisin in a container and shake it, asking the children to decide if this is the raisin or the popcorn just by listening.

Reinforce the idea that they can use one, two, three, four or all five senses when they are learning. Have the children identify ways they have used one or more of their senses that day. Examples are:

1) heard alarm
2) smelled toast
3) felt shirt being buttoned
4) saw sun shining
5) tasted cold milk
6) heard school bus
7) felt snow pack underfoot
8) smelled smoke
9) saw a picture on the chalkboard
10) heard a story

II. Since individuals are different, they are also different in the ways in which they learn.

Introduce this concept with the story, "A Gift of Feeling," on page 80. Before you read the story, ask the children to remember all the ways by which they learned what was in the surprise package. Review how they used their five senses to identify the raisin and the popcorn. Explain that all of the senses were used to help them learn about the raisin and the piece of popcorn, but that sometimes it is not possible to use all the senses. In the story, "A Gift of Feeling," Steve uses his sense of touch the most, and Maria helps Steve to read in a very special way. Have the children listen to discover how Steve learns. After reading the story to the children, talk together about Steve's blindness and what he has to do to learn things that other people learn by seeing with their eyes.

Ask the children to think about how a hearing-impaired or physically-impaired child learns by adapting. Emphasize the beauty of having five senses, so that they can learn in different ways.

Engage in activities that help the children to be aware of the use of each sense. Always point out that each person is unique. Therefore, each does not see, hear, taste, feel and smell in the same way, nor does each person receive the same information from a source of sensory stimulation. Example activities are:

See

Have the children:
1) match like shapes, colors, objects.
2) describe a picture after a ten-second viewing.
3) close their eyes and describe an object in the classroom. (Ask questions about some objects, for example, Is there a picture of a bird in our class? How many doors are in our room?)
4) do a hidden picture activity.

Hear

Have the children:
1) match shaker boxes by sound (place rice, blocks, coins and salt in several separate packages with plastic lids). The children shake the packages and match those with like sounds.
2) identify sounds heard in the classroom.
3) make drum sticks from a cardboard roll. Have the children listen to a series of beats and repeat the series they heard.
4) identify sounds that protect them, such as sirens, teakettle whistles, fire alarms, horns, buzzers, whistles, voices.
5) follow spoken directions to make a picture.
   Example: Draw a long box.
             Draw two circles under the beginning and two circles under the end
               of the box.
             Draw slanted lines from the corners across to the other corners.

Touch/Move

Have the children:
1) feel common objects found in the classroom and then describe their size, texture, and shape.

2) State which of the objects below are rough and which are smooth.

stone	pineapple
banana	grass
carpet	balloon
sandpaper	apple

3) State which of these are hot and which are cold.

icicles	refrigerator	fire
skillet	snow	soup cooking
tea kettle	ice cream	

Smell

1) Collect objects that have distinct odors, such as flower, pickle, soap, pine cone. Wrap each of them so as to hide their shapes. Have a smelling contest to see who can guess the items.
2) Have the children identify their favorite smells and their least favorite smells.
3) Have the children think about smells that are helpful, for example, smoke warns of fire, food burning warns the cook to look, fragrance of plants helps with plant identity.
4) Have the children state which of these are easy to recognize by smell.

sauerkraut	paint	flower
guitar	paper	squirrel
onions	fish frying	peanuts
chair	vinegar	glasses

5) Read the story "Bobby Sniffs Around the Block," on page 82.

Taste

Have the children:
1) state which foods are usually eaten cold and which are eaten hot.

watermelon	soup
toast	pears
gelatin	corn

2) identify foods that are sour and foods that are sweet.
3) paste pictures of food on a paper plate and ask the children to describe how the foods taste. Encourage descriptive words. Examples are *sweet, sour, salty, bitter.* Talk about the textures of the foods. Encourage descriptions such as *smooth, hard, crunchy, hot, cold, slippery, soft.*
4) conduct a taste party. In a muffin tin place food items that are cut into bite size portions. Use cheese, apples, bananas, crackers, dates, dried beef, pretzels. Have each child select one food and taste. Then after each has tasted one food, have a child describe what he or she ate, without saying the food's name. Those children who think they ate the same food should stand up and name the food.
5) make a no-cook recipe (pudding or peanut butter) and taste it.

III. Special body parts are used for receiving information.

Have the children look at the chart that was made earlier listing the five senses with the rebus illustrations. Ask the children to tell what body part helps them to see, hear, touch/move, taste, smell. Read "How A Body Does," page 84, to the children.

Discuss each of the body parts listed and how they work to bring the information they receive to the brain. Have the children look at each body part (pair students so they can look at each other's ears, mouths and noses). Discuss the shapes and special features. Examples are:

eye—explain that the retina acts like a camera, eyelid acts as a cover, eyebrows and eyelashes protects from dirt, liquid (tears) keeps it moist.

ear—explain that the outside helps to catch sounds and channel vibrations to the inner ear; (compare the ear to a tape recorder.)

nose—have the children look at the two openings called nostrils and the fine hairs that catch the dust so as to protect the lungs. Have the children sniff and observe the movement of the nostrils.

mouth/tongue—explain that taste buds are located on the tongue, and that different parts of the tongue pick up different tastes.

hands—explain that the hand has five moveable fingers that have tender surfaces to help grab, hold, and feel.

IV. The body parts that help the children learn should be protected.

Encourage the children to think about how each body part has built-in protection. This would include the hair around the eyes and nose, the outer ear and the small opening to the inner ear, the lips that close in front of the tongue and the muscles that let the tongue move, and fingers that can curl or move quickly and have a protective nail covering. Discuss with the children ways to protect their sense organs. Avoid telling children what "not" to do, but rather state ideas in a positive manner. Examples are:

Keep sharp objects away from eyes.

Avoid dust by closing eyes.

Keep ears clean and free from objects.

Keep hands away from motors or machinery that is moving.

V. A person has feelings about the things he learns.

Hold up a red or yellow color card. Ask the children to close their eyes and think about the color. Ask, "What did you think about?" Encourage children to express any ideas they had, including food or household items. If no one mentions feelings, tell them that some colors seem to make people feel happier, sadder, warmer than other colors.

Explain to the children that while they are learning, they are also having feelings about what they see, hear, touch, taste or smell. Have the children look at magazines and find pictures that make them feel happy. Give them opportunities to share happy pictures.

Discuss with the children that everyone is different. People look different, they think differently and they feel differently about what they learn. Emphasize how dull the world would be if everyone liked the same food, color, book, television program or game. Encourage the children to perceive that differences are nice and that they must respect another's right to think and feel differently.

Thinking and Reasoning

Ask your children these questions:

Which has bigger ears, you or a dog?

Would it be fun to stand barefoot on ice?

When you hold snow in your hand, does it feel warm or cold?

Billy reached into a box and quickly pulled out his hand, saying, "A mouse is in there!" How could he know this without seeing the mouse?

Do you listen to music with your eyes or your ears?

Amy and her mother were in the kitchen. Suddenly Amy said, "Somebody is at the front door." She couldn't see or hear anybody from where she was. How could she know somebody was at the door?

"Oh, you have just painted this room," said the blind lady. How could she have known this?

Do you smell with your ears?

When you hear a whistle blowing, how do you know it is not a bell ringing?

Can you feel the wind? Can you hear it?

Which is more sour, a lollipop or a pickle?

Which tastes colder, ice cream or cake?

"Oh, we are having bacon for breakfast," said Sharon. No one had told her. How could Sharon know they were having bacon for breakfast?

How can you tell that your nine-month-old baby brother can hear?

Do sugar and salt look very much alike? Do they taste the same?

If you heard some children in another room talking but had never seen them, would you know whether they were boys or girls?

Can you taste anything before putting it into your mouth?

Can you hear another person when he coughs? Can you hear him when he thinks? Can you hear him when he swallows? Can you always hear him when he cries?

Mrs. Corey was so hard of hearing, she couldn't hear a word! Yet when Mrs. Stone told her about an accident, she understood what Mrs. Stone said. How did she understand it?

Are cookies sweet or sour?

"What happened to your thumb?", Lois asked Janet. What could have caused Lois to ask this question?

When your food is too hot to eat, what should you do?

"This lamp bulb has burned out," said Sid. How could he know it had?

Did you ever see a loud noise?

Do we eat flowers in order to enjoy them? How do we enjoy flowers?

Is maple syrup sour or sweet?

Why don't tiny babies wear glasses?

Can you see it thunder?

Name some things you could recognize from their odor without seeing them.

Can you hear and see at the same time?

How could a blind person know when food on the stove is burning?

Can you hear a person smile? (Laugh?)

Can you find the hidden nose, hand, eye, mouth, and ear in this picture?

Circle what's wrong in this picture.

Using Your Senses

Which may you enjoy by hearing?
by seeing?   by smelling?
by tasting?   by handling?

Things We Feel

Which is more smooth?

a window pane or a stuffed chair

a baby's face or her father's face

a gravel walk or a bare waxed floor

a handkerchief or a washcloth

the tread on a tire of a car or the car windows

a ripe tomato or a ripe strawberry

a newspaper or a sheet of sandpaper

new ice on a pond or ice frozen from slush in the street

a board just sawed or this board after sanding

a leather coat or a burlap bag

a turtle or an eel

your eyebrows or your lips

woolen mitts or cotton gloves

Would you like to walk barefoot:

over a floor covered with soft thick carpet?

over a soft, muddy road on a warm day?

over a field covered with three inches of snow?

over a soft newly plowed field?

over a grassy lawn?

over a road covered with sharp, rough gravel?

over the sand by the seashore?

over a field from which grain or hay was lately cut?

over a concrete sidewalk on a very hot day?

Which of these things are heavy and which are light?

house	sponge
car	typewriter
egg	balloon
kite	pencil
table	couch

Which is softer?

a glass bottle or a cardboard carton

mud or a stone

a piece of wire or a rubber band

a pretzel or a pancake

the coat of a cat or the coat of a pig

your cheek or your forehead

a ripe apple or an apple not yet ripe

a fresh slice of bread or a slice of toast

Which of these are hot? Which are cold?

icicles	refrigerator
fireplace	soup
ice cream	sun
teakettle	snow

Which are rough?
Which are smooth?

stone   balloon
pineapple   carpet
banana   sandpaper
grass   apple

Which is easier to hold in one hand?

a rooster or a mouse
a peanut or a saucer
a grasshopper or a rabbit
a teacup or a thimble
a rubber ball or four eggs
a baseball bat or a button
a baseball or a football

Which of these things are soft and which are hard?

marshmallow   sweater
desk   sponge
snow   pencil
brick   kitten
pillow   feather
wall   water
stone   nail
car   tree
couch   chalk

Which of these things could be made smaller by squeezing it in your hand?

handkerchief   envelope
spool   sponge
clothespin   block
flower   pencil
nail   pebble
mitten   strawberry

Which of these things would melt if you held them in your hand?

ice
spoon
sugar
butter
candle
chocolate
apple
stone
ice cream
salt

Which are slippery?
Which are smooth but not slippery?

the top of a desk
new ice on a pond
a tile floor in a bathroom
a live fish
writing paper
the skin of a tomato
a man's face after shaving
a wet, muddy road

Which can you easily separate or unmix?

Snow and ice mixed in a pan of hot water.

Milk and sugar mixed in a cup of water.

Screws, marbles, and buttons mixed together in a pan.

Chocolate chips baked in cookies.

Green jelly beans mixed with red ones and black ones.

Quarters, dimes, and half-dollars put together in a box.

Sounds

Can you recognize and describe these sounds when you do not see the source? Make any of the sounds that you can.

an airplane overhead
a motor-driven lawn mower
thunder
a violin playing
an explosion
a car starting
a baby crying
a person driving a nail
a trombone playing
a dog barking
two cars crashing
a duck quacking
a cow mooing
a drum being beaten
screeching brakes of a car
a church bell ringing
a bee buzzing
a rooster crowing
a lion roaring
a frog croaking
a doorbell ringing
a watch ticking
a balloon bursting
a telephone ringing
a cat meowing

Pretend you are alone in a dark, quiet room and you hear a sound like *sssssss*. How many things can you think of that might make that sound?

Suppose you heard, "drip-drip-drip". How many things could make that sound?

Suppose you heard a banging sound. What could cause that?

Suppose you heard music. How many things can you think of that might make music?

Which sounds do you like to hear? Which sounds do you not like to hear?

a cricket chirping
waves dashing against a rocky shore
a child crying
dishes falling from a tray
a person moaning with pain
water dripping from a roof
a door slamming
a kitty purring
a siren on a fire engine
a door screeching
the wind blowing through trees
a clock ticking

Which of these make sounds and which do not make sounds?

boy
butterfly
swan
apple
caterpillar
chalk
dog
milk
girl
automobile
hat
cup
radio
desk
typewriter

If you could not use words, what sounds could you make:
to tell someone to be quiet?
to call a cat or a dog?
to show you enjoyed your food?
to show you are cold?

Do we usually eat these foods cold or hot?

Which part or parts of these foods do we eat?
Which get softer as they are cooked? Which get harder?

Using Your Senses

In each pair, which makes more noise when walking or running?

Which of these have you heard walking or running?

a turtle or a rabbit
a puppy or a lamb
a cat or a boy
a fox or a pony
a donkey or a pig
a mouse or a squirrel
a deer or a goat

In each pair, which would feel softer?

a mouse or a pig
a squirrel or a fish
a chicken or a turtle
a balloon or a block
a sponge or a brick
a baby's hand or a grown-up's hand
a baked potato or a raw potato
a stone or a ripe tomato

What's the Sense?

Before each statement below could have been made, which sense was used—smell, taste, sight, hearing?

"My, she has a beautiful voice."

"During the night an airplane flew low over our house."

"Sauerkraut must be cooking in the kitchen."

"That picture is so colorful!"

"There must be someone at the door."

"The dog wants to come in now."

"You certainly have lost a lot of weight."

"Mr. Jones must be having a barbecue."

"This apple is delicious."

Animal Ear Muffs

Cut a 3-inch by 20-inch piece of felt. Using a pair of scissors, round the ends of the felt.

From a different color felt, cut four small triangles for ears. Glue a pair of ears about 3 inches from each rounded end. Below each set of ears, glue or sew a pair of buttons for eyes and a small wool pompon for a nose.

Sew a shoelace under each newly made animal face, and tie your new muffs over your ears.

Which of these things smell pleasant?

Which of these things smell unpleasant?

What are some other things that smell pleasant or unpleasant?

Which smell might protect you from harm?

Connect the picture on the left to the matching picture on the right by drawing a line.

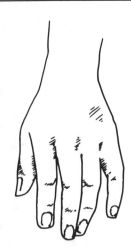

How many differences can you find in the two pictures? Circle them.

Melvin Mole

BETH LIPSEY, Age 9

One day Melvin Mole, sitting inside his tunnel, heard a knock on his door. "Who is it? Come right in. The door's open."

Now, you might wonder who would visit a mole, but Melvin was a very bright and polite mole. Many forest folks visited him. Today it was Susie Squirrel.

"Melvin, I was wondering about your eyesight," Susie exclaimed. "Did you ever see flowers? Did you ever see trees?"

Melvin's happy-to-see-a-friend expression turned to an unhappy-to-hear-what-he-didn't-want-to-hear expression. "Susie," Melvin said, after a pause, "Susie, I've always wanted to." Then he burst into tears.

"Now, now, quiet down, Melvin. I've got just the thing for you," Susie said. "Rory Raccoon just moved into Merry Meadow. He's an eye doctor, and he can give you a pair of these." Susie reached into her pocket, tugged and pulled, and finally came up with her own new eyeglasses.

Melvin was flabbergasted. He knew that humans could get eyeglasses, but animals . . .?

"Come on," said Susie. "Let's pay a visit to Doctor Raccoon."

Once there, Melvin got scared. He was calmed down by the thought of a no-more-nearsighted Melvin! Lost in thoughts, Melvin was startled by a voice saying "Come in!"

Melvin Mole, one of the most nearsighted moles in Fairy Forest, now can read, write, and is much brighter than before. He owes it all to Susie Squirrel and her new eyeglasses.

Sounds

JOSEPH JACOBS

Some of the most common things in our lives are very interesting. They are so common that we do not notice them. This is true of sound. The tick of the clock, the toot of the automobile horn, the fire siren, the school bell, the song of the birds, music, and speech are all sounds.

Have you noticed that some sounds are pleasant, while others are not? The rattle of the train wheels on the hard rails is not pleasing, yet we like the song of the bird and the soft tone of the violin. What makes the difference?

What is sound? You might say,

"When I strike a bell with a hard object I make sound." You are right, but what makes the sound? If you place your finger on the bell just as soon as possible after you strike it, you will notice that the bell is vibrating, though it is moving so rapidly you cannot see it move. You also notice that when you touch the bell the rapid motion stops, and there is no more sound. While the bell is vibrating it makes air waves, waves somewhat like the ones you see in the water after a stone has been dropped. These air waves finally reach your eardrum and you hear sound.

A Gift of Feeling

BARBARA SCHENCK

Maria slowly counted the money in her hand. Two dollars and seven cents. No matter how many times she counted it, it was the same. And it was never enough. She stuffed the coins back in her pocket and sat leaning against the oak tree, staring at the sky. The book catalog under her arm dropped to the ground. She had wanted to buy her brother Steve a book for his birthday—a braille book because Steve was blind and was just learning to read braille.

"He's never had a book he could read himself," Maria had told her mother. "His own—to keep, I mean."

Her mother nodded. "I know," she said. "You read so much to him, though, Maria. He likes that. And braille books are expensive. He's only going to be eight. There will be time for his own books later on." She laid a hand on Maria's shoulder and smiled.

Maria knew she was right. Steve did like it when Maria read him books and stories. But Maria also remembered something her mother did not. One night after she had finished reading to Steve, her brother remained still for a very long time. Then he said, "You really love that story, don't you, Maria?"

Maria looked at the worn, often-turned pages. "Yes," she said.

"And it's there any time you want to read it." Steve's voice was getting excited and he sat up.

"Yes," Maria agreed.

"I wish I had a book," Steve said simply, and then he lay back down. "I wish I had a book that I could pick up and make the story come alive again, too. All these books are the same for me."

So it had to be a book—a braille book—because regular ones all felt alike to someone who couldn't see.

Suddenly, Maria sat upright. That's it, she thought. If a book didn't feel like the rest—even if it weren't a real braille book—wouldn't Steve be really able to know that book? Her excitement grew, and the more she mulled over the idea the more she knew what she would do.

For the next few weeks Maria disappeared after school. She had a lot of work to do before Steve's birthday. During that exciting month she visited Steve's braille teacher, Mr. Gage, the librarian at the public library, the hardware and art supply stores, and soon she had everything she needed to begin work.

Finally, Steve's birthday arrived. That Sunday morning Maria was awake even before her brother. She got up quietly, dressed, and slipped outside to her dad's workshop. There she checked over Steve's present once again. Then carefully she wrapped the package. Tucking it under her arm, she went back into the house.

Her mother was making waffles, Steve's favorite. "Good morning," she said with a smile. "Is that for Steve?"

Maria nodded. She put it on the table by her brother's place with the other gifts.

"Where's Steve?" Maria asked.

"Right here," her dad answered as he opened the door to the kitchen. He and Steve came in smiling.

"Happy birthday," Maria said. She caught her brother by the arm. "Do you want your eight swats now or later?"

Steve laughed. "Just try to get them." Then, sniffing, he said, "Mm, waffles."

"Aren't you going to open your presents?" Dad asked.

Steve went to his chair. He began opening his gifts as Maria handed them to him, reserving her own for last. Mom and Dad gave Steve a jacket and a sack of red clay because he loved to make things with his hands. From his grandfather came the knapsack Steve had talked of but never dreamed of getting. At last Maria handed him a flat box. "This one's from me," she said. "Be careful."

"OK," Steve said. Slowly and deliberately, he removed the wrapping. Mom and Dad looked at Maria questioningly. She smiled slightly at them but turned to watch her brother. Steve took the lid off the box and lifted out his gift. His hands moved slowly over it.

"A book," he breathed. His hands brushed the poster-board cover. "Hey!" he exclaimed. "Letters! I can feel letters. Is it sandpaper or what?" He stopped and slowly traced the letters on the cover—sandpaper letters spelling Steve. And after he had done it once, he did it again.

"It's *my* book," he said joyously, opening the first page. On heavy paper there were raised, cut-out cardboard outlines of four people—a man, a woman, a girl and a boy. Steve's story, as Maria had written it carefully in newly learned braille, began at the bottom of the page.

Stumbling a bit, Steve read the two or three sentences on each page. He read that he always had eaten more graham crackers than Maria when he was little, and he felt the graham cracker Maria had glued in on that page. One page recalled their vacation at the beach and had sand, pebbles, and shells on it. Another told of Uncle Bill's farm with glued-on corn, soybeans, and straw. On each page Maria had told the story in braille and, as Dad said, "With illustrations."

"I've got a book," Steve said as he closed the last page. "And it really is my own story. I can read it again and again, and I can keep it forever." He turned to where Maria was sitting at the table watching him. "Oh, Maria, thank you. It's the best gift ever."

Maria looked at Steve's smiling face, at his hands which still moved quietly over the cover, and knew it had been worth it. Steve's own book was worth every hour Maria had spent learning the braille alphabet, every error she had made transcribing the story with the stylus Mr. Gage had shown her how to use, every new beginning to make Steve's story simple, yet alive and able to be felt and read by her brother alone.

"It was fun, Steve," Maria said. "I'm glad I made it. Maybe together we can make you a whole library!"

Bobby Sniffs Around the Block

LUCY FUCHS

Bobby loved dogs. On his birthday Daddy came home with a beautiful brown dog with floppy ears. The dog was excited when Bobby took her. She wagged her tail and licked Bobby's face. She sniffed Bobby all over. She sniffed at Mother and Daddy, too.

"Thank you for the dog," Bobby said to Mother and Daddy. "I'm going to name her Ginger."

"You'll have to feed her every day and give her baths," said mother.

"Oh, I will," said Bobby.

Bobby showed Ginger his room. He showed her all around the house. Ginger sniffed at everything.

"Mother," Bobby asked, "why does Ginger sniff at everything?"

"That is how she learns to know things," Mother said. "She knows things by their smell."

Bobby sniffed the air. "I think I'll try that, too," he said.

When Bobby woke up the next morning he thought of Ginger. Then he closed his eyes again. He sniffed hard. "Bacon and eggs for breakfast," he called to Mother.

"Come and see," Mother said. Bobby was right. There was bacon and eggs and there was toast with butter and jelly.

Mother brought him a large glass of milk. He sniffed at it. It smelled cold and good.

He sniffed at Mother. She smelled like a mother—clean and sweet and a little bit like buttered toast.

Bobby's daddy was reading the paper. Bobby sniffed at the newspaper. "Did it rain this morning?" he asked.

"Yes, it did," Daddy said. "Very early this morning. Why?"

"The paper smells a little like rain," Bobby said. He sniffed at Daddy. Daddy smelled a little like shaving cream.

"You'd better feed Ginger," Daddy said after breakfast.

Bobby sniffed at the dog food. It smelled like meat, but not meat for people. He took it to Ginger. He sniffed at Ginger, and Ginger sniffed at him.

Bobby and Ginger took a walk around the block. They both sniffed at everything. When they came to the field where he and Paul and Diane played ball, he closed his eyes and sniffed hard. It smelled like dirt and balls and fun.

They walked on to Mrs. Brown's flower garden. Again Bobby closed his eyes and sniffed. Ginger sniffed, too. Mrs. Brown's garden smelled like roses and gardenias.

Mrs. Brown was working in the garden. "Your garden smells good," he said.

"Thank you," she called, and she went back to work.

Next to Mrs. Brown's flower garden was Mr. Jones's vegetable garden. Bobby and Ginger sniffed hard. Bobby could smell onions and tomatoes and strawberries. Mr. Jones was watching him. "What are you doing?" he asked.

"I am smelling your garden. It smells like good food," Bobby said. Ginger barked and wagged her tail.

Bobby and Ginger walked on past more houses. They sniffed at the trees as they went. Some trees smelled exactly like Christmas trees. Others smelled like nuts and acorns.

Bobby stopped in front of a little store. He closed his eyes and sniffed. He smelled spices and fruit and many other good things. He smelled peppermint candy and jelly beans. Ginger sniffed and wagged her tail.

Bobby went on and on. At last he stopped in front of a little yellow house. It was the house of the Smith family. He sniffed. He smelled something funny. It was something that was wrong. He smelled smoke.

He ran to the door and rang the doorbell. Ginger barked. Mrs. Smith came to the door in an apron. "I smell smoke," he told her. "Maybe your house is on fire."

Mrs. Smith laughed. "Come and see," she said.

Bobby and Ginger went with her to the back of the house. There she was burning some trash. "See, that's the smoke you smelled," Mrs. Smith told Bobby.

"But I have something for you," she said as she went into the kitchen. Bobby closed his eyes when she brought it to him. He sniffed. He smelled something cold and sweet and good. And he smelled chocolate.

"Chocolate ice cream!" he cried.

"No," said Mrs. Smith, "take a look."

It was white ice cream covered with chocolate syrup.

"Thank you, Mrs. Smith," Bobby said.

Ginger sniffed and barked. She wagged her tail. Mrs. Smith looked at Ginger. Then she got a dog biscuit for her. Ginger barked to say thank you.

"Thank you both, Bobby and Ginger, for smelling my fire," Mrs. Smith said. "But now I think that you two had better sniff your way home."

Why Do Mice Have Pink Ears?

Long ago there lived a farm mouse. His name was Charlie. He lived in a little cubbyhole under the ground. He was a smart mouse but he had a problem—a very bad, bad problem. You know that in the old, old days the mice had gray ears and the cats could see the mice very well. Many of the mice were caught. The cats had pretty good dinners.

Well, one day the little mouse saw a pretty pink rose. He thought that if he had pink inside of his ears and gray on the outside, the pink would look like the rose and the gray would look like the ground. He picked the rose and went to the village to get his ears colored pink. When he got to the village, he said to a boy, "Please color the inside of my ears pink."

He said, "I'll be glad to."

He colored the mouse's ears pink. The mouse went home and he never got caught by the cats. He passed his pink ears on to other mice and the mice hardly get caught any more. Only the smart cats can catch them.

KAROLYN DASCHBACH, Age 8

How a Body Does

MARCUS O'BRIEN

Susan and Sax were sitting on Uncle Jim's front porch waiting for him to come home. They petted Duke, the big collie dog, and listened to the cars on the main street and watched to see which would turn off and bring their uncle. All of a sudden Duke pricked up his ears and wagged his tail. He was already running out on the lawn when the car turned the corner and pulled into the driveway.

"Duke beat us again," said Susan. "He knew you were coming even before we could see your car. How could he know?"

"I guess he just has sharp ears and knows the sound of my car," answered Uncle Jim.

"But how can you know just by hearing?" asked Susan.

"Well, how do you know just by seeing? How do you know that Duke is wagging his tail?"

"Don't make fun of me, Uncle Jim," said Susan, just a little bit peeved. "I can see him wag his tail."

"I wasn't trying to make fun of you, Susan. You really have a pretty big question. How do we know about the things around us? Do you want me to tell you how your body does it?"

"Oh, yes," said Susan and Sax.

Uncle Jim thought a minute and then said, "Most of us think of the things around us as if we were seeing them. But seeing, or SIGHT, is just one of our five senses. Close your eyes, Susan. Now, tell me what Duke is doing."

"He is panting," said Susan. "I can HEAR him."

"HEARING is a sense, just as seeing is. Now, Sax, tell me what Aunt Martha is cooking for supper."

"It smells like fish," said Sax.

"And when you eat it, it will taste like fish, won't it? TASTE and SMELL are two senses. There is one more. Close your eyes again, Susan. Now what did I put into your hand?"

"It's your fountain pen, Uncle Jim. I can feel the clip."

"That's your fifth sense, the sense of TOUCH. It works all over the outside of your body and tells you whether things are hot or cold, too."

"My, I didn't know my fingers were so smart," said Susan.

"They aren't," said Uncle Jim. "The only part of you that is smart is your brain. It has a kind of telephone system that reaches out to all parts of your body. All together it is called the NERVOUS SYSTEM. There are little receivers in your skin that respond to touch just as there are other receivers in the back of your eye that respond to light. There are still other kinds of receivers in your ear for sound, at the back of your tongue for taste, and in the lining of your nose for smell.

"There are just thousands of these little receivers hooked up to the brain by nerve fibers that carry messages just as if they were little wires. It is your brain that sorts out the different kinds of messages and tells you just what each of them means. So you see that it is because of your brain that you know what things are by tasting or smelling or touching or hearing or seeing them."

Galoshes

RHODA W. BACMEISTER

Susie's galoshes
Make splishes and sploshes
And slooshes and sloshes,
As Susie steps slowly
Along in the slush.

They stamp and they tramp
On the ice and concrete,
They get stuck in the muck and the mud;
But Susie likes much better to hear

The slippery slush
As it slooshes and sloshes,
And splishes and sploshes,
All round her galoshes!

Poems

Cotton Candy

S. LAVERN WILBER

I love a cotton candy,
Spun up rosy pink,
But when I touch it with my tongue,
The candy starts to shrink!

I'd like to keep it always;
I'd like to make it last;
But it disappears before me
Unless I eat it fast!

Rain

I like to listen
To the beat of the rain.
Drip, drop, drip, drop!
I think the beat is very sweet.
The rhythm is just like a band.
Drip, drop, drip, drop, drip, drop!

BONNI LU NASE, Age 8

The Sea

The wonderful sea is a beautiful place,
Where starfish and seashells are found,
And all of the people that come to the sea
Admire the beautiful sound.

LINDA RIDGE, Age 8

The Fire

I like the fire, it is bright and warm
And dries me out after a storm.

I love the colors, red, yellow, and gold.
It keeps me warm when I feel cold.

It crackles and spits as up the flames fly
And the fiery sparks drift up to the sky.

All stretched out sleeps my little dog
In front of my fire with the nice flaming log.

KATHARINE FRANKS, Age 7

Senses

KEVIN O'HARA

I think it would be rather queer
To wake and find I had no ear.
Or to bend down to smell a rose
And find myself without a nose.
Or miss my hand, my mouth, my eye,
Their loss would make me want to cry.
I'm glad I have my senses five,
They make it fun to be alive.

When It's Cold

My feet twinkle.
My hands shiver.
My teeth chatter.
My fingers shake.
And that's how I feel when it's cold.

CARTER GLIDEWELL, Age 8

Favorites

KEVIN O'HARA

So many things I like to see,
   A dog, a pig, an apple tree,
   A railroad train, a bumble bee,
   And in a mirror, even me.

So many things I like to hear,
   The tooting horns of the New Year,
   The gentle voice of someone dear,
   A marching band as it comes near.

So many things I like to feel,
   A big fish tugging on my reel,
   A furry kitten, not an eel,
   A bicycle of shining steel.

So many things I like to smell,
   A tulip, lilac and bluebell,
   A rose or daisy in the dell,
   A roasted peanut in its shell.

So many things I like to taste,
   A big, fat turkey that you baste,
   A frosted cake with candles graced,
   A glass of water when I've raced.

So many things I like, that's true,
How many things are liked by you?

The Sounds I Like To Hear

The sounds I like
are not the same,
but I hear them all
at my favorite game.
One of the sounds I must
report
is a basketball bouncing
on the court.
The sound of the people
up in the stands,
as they whistle and shout
and clap their hands.
The sound of the buzzer
as the game begins,
the shouts of encouragement
from all of my friends.
The sound I like better yet
is the sound of the ball
swishing the net.
The sound of all the running
feet,
the sound of victory,
oh, how sweet.
The sound of joy when
the game is won
The sound of the coach saying,
"A job well done."

SCOTT FOGLE, Age 10

Sounds Around Us

RUTH MANLEY POWERS

A goose can honk like an automobile.
A snake can hiss
Like this-s-s-s-s-s.
An owl can hoot like a railroad train.
A bee can buzz
And does-z-z-z-z-z.
A cow can moo like an old foghorn.
What pigeons do

Is coo-oo-oo-oo-oo-oo.
   But nicer than hisses
     or buzzes
     or coos
Is the pur-r-r-r-r-r-
     that I hear
From my kitty.
It's pretty.

Finger Plays

The Parade

Clap your hands.
(clap hands)

Stamp your feet.
(stamp feet)

A parade is coming down the street.
(shade eyes with right hand, looking to the left)

Rum-tum-tum booms the big red drum.
(beat imaginary drum)

Root-toot-toot tweets the little flute.
(blow imaginary flute)

Bong-bong-bong clangs the big brass gong.
(hit imaginary gong)

Clap your hands.
(clap hands)

Stamp your feet.
(stamp feet)

A parade is marching down the street.
(shade eyes with right hand, looking to the right)

Fun With Fingers

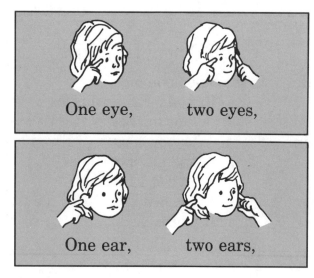

One eye, two eyes,

One ear, two ears,

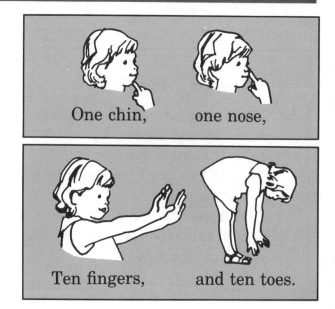

One chin, one nose,

Ten fingers, and ten toes.

More Finger Fun

All for Benny

Here's a ball for Benny
Big and soft and round.
Here is Benny's hammer,
Oh, how he can pound!

Here is Benny's music,
Clapping, clapping so.
Here are Benny's soldiers
Standing in a row.

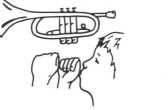

Here is Benny's trumpet.
Toot, toot, toot, too, too.
Here's the way that Benny
Plays at peek a boo.

Here's a big umbrella
Keeps our Benny dry.
Here is Benny's cradle.
Rock-a-Benny-bye.

Fun With Fingers

These are mother's knives and forks.

This is mother's table.

This is sister's looking glass.

And this is baby's cradle.

Games

Where Is Headley?

Have the players stand or sit where they can move their hands freely. One person, the leader, stands in front of the group and leads off. Everything should be said slowly at first until everyone knows the words and the actions.

Begin with "warm-up" questions: "Which part of your body talks?" (Touch your mouth.) "Which part hears?" (Touch your ears.)

Then the leader says: "Now I want you to say what I say and do what I do. Ready? Let's begin." Then, using both hands, the leader says: "Say (touching mouth), have you seen (touching eyes) or heard (touching ears) from Headley? (touching head). He is needed (touching knees) in the army (folding arms). Now he is back (touching back) from the front (touching chest) with a hip, hip (slapping hips), hurrah! (throwing hands in air)."

Keep repeating this faster and faster to see who can do it quickly without making any errors. For instance, to say "seen" and touch the ears is wrong. Those who make errors drop out and watch the rest. The person remaining is declared the winner.

Seeing With Your Hands

One child is blindfolded. Another child hands to the blindfolded child different objects, one at a time. The blindfolded child feels and handles each object so as to tell what it is.

Any familiar object may be used. A few good ones are: banana, apple, comb, clothesbrush, key, cup.

What is in the Box?

Choose sides, two teams with an equal number of players. Arrange two rows of chairs, as many as each team has players, facing each other. You will need one large empty oatmeal box with cover. One team selects an item to put in the box while the other team either goes out of the room or closes their eyes.

The team which is guessing is given clues. The first clue tells where the item is usually found, such as kitchen or playground. Each member of the guessing team has a chance to shake the box and guess its contents. If no one guesses correctly, the team is given another clue. The second clue describes the item in some way—its shape or color or what it is made of. If no one guesses correctly, a third clue is given, also describing the item. The guessing team is then given one last chance.

Musical Sponge

Play music and pass around a wet sponge; have the players standing or sitting in a circle. The one holding the sponge when the music stops is OUT. The last one left is the winner.

Feel the Sponge

Use the flat rectangular type of sponges used for washing dishes. They can be cut easily with scissors. Cut several different shapes.

A triangle, fish, star, doughnut, and letters T and S are some that are easy to identify. Fill a small wading pool or large dishpan or baby bathtub with water and place these sponge shapes in it. Blindfold the players one at a time and let each kneel down and find as many sponges as possible, identifying them by feeling. The player who identifies the most shapes correctly wins.

Sound Activities

Sound Games

Place on a tray several objects found in the kitchen. Show the objects to the children. One child goes to the back of the room where the sound objects are then placed. The other children close their eyes and listen while the one child makes a sound with a kitchen object. The other children guess which object was used to make the sound. Objects that might be used are: lid, wooden spoon, plastic bowl, pan, vegetable brush.

Select one child to be 'it'. Have the other children close their eyes and listen. The teacher whispers a direction to the child, so the children can't hear. Then the children open their eyes and guess what 'it' was doing. Directions that might be given are:

1) walk to door and back 4) sharpen a pencil
2) hop around on one foot 5) bounce a ball
3) knock on the desk top 6) crumple paper

Whirring Button

Find a large button and a piece of string about 2½ feet long (a round piece of cardboard will also work). Thread the string through two of the holes in the button—then tie the ends of the string together.

Center the button on the string. Place the looped ends of the string over your middle fingers.

Make a circular motion so that the string twists and winds up. When it is tightly wound, make a motion with your hands toward the button and away from it. The string will keep coiling and uncoiling by itself. The button will make a whirring noise.

It is fun to paint the button or cardboard with various colors and designs. Then watch the bright colors when it spins.

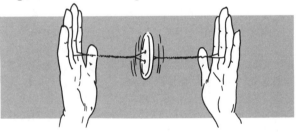

Circus Parade

Each player is given a "band" instrument, such as a dishpan, pie, or cake tin, an old pan, a heavy spoon, a horn, a drum, a whistle, a harmonica—in fact, anything that makes a noise. The band leader, should be appropriately dressed with a colorful coat, sash or hat, plus a stick for a baton. Let some of the children wheel pets or stuffed animals in wagons, doll buggies, wheelbarrows, and the like, to add to the fun. The leader puts the band through its paces.

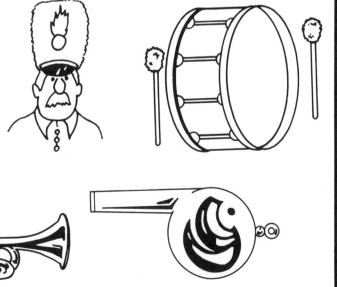

Musical Glasses

You have musical instruments in your kitchen. In fact, you probably use them every day without even thinking about them as musical instruments.

What am I talking about? Ordinary drinking glasses.

Now maybe you have never thought of a glass as an instrument, but you can easily turn eight glasses into eight notes. And if you have eight notes, you can play many familiar songs.

How? It's easy. Get yourself eight glasses. They do not have to be a good set, although different types of glasses make different sounds.

Place the glasses in a row. Number them 1 through 8, starting with number 1 on the left. Fill a pitcher or milk carton with water because you'll need plenty of water to complete the scale. Fill glass number 1 with water, then put a little less water in number 2, and so on. The last glass on the right, number 8, will be empty.

Next, begin tapping each glass with a knife or wooden spoon. You should be able to hear the different notes of the scale. You will probably have to pour a little more water in some glasses and remove a little from others.

Be patient. It will take some time to form a perfect scale, but it is important that the scale be accurate. Your ear will tell you if it sounds right.

Once your scale is perfect, put a little strip of adhesive tape on each glass at the water level. This will help you know exactly how much water to put in each glass the next time.

Most likely you will be able to figure out songs just by experimenting with the different notes. But to get you started, here are the numbers for three songs which can be played using an eight-note scale and a knife (or wooden spoon).

One more thing: Strike the glasses very lightly while playing. Otherwise, you'll have broken glass and water to clean up when you're finished—and a very short musical career!

Three Blind Mice
3 - 2 - 1, 3 - 2 - 1
5 - 4 - 4 - 3, 5 - 4 - 4 - 3
5 - 8 - 8 - 7 - 6 - 7 - 8 - 5 - 5
5 - 5 - 8 - 8 - 7 - 6 - 7 - 8 - 5 - 5
5 - 5 - 8 - 8 - 7
6 - 7 - 8 - 5 - 5 - 5
4 - 3 - 2 - 1

Twinkle, Twinkle, Little Star
1 - 1 - 5 - 5 - 6 - 6 - 5
4 - 4 - 3 - 3 - 2 - 2 - 1
5 - 5 - 4 - 4 - 3 - 3 - 2
5 - 5 - 4 - 4 - 3 - 3 - 2
1 - 1 - 5 - 5 - 6 - 6 - 5
4 - 4 - 3 - 3 - 2 - 2 - 1

This Land Is Your Land
1 - 2 - 3 - 4 - 4
4 - 1 - 2 - 3 - 3
5 - 5 - 3 - 2 - 2
2 - 2 - 1 - 2 - 3 - 3
1 - 1 - 2 - 3 - 4 - 4
4 - 4 - 1 - 2 - 3 - 3
2 - 2 - 2 - 2 - 4 - 3 - 2 - 1

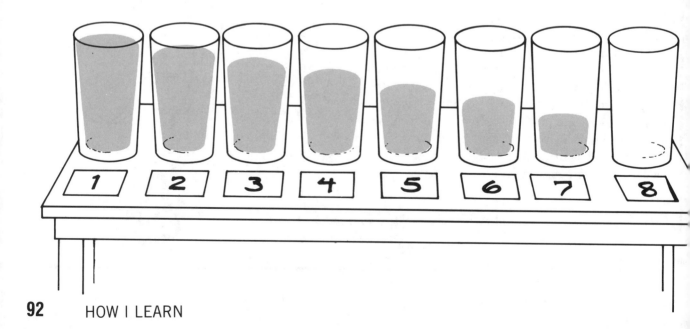

Musical Instruments

You and your friends can make a whole band of box instruments and have your own Fourth of July parade.

These instruments are all made out of round boxes (the kind some hot cereal comes in).

All of these instruments will look nicer if you paste construction paper over the boxes and decorate with cut-paper designs. For the Strummer and Jingles, cover and decorate before putting the instrument together.

Shaker: Cut a round box down to about 2 inches in height. Put a few jingle bells inside this little box and glue the lid on it. Poke a stick through one side of the box and out the other. Secure the stick with masking tape.

Twanger: Take a piece of string as long as from one hand to the other when your arms are stretched out. Make a small hole in the middle of a round box lid. Poke one end of the string through the hole from the top to the inside. Put that end of the string through one hole in a button and back through another hole.

Then put the string back through the hole in the lid. Make the ends of the string even and tie them together. To play, hold the box tightly under one arm, hold the end of the string in your hand, and stretch it out full length. "Twang" by plucking on the string.

Rattler: Put small pebbles or beans inside a round box and tape the lid in place. Shake the Rattler or hold it in one hand and slap it with the other.

Three-Tone Drum: Cut two triangles in the cover of a round box. Glue a piece of typing paper under one hole; a piece of heavier paper under the other. Thump on the two triangles and the lid to make three different sounds.

Strummer: Find several different widths of rubber bands. Stretch them over a round box (without lid). If your rubber bands are too short, try cutting the box down. Pluck on the rubber bands to make different tones.

Jingles: Cut a 1½-inch ring from what's left of the box you used for the Shaker. With hammer and nail, pound a hole in each of ten bottle caps. Place the caps in pairs, flat sides together. Put a brass two-pronged fastener through each pair of caps and through the ring. Open the prongs to secure in place. Do the same with the other pairs of caps, leaving an open space on the ring to hold it by.

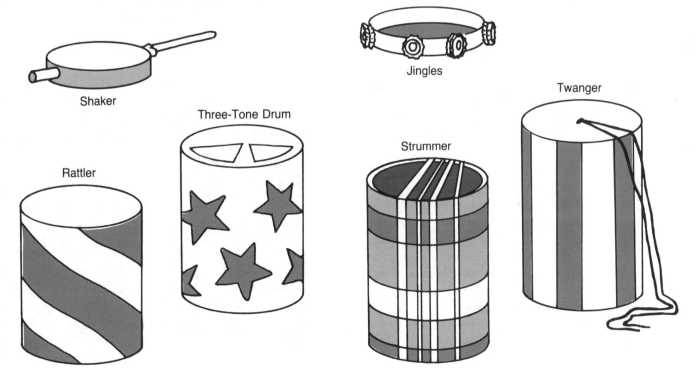

Jingles

Twanger

Shaker

Three-Tone Drum

Rattler

Strummer

More Music

A Whistle

To make a whistle, use a piece of paper, a pencil and scissors.

Draw figure *1* (twice size shown) on a piece of paper. Cut out and fold on the line shown in the center of the figure. Cut a triangle at the center fold.

Now fold the end tabs on the dotted lines as shown in illustration.

Place the tab folds against your lips—then blow very hard. Your whistle should make a loud noise.

Color your whistle to make it more interesting.

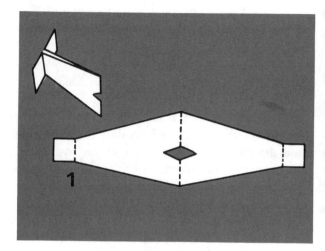

Bongo Drums

Use three large cans (such as the stacked potato-chip cans with plastic lids) for this project. Trim down two of them so you have small, medium, and large sizes. Glue the lids on. Cover with paste and one layer of paper. Paint with tempera. Decorate each can with yarn. Tie the three together with yarn, keeping the lids at the same level. Make a shoulder strap by braiding yarn together. Tie the strap to the drums. Tap the lids and notice how the sounds vary with the size of the drum.

Pie-pan Tambourine

Use an aluminum pie pan to make a tambourine. These pans come in many sizes—small ones with meat pies, larger ones with dessert pies or cakes. Poke holes one to two inches apart just inside the rim. Make the holes closer on small pans, farther apart on larger ones. Leave one larger space so you can hold your "tambourine."

Use ties from bread wrappers to tie on the "jangles." You might cut circles from another pie pan to make jangles, or use the tops of flip-top beverage cans. Twist the ties at the very ends so the jangles will hang loosely.

Now shake your tambourine or hit it against your fist to make rhythm sounds.

Things to Make

Colored Glasses

Would you like to see the world through a pair of rose-colored glasses? The next time you have a piece of red cellophane, you might try making a pair.

Out of lightweight cardboard cut one piece as shown. Cut out the shaded portion and make a slit at A and B. Now, out of cardboard cut two ear pieces. Fold on the dotted lines C and D and slip one piece through slot A and one through slot B. Open out the folded pieces and fasten down to glasses with a piece of Scotch tape.

Cut two pieces of the red cellophane large enough to make the lenses. Fasten back of cardboard with several small strips of Scotch tape. You might also make other pairs of colored glasses with yellow, green, or blue cellophane.

Homemade Drinking Cup

Imagine sitting down to each lunch. You fold a square piece of paper five times and fill it with milk. Imagine what your friends will think. It's easy. Here's how.

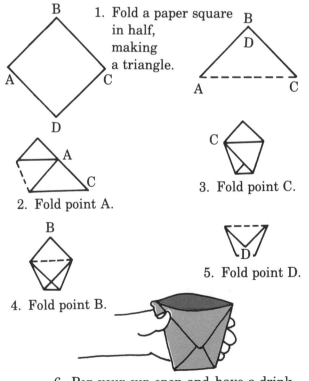

1. Fold a paper square in half, making a triangle.

2. Fold point A.

3. Fold point C.

4. Fold point B.

5. Fold point D.

6. Pop your cup open and have a drink.

Owl Napkin Holder

Use cardboard tubing 4½ inches long. Draw two V-shapes, one on the front and one on the back. Repeat this on the other end of the tube. Cut out the four V's. Bend and paste on two of them for ears. Add a paper nose, and eyes with inked outlines and pupils.

Japanese Paper Folding

Paper-folding (called *origami*) was developed into a fine art in Japan over many centuries. Usually a rather thin paper colored on one side only is used for the foldings, but any thin paper will do. Many Japanese children have become very skillful in folding a great variety of different designs. Maybe you would like to try this simple example of the ancient art of *origami*.

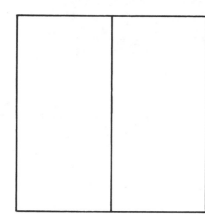

1. Mark the center line on a square piece of paper.

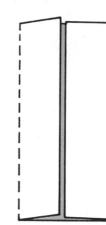

2. Fold both sides in to meet at the center.

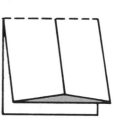

3. Turn it over, and fold in half from top to bottom.

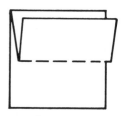

4. Fold the front half up to the top.

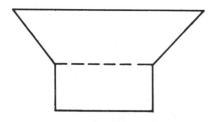

5. Put your fingers under the first layer on the top and pull out the corners. Crease.

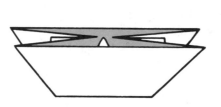

6. Turn it over and do steps 4 and 5 on the other side.

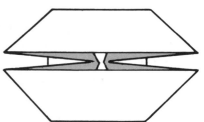

7. Open out center fold.

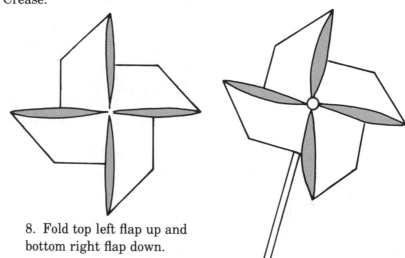

8. Fold top left flap up and bottom right flap down.

Flower Crafts

Tiny Flowerpots

Cut pieces of colored sponge into flower shapes. Stick them onto green pipe-cleaner stems. Cut leaves from green construction paper and glue to the stems.

The pots are tops from old toothpaste tubes, filled with modeling clay to hold the flowers in place.

Cotton-Ball Pictures

Pull several cotton balls into petal shapes. Glue them around a cottonball center. Add a pipe-cleaner stem and cotton-ball leaves.

Paint with tempera. (For an unusual effect, apply small dabs of paint on the petals.)

Use cotton balls to make other things like butterflies and bugs. Add details with a felt-tipped marker.

Sand Flowers

Color sand by placing it in a plastic bag and adding a few drops of food coloring. Shake well.

Design a flower with the end of a glue bottle, allowing the glue to flow onto the paper. Sprinkle the design with sand. Form another flower and sprinkle it, and so on. You may outline the flower with yarn or add centers of small balls of yarn.

Flora Fun

Vegetable Window Garden

If you cannot have a vegetable garden, "plant" a garden to hang in your window!

On a piece of cardboard draw the outline of a vegetable. Cover the cardboard with plastic kitchen wrap. On the plastic wrap squeeze white glue along the vegetable outline. Press two thicknesses of yarn along the outline. Mix a few drops of food coloring in white glue. Paint the inside of the vegetable outline very thickly. Dry for several days. Peel the glue from the plastic wrap. Add a thread-loop hanger. Hang the vegetable in your window.

Apple or Pear Decoration

Cut three apple or pear shapes from folded paper. Cut a hole in the center of each shape. Slit one from the top and bottom (No. 1) and the other two from the center (No. 2). Insert, forming a fruit. Glue the tops together at the fold. Thread seeds onto a cotton thread and secure with a knot at the top of the fruit. Seeds will hang in the open space. Remaining thread will be used for hanging. Make a leaf.

Cloth Blossoms

Twist six pipe cleaners into petal loops and three into leaf loops. Leave a little of each end of the pipe cleaner free for attaching. Squeeze glue on one side of each loop and press onto a piece of cloth. When the glue is dry, trim away the extra cloth.

Twist the petal loops together at the center and attach to a stem made of a piece of wire. Use glue to hold the blossom in place on the stem. Attach leaves by twisting the pipe cleaner ends around the stem. To "plant" your blossom, push the stem into a ball of clay in a flowerpot.

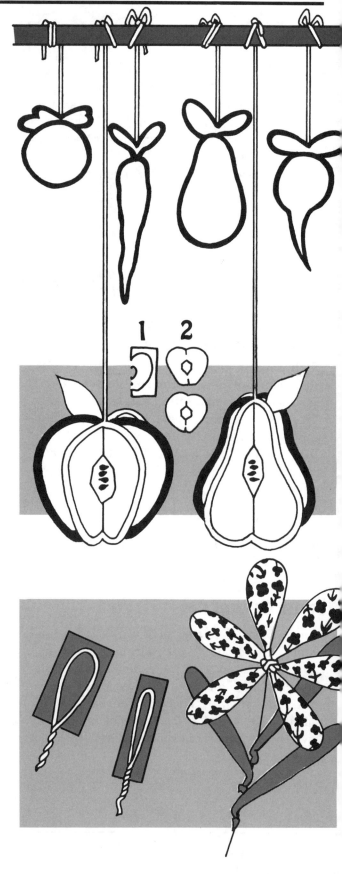

Color the fruits and vegetables.

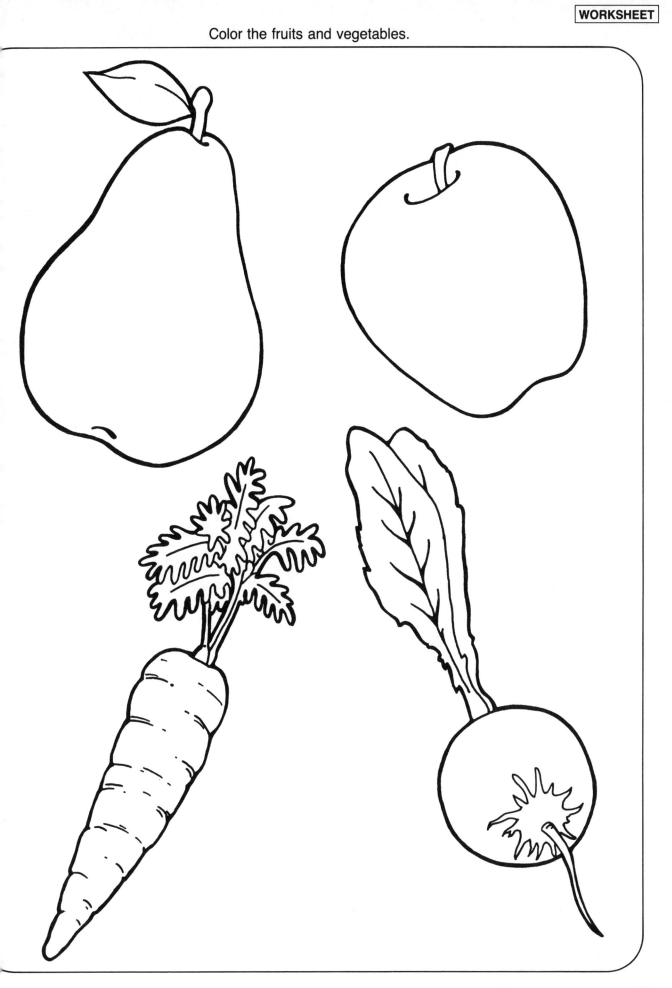

Notes

Looby-Loo

Traditional

Moderately, in 2 (♩. = 1 beat)

Here we go loo - by loo, Here we go loo - by light, ___

Here we go loo - by loo, All on a Sat - ur - day night.

Last time end here

(previous ♩.= ♩)

I put my right hand* in, I take my right hand out, I

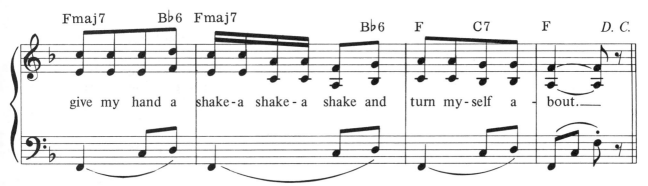

give my hand a shake-a shake-a shake and turn my-self a-bout.___

*Continue similarly with "left hand," "right foot," "left foot," "little head" etc., finishing up with "whole self."

These Are My Eyes I Use To See

Moderately, in two (♩. = 1 beat)

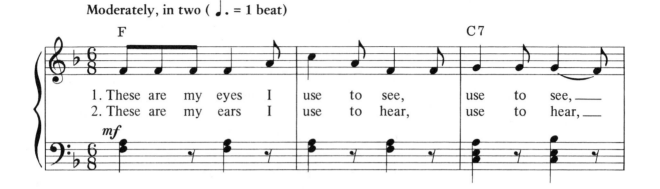

1. These are my eyes I use to see, use to see, ___
2. These are my ears I use to hear, use to hear, ___

use to see. These are my eyes I use to see,
use to hear. These are my ears I use to hear,

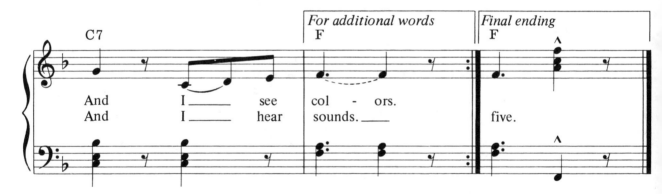

For additional words

Final ending

And I ___ see col - ors.
And I ___ hear sounds. ___
five.

3. This is my nose I use to smell,
    use to smell,
    use to smell,
This is my nose I use to smell,
And I smell roses.

4. This is my mouth I use to taste,
    use to taste,
    use to taste,
This is my mouth I use to taste,
And I taste food.

5. These are my senses I use to learn,
    use to learn,
    use to learn,
These are my senses I use to learn,
And I have five.

Exploring My World

Introduction

In the prior units, the child's attention has been narrowly focused on school, the person, the senses. By allowing a child the opportunity to examine his or her identity first, the capability for a smooth transition to the school world will increase. This unit is designed to create an awareness of all living things and their needs and to investigate people, animals, and plants.

No child comes to kindergarten without some perceptions and experiences of the world. But often, these experiences are isolated in the child's mind. This section attempts to relate separate concepts, to develop systematic learning.

The child examines the similarities and differences among a myriad of familiar and unfamiliar living things. Patterns begin to emerge, understanding grows, linguistic expression expands. And through this process, the interdependence of all living things becomes evident. The child faces an intertwined universe and sees that, within its intricate structure, he or she has a unique place.

Concepts To Be Taught

I. People, animals and plants live on the earth.

II. People live in many locations and have many types of homes.

III. Animals live in many locations and have many types of homes.

IV. Animals differ in many ways.

V. Animals and people need plants.

Information For Teaching Concepts

I. People, animals, and plants live on the earth.

Have the children close their eyes and imagine that they are climbing the tallest tree in the world. In their minds, they are to climb and climb until they are at the very top where they sit down in a comfortable crook of the tree and look out at the earth below. Direct them to keep their eyes closed and ask them to describe what they see. Encourage them to think about the people, animals, and plants that might be in view.

After reading the poem, explain to the children that there are three types of living things in the world. Have the children name different people, animals and plants. Remind them about the differences in people and how each person is unique. Explain that there are differences in all living things but also similarities. One of the similarities is that all have a home which provides shelter. One of the differences is *where* they live. People can live in the city or country, animals can live in water, trees, under the ground or on the land, and plants can grow almost anywhere we might look.

II. People live in many locations and have many types of homes.

Read the poem, "City Street at Night", on page 138.

Ask the children, "Why do animals and people need homes?" Stimulate the children's responses to include the joy of belonging, living together with a family, protection from the weather, a place to keep possessions, comfort, and any other ideas that can be gathered. Next ask, "Do all people live in the same type of a house?" Again encourage a variety of responses that might include:

single-family dwelling	mobile home
double-family dwelling	lighthouse
apartment	log cabin
condominium	igloo
adobe hut	tent

Read the story, "Jonathan's House," page 129. Ask, "Was Jonathan happy to be in his house?" "Was the house right where it should have been?" Discuss with the children that homes are built in many locations. Have the children tell the kind of home in which they live and where it is located. If possible, make a collage of the various kinds of homes in your community.

Discuss what you might find inside a home. Be sure to elicit that most homes have different rooms. Then, do the activity, "Moving Day," page 112.

III. Animals live in many locations and have a variety of homes.

Draw on the chalkboard land, water, and air. Ask the children to listen as you say the name of an animal and think about where the animal lives. If the animal lives on land, they stand up, if the animal lives in the water, they move their arms as though swimming;

if the animal lives on land but flies in the air, they stretch their hands high over their heads. Say:

whale	rabbit	zebra	tiger	eagle	fox
sunfish	mouse	penguin	owl	frog	robin

Read the story, "Why is Mr. Tortoise So Slow?" page 130. Ask, "Where were all the animals hurrying to?" "Why?" Discuss how the turtle's shell protects it from its enemies, yet is heavy and causes the turtle to move slowly. Have the class think about ways animals build their homes for protection against their enemies. Examples are:

moles have tunnels under the ground

birds build nests high out of the reach of many animals

owls have homes inside a tree

wasps build hard nests

IV. Animals differ in many ways.

Read the story, "Little Mistake," page 128 to the children. Ask the children how the lost baby skunk and the lost kitten were alike (both were black and white, had four legs, were fur covered). Ask how they were different (skunk had a white stripe down its back, skunk waddled, kitten was frisky, kitten meowed). Discuss some of the ways animals are different: size, shape, color, sound, etc.

List different kinds of animal coverings and have the class identify animals for each covering. Examples are:

feathers—owl, chicken, canary, (birds)

fur—rabbit, cat, squirrel, bear

hair—horse, cow, opossum

skin—elephant, pig

wool—sheep

scales—fish, snake, alligators

Read the poems, "The Hippopotamus," page 140, and "I Envy the Chimp," page 140. Ask the class to think about what each animal could do that was special. Ask the children, "Which was the largest?" "Which was the smallest?" Have them name the largest animals they can think of and then the smallest animals. Tell the children that the largest animal in the world is the blue whale.

Place color cards across the chalkboard and ask the children to think of an animal to go with each color (some animals can be various colors). Examples are:

red—rooster, cardinal

green—frog, parrot, lizard

yellow—lion, canary

orange—fish, cat

blue—bluejay, blue whale

black—skunk, dog, horse

grey—squirrel, elephant

Explain to the children that another way animals are different from each other is that they make different sounds. Ask children to identify an animal that:

crows	chatters	moos
hisses	trumpets	thumps its feet
shrieks	barks	meows

Explain that these sounds are used to give warnings, gain attention and show affection.

V. Animals and people need plants.

Watching a plant grow is an interesting process and can quickly show children that plants need air, sunlight and water. Read the story, "Little Things Grow Big," page 127. Take sunflower seeds to school and show the children how small they are. Then give each child a seed to eat. Talk about all the animals that eat seeds and that some animals (cows or deer) would eat the stalk as well. Explain that in the story Betsy made sure the plant had air, sunlight, and water so that it could grow.

Read, "Trees," page 140. Ask the children to listen for all the ways that trees help people.

Tell the children about the many things trees provide. Explain that:
trees give us nuts and fruit, seeds, bark, leaves.
wood is used for fires to keep us warm.
wood is used to build houses.
wood is crushed and used for making paper.
trees provide homes for many animals.

Help the children to become aware of the many ways plants take care of people and how much animals and people depend upon them.

Thinking and Reasoning

Ask your children these questions.

Why is there an eraser on a pencil?

What is used most often to put out a fire?

On a clear night, what might you see in the sky?

How is television different from radio?

Name some things in your home that are run by electricity.

Do we go down to the attic or up to the attic?

Does a chair ever get frightened?

Is it easier to stack six cups or to stack six saucers?

Do animal children have birthday parties?

Which makes more noise while walking, a horse or a dog? Why?

Is the outside of your home made of brick, wood, or stone?

After a heavy summer rain there may be a number of puddles of water in the street. What may cause them to disappear?

At what place on an envelope do we put the stamp?

Does a pig have fur?

What is the difference between a straight pin and a safety pin?

What do you use to unlock a door?

Is pudding thicker or thinner than soup?

How do you know a stone is heavier than water?

Name everything you can that has a head. Which of these heads will feel no pain when hit? Which will feel pain when hit?

How many wings has a bird?

Does an egg have bones in it?

Did you ever see a dog catch a ball?

Explain the difference between the way you open and close a door, and the way you open and close a drawer.

Why do we put the stems of cut flowers into water?

When you wash your hands, what do you need besides soap?

How many legs has a chair? What is the difference between its legs and yours?

Give two reasons why we paint buildings.

Does smoke always go straight up from the chimney?

How do you know when water is boiling?

Does a baby bird have a mother?

Are the streets icy on hot summer days?

What is the difference between a needle and a pin? A spoon and a fork?

What do we call the sharp end of a pin? The other end?

Why do we cook foods?

In what ways are a pancake, a saucer, and a pie pan alike?

Do you button your coat in the back or in the front?

Is an apple round or square?

Which would be harder to pick up after spilling, a pail of eggs or a pail of apples? A pail of sand or a pail of blocks?

Do wild bears have heated houses in which to live?

Which looks larger, the moon or a star?

In what way are milk and water alike?

If you could touch the sun, would it feel hot?

Which is easier to cut with scissors, cardboard or paper?

You wear a pair of socks. Name some other things you wear that are always in pairs.

How many shoes are in a pair?

Which would harm a clean suit or dress more, if you got wet paint on it or if you got dry flour on it?

Can a fish talk?

Does a bird sleep in bed as you do?

Which do you see more often in a person's house, a wolf or a dog? A cat or a fox?

Could you touch the sky from the top of a tall tree?

Which could you carry in a strainer: sand, water, or nuts?

When it rains, why does less water fall right at the foot of a tree than several feet from the foot?

"When did you burn that hole in your coat, Father?", the daughter asked. How did she know the hole had been burned in?

When ice melts, where does it go?

As Mrs. Murphy was hanging up the clothes, she said, "They should be dry in a little while." How could she know this?

Tell the different ways by which a person in London might send a message to a person in New York.

Why doesn't a snowflake fall to the ground as fast as a raindrop falls?

Name all the reasons you can for wearing gloves.

Which is harder, glass or butter?

Why couldn't a horse drink from your glass or cup?

Which is farthest away, the sun, the top of the highest tree, or the clouds?

Name all the trees whose names you know.

All elephants have four feet. Are all animals with four feet elephants?

Where is the roof of your house?

Why are bees not good to play with?

Can a mouse take as big a bite of cheese as you can?

Do horses keep their shoes on at night?

Do we use an umbrella when the sun is shining or when it is raining?

"Jane, you will need to wear rubbers to school this morning," said Jane's mother. What could have made the mother say this?

When you are standing on the bank of a stream are you higher or lower than the top of the water in the stream?

Are all cats grey?

Connect the picture on the left to the matching picture on the right by drawing a line.

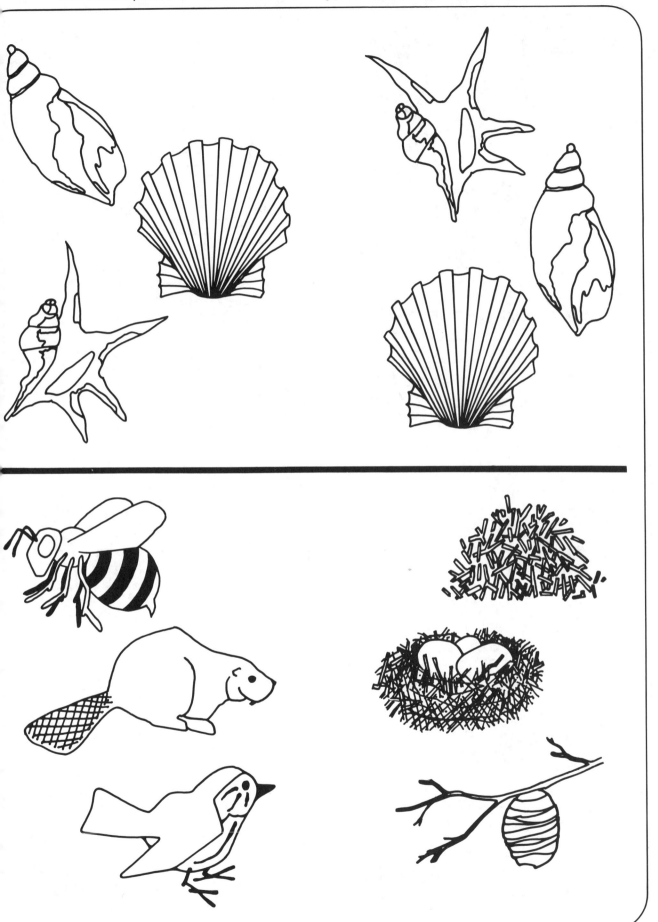

Connect the picture on the left to the matching picture on the right by drawing a line.

Name each one of these things.
Tell when and how we use each of these at mealtime.
Which do we use the most?
What are some of the other things we use at mealtime?

Things In Your Home

In each of these pairs, how are they alike? How are they different?

sofa and chair
recliner and rocker
table and chair

Which of these belong in the kitchen?

refrigerator   TV set
dining table   teakettle
bed   high chair
rocking chair   bathtub
medicine chest   stove

In each of these pairs, which are there more of in your kitchen?

kettle or spoon
egg beater or pan
cup or skillet
toaster or fork
plate or can opener

In what room of your home would you

eat breakfast   brush your teeth
sleep   get dressed
watch television   look at a book
play with your toys

If you were going to build a house, which of these things would you have to do?

buy the land
gather lumber and bricks
plant a garden
have a plumber help you
put up the framework
put up a television antenna
make a roof
paint
write letters

Pretend your family is moving into a new house. Name all the rooms that might be found in the new house. Your parents have asked you to tell the movers where to put things. In which rooms would these things go?

radio   bed
skillet   tools
clothes   refrigerator
dresser   garden hose
dog bowl   teddy bear
television   mop
alarm clock   sheets
shower curtain   lawn mower
mailbox   car
washcloth   piano
bedspread   rocking horse
end table   teakettle

Pets have to have homes, too. What do you need to make a proper home for your:

goldfish
cat
hamster
parakeet
dog

What things do you do to take care of these pets?

In each column circle the item that does not belong.

How many things can you find wrong in this picture?

All About Animals

Tell if the following creatures live on land, live in the water, or live both in water and on land.

fish   mouse
robin   penguin
frog   elephant
bear   whale
lobster   seal

Which of these might bark?
Dog or cat or bird.
Which has the sharpest claws?
Cat or bird or rabbit.
Which has the shortest tail?
Bird or rabbit or fish.
Which has no feet?
Rabbit or fish or bird.
Which may sing?
Fish or bird or dog.

What would be the name for the baby animal each of these would have?

dog?   puppy
cow?   calf
sheep?   lamb
cat?   kitten
lion?   cub

Which one in these groups is a food, a flower and an animal?
Camel, pear and rose.
Lily, potato, and giraffe.
Carrot, tulip and squirrel.
Daisy, bear and raisin.

In each pair, which wears the warmer or thicker coat?
elephant or bear
sheep or goat
pig or calf
mouse or cat
rabbit or bird
cow or tiger

In each pair, which is taller?

poodle or Great Dane
horse or sheep
duck or stork
giraffe or rhinoceros
camel or mule
pig or cow

In each pair, which can move faster?
bird or butterfly
turtle or mouse
rabbit or woodchuck
grasshopper or caterpillar
pig or squirrel
cow or deer

Which of these animals could you pick up?

hamster   cat
horse   rhinoceros
cow   elephant
whale   dog

Which has feathers?
Which has hair?
Which has no hair, no wool and no feathers?
Name some things you can do that none of these creatures can do.
Name some things that each of these animals do that you cannot do.

Connect the picture on the left to the matching picture on the right by drawing a line.

In each pair, circle the animal that has a longer tail.

Connect the picture on the left to the matching picture on the right by drawing a line.

In what way does each of these things use water?
Does an automobile use water the same way as a fire engine?
How do you use water?
Name some other things that use water.

Fruits and Vegetables

Use these choices to answer the questions below:

Apple, potato and banana.
Beets, peach and celery.
Carrot, cherries and cabbage.

Which have one or more seeds?
Which grows under the ground?
Which grows on trees?
Which are fruit? Which are vegetables?
Which do you like to eat raw?
Which can be used in soup?
Which are usually peeled?
Which may be used in a pie?

Which of these are vegetables and which are flowers?

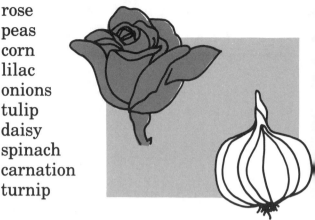

rose
peas
corn
lilac
onions
tulip
daisy
spinach
carnation
turnip

Do we usually eat these foods with a spoon, a fork, or with our bare hands? Which do we cut up with a knife? Which do we drink?

cereal
cake
cocoa
milk
orange
steak
soup
hamburger
celery
egg
sandwich
potato salad

Flower See-Throughs

KENT DOUGLAS

Unfold a facial tissue. Separate tissue into two layers. Lay one tissue layer on a piece of paper towel. With watercolors, paint flowers on the tissue. Dry. Glue to a paper frame. Hang in a window.

Pretend you are going to plant a vegetable garden. How many vegetables can you name to plant in the garden?

Pretend you are going to plant a fruit orchard. How many fruits can you name to plant in the orchard?

Pretend you are going to plant a flower garden. How many flowers can you name to plant in the garden?

Connect the picture on the left to the matching picture on the right by drawing a line.

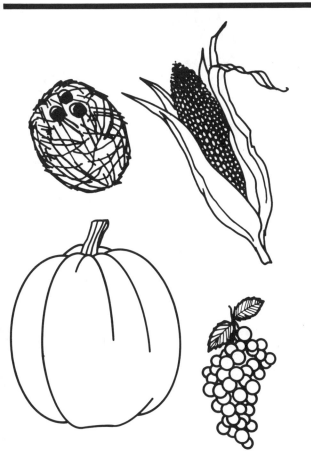

EXPLORING MY WORLD **121**

In the left column are two parts from each of the objects in the right column. Connect them by drawing a line.

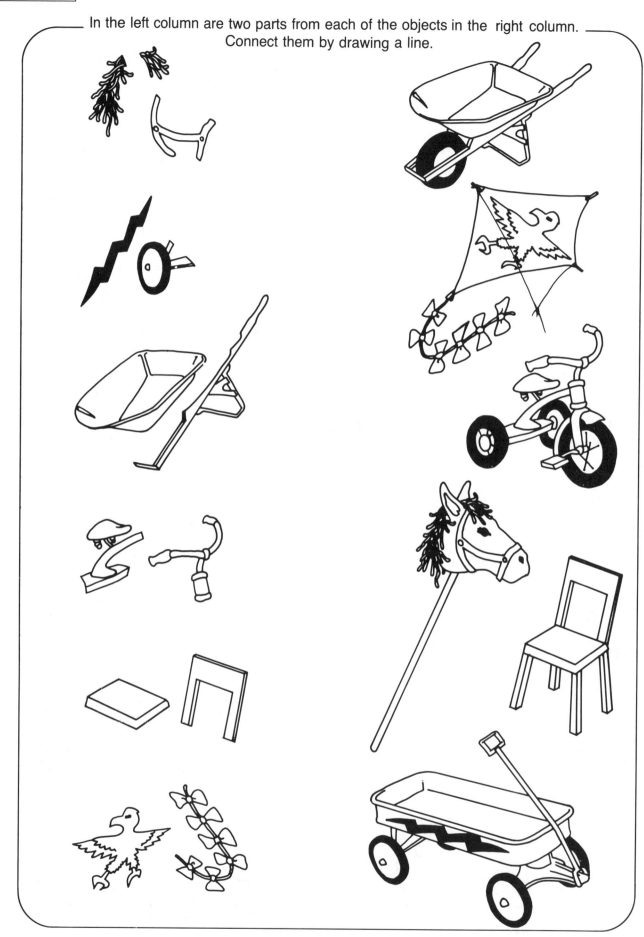

Alike But Different

How are the things in each pair alike? How are they different?

ax—saw
handbag—suitcase
flashlight—electric bulb
suspenders—belt
socks—shoes
car—truck
cat—dog
knife—fork
apple—tomato
mitten—glove
hat—shoe
scissors—knife

In each pair, which can stand more cold?

polar bear—man
robin—dog
tomato—pine tree
fish—fly
seal—frog

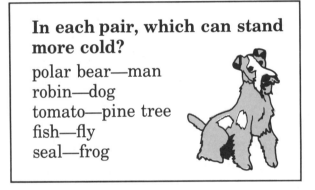

Which of these things do we eat and which do we wear?

carrot   shoes
coat   grapes
apple   beet
hat   bread
sweater   banana

If you covered these things with water which would get softer?
nail   pencil
doughnut   sandwich
pretzel   fork

Name a creature:
    that barks
    that grunts
    that quacks
    that meows
    that moos
    that crows
    that neighs
    that baas
    that cackles.

Listen and tell which one of the group does not belong.

chair, table, dresser, owl, bed
chicken, baby, turkey, bird, duck
horse, lamb, clock, donkey, pig
spinach, lettuce, stove, carrot, onion
corn, bread, potato, chair, banana
turtle, hammer, fish, bird, dog
bus, boat, car, tree, plane

Which of these are made of cloth? What are the other things made of?
ax   football
boot   towel
shirt   sneaker
watch   saw

Which of these things do we use to make light and which do we read?
candle
book
lamp
letter
newspaper
flashlight

Listen and tell which one of the group does not belong.

hammer, nail, screwdriver, cheese
red, blue, giraffe, purple
house, bell, horn, drum
sun, train, moon, star
ball, doll, crayon, elephant
bench, balloon, chair, stool

Which of these things do we use to make light and which do we read?

candle	letter
book	newpaper
lamp	flashlight

In each pair, which one grows?

a tree or a window
a book or a fingernail
a stone or a dog
a bed or a baby
a hair brush or your hair

In each pair, which one is easier to roll?

ball or block
book or pencil
apple or banana
domino or checker

Is it easier to hold

a pencil or a bus?
a pile of bricks or a shoe?
a sandwich or a donkey?
a hot pan or a jacket?
sand or a leaf?

In each pair, which one is easier to roll?

ball or block
book or pencil
apple or banana
domino or checker

In each pair, which jumps more?

squirrel or dog
frog or fish
butterfly or grasshopper

In each pair, which moves faster?

butterfly or bird
rabbit or turtle
snail or mouse
deer or elephant.

Which of these are made of cloth? What are the other things made of?

ax	football
boot	towel
shirt	sneaker
watch	saw

Which of these things do we eat and which do we wear?

carrot	shoes
coat	grapes
apple	dress
hat	beet
sweater	bread
banana	

In this group, find three things that are alike in some way.
How are they alike?
Find a different group of three things here that are alike
in another way.
Name some other things that can fly.

EXPLORING MY WORLD   **125**

The first pail is full of apples, the second full of water, and the third full of blocks.

Suppose you quickly turned each pail upside down, emptying it on a level sidewalk.
Which would scatter widest on the sidewalk?
Which would scatter least?
Which would be hardest to put back into the pail?
Why?

Little Things Grow Big

ANNIE TATABERE

Betsy and Pete sat on the sunbaked steps and munched sunflower seeds.

"My grandma says a little old seed like this"—Betsy held up a seed, then cracked the shell to get the soft kernel inside—"would grow six feet high."

Peter laughed. "I don't believe it," he said as he tossed a handful of shells to the sidewalk.

"My grandma should know," Betsy insisted. "When she was little, she lived on a farm near a small town."

"Yeah—but she might be fooling us," Peter argued. "I just don't believe it."

The children lived in a tall old building in a crowded city. No one ever planted flowers or grass anymore.

Betsy poured the last few seeds into her hand and stared at them. "I'm going to plant these," she said, "just to see what happens."

"Where will you plant them?" Pete laughed again. "Don't be silly!"

"Well—let's see." Betsy put the seeds into her pocket. Then she walked around the building. She found a place where a narrow walk led to the back entrance. There where the porch joined the house was a corner of ground. Paper sacks and cans littered the spot. Betsy filled a sack with the rubbish until the spot was cleared. They soaked the spot.

"Now let's plant the seeds!" Betsy said grandly. "There are six left."

The children placed sticks around their garden so no one would walk on it.

Several days passed. Nothing happened. Then suddenly, the ground rose in one spot and a little bent shoot of green came out. Then another. And another. And another. All the children in the neighborhood watched Betsy's garden.

Peter wouldn't pay much attention to it but he didn't laugh anymore. Four brave little green shoots pushed out of the ground.

One day when no one was around, Peter came over and looked at the garden.

"I don't believe it," he muttered. Then he stooped down and pulled one of the green shoots out. Sure enough, there was a split sunflower seed clinging to the green shoot and white roots hanging down.

Pete didn't want anyone to see what he had done so he tossed the bit of green out into the street. Cars and trucks soon mashed it flat.

Next morning, Betsy counted her little plants. "One is gone. What happened?" she asked the children. No one knew. Pete tried to look innocent.

Every day the three little plants grew. Then for two days, Betsy forgot them. When Betsy remembered her garden, the three little plants were limp and wilted. She poured water on them. Two slowly revived but one turned yellow and died.

"I think a dog stepped on it," Betsy said. "It is broken off."

Now the children took better care of the two that were left. They grew and grew—until the baby in the downstairs apartment wandered out on the walk. She saw the green plants, something new in her world. She wrapped her little fingers around one and pulled.

When Betsy found her, she was

happily chewing her sunflower plant and had already swallowed most of it, dirt and all. Betsy became discouraged.

But the sunny days slipped past. Every day she watered her one plant. Up it grew and up. After a while it was taller than the children.

When it was taller than Daddy, a big round yellow bloom topped the plant. It looked like pictures of the sun that the children drew in school.

"That's why it is called a sun-flower, I guess," Betsy said proudly.

Soon the center grew bigger and bigger and then the yellow petals dropped off.

"It's full of seeds," Pete said one day.

"Enough for all of us," Betsy added.

"From just one little old seed. I still don't believe it!" Pete laughed.

"I've been thinking," Betsy said slowly. "Most everything starts from something small."

Little Mistake

DEANNE DURRETT

Butter lay quietly in her nest. She had picked a cozy spot between the sacks of oats and the hay. She purred softly and nuzzled her six kittens. Then she lay back and worked her claws in and out. She was so proud of her newborn family.

Butter stayed in the nest with her kittens as long as she could. But finally she knew she must get food.

She was only gone long enough to eat and drink. (Well, she did linger just a minute to have her throat scratched.) When she returned to the nest, she nuzzled each kitten. One . . . two . . . three . . . four . . . five. Number six was missing!

She leaped from the nest and sniffed the hay where the kitten might have fallen. Where could he be? She searched the hay, making short purring noises, calling her black-and-white kitten. She had to find him. His eyes weren't open yet and he needed his mother's care.

Suddenly she froze! She cocked her head to listen. Had she heard something? Yes, there it was again. A tiny meow. It sounded so far away. Somewhere in that stack of oats.

She crept silently around the sacks of oats. She heard it again. In the moonlight she could see the sacks were stacked tightly. There seemed to be no way to reach the kitten. Then she saw it! There, between the sacks and the wall, was a tunnel. Butter crawled in.

Her nose touched something warm and soft. She took it by the scruff of the neck and carried it back to her nest.

When dawn came, Butter nuzzled and bathed her kittens. My, but the wanderer needed a bath. He didn't smell anything like a kitten. For that matter he didn't look like a kitten. He was black-and-white all right. But his white was all in one place—a stripe running right down the middle of his back! How could Butter have made such a strange mistake? Well, she might as well make the best of it.

The five kittens soon grew to be a playful bunch. They jumped at each other and wrestled. They chased and attacked anything that moved, whether it was Mother's tail, a feather floating on the breeze, or Little Mistake.

Now, Little Mistake just didn't understand this wrestling business. He was good-natured but not quite as eager for play as the kittens. He walked with a waddle, his graceful tail held proudly in the air. He never seemed to get where he wanted to go; he was always attacked on the way.

This day, in particular, he had just about had enough of those kittens. He stamped his front feet two times as a warning. Then with a sudden jump he twisted his backside around, ready to do battle.

Just about that time Mother Skunk ambled out from behind the oat sacks. One . . . two . . . three . . . four . . . five little skunks followed. And six? Number six was a black-and-white kitten!

Well, it was a big decision, but somewhere in the back of Little Mistake's memory there was something familiar about Mother Skunk. He liked her right away. He just couldn't help himself. He fell right in line and didn't mind being last at all.

As for the kitten, he didn't even see the skunks go. He was too busy jumping, attacking, and wrestling. That other bunch had been just too slow for him.

Jonathan's House

IVY O. EASTWICK

North, South, East, or West—the house where you live is surely the best. Except to Jonathan James O'Shay who was always threatening to run away.

His mother pleaded, "Oh, Jon! Don't go. Your father and I would miss you so."

His uncle begged and his auntie sighed. "Oh, Jonathan, the world's so wide, so please don't run away."

"I'm GOING!" snapped Jonathan James O'Shay. "Maybe tomorrow. Maybe today."

The house where he lived was a cheerful place (except for Jonathan's scowling face). It had painted walls and pictures gay and windows which caught the sun each day.

"North! South! East! West! Home is the place you love the best," muttered the house to itself one day while Jon was threatening to run away.

"I'm tired," said the house, "of this stupid Jon who has always threatened but never gone. So—when he returns from school today, he will find that I have run away."

And so it was.

At half-past four there was not a sign of house, or door, or balcony red, or garden green. There was just a gap where the house had been.

Jon's mouth became a BIG ROUND O. "My house has gone! Did you see it go? It was here at lunchtime, from twelve till two. Has anyone seen it? You? Or you?" he asked the neighbors, who said:

"Jon J! Why shouldn't your nice house run away? You've no cause to grumble, oh dear, no. You were always threatening YOU would go."

Jon ran to the East.

He rushed to the South.

He dashed right down to the river's mouth.

He asked fish, and rabbit, and little dormouse:

"Have you seen a sign of a runaway house?"

Rabbit said, "No."

Dormouse said, "No."

Fish in the river's mouth said, "Oh, I've seen whales and sharks and mermaids green, but a runaway house I have never seen."

Jon searched the North, South, East, and West. He sighed. "Of all places home was best. If only the house would return to me I'd be TWICE as good as a boy should be."

He flung himself down on the clovery grass and watched the sun and the shadows pass.

He saw the birds fly away to rest— each had a home. A treetop nest.

He watched the rabbits run home to sleep in hideaway burrows safe and deep.

He watched the muskrats swim with speed to their houses built among rush-and-reed.

Everyone had a place to stay.

Excepting Jonathan James O'Shay.

Jonathan's house had run away.

Then he hid his face in the grass and clover and fell asleep while the night passed over.

When he awakened—where was he?

In exactly the place where he wished to be.

In his own bright room with the sun looking in through the curtains with, oh, such a cheerful grin.

Here were his books and toys and things—his clockwork dragon with whirring wings, the model cars, the giant jet plane—

Oh, Jon O'Shay was home again.

"I'm back! It's back! We have come to stay. We have both been dreaming," said Jon O'Shay. "My good little house did not run away."

Why Is Mr. Tortoise So Slow?

ANN DEVENDORF

Once upon a time
Mr. Tortoise walked on a path in
the woods.

Far behind him on the path
ran Sniff and Snuff.
Sniff and Snuff were field mice.

A cold wind fluffed their fur and

chased them along.
"Brrr, I'm cold," said Sniff.
"So am I," said Snuff.
"Let's run faster."

They ran faster.
They ran so fast
they ran right over the top
of Mr. Tortoise.

"Pardon me!" said Snuff.
"Pardon me!" said Sniff.

They hurried on their way.
Soon they were in their nest.
"Why is Mr. Tortoise so slow?"
Sniff asked Snuff.
"I don't know," said Snuff.

Next, along the path
hopped Peg Rabbit.
She hopped fast.
The cold wind turned her
pink ears to red.

She saw Mr. Tortoise in the path.
She hopped over him.
"Pardon me!" she called.
"Why is Mr. Tortoise so slow?"
said Peg Rabbit to herself when she
got to her burrow. "Why?"

Next, down the path came I.Q. Fox.
He came at a fast trot.
He saw Mr. Tortoise ahead of him.

Then the wind whipped his tail
into his eyes! BANG!
He bumped into Mr. Tortoise.

"Pardon me!" he said.
"But why did you stop?"
"I didn't stop!" said Mr. Tortoise.
"You didn't!" said I.Q. Fox in surprise.
"No!" said Mr. Tortoise.

I.Q. Fox trotted on his way.
He got to his den.
"Why is Mr. Tortoise so slow?"
he said aloud. "Why?"

"I know," said Pokey Snail
passing by the den. "I know
why Mr. Tortoise is so slow. And I
have told Sniff and Snuff and Peg."
"Tell me, too," said I.Q. Fox.

Pokey Snail said,
"Mr. Tortoise is slow because he does
not have to hurry home. Mr. Tortoise
has his home with him all the time!"

Cats, Kittens, and Kenneth

BETTY HOLDEN

Kenneth was visiting Aunt Clara. He liked the small house on Spring Road.

Kenneth helped Aunt Clara by feeding the hens, watering the garden, and putting out milk for Calico Cat and her five kittens. One day he discovered that Aunt Clara was worried about the kittens.

"I must find homes for them," she told him. "I can't have six cats, but no one wants cats anymore."

"I'll find homes for them," offered Kenneth.

"I hope you can," sighed Aunt Clara.

Kenneth took the five kittens out into the yard to play. They batted at leaves, wrestled, and finally cuddled all together in Kenneth's lap.

When Kenneth went up to bed that night, he told Aunt Clara, "I'll find homes for the kittens tomorrow."

"I do hope so," said Aunt Clara. He lay in bed, thinking and thinking. Finally he fell asleep.

In the morning he borrowed Aunt Clara's big wicker flower basket and put the five kittens in it.

"Good-bye," he called to Aunt Clara as he started down Spring Road.

At the first house Mrs. Forrest answered the door. She was holding a broom.

"Come in, Kenneth," she said. "Take this broom and chase a mouse from under my sink."

"I would, but I have something better than a broom for chasing mice." And Kenneth handed Mrs. Forrest a kitten marked just like its mother.

"Of course, a cat!" said Mrs. Forrest. "Thank you, Kenneth."

Kenneth whistled as he went next door and rang old Mr. Clark's doorbell. He had to wait a long time for the man to answer.

"Oh, it's you, Kenneth. I was just filling the hot-water bottle to put on my aching knees."

"I have a knee warmer for you," said Kenneth. "It never cools off." And he handed Mr. Clark a small gray-and-white-striped kitten.

"Of course, a cat!" said Mr. Clark. "Thank you."

Kenneth stopped at Mrs. Wilson's house. When Mrs. Wilson answered his ring, she was holding little Carol.

"Hello, Kenneth. Would you have time to play a game with Carol? I must finish my housework."

"I would," said Kenneth, "but here is a present for Carol that will play as long as Carol wants to play." He handed the little girl a small yellow-and-white kitten.

"Of course, a cat!" said Mrs. Wilson. "Thank you!"

"This is easy," thought Kenneth, strutting to the next house. "Miss Hanks will take a kitten, just like that," and he snapped his fingers. But Miss Hanks looked cross and grumpy.

"Humph, trying to give away kittens?" she asked. "Well, I don't want one. I have been busy fixing over my house and trying to find an ornament for the fireplace hearth."

"Wouldn't a white kitten with blue eyes be very pretty against the red bricks?" asked Kenneth.

"Huh?" said Miss Hanks. "Let me see the kitten." She carried it to the living room. When the kitten looked up at her with big blue eyes and meowed, Miss Hanks said, "Perfect! Thank you, Kenneth."

He went up the steps of the house where Mrs. Abbott lived all alone.

"Come in, come in," she said. "I was hoping someone would stop for a cup of tea and a cookie. I do like to have someone to visit."

"I am sorry you are lonesome," said Kenneth, "and I have someone who would like to be your friend and stay with you all the time." He showed Mrs. Abbott the inky-dark kitten.

"They like to be friendly," said Kenneth.

Mrs. Abbott nodded. "Indeed they do, and I do need a friend."

Kenneth gave her the little inky-dark kitten.

"Thank you," said Mrs. Abbott.

Kenneth swung the empty basket as he ran back to Aunt Clara's house.

"I did it! I did it!" he cried. "Every kitten has a good home."

"My goodness," said Aunt Clara. "I don't know how you did it!"

Kenneth laughed. "It was sort of easy," he confessed. "They all really wanted a cat. They just didn't know it."

There's Something Special About the City

SANDRA FENICHEL ASHER

City Squirrel saw an acorn across the street. But as he dashed out to get it, cars and trucks screeched to a stop and honked their horns angrily. He raced back to the sidewalk.

"Oh, dear!" he cried, trembling from the tops of his tiny pointed ears to the tip of his long bushy tail. "That was very careless of me. But I have not found an acorn all day, and I must store away food for the winter."

A sparrow hopped by and said, "Why not come to the forest with me? There are no cars or trucks there."

"I have been to the forest," said City Squirrel, "but I missed the city. There's something special about the city."

"What?" asked the sparrow.

"I do not know exactly," said City Squirrel, "but I like it here."

"Good-bye then," said the sparrow. And she flew away.

City Squirrel hopped back to the park. A child was sitting on a bench with her mother. The child waved at City Squirrel. That made City Squirrel feel good. Suddenly, he spotted a nut lying on the path. He rushed over to it. But it was only an empty peanut shell.

"Oh, dear," he sighed. "I have not found a bit of food for the winter."

A rabbit hopped by and said, "Why not come to the country with me? There are lots of nuts there and fruits and berries, too."

"I have been to the country," said City Squirrel, "but I missed the city. There's something special about the city."

"What?" asked the rabbit.

"I do not know exactly," said City Squirrel, "but I like it here."

"Good-bye then," said the rabbit, and he hopped away.

City Squirrel was tired. He decided to rest before looking for food again. He climbed up to his home in the hollow of a tall, old tree, curled up into a little, furry ball and fell asleep.

When he woke up, the sun was setting. City Squirrel rushed down from his tree.

He hopped past an old man sitting on a bench. The old man took a small paper bag out of his pocket.

The old man took something out of the bag and threw it on the path.

City Squirrel twitched his nose and flipped his tail.

"A peanut!" he cried. He rushed over to the path and picked it up.

"Here is another one," smiled the old man.

City Squirrel ate the first peanut. Then he carried the second one back to his home in the hollow of the tall, old tree. When he hopped back to the bench, the old man had another peanut waiting for him. And another one after that. And another and another and another.

"That is all for today," said the old man at last.

City Squirrel had carried so many peanuts, he could hardly climb his tree one last time to go to bed.

A robin sat on a branch and said, "My, you look tired. Why not go away for a vacation as I do?"

"Oh, no," said City Squirrel. "I

would miss the city. There's something special about the city."

"What?" asked the robin.

This time, City Squirrel thought about it. He thought about the child who waved at him and the old man who gave him peanuts.

"The people!" he cried happily. "It is the people who make the city special! I like it here!"

Charley Chipmunk

ANN DEVLIN

Charley Chipmunk sat up on his tail and sniffed. He felt the wind begin to blow. It blew his short, white whiskers sideways.

It rumpled his fur up and down.

It blew leaves and sticks all about the woods.

Suddenly a strange thing blew out of the sky. It rolled over to Charley Chipmunk's feet. It was yellow and silky. It had a long glass handle.

Charley Chipmunk had never seen an umbrella.

"What a lovely bright thing this thing is!" he said to himself.

He crept up on the handle.

"Swoosh!" The wind rushed along the ground.

"Swoosh!" It lifted up the umbrella.

Charley clung tightly to the spokes.

Up, up, up he went, over the tops of the tall trees.

"Whee!" Charley shouted happily, "I'm flying."

On, on, on the gay umbrella sailed. Charley looked over the edge. He saw tall chimneys and white buildings beneath him.

"Oh," Charley said happily, "I'm flying over a city. But where down there would I ever live? There is no black, wet earth. There is no tall grass. The ground is all white stone."

The wind stopped blowing.

Down,
  down,
    down Charley sailed in the yellow umbrella. Over the tops of houses. Over the tops of automobiles. Over the tops of people.

Some children were playing tag in a park. "Swoosh!" Charley's umbrella sailed right over them.

"It's a runaway umbrella," one of the boys cried. He began to run and chase the umbrella. The other children laughed and ran, too.

The umbrella handle caught on a bush. Charley ran down the handle to the soft green grass. A lovely rosebush spread out over the ground. Around it was dark, sweet earth.

"What a lovely place for a home," Charley said.

He dug a hole at the front of the bush.

He dug a hole at the back of the bush.

He dug a tunnel between the holes. Then he sat down to rest.

The children were playing with the umbrella. They laughed. They ran. They were happy.

Charley sighed gratefully.
"Thank you, Mr. Wind," he said, "for bringing me to a lovely home."

The Tomato Thief

ANN DEVENDORF

Mr. Burns grew tomatoes in his garden. He grew big, red, ripe, fine tomatoes.

One morning, Mr. Burns went out to look at his tomato plants. He looked at the tomatoes on them. His eyes got big and round. His mouth flew open.

"Who took a bite out of my tomatoes?" he roared.

Mrs. Burns came running from the house. "Oh dear," she said.

"Did you bite my tomatoes?" asked Mr. Burns.

"Not I," said Mrs. Burns. "Indeed not!"

"I know you like fresh tomatoes," said Mr. Burns.

"Not *that* fresh," said Mrs. Burns. "Maybe a bird took a bite."

"Birds do not bite," said Mr. Burns. "Birds peck."

Mrs. Burns went into the house.

"Who took a bite out of my tomatoes?" shouted Mr. Burns.

His neighbor, Mr. Green, came to Mr. Burns' yard.

"Your tomatoes are very good," said Mr. Green. "But I like them on a plate with salt and pepper, not on a plant!"

"Who took a bite out of my tomatoes?" Mr. Burns hollered.

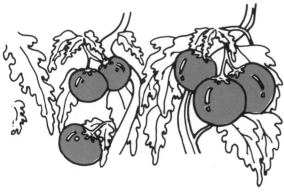

"Not I," called young Bobby Jones from down the street. "I like to look at tomatoes but I don't like to eat them."

"You would like mine," said Mr. Burns.

Bobby Jones skipped away.

"I'll get that tomato thief," said Mr. Burns. "I'll get him. I'll get him if I have to sit up all night and wait for him. When he comes, I'll grab him. I'll tie him. I'll call the police!"

That night Mr. Burns sat on his porch. He looked at his tomato plants. The moon made the night bright.

Mr. Burns sat very still.

He saw the thief run from the shadows and pitty-pat to his tomato plants! Behind the thief came two more little thieves!

"Skunks!" said Mr. Burns to himself. "Skunks are eating my tomatoes!"

Mr. Burns did not grab the thieves nor tie them or call the police. Oh no!

He sat and watched them.

In the morning, Mrs. Burns asked, "Did you catch the thief?"

Mr. Burns laughed. "No," he said. "The thief was a mother skunk with two little skunks."

"What will you do?" asked Mrs. Burns.

"I will put mothballs around the tomato plants," said Mr. Burns. "Skunks do not like the smell of mothballs."

"You *are* smart," said Mrs. Burns.

"I will not put mothballs around all the plants," said Mr. Burns. "I will leave some plants for the skunks."

"You are more than smart," said Mrs. Burns.

Just Perfect!

CAROLYN GLOECKNER

Once upon a time there was a hermit crab named Humphrey. His house was a silvery, shiny, speckled, spiny seashell shaped like a horn. Wherever Humphrey went, he carried his house on his back. Then, when he felt like it, he could fold up his ten legs and pull himself inside.

As Humphrey strolled along the beach one sunny morning, a sea gull swooped down and settled beside him.

"What a dinky little shell," the sea gull said rudely. "I don't see how you squeeze yourself inside it."

"I like this shell," Humphrey replied. "It's very comfortable."

The sea gull squinted down at Humphrey's shell. "I doubt that," he said. Then he flew off to hunt for fish.

Humphrey thought over what the sea gull had said. "Maybe my shell is too small," he said to himself. "Perhaps I should look for a bigger home."

Just then he saw a shell nearby on the sand. It wasn't as nice as his, for it was greenish-gray. But it was a little bit bigger.

"I'll try it on," Humphrey said to himself, "just to see how it feels." He slipped out of his silvery, shiny, speckled spiny house and into the greenish-gray shell.

"Well, this *is* roomy," Humphrey said. "It isn't nearly as pretty as my old shell. But it's very comfortable."

Then he saw an even bigger shell than the greenish-gray one. This one was a pale purple color.

"I'll try it on," Humphrey said.

"This is very comfortable, indeed," he said once he was inside. But it was too big for Humphrey.

Farther on, Humphrey saw the biggest, most beautiful sparkling pink shell of all. Without a second thought, he slipped out of the pale, pearly purple shell and into the big pink shell. But the pink shell was so big that Humphrey could scarcely carry it.

"After all, it's such a beautiful shell," Humphrey told himself. "I won't mind the extra weight."

So he staggered proudly along the edge of the ocean, showing off his new home to everyone.

"Goodness, but I'm tired!" Humphrey exclaimed. "Carrying this shell around is hard, hard work." Soon he was asleep inside his new home.

While Humphrey slept, the waves crept up the sandy beach.

When Humphrey awoke, his big new home was flooded with water! He tried to get away, but he couldn't. The shell was so heavy that it stuck fast in the sand.

He pulled and he tugged. He wiggled and he squirmed. But the big pink shell wouldn't budge. And all the while waves pounded the beach and poured over Humphrey and his shell.

Then a giant green wave rumbled in and washed Humphrey and his shell far up the beach. Over and over they rolled. At last they stopped, high up on dry sand.

Humphrey didn't waste a minute! He scooted out of the beautiful pink shell and hurried as fast as his ten legs could carry him back up the beach.

When he came to his old home, the silvery, shiny, speckled, spiny seashell shaped like a horn, he stopped.

He slipped happily inside it and

curled up. It was good to be back!

"Well!" said a grumpy voice outside. It was the sea gull again.

"Ha!" said the sea gull. "I see you haven't taken my advice. You're still living in that little, tiny shell."

"That's right!" Humphrey answered cheerfully. "I don't need a new home. This shell is just perfect for me!"

Flip-Flop Turtle

DOROTHY GORDON

Turtle liked to travel over rocks. Sometimes he slipped. Then he went flip-flop over on his back. He did this so often his friends called him Flip-Flop.

Turtle did not mind going flip-flop over on his back. One of his friends always came along and turned him over again. Sometimes Rabbit turned him over. Sometimes Squirrel turned him over. Woodchuck helped him and so did Deer and Owl. So Turtle never tried to turn himself over. He just waited for some friend to come along.

One day Owl, the wise one, said to the other animals, "We must stop helping Turtle. He must learn to turn himself over."

"Why should we stop helping him, Owl?" asked Rabbit.

"Because some time we might not see him. He might just lie there on his back until he died."

The animals thought about what Owl had said. They agreed not to help Turtle the next time he went flip-flop.

Turtle was traveling over some rocks one day. All at once over he went, flip-flop on his back. "I'll just rest here," he thought. "One of my friends will come along to help me."

Rabbit, Squirrel, Woodchuck, Deer, and some other animals gathered around. But none of them would help.

Owl flew to a tree overhead. "You must turn yourself over, Turtle," she said. "We won't help you anymore. You must help yourself."

"I can't!" cried Turtle. "Help me, Rabbit! Help me, Squirrel! Help me, someone!"

But the animals would not.

"Squirm, Turtle," called Owl. "Squirm and try to turn yourself over!"

"I can't!" cried Turtle.

"Squirm," chanted all of the animals. "Squirm, squirm, squirm!"

Turtle squirmed but he could not turn himself over. "My shell is caught under a rock!" he cried.

"Then squirm and heave upward," advised Owl.

"Squirm and heave!" chanted the animals. "Squirm and heave, squirm and heave!"

Turtle squirmed and then he heaved himself upward. His shell came out from under the rock. All at once he was right side up.

"Hurrah!" shouted his friends. "You did it! You turned yourself over!" The animals were proud of him.

Turtle was proud, too. After that he did not depend upon his friends. He still often went flip-flop over on his back. But now he knew how to flip-flop himself right side up again.

Poems

City Street at Night

NONA KEEN DUFFY

A city street at night
Is a fascinating sight.
I like to watch the antics
Of the signs.

I like the jolly winking,
The unexpected blinking
Of the buildings all ablaze
With gay designs.

Mice

ROSE FYLEMAN

I think mice
Are rather nice.
Their tails are long
Their faces small,
They haven't any
Chins at all.
Their ears are pink
Their teeth are white,
They run about
The house at night.
They nibble things
They shouldn't touch
And no one seems
to like them much.
But I think mice
Are nice.

The Sun

JOHN DRINKWATER

I told the Sun that I was glad,
I'm sure I don't know why;
Somehow the pleasant way he had
Of shining in the sky,
Just put a notion in my head
That wouldn't it be fun
If, walking on the hill, I said
"I'm happy" to the Sun.

The Garden

AILEEN FISHER

We wanted a garden,
and oh, what fun
to plan a garden and dig in one!

But was it awful
the way the weeds
grew every place we wanted seeds!

And was it frightful
how rain and such
was either too little or else too much!

And was it weary
to weed and hoe
when there were places we wanted to go!

But was it jolly
the day we spied
little green pods growing peas inside!

Chums

ARTHUR GUITERMAN

He sits and begs, he gives a paw,
He is, as you can see,
The finest dog you ever saw,
And he belongs to me.

He follows everywhere I go
And even when I swim.
I laugh because he thinks, you
know,
That I belong to him.

But still no matter what we do
We never have a fuss;
And so I guess it must be true
That we belong to us.

Poems

Trees

HARRY BEHN

Trees are the kindest things I know,
They do no harm, they simply grow

And spread a shade for sleepy cows,
And gather birds among their boughs.

They give us fruit in leaves above,
And wood to make our houses of,

And leaves to burn on Hallowe'en,
And in the Spring new buds of green.

They are the first when day's begun
To touch the beams of morning sun,

They are the last to hold the light
When evening changes into night,

And when a moon floats on the sky
They hum a drowsy lullaby

Of sleepy children long ago . . .
Trees are the kindest things I know.

The Hippopotamus

GEORGIA ROBERTS DURSTON

In the squdgy river,
Down the oozely bank,
Where the ripples shiver,
And the reeds are rank—

Where the purple Kippo
Makes an awful fuss,
Lives the hip-hip-hippo
Hippo-pot-a-mus!

Broad his back and steady;
Broad and flat his nose;
Sharp and keen and ready
Little eyes are those.

You would think him dreaming
Where the mud is deep.
It is only seeming—
He is not asleep.

Better not disturb him,
There'd be an awful fuss
If you touched the Hippo,
Hippo-pot-a-mus.

I Envy the Chimp

JACOB KISNER

Oh, I envy the chimp,
For he makes quite a stir
As he ambles about
In his custom-made fur.

Oh, I envy the chimp
For his devil-may-care,
Unhurried, unworried,
Unflappable air.

Oh, I envy the chimp,
For he keeps himself trim
And never gets worried
When out on a limb.

Oh, I envy the chimp;
Not a trick does he lack.
His arms are so long
He can scratch his own back.

A Finger Play

1. Here is the alligator, (right hand forms alligator)

2. Sitting on a log. (right hand on left forearm)

3. Down in the pool, (make horizontal circle of arms)

4. He sees a little frog. (put hands around eyes like binoculars)

5. In goes the alligator, (diving motion with hands)

6. Round goes the log, (forearms go around each other)

7. Splash goes the water, (hands to up in air)

8. Away swims the frog! (swimming motion with hands)

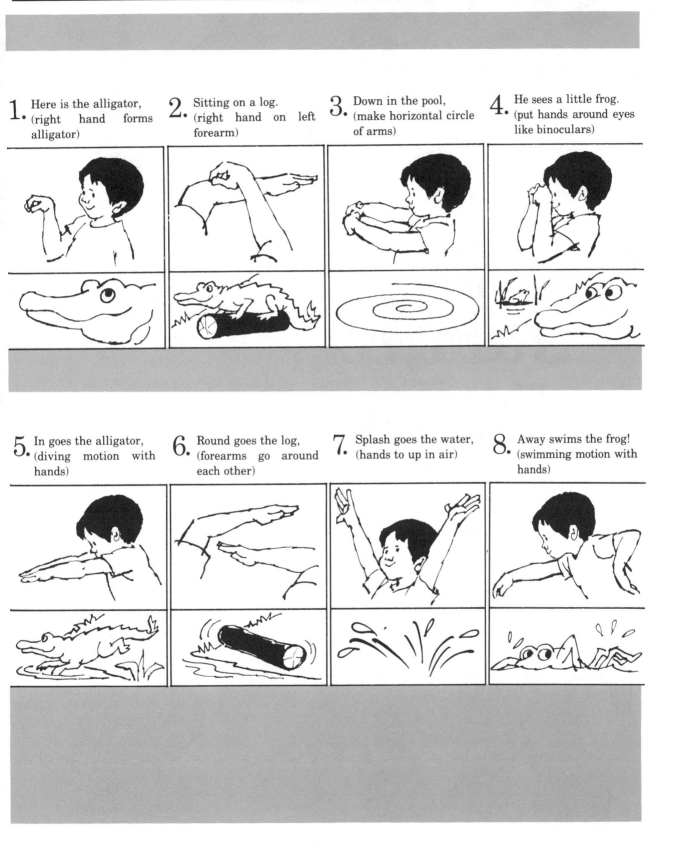

A Jungle Jingle

MARY E. MATTHEWS

A big, gray elephant lives in the jungle,
(bend over, hands clasped to form trunk)

And when he walks, he walks with a rumble.
(big, giant-sized steps, making noise with shoes)

He tosses his trunk high in the sky,
(hands still clasped, above head)

Kicks his back legs, and winks one great eye,
(kick one foot, then the other, wink)

Then slowly goes back to the jungle.
(bend over again, arms together, walk other way slowly

Finger Plays

1. Here's a nest for Bobbie Redbreast.

2. Here's a hive for Bessie Bee.

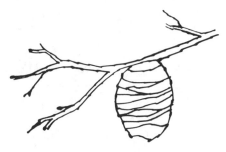

3. Here's a hole for Jackie Rabbit.

4. Here's a house for me.

The fish live in the little brook,

(wiggle hands, move forward)

The birds live in the tree.
(arms make spreading motion)

But home's the very nicest place
For a little child like me.

Fun With Fingers

Here are the bee hives,
(hands clenched)

But where are the bees?
Hidden away where nobody sees.

Soon they'll come creeping
Out of their hives

One -   two-   three -

four-   five

Bzzzz-zzzz-zzzz-zzzz-zzzz
(flying motion with the fingers)

This little dog said
"Let's go out to play."

This little dog said
"Let's run away."

This little dog said
"Let's stay out till dark."

This little dog said
"Let's bark,
        bark,
            bark!"

This little dog said
"I think
it would be fun
To go straight home

So let's   run
            run
                run!

(all doggies run
across lap)

Animal Crafts

Loop Zoo

With paper loops and a few cut-paper details, you can make a whole zoo. Cut colored construction paper into 1-inch-wide strips lengthwise. Hold two of the strips together, one on top of the other, and staple or glue the ends together. Make a smaller loop and attach it to the first one. Now you have a body and head. You can make legs, tail, and other parts from different sized loops.

Details such as feathers, eyes, and ears can be cut to shape from construction paper and glued on. For a rounder effect, such as the caterpillar's head, make two loops the same size. Put one inside the other so that they criss-cross. The turtle's body is made in a similar way, but with four loops, squeezed gently until it resembles the turtle's squatty shape.

Paper Lion

Cut a "hill" from the bottom of a rectangular piece of yellow construction paper. The "hill" will be the lion's head; the remaining part of the yellow paper will be his body. Paste the yellow head in the center of a square piece of brown construction paper. Cut the edges of the brown square jagged to represent the lion's mane. Paste the mane and head to the upper left-hand corner of the body shape. Cut ears from another piece of yellow paper, and paste in place.

Make the eyes, nose, tongue, whiskers, and tail from different colors of paper.

Foil Turtle

Cut a turtle shape from lightweight cardboard. Also cut cardboard flower shapes. Glue flower shapes onto one side of the turtle. Cover turtle with foil. Use a few drops of glue to hold the foil in place. Rub gently with fingertips and you will feel and see the shapes come through. For an antiqued look, gently rub black shoe polish over the foil surface.

Animal Crafts

Box and Egg-Carton Zoo

Collect an assortment of small boxes. Use each box as the body of the animal or bird. Cut a papier-mache egg carton apart. Use the cups and pillars as legs, heads, and eyes. Glue onto the box and paint with tempera. To make the paint stick, add a few drops of liquid detergent to the paint or rub the brush across a cake of soap.

Box-and-bag Animals

Stuff a small bag about half-full of paper. Twist and glue the top shut. Use this for the head. For the elephant and bird, twist the top of the bag into a trunk or beak. Glue the head to a small box. Cut the legs from cardboard. Glue to the box and paint with tempera. Cut features from paper and glue in place.

Lucy Rabbit

American Folk Song

Lu - cy Rab - bit, Hey! Hey! In my gar - den, Hey! Hey!

Cut my col - lards, Hey! Hey! Cut my car - rots, Hey! Hey!

Cut my tur - nips, Hey! Hey! All night long,— Hey! Hey!

Shoo rab - bit 'way, Hey! Hey! *Shoo!*
(Spoken loudly by everyone)

The Bear Lives in a Cave

Moderately, in two (♩. = 1 beat)

1. The bear lives in a cave,
2. The bee lives in a hive,

The bear lives in a cave, Ev - 'ry - bod - y
The bee lives in a hive, Ev - 'ry - bod - y

has a home, The bear lives in a cave.
has a home, The bee lives in a hive.

3. The bird lives in a nest,
The bird lives in a nest,
Everybody has a home,
The bird lives in a nest.

4. The cow lives in a barn,
The cow lives in a barn,
Everybody has a home,
The cow lives in a barn.

5. The fish lives in a brook,
The fish lives in a brook,
Everybody has a home,
The fish lives in a brook.

6. The squirrel lives in a tree,
The squirrel lives in a tree,
Everybody has a home,
The squirrel lives in a tree.

7. The worm lives in the ground,
The worm lives in the ground,
Everybody has a home,
The worm lives in the ground.

8. I live in a house,
I live in a house,
Everybody has a home,
I live in a house.

9. No matter where I roam,
No matter where I roam,
I will always have a home,
No matter where I roam.

Moving About

Introduction

The desire to move about is intrinsic in human beings. It is the means to satisfy their innate curiosity for exploring the world. Beginning with the struggles of an infant to turn over, stand and crawl, this desire does not end until the end of life itself.

Various methods of transportation, each with its own particular characteristics, have been developed to meet this urge to move about. From animals to space ships, human beings have attempted to increase the ease and efficiency with which they can travel, to master land, sea and air, to compress distances. This unit seeks to enlarge the child's understanding of this process, capitalizing on his or her strong natural interest.

Transportation also brings people the many products they eat, wear and use every day. Kindergarten children need to learn something of the nature, function and means of transportation in order to appreciate how it vitally affects their lives.

Concepts To Be Taught

I. **There are various ways to move about.**

II. **Various forms of transportation serve many important purposes.**

III. **People and things travel on land, on and under water, and in the air.**

IV. **There are differences between early forms of transportation and modern ones.**

V. **Some people associated with moving about are drivers, pilots, boat captains, railroad engineers and riders.**

Information For Teaching Concepts

I. There are various ways to move about.

Direct the class to be seated. Then, tell them to look about and name objects they can see. Ask, "How many of you can see your house from where you are sitting?" After they respond, ask why the children can not see their houses. Encourage them to think about other things they cannot see from their seated positions. Allow them to walk around the classroom for a brief time to locate something they could not see when they were seated. After they have returned to their seats, discuss how they were able to see more once they were able to move about.

Ask how they moved around the classroom (walked). Have the children discuss the various ways they and other children get from home to school (on foot, on bicycle, by bus or car).

Read the story, "The Girl Who Could Fly," page 168. Ask these questions:
  "Where did Jenny want to go?"
  "How was Jenny going to get to her grandmother's house?"
  "What are some other ways Jenny could travel to visit Grandmother?"
Locate pictures of various forms of transportation including:

bicycle	boat	horse	truck	car
person walking	airplane	sled	train	bus

Have the children name each form of transportation. Ask them which form would be the slowest and which would be the fastest. Ask them to name the transportation forms that have wheels and those that have motors.

II. Various forms of transportation serve many important purposes.

Place a stack of books or blocks in front of the classroom and ask one child to carry them to the back of the room while the rest of the class observes. Make certain that the task will require two or more trips. Next, ask the children to consider what might be an easier way to move the items from one place to the other.

If a wagon or other vehicle is available, demonstrate the comparative ease with which the task is performed when a vehicle is used to transport the items. Point out the comparative saving in time.

Have the children consider the items they find in the school and discuss how they may have arrived at the school building. Emphasize the use of trucks in carrying food, desks, paper, mail, etc. Present a picture of a truck and discuss how the truck moves about on wheels. Share with the children the activity "What Is Each Truck Used For?" page 161. Talk with the class about trucks and their uses.

Explain to the children that people and goods are moved by various means of transportation. Have them consider trains, both passenger and freight trains, and discuss the ways in which trains move people, cattle, cars, fruit, tractors, lumber and other goods.

Read the story, "Tiny Toot," page 166. Also, you might make a train, following the pattern for *The Cardboard Express,* page 182.

III. People and things travel on land, on and under water, and in the air.

Have the children recall the story, "The Girl Who Could Fly." Then ask:
"How was it possible for Jenny to fly?"
"What are some other things that can fly?"
"What helps each of these things to fly?"
Experiment with balloons and feathers. Demonstrate how easy it is to keep a balloon or a feather in the air by blowing on it. Hold a balloon full of air and then release the air. Have the children observe how fast the balloon moves as the air rushes out. Explain that movement of air causes the balloon, as well as planes and kites, to fly.

Locate pictures of several different types of boats and ships. Ask the children to tell whether each vessel would ordinarily be found on a lake, a river, or an ocean. Explain that different boats are powered by different means. Have the children name vessels that use paddles, oars, motors and/or wind. Talk about submarines and how they travel under the water; houseboats, where people make their homes; tugboats, which guide other boats into the docks; and ferry boats, which carry people and sometimes cars across a body of water. Read the poem, "Where Go the Boats?", on page 177.

Show a road map to the children and ask who uses such a map. Have them explain what the lines on the map tell the driver. Discuss how a road map shows the driver different routes he can follow across a city, a state or even an entire country. Ask the class to think about all the streets, avenues, roads, and highways each of them has traveled on. Have them name the various kinds of vehicles or other modes of transportation they might see on a road (car, truck, motorcycle, bus, jeep, horse).

Talk about safety on the road and devices that are used to protect drivers and their passengers. Examples are:

1) driver's licenses	3) highway signs	5) highway crews
2) speed limits	4) police officers	6) safety belts

Draw railroad signs on the chalkboard. Ask the children where they would find such signs. Have them listen as you say "rail*road*," emphasizing *road*. Explain that this is a special road and ask them to describe the difference between a *rail*road and a road where cars and trucks travel. Have the children look at a picture of railroad tracks and the wheels found on a train. If a toy train is available, use it to demonstrate the grooved wheels on a railway car and to show how they grip the tracks in a special way. Explain that passenger trains move people and that other types of trains, freight trains, move food and commercial products. Show the children a picture of a freight train and discuss how this train moves goods across cities, states and even the nation.

IV. There are differences between early modes of transportation and modern ones.

Have the children pretend that wheels and motors have not yet been invented. Ask them to imagine what it was like before cars, trucks, trains and planes were invented. Explain that in earliest times, when people wanted to move their belongings, they would carry them on their backs. Later, people learned to tame animals to help move them and their goods about. Horses, oxen, camels, goats, elephants and dogs were taught to carry people and/or burdens on their backs and to pull wagons and sleds. Have the class compare the advantages and disadvantages of the early horse-drawn wagon with modern cars and trucks.

Discuss the ways people traveled on water before the invention of the steam engine. Explain that before boats were used people floated on logs in the water. Hands or poles were used to guide the direction of the log. Later, the logs were hollowed out to form canoes, or lashed together to form rafts. Oars and sails were invented to assist water transportation. Ask the class how oars or sails would improve water transportation. Point out to the class that; early in the history of people, ships were constructed of large wooden boards, shaped and fitted together. Ask the class if they know what materials modern boats and ships are made of.

Use the activities on advantages and disadvantages of various types of transportation, page 154; train crafts, page 182 and boat crafts, page 180.

V. Some people associated with moving about are drivers, pilots, boat captains, railroad engineers and riders.

Line up the chairs in the classroom to form a bus. Ask the class, "Who rides on a bus?" Discuss what a bus driver does (opens and closes the door, greets people, turns the key, pushes on the gas pedal, steers, brakes). Have one child imitate the school bus driver while the others pretend to be passengers. As the "driver" opens the door, have the "passengers" take seats on the bus.

Have the children name drivers of other types of vehicles. Examples are:

truck drivers	bus drivers	mail truck drivers
taxi drivers	ambulance drivers	
fire engine drivers	tow truck drivers	

Read "Jumbo Jet Flight", page 176, to the children. Talk about members of the flight crew. Ask what the person who flies a plane is called. Have the children describe how a pilot guides a plane.

Show the children a picture of a large boat or a ship. Ask what the person who is responsible for guiding the boat is called. Show a picture of a locomotive to the class and ask who is responsible for guiding the train.

Try to locate hats that are associated with each of the special drivers discussed in the lesson plan. Teach the children to associate actions with each type of driver and then place the hats in a special area for the children to use in role-playing activities.

Encourage the children to think about places they would like to go, what they would like to see and how they would travel to get there. Have the children make a mural that shows the many ways people can move about.

Thinking and Reasoning

Ask your children these questions:

Why do we not turn on headlights when the sun is shining?

Does a boat run on the ground or in the water?

Which makes more noise when it flies, a bird or an airplane?

Why are there license plates on automobiles?

What do we mean when we say a car gets good mileage?

Which can land in a smaller space, an airplane or a helicopter?

When a car is driven at night, what color are the lights on the rear of the car?

Name something that isn't alive but can fly.

At which end of a boat is its rudder?

What is the difference between a bus and a truck? Between a truck and an automobile?

Where are the wheels of an airplane while it is flying?

How may the driver of a car see another car coming close behind his car?

How is a jeep different from a regular car?

Why does a traffic light usually signal yellow before red appears?

"Someone has driven this car since I came home in it last evening," said Mr. Ross. How could he have known this?

In what part of an airplane does the pilot sit? The navigator? The flight attendant?

Why might a wheelchair be made to fold up?

If an island is far from land and there is no bridge, how might you get there?

How would life on a small island far from land be different from life in a large city?

Does an automobile run on tracks as a train does? Does an airplane?

What safety devices does a car have? How do signs along the road help a driver be safe?

What is the wheel inside a car used for?

Which is bigger, a bus or an automobile?

Name three ways of going from one floor to another in a big department store.

Does a helicopter fly as fast as a jet plane?

Can you travel on an elevator from one side of a building to the other?

Does an airplane flap its wings when it flies?

How does your mother know how fast she is driving the car?

How would a person go to the moon?

Four people started at the same time to travel to a place 100 miles away. One went by bicycle, one went in an airplane, one went in an automobile, and one walked. Who arrived first, who second, who third, who last?

Can an airplane fly above the clouds?

Which move on legs?
Which move on wheels?
Which move on wings?
Name some other things that move on legs, on wheels, and on wings.
What is the difference between the bird's wings and the plane's wings?
How do you move? Could you move in or on all of the things shown?

Connect the picture on the left to the matching picture on the right by drawing a line.

Draw a line to show where each wheel belongs.

Which one travels in the air?
Which one travels on water?
Which one travels on land?
Name some other things that travel in the air, on water and on land.
What are some good things about each type of transportation?
What are some bad things about each type of transportation?

MOVING ABOUT IN MY WORLD   **157**

Which has four wheels?
Which has three wheels?
Which has two wheels?
Which has no wheels?
How does each of these things move?
What else moves on four wheels? on three wheels?
on two wheels? on one wheel?

Thinking Questions

Answer these questions using the choices below:

tricycle, canoe, sled, sailboat, kite, automobile

What makes each of these go?

Which may move high in the air?

Which are driven by the wind?

Which may coast down a hill?

Which is driven by a motor?

Which runs on bare ground?

Which of these can walk but not fly?
crow, bear, airplane, elephant

Which of these can fly but not walk?
eagle, dog, airplane, tiger

Which of these can walk and fly?
crow, tiger, helicopter, bear

Something Larger

Each of the following belongs to something larger. What is it?

caboose	animal's tail
taillights	radiator
animal's head	exhaust pipe
spare tire	headlight
locomotive	outboard motor
windshield	rudder
handlebars	windshield wipers
gas tank	propeller

Which are at the rear?
Which are at the front?

Tell how each of these flies:

helicopter	honeybee
pigeon	airplane
kite	balloon

Answer these questions using the choices below.

snake, kangaroo, grasshopper, baby

Which of these creatures usually crawl?

What other creatures crawl?

Which of these creatures can jump?

What other creatures can jump?

What special ways are curbs at street corners made to help persons using wheelchairs?

"That taxi won't stop. The driver is off duty," said Mrs. Gonsalves to her friend. How did she know?

Sometimes trains on the same subway will be marked "local" and "express". What is the difference?

How many doors might a car have?

Some companies have a special parking place for employees who are in a car pool. Why is this, do you suppose?

Does an airplane have wheels? Does a boat?

Why doesn't a fire engine always stop at a red traffic light?

Why are some streets marked "One Way"?

Which of these moves on land?
Which moves through water?
Which moves in snow?
Do you know of any other ways of moving through water?
Which of these three would be the easiest to steer? Why?

Trucks

What is each truck used for?
Name some other kinds of trucks and tell what they are used for.
What can a truck do that a car can not do?

MOVING ABOUT IN MY WORLD **161**

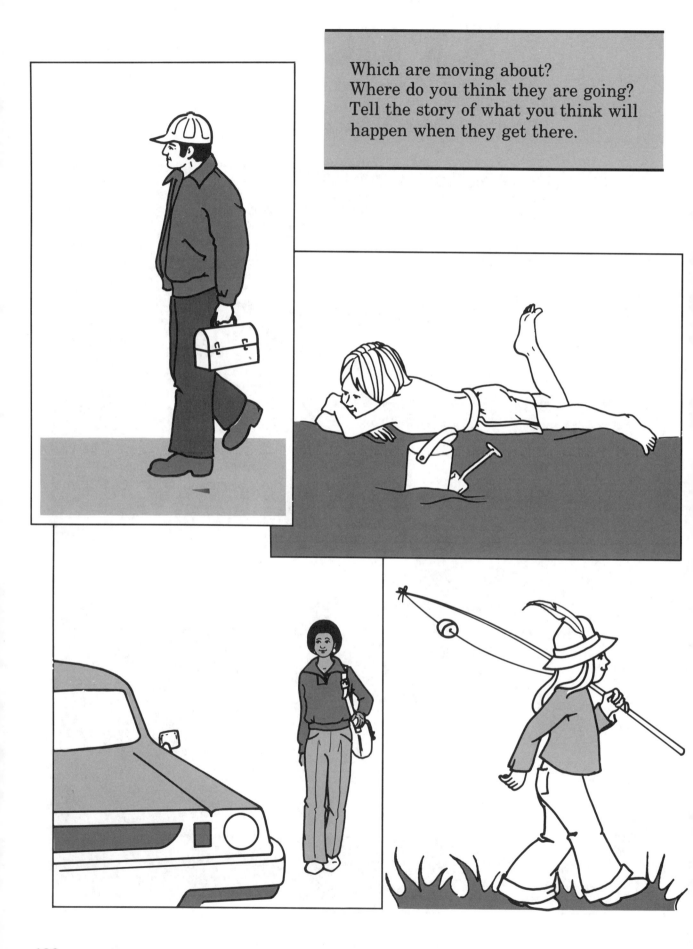

Which are moving about?
Where do you think they are going?
Tell the story of what you think will happen when they get there.

Match each person to the way he or she moves about.

Cut out and paste in order from first to last.

In a short race, which will go the fastest? the slowest?
Which can go the longest distance without slowing down?
If they came to a pond, which could get across it best?
Which would go better in the woods, the girl on the bicycle or the rabbit? Why?
Why do you suppose they are racing?

Tiny Toot

JULIET EARLE WELTON

Tiny Toot was the smallest switch engine of them all. He ran up and down the repair yard tooting to himself as he went. He was very busy. His jobs were not really big important ones, but they were things that had to be done, and it was up to him to do them.

He scampered up and down and around the great streamliners, passenger, and freight cars. His little piston rods pushed back and forth, and his wheels kept time with his tooting:

"Clickety-clack, clickety-clack,
Up and down the railroad track,
All day long I'll toot my song,
Clickety-clack, clickety-clack,
Away I'll go, but I'll toot back."

He pushed the streamliners and steam engines into the roundhouse when they went for repairs, or oiling and checking over. He pulled them out, and pushed them over to be coupled with their lines of passenger or freight cars. It was a little like a game of tag; for they never knew which one he would catch and drag to some other part of the yard.

The engines who used the repair yard treated Tiny Toot as a little brother. They often called him "T.T." for short. They told him stories about their long trips, about the wonderful things they had seen, and the faraway places they had visited. They tried, too, to make Tiny Toot feel important. They showed him how they appreciated his efficient service. They knew his little jobs were as important to him as their cross-country runs were to them.

One day a very long, new, shiny streamliner glided into their midst. He was so new and shiny that Tiny Toot couldn't believe that he needed repairs. With nose in the air he slid past Toot and the others without so much as a nod of greeting in answer to their smiles of welcome.

In fact, he had his nose so high in the air, and was trying so to impress the others with his sleek beauty, that he didn't see the curve in the track. Instead of continuing around the curve, his front wheels jumped the track.

Tiny Toot rushed over to help put him back on the track.

"Keep away, Tiny," said the streamliner. "I don't need you to help me. If I can't get back myself, one of the large engines will help me."

Poor Toot had never been treated like that before. He turned and sped away. This time he didn't whistle to himself, "Clickety-clack, clickety-clack," but just blew a sad "toot, toot, toot, toot," as his headlight was so misty that he couldn't see very well, and he didn't want to run into anything. His feelings were so hurt that he hid in the darkest place in the roundhouse.

The streamliner tried and tried to get his front wheels back on the track. The other engines just stood around and watched him. Finally he called impatiently to the other engines:

"One of you fellows come over here and give me a push. I can't quite make it."

"None of us can do it as well and

carefully as Tiny Toot," said Steamie. "He knows just how hard and when to push. We might bump you too hard and make a dent in your smooth outer shell."

"Well, get Tiny Toot," said the Streamliner, "and tell him to hurry, as I am due to leave at six twenty-five."

"You weren't very kind to Toot, and I don't know if he will come, but I'll go ask him," said Steamie.

Steamie puffed over to the roundhouse.

"T.T., we need you very much. There is a job that none of us can do as well as you can. Will you help Streamliner get back on the track? He is due to leave soon. You are the only one careful enough to bump him so as not to dent his shell or scratch his paint and get him back on the track."

Tiny Toot ran right out of the roundhouse and over to the siding. He didn't need to "toot, toot" now as his headlight was clear and he could see. As he went, his wheels sang, "Clickety-clack, clickety-clack."

In a very short time Tiny Toot had pulled and pushed the Streamliner back on the track. He had done it so carefully that there wasn't a single dent or a bit of paint scratched off. The other engines stood around looking very proud of Toot.

"I'm sorry, Toot, that I was so cross to you," said the Streamliner. "I didn't realize that you little fellows have jobs that are just as important as our big ones. If you don't do your jobs we can't do ours. If it hadn't been for you I wouldn't be ready to leave now. I know now we all have to work together. Thank you, Tiny Toot, for helping me."

As the Streamliner left the yard, Toot ran alongside of him to see him safely out of the repair yard.

As the Streamliner started on his cross-country run, the last thing he heard from the repair yard was Tiny Toot's happy song:

"Clickety-clack, clickety-clack,
Up and down the railroad track,
All day long I'll toot my song,
Clickety-clack, clickety-clack,
Away I'll go, but I'll toot back."

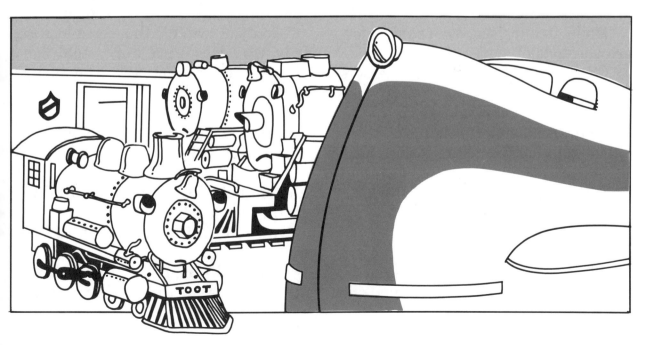

The Girl Who Could Fly

ALAN CLIBURN

Jenny went shopping with her mother one Tuesday morning. While she was getting some milk from the dairy case, Jenny walked up to a woman putting cans of dog food on a shelf.

"I can fly!" Jenny announced excitedly.

The woman smiled. "That's nice. Can you fly around the store?"

Jenny shook her head. "No. But I can fly!" Then she ran to catch up with her mother.

A lady with gray hair was checking her grocery list when Jenny and her mother turned up the bakery aisle to get a loaf of bread.

"I can fly!" Jenny told the lady.

"Fly?" she repeated, a twinkle in her eye. "Do you have wings?"

"No," Jenny replied. "But I can fly!"

While Jenny's mother was picking out some ripe red tomatoes for dinner, Jenny marched over to the produce man, who was busy spraying celery with cold water.

"Hello, Jenny," the man said. "How are you today?"

"Fine," Jenny answered. "And guess what!"

"What?" the man asked.

"I can fly!" Jenny exclaimed.

The man laughed. "I'm glad to hear it. The potato truck is late. Can you fly out to the farm and see what's wrong?"

"No," Jenny said. "I don't even know where the potato farm is. But I can fly!"

As Jenny's mother went around the store, up one aisle and down the next, Jenny followed closely behind. She told almost everyone the good news.

"I can fly!" she said to an old man.

"I wish I could," the old man replied. "I get tired walking."

"I can fly!" she said to a cross-looking lady who was in a hurry.

"Don't be silly!" she answered sharply. "Little girls *cannot fly*!"

"I can," Jenny told her.

Finally, Jenny's mother pushed her cart to the checkout stand. Many of the people Jenny had spoken to were standing in line.

"Well, here comes the girl who can fly," the lady with gray hair said.

"That's her, all right," the old man agreed.

"What's that?" the store manager wanted to know. "I have someone in my store who can fly?"

"I can!" Jenny replied. "I can fly!"

"Can you fly high, Jenny?" the manager asked.

"Very high," Jenny said. "Higher than this store even!"

"No, you can't," the cross-looking lady who was in a hurry told her. "Little girls cannot fly!" She turned to Jenny's mother. "Why do you let your little girl go around telling people she can fly? Children should tell only the truth!"

Jenny's mother looked at the lady and smiled. "But Jenny is telling the truth. She can fly!"

Everyone stared at Jenny and her mother.

"She really can fly?" the manager questioned, a surprised look on his face.

"Up in the sky?" the old man asked.

"Like a bird?" the gray-haired lady wanted to know.

"Well, not quite like a bird," Jenny's mother admitted. "But she can fly."

The cross-looking lady who was in a hurry gave a snort. "Humph! A girl who can fly! Can you prove it?"

"Oh, yes," Jenny's mother replied.

Everyone stared at Jenny, expecting her to fly off at any second. But she just stood quietly next to her mother.

"Here it is," Jenny's mother said, pulling an envelope out of her purse.

"What is it?" the cross-looking lady asked.

"An airplane ticket," Jenny's mother told her. "Jenny's grandmother wants her to come for a visit. She's always gone on the train before, but not this time."

"This time I can fly!" Jenny announced proudly. "I can fly to my Grandma's!"

Everyone at the store smiled. Jenny hadn't been pretending, after all.

Poems

How Do We Go?

KEVIN O'HARA

Listen folks, I want to shout
Of the many ways to move about.

Of shiny autos on the roads
And big trucks with their heavy loads.
Of freight cars, tank cars, let's be plain,
I love each and every train.
Of row boats, speed boats, tug boats, too,
And ships that sail the ocean blue.
Of planes that fly so very high
Leaving smoke trails in the sky.

Each way of moving is a treat,
But most of all I use my feet.

The Horse Came First

LLOYD ERIC REEVE

It's "horsepower" which makes an automobile glide swiftly along the highway. It hastens the motorcyclist along and pulls the heavy loads of huge trucks. It speeds cars and trucks and trains over high mountains. It hurtles planes through the air and spaceships to the moon. It propels small boats along turbulent rivers, submarines beneath the sea, and ocean liners to the far corners of the world.

Did you ever wonder why this magic power of a mechanical engine is called *horse*power? Well, the answer is simple. In the time before people had motors to do their work, the horse was one of their most important helpers.

Human beings were their own first beasts of burden, carrying whatever they wanted to transport and later pulling their primitive carts. As time went on, however, people gradually replaced themselves with other animals: horses, oxen, camels, goats, llamas, elephants, dogs.

It was the horse that pulled stagecoaches and wagons. Roads were often muddy and had deep ruts. Finally, someone thought of a better kind of road. Wooden rails were put down on the road and the wheels of the horse-drawn coaches and wagons ran along these rails instead of on the ground.

Next thing tried was hitching several wagons and coaches together with just one driver up front driving the horses. This was called a train. Because it ran on rails laid along the road it was called a railroad train.

In this horse-drawn train, passengers rode in the carriages. Freight was hauled in the wagons. When there were only passengers, it was called a passenger train. When only freight was carried, it was called a freight train.

The first American railway to carry both passengers and freight was the Baltimore and Ohio Railroad. It was horse-drawn and the "engineer" sat up front, driving the horses which pulled the train along the rails.

Construction of that railroad was started on July 4, 1828. It was considered so important an event in American history that Charles Carroll was asked to turn the first shovelful of dirt in the groundbreaking ceremony. He was given this honor because he was the last living signer of the Declaration of Independence.

A variation of these early horse-drawn trains was the treadmill car. It was horse powered, but the horse didn't pull it along the rails. Instead it walked on a treadmill mounted in a cage-like car. This made the wheels, to which it was connected, revolve along the train tracks below.

Boats on the great canals of early times were also horse powered. They were towed by horses or mules walking along the bank of the canal on a path called a tow path. Many of the long narrow canal boats had little barns at one end where the animals stayed at night.

Horses were once streetcar "motors," too. Like the railway engineers, the motormen sat up front driving the horses.

Two or more horses pulling a wagon are called a "team." Their driver is called a "teamster." Even today the labor union of truckdrivers is called the Teamsters Union.

The Scottish inventor, James Watt, is best known for his development of the steam engine. Watt needed some kind of measure to tell how good his engines were. He needed to measure their power, how fast they could do work. It was natural to compare an engine to a horse. So the question was: How fast can a horse do work? By using a rope with pulleys and weights, Watt found that a horse could do the work of lifting weight at the rate of 550 pounds per second. He called that rate of doing work one horsepower.

Of course, unlike a machine, the average horse cannot work that fast for very long. But the purpose of Watt's experiments was only to determine some unit for power measurement in terms of the maximum power of a horse. There are also other units for measurement of power. For electrical measurements one horsepower equals 746 watts. The unit of electrical power came to be named for James Watt, the man who showed us how to think about power. So you

will find his name printed on any light bulb.

Watt's steam engine made possible the first steam wagons. Later, steam was replaced by the internal combustion engine using gasoline as fuel. Yet for many years people still continued to refer to the automobile as the horse*less* carriage.

On the other hand the early locomotive was promptly nicknamed the Iron *Horse*. Steam locomotives began to replace horses in American railroads in 1830.

Cowboys in the Wild West of those frontier times often raced their ponies alongside these early trains. Swirling their ropes over their heads, they would even try to lasso the snorting, funnel-shaped smokestack of the Iron Horse engine.

Cowboys still depend on their horses to work cattle. But as often as not these days they transport them to and from the cattle in distant range areas in a truck. The truck has a lot more horsepower than the horse it carries. But the quick-moving little cow pony is a lot smarter.

But it's still the real horse that started it all. Even today we describe a feat of great strength by saying, "That's real horsepower."

Trucks

GARY M. LABELLA

Do you know how the clothes, food, toys, school supplies, books, and the other things you use each day were delivered to the stores you bought them from?

Most likely they were shipped there by trucks. Trucks deliver most of this country's goods. Even when your goods are delivered by train or airplane, a truck is needed to carry the freight from the airport or railroad station to the store.

Trucks are the most common kind of freight transportation in the United States today because they can travel anywhere there is a road.

The early trucks were nothing more than automobiles with wagons hooked on the back. They were called "horse-less wagons" because Americans used horses to haul their freight before the motor-driven vehicle was invented.

The early trucks had very few of the comforts modern trucks do. They had no windshields to protect against bad weather and no soft tires to absorb the bumps of old dirt roads.

Manufacturers learned quickly, however, to build trucks that were both lasting and comfortable. As they did, more and more merchants and businessmen bought trucks, and the trucking industry grew rapidly.

In the beginning, there were very few trucks on the road but today in the United States there are lots and lots of them. In fact, if you lined them all up one behind the other, there would be enough trucks to circle the earth.

The horse-drawn wagon was in use before the truck was invented. For a long time in the late 1800's, horse and wagon teams provided the best transportation between many towns and settlements. They weren't as fast as railroads, but they would reach far away areas that rails couldn't. It took several days, though, for horse and wagon teams to travel distances that trucks now travel in hours.

The first trucks offered little protection and comfort for the driver. The ride was jerky because the solid rubber tires did not absorb the bumps of dirt roads well. The drivers wore goggles to protect against dust and stones. It was almost like driving a horse and wagon. This early truck was called the "Auto Wagon" and its top speed was 20 miles per hour.

Later, the driver's compartment was closed in, safe from the wind and rain. Then, trucks were designed to come apart. The front part, which did the driving, could be attached to different trailers carrying many kinds of loads. Inflatable tires were added to make the ride smoother.

Modern trucks are bigger, stronger and faster than those of the past. They carry all kinds of goods on both long and short trips. Without trucks we would never be able to enjoy all the things we use every day.

Trucks

What are the differences between the early trucks and the modern trucks?

What is the same?
How many kinds of trucks can you name?
What is the biggest truck you have seen? The smallest?
Would you like to be a truck driver? Why?

From Adventure to Comfort

WALTER B. HENDRICKSON, Jr.

The first scheduled airline provided more adventure than comfort. Mail was more important than passengers in the early years of flight in the United States. The one passenger had to find room among the mail sacks. Because the biplane (two wing airplane) had an open cockpit, the passenger had to dress according to the weather, and needed to wear a helmet and goggles just like the pilot.

Later, the space for passengers and crew was enclosed in the plane. But air travel was still short on comfort. The roar of the motors on these airliners caused a ringing in passengers' ears long after the flight landed. Passenger air vents leading to the outside admitted rain as well as air.

Planes were built that could fly even if one engine failed. Then, an all-metal airliner was made to solve the problem of the rotting of wooden frames in earlier aircraft. These planes were the beginning of real airline service.

Using many new ideas, airplane companies built planes that could fly higher and longer and faster. The engines on the planes were changed from propellers to jets. Today, passengers are served almost entirely by jets, such as the very big jumbo jets and the very fast supersonic transport planes. More and more people have had a chance to fly. Passenger flying has changed from adventure for a few to comfort for everyone.

How are the biplane and the jet the same?
How are they different?
Which would you like to fly in? Why?
What do you think the airplanes of the future will be like?

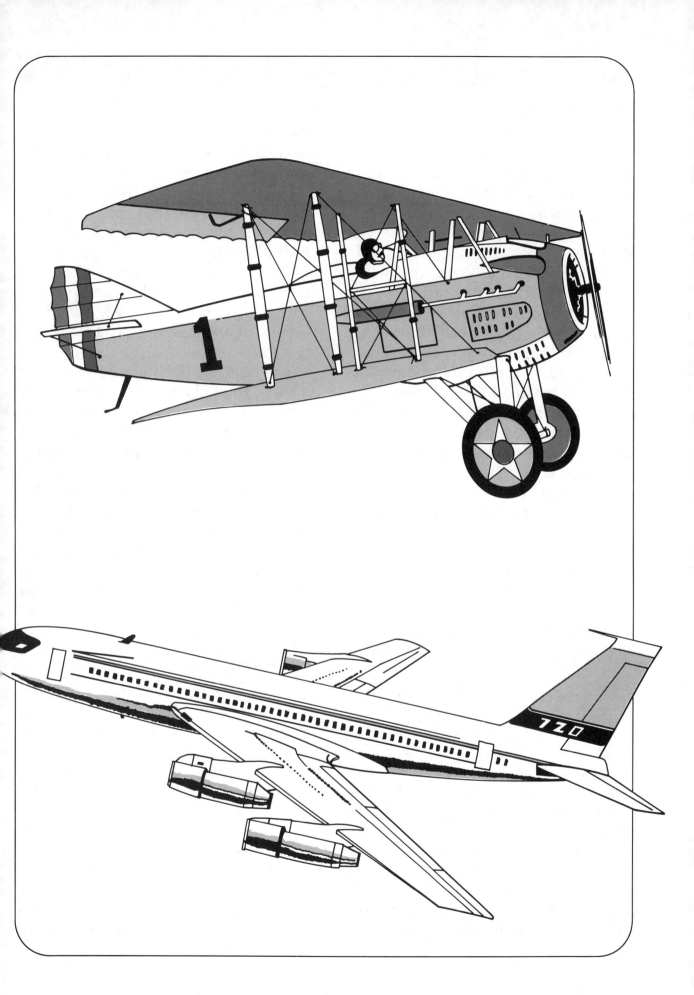

Jumbo Jet Flight

MARVIN MILES

The big 747 jumbo jet moved slowly down the taxi strip at Los Angeles International Airport and paused near the head of the runway. Finally the control tower cleared it for takeoff and the giant ship swung slowly upwind, ready to roll.

Captain Charles Beck completed the takeoff check list with copilot Mike Freebairn and flight engineer Jill Manning. "All set?" he asked, without taking his eyes off the runway. "Ready," came replies from his crew who watched their crowded instrument panels.

Many checks were made with different questions and answers to make sure that all of the jumbo's systems were working properly.

"Flight control power switches?"

"On."

"Instrument warning system?"

"Tested."

"Gear handle?"

"Down and in."

The Boeing 747 is the largest public passenger airplane flying today. It has a huge cabin stretching almost as long as a football field to a tail that is as high as a big building. But the cockpit at the front of the airplane where the captain and crew sit is like a small, crowded room. From there, you can't see the engines or the tips of the wings. Nor can you see the nose of the jet because it curves downward sharply in front.

A maze of instruments stares at you from the wide panel just in front of the captain and the copilot and also from the flight engineer's station on the right side of the flight deck.

Orange, red, and green lights dot the instrument sections, and overhead, rows of switches fill another panel.

Holding the control wheel with his left hand, the captain spread the fingers of his right hand across the four gray throttle knobs and moved them forward gradually as he released the brakes. Instantly, the plane began gathering speed. For a few seconds it seemed it was moving much to slowly to become airborne.

The captain did not speak a word during the takeoff. Not once did he take his eyes off the runway that streamed faster and faster beneath him. In a little while, the copilot called out, "V-1."

V-1 was the last speed at which the captain could turn off his engines, hit his brakes, and stop the plane before the end of the runway. If it had lost an engine before V-1, Captain Beck would have stopped the takeoff. Once he passed V-1 speed, he could take off on three engines, if necessary.

Seconds later, the copilot called out: "V-R—Rotate!". At once, the captain eased back on the controls, raising the jumbo's nose high above the runway before all of its main wheels left the concrete.

In a second or so came the final call: "V-2." This told the captain that the 747 had reached 165 miles per hour as it swept off the ground and began to climb.

At a sign from the captain, Mike Freebairn flipped a switch that raised the wheels of the landing gear out of sight. They were off on the long flight to New York.

Where Go the Boats?

ROBERT LOUIS STEVENSON

Dark brown is the river,
Golden is the sand.
It flows along forever,
With trees on either hand.

Green leaves a-floating,
Castles of the foam,
Boats of mine a-boating—
Where will all come home?

On goes the river
And out past the mill,
Away down the valley,
Away down the hill.

Away down the river,
A hundred miles or more,
Other little children
Shall bring my boats ashore.

Poems

Roads

RACHEL FIELD

A road might lead to anywhere—
To harbor towns and quays,
Or to a witch's pointed house
Hidden by bristly trees.
It might lead past the tailor's door,
Where he sews with needle and
thread,
Or by Miss Pim the milliner's,
With her hats for every head.
It might be a road to a great, dark
cave
With treasure and gold piled high,
Or a road with a mountain tied to its
end,
Blue-humped against the sky.
Oh, a road might lead you anywhere—

To Mexico or Maine.
But then, it might just fool you,
and—
Lead you back home again!

Planes, Rockets, and Jets

Flying high! Flying low!
Look how those planes and jets go!
Rockets launching up in the sky.
Oh! There's a jet speeding by.

MACK HAGOOD, Age 7

Trains

Trains are big,
Long, and strong.
If you listen to the wheels,
You sometimes hear a song
As they roll along.

MATTHEW MARCHIORETTO, Age 8

People Movers

How do people move around
From here to there along the
ground?
Heavy traffic everywhere
Crowds the roads, pollutes the air.
Traffic's getting worse each day.
Could we move some other way?

DAWN CHESLEY, Age 9

The Jet

One day as I was walking by,
I heard a noise from up high.
First it was soft, then a roar,
And from the sky a jet did soar.
It did a loop and a turn or two.
It was beautiful next to
the sky of blue.
First it was there, then it was
gone,
And away it flew on and on.

MIKE LAMAR, Age 10

Foreign?

ETHEL BLAIR JORDAN

I thought that foreign children
    Lived far across the sea
Until I got a letter
    From a boy in Italy.

"Dear little foreign friend," it said
    As plainly as could be.
Now I wonder which is "foreign,"
    The other child or me.

Trains in Motion

Here is a train,

"Toot! Toot!" it says,

Fun with Fingers

It runs on a track—

And then it runs back.

Here is the train
(make fist with
right hand)

And here is the track—
(hold left arm level)

Choo-choo forward!
Choo-choo back!
(place fist on arm,
move forward and back)

Here are the wheels,
Going clackety-clack.
(rotate hands around
each other)

POOF! goes the smoke
From the big smokestack!
(move hands up quickly in
mushroom shape)

The Moving Stencil

On a piece of heavy construction paper draw a
simple picture. With scissors, cut out the major
parts of your picture. The picture with the parts
cut out is a stencil.

Place this stencil on a piece of paper. With a
crayon outline all of the areas in the cut-out
parts. Move the stencil over just a little bit and
then outline the cut-out areas again in a different color.

Repeat as many times as you wish until the
moving stencil picture looks pleasing to you.

Boats To Make

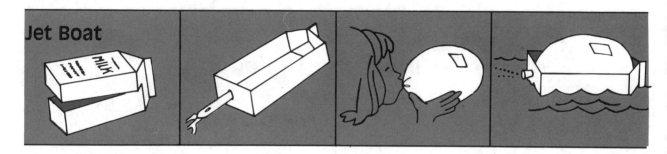

Jet Boat

Box Boats

For a steamer, cut the end-flaps from both ends of a small box. Staple or glue the ends together. Glue on a box for a cabin. Cut holes in the cabin and glue in paper chimneys. Paint with tempera. Glue on paper-circle portholes.

To make a submarine, follow the same directions, but add a pipe cleaner for the periscope.

What other ships can you make?

Racing Sailboats

Cut the bottom of each sailboat from a plastic-foam meat tray. The sail is a small triangle of paper. Decorate the sail with crayon or marker. Run a toothpick through the side of the sail and stick it into the plastic boat. Make several boats for your pool or bathtub. Blow on them gently, and see which one wins the race.

Toothpaste-Box Sailboat

Tape the end flaps of a toothpaste box together. Cover the box with a layer of pasted paper. Paint. To make the boat waterproof, cover it with a piece of plastic kitchen wrap. Cut a sail from paper. Glue to a stick and attach to the boat by sticking it in the box. Now sail your boat in the bathtub or a tub of water.

Fun Projects

Parachute Kite

Take a paper napkin and paste reinforcement rings in each corner. Punch holes through the rings, and tie a 12-inch thread to each corner. Bring the four threads together and tie.

Cut a flight string any length desired. Tie one end of it to the four-string knot, and the other to a small plastic soda straw for a finger-hold.

Pictures With Rice

Draw a picture on heavy paper or cardboard. Instead of coloring it with crayons or paint, fill in each area with grains of rice in the color you want. To color the rice, fill a small jar half-full with raw rice. Add three or four drops of food coloring and shake to distribute the color. Make purple by combining red and blue coloring, orange with red and yellow, and so on. When coloring has dried, attach the rice by covering one area at a time with glue and sprinkling the rice over the glue. When dry, blow away any rice that has not stuck in place.

High-flying Balloon

A plastic egg (such as the kind some hosiery comes in) serves as the balloon. It can be decorated with pieces of colored construction paper. A small paper cup is the basket, also decorated with pieces of construction paper. Measure and cut a strip of cardboard to fit around the midsection of the balloon. Punch five holes in the cardboard and staple it to fit around the balloon. Make five pin-holes in the paper cup, and attach the balloon to the basket by inserting five pipe cleaners in the holes and adjusting them. Take two pipe cleaners or a piece of cord and loop around the paper cup.

Paper-Plate Car

Cut a small paper plate in half, leaving two rounded sections at the bottom for wheels. Do this again with another plate, using the first one for tracing. Attach the plates with pieces of pipe cleaner. Using tempera or a felt-tipped marker, color the wheels black and draw on windows and a door.

Crafts for Travel

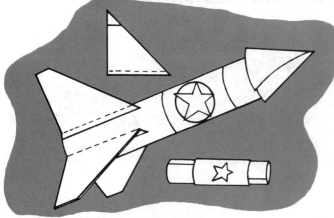

Three-Stage Rocket

Cut a cardboard tube, like the ones found inside rolls of waxed paper, into three sections. Cover all sections with construction paper.

For fins, cut two 3-inch squares from construction paper of a contrasting color. Cut each square in half diagonally. Snip off corner as shown and bend back small bands (see illustration). Attach the four fins to the bottom of the rocket by gluing the narrow bands in place.

For the nose cone, cut a 6-inch circle of paper in half. Roll one half into a cone and glue the edges together. Attach with glue to the top section.

Roll two pieces of construction paper to make tubes about 3 inches high and just large enough to fit inside the cardboard tube. Glue these inside the center section of the rocket so that some of the paper tubes extend from the cardboard at the top and the bottom.

Slip the top and the bottom sections over the paper extensions to assemble the rocket.

Old-time Locomotive

Use an empty salt box for the engine body, a small pudding box for the cab, and a baking soda box for the coal car.

Cover the boxes with construction paper, taping or pasting in place. Cut the wheels out of cardboard, and cover with construction paper. Cut the grill and narrow strips connecting the wheels from black construction paper. Use a thread spool for the smokestack. Glue the parts together as shown. Paint the smokestack black.

Make a window on each side of the cab by cutting holes in the box or by gluing a small square of construction paper to each side. Add any other markings you might like.

For the coupling, cut two strips of cardboard about 3/4 inch wide and 1 1/2 inches long. Cut one end of each to a point and connect the pointed ends with two staples. Glue one straight edge to the locomotive, the other to the coal car.

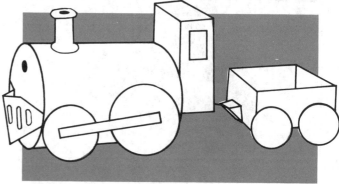

Helicopter

Cut two corners, the same size, from a lightweight cardboard box. Use other portions of the box to cut out a base, large rotor, tail section, and tail rotor. Make a slit in one of the corner sections, insert the tail, and glue in place. Next, glue the two corners together to form the cabin and add the base and tail rotor. Poke a hole at the top of the cabin, insert a section of pipe cleaner, and attach the large rotor at the top. Paint the various sections in contrasting colors and, when dry, add windows and other details.

Cut out the pieces and draw around them on a plastic-foam meat tray. Cut out the plastic-foam pieces and put the airplane together. A paper clip on the nose of your plane may make it fly better.

Notes

Let's Go Riding Together

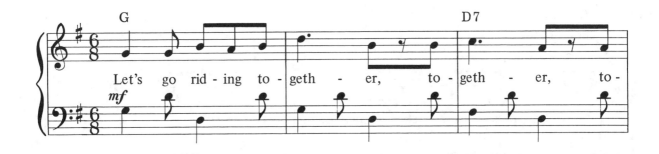

MOVING ABOUT IN MY WORLD **185**

Trucks

Music by
FRANCIS HILLIARD

Words by
JAMES S. TIPPETT

We're Going to the City

Mary Jaye

Traditional Singing Game

Happily

1. We're going to the city, We're going to the
(2. Go) in and out the tunnels, Go in and out the
(3. We'll) drive across the bridges We'll drive across the

mf

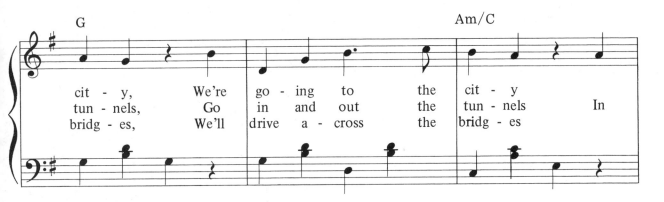

city, We're going to the city
tunnels, Go in and out the tunnels In
bridges, We'll drive across the bridges

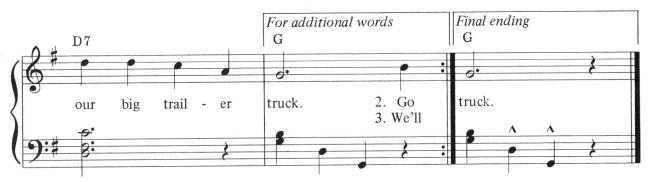

For additional words G

Final ending G

our big trailer truck. 2. Go truck.
3. We'll

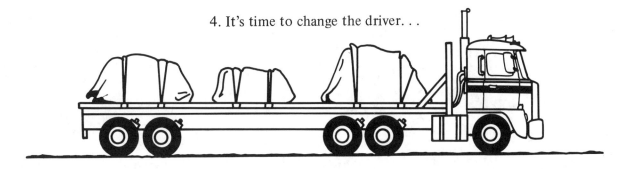

4. It's time to change the driver. . .

Work To Do

Introduction

Work plays a vital part in the lives of most people. It is one way a person identifies herself or himself, "I am a mechanic" or "I work at ABC Company." People invest great parts of themselves, their time and their efforts in their jobs.

But work itself is more than just a job for pay; it is the process of performing a task or tasks to accomplish some end. The initiation and completion of a task generates a feeling of self-worth and purpose in the worker and can provide deep personal satisfaction.

Kindergarten children are ready to learn how the home, school and community depend on workers. They are ready to examine what jobs need to be done and who will perform them. They will find that, in the scheme of things, they, too, have significant tasks to perform.

This unit aims to foster a respect for work and workers on the part of each child. The children will see how work can effect changes and improve people's lives, including their own. The children's major work now is school; understanding this increases the likelihood of their successful completion of that task.

Concepts To Be Taught

I. Workers can be seen in different locations and can be identified by the jobs they do.

II. Different workers use different tools in their work.

III. Certain workers wear special clothing.

IV. Some workers are paid money for their work. Others receive different kinds of benefits.

V. Workers provide goods and services. Consumers use the goods and services.

VI. Kindergarten children are workers.

Information For Teaching Concepts

I. Workers can be seen in different locations and can be identified by the jobs they do.

A. Workers in the school

Ask the children to name the people they might meet if they were to walk around the school. Then, have them discuss why those people are at the school and what purpose each person serves.

Examples are:
teacher	cook
principal	bus driver
librarian	custodian
students	nurse

Describe for the children the jobs the teacher does in school:

> selects books   writes lessons on chalkboard   prepares supplies   keeps records
> prepares papers   arranges tables and chairs   grades papers   reads poems and stories

Tell the children that because there are so many jobs to be done in the classroom you need their help. List all the potential jobs. Examples are:

> clean the paintbrushes   feed the fish   hold the flag   clean the chalkboard
> pick-up papers   water the plants   pass out supplies   dust the shelves

Discuss with the class how these jobs can be shared. Plan with the children a job-board and a schedule for doing the work. Encourage the children to discuss the responsibilities of each worker.

B. Workers in the Home

Show the children a picture of a school and a house and say, "We already know there are many workers that keep a school working. But, what about workers in the home? Who are the home workers?" Assist the children to identify people who work in or about the home:

a) family members b) outsiders who provide services

With the children's assistance, make a list of jobs that are done in the home. Examples are:

> dumping trash   putting toys away   raking leaves   dusting
> washing dishes   setting the table   sorting laundry   clearing the table
> feeding pets   hanging up clothes

C. Workers in the community

Have the children look about the classroom and name as many things as they can see. Explain that you and the children use these items and ask, "Who made each of these things?" Examples are:

furniture makers/carpenters	printers	glassmakers
lamp manufacturers	bookbinders	paper manufacturers

Then, explain that some workers do not provide products, but they instead provide services. Examples are:

repair person	librarian	bus driver	teacher
sales clerk	dry cleaner	homemaker	sanitation worker
medical worker	baby sitter	waiter/waitress	delivery person

II. Different workers use different tools in their work.

A. Tools used in the classroom

Tell the children they are the most important workers in the school. Reinforce the earlier concepts about the classroom work. Ask the children to think of the tools they use in their classroom work. Examples are:

pencils   erasers   scissors   staplers   paper   crayons   paints   chalk

Discuss how each classroom tool is used and why the tool makes the child's work easier.

B. Tools used in the home

Encourage the children to think of home tools, especially as they relate to the tasks discussed in the section on workers in the home. Ask the children what tools might be used for:

Cleaning: vacuum, dust mop, washer, broom

Repair: screwdriver, hammer, ladder, paint brush

Personal Care: comb, brush, toothbrush, scissors

Food Preparation: mixer, stove, rolling pin, spoon

C. Tools used by workers in the community

Name several of the workers previously identified as producers or service workers in the community. Ask the children to name all the tools they can think of related to each worker. Examples are:

carpenter: saw, hammer, level, pliers   firefighter: firetruck, ladder, hose, ax

sales clerk: cash register, pencil, pad   farmer: tractor, plow, seeder, shovel

III. Certain workers wear special clothing.

Explain to the children that many people wear ordinary street clothes to work. However, certain workers wear special types of clothing.

Make a collage of examples of special clothing and ask the children why the clothing is used. Examples are:

	TYPE	PURPOSE
Hats	Hard	Protects the head from falling objects.
	Sunvisor bills	Protects eyes and makes it easier to see in bright sunlight.
	Surgical	Keeps hair from falling into surgery area.

Masks	Chef's	Keeps hair from falling into food.
	Firefighter's	Protects firefighter from burns and falling objects.
	Surgical	Keeps germs away from the patient.
	Catcher's	Protects catcher's face from balls and bats.
	Scuba	Protects diver's eyes under water.
Uniforms	Police Officer	Identifies police officer to the public.
	Dentist	Provides sanitary covering, pockets for essential tools, and permits ease of movement.
	Waitress	Provides a sanitary, washable outfit, identifies her to customers; apron provides protection for clothes.

IV. Some workers are paid for their work. Others receive different kinds of benefits.

Ask the children if they have every wished for some *thing*. Then, inquire if the thing wished for cost money. Ask where the money to buy things comes from. Encourage the children to realize that money is earned by jobs done.

Discuss whether everyone gets paid money for the work they do. Have the children give examples of situations where they have rendered service without pay. Examples are:

raking leaves   delivering dessert to a sick friend
caring for family members   feeding a pet
picking up litter

Talk about the satisfaction a person receives when a job is completed. Encourage the children to perceive that working can make a person feel good about himself or herself.

V. Workers provide goods and services. Consumers use the goods and services.

Review the concepts covered in the "Workers in the community" section of this unit. Encourage the children to walk about in their community. Ask them to identify the products they have seen or the services they have seen rendered.

Ask them if they have ever used these goods or services. Explain to them that a person who uses the goods or services provided by another is called a *consumer*. Tell them that *to consume* means *to use*, so that a *consumer* is a *user* of the goods that workers make or the services that workers perform.

Plan a trip to a plant where something is made. A bakery is one example of a plant found in almost every community.

VI. Kindergarten children are workers.

Discuss important attitudes that workers must remember. Examples are:

1. Listen carefully to directions.   4. Complete each job.   6. Follow safety rules.
2. Follow directions.   5. Take care of tools.   7. Be thoughtful of others.
3. Remember that everybody's work is important.

Thinking and Reasoning

Ask your children these questions.

What does a carpenter do?

What do you do with a broom?

Mr. Lee fixed a loose bolt in the handle of the lawn mower. Did he use a hammer, a wrench, or a screwdriver to fix it?

What would you use to drive a nail into a board?

To get your hair cut, do you go to a dentist, doctor, barber, butcher or baker? To which would you go if you were sick? If you wished to buy bread? If you wished to buy meat?

Why does a painter begin at the top of a wall and paint down instead of beginning at the bottom and painting up?

Which of these chores are you able to do? Make your own bed? Empty the wastebasket? Carry food to the table? Clear the table after a meal? Wash the dishes? Tidy up the living room? Rake leaves? Scrub the porch and steps? Mow the lawn? Run the vacuum cleaner?

What do we call the funny man at the circus?

Do we peel an apple with scissors or with a knife?

Which is bigger, a nickel or a dime? Which will buy more?

What tool is used to lift a car in order to change a flat tire?

What is the difference between work and play?

When Jane's mother came home, she said to Jane: "I've had a busy day. I performed two operations this morning and saw seventeen patients this afternoon." What does Jane's mother do?

Why do we have clocks?

What is money used for?

How does the mail carrier know which letters are for you?

"You didn't dust this chair carefully," Joe's mother said to him. Why did she make this remark, do you suppose?

Do you have a mailbox?

Which person might get more physical exercise while working, a lawyer or a carpenter? A baker or a clerk?

Name six tools a carpenter uses. How is each used?

What kinds of jobs can't be done when it is raining?

Name some workers who wear uniforms. Why do you think they wear them?

Jack dialed Sue's number on the telephone. After a few minutes Jack said, "No one was home at Sue's house." How did Jack know this?

What are some ways that you might earn money?

What kind of work is done with a needle and thread?

How can you tell when a store is closed?

Why do we shovel snow from the sidewalk?

Would you wear a new suit or dress while painting your house? Why?

Why do you need a shopping cart in the grocery store?

Who Are They?

Connect the picture on the left to the matching picture on the right by drawing a line.

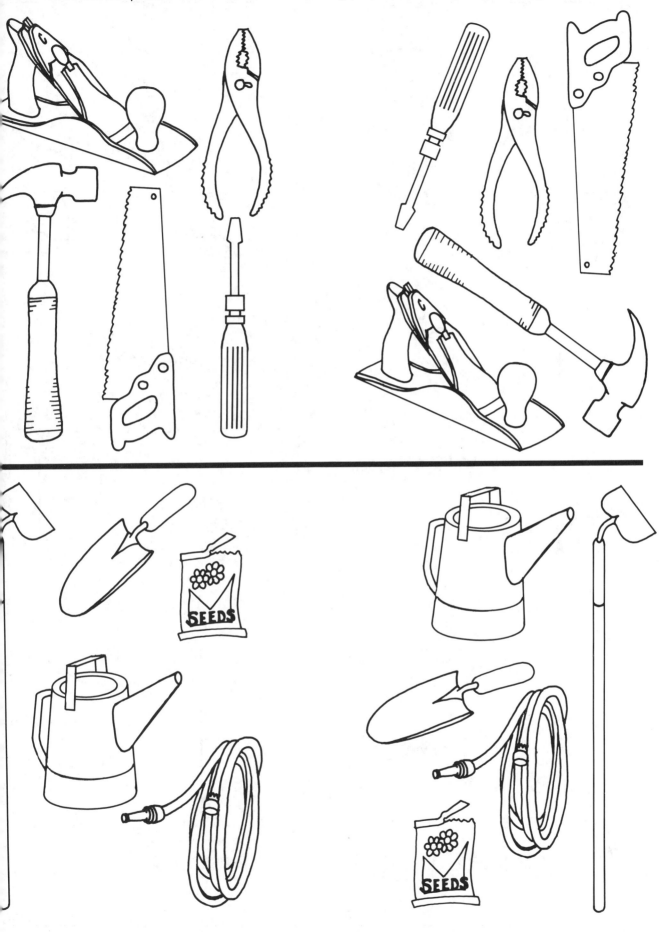

WORK TO DO **195**

Connect the picture on the left to the matching picture on the right by drawing a line.

Tools

Which are used for digging and which for cutting?

shovel	saw
scissors	ax
spading fork	trowel

Can you name anything else used for digging? for cutting?

Which are used for sewing? Which are used for cleaning? Which are used for writing?

broom	pencil
needle	thimble
chalk	mop

Name some other things used for sewing, for cleaning and for writing.

Why do many power tools have a guard?

Why are there life preservers in a boat?

Why do you have reflectors on your bicycle?

Why does the bus driver close the door before starting out?

Why don't you park in front of a fire hydrant?

Why should you keep away from a house fire?

Why do you wash your hands before meals?

How are the things in each group alike?

saw	scissors	knife
hoe	shovel	rake
basket	pail	bag
pencil	pen	chalk
broom	mop	dustrag

Memo Holders

KENT DOUGLAS

Use different-sized corks as the bodies. Glue several together for the caterpillar and cover with yarn. Glue on paper-punch dot eyes and pipe-cleaner antennae. The butterfly is three corks glued together and painted black, with pipe-cleaner wings.

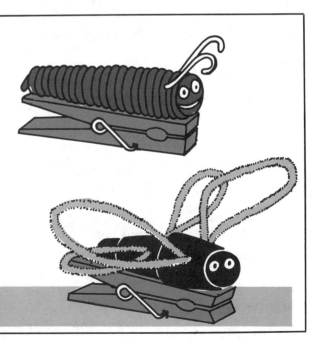

WORK TO DO

Work Questions

Which work mostly indoors? Mostly outdoors?

marine biologist	teacher
violinist	farmer
park ranger	computer operator
doctor	electrician
letter carrier	banker
TV camera operator	air traffic controller

Where would you go?

to get a tetanus shot?

to have your teeth examined or repaired?

to have clothes cleaned?

to have your shoes mended?

to find information for a school report?

to buy a newspaper?

to get a prescription filled?

to buy a dog license?

to borrow a book to read?

to have your hair cut?

Which come to you?

Which persons may come to your home?

Which come regularly?

Which ones might you visit at their office?

dentist	mail carrier
plumber	barber
druggist	electrician
tailor	telephone installer
carpenter	
doctor	newspaper carrier

At which places are you asked to pay when entering? When leaving?

At which places do you use money or a ticket?

At which places do you not have to pay?

a circus

a church or synagogue

a movie theater

a Sunday school

a restaurant

a hotel

a post office

a doctor's office

a garage

a grandstand at a ball park

a dentist's office

a plane, train, or bus

a telephone pay station

a concert hall

a toll bridge

a turnpike

a zoo

a public library

a state park

a national park

Name some other places where you pay when entering.

Name some places where you pay when leaving.

Name some places where you don't pay at all.

Name some places where you pay less than adults pay.

What is each person wearing?
How is each one used?
Why are they used?
Can you name some other things used
for safety?

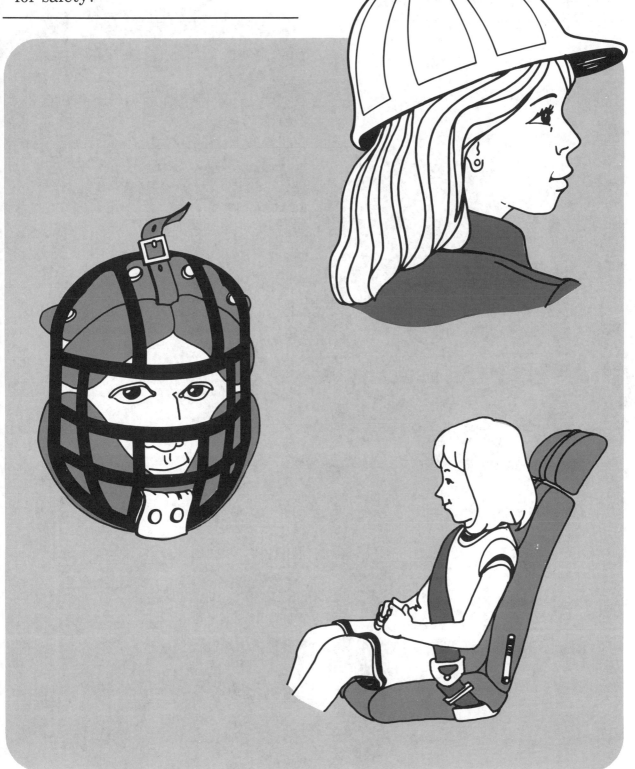

How is each one used differently?
Which would hold the most?
Which would be easiest to carry?
What else do we use to carry things?

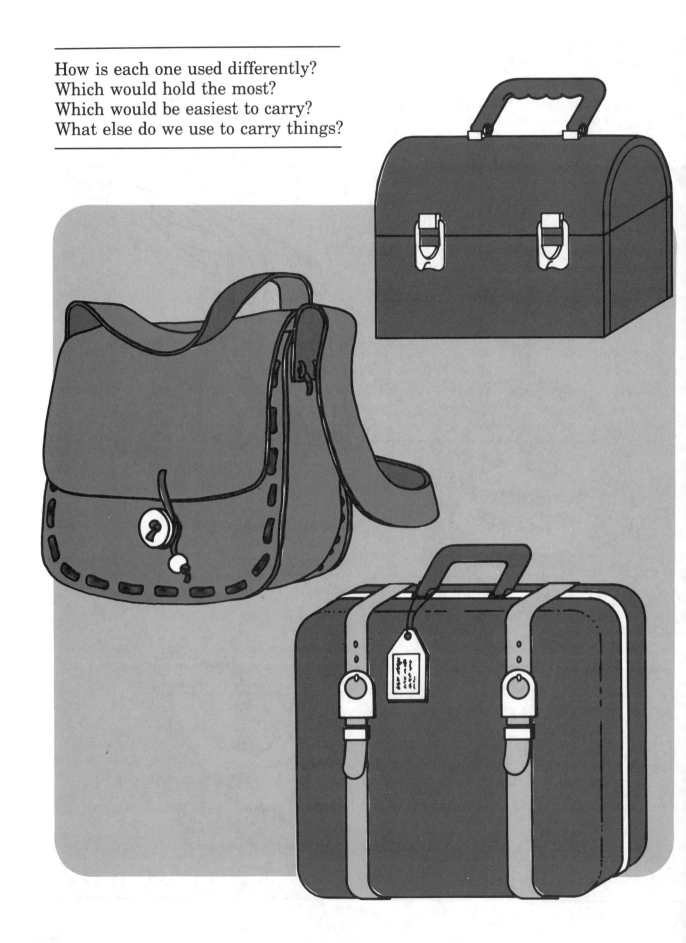

Cut out each picture and paste them in the order in which they happened.

WORK TO DO   **201**

Find a handle to match each of the items in the bottom square.

How Do You Wash an Elephant?

JOY MARSH

Yesterday, my mother said to me:
"Tom, about your elephant—
You've got to wash him.
He's dirty as can be."

Well, I looked him over;
I decided she was right.
He was dirty behind his ears.
His feet were an awful sight.
I began to plan and plot
Exactly what I'd do
But
I don't know how to wash an elephant.
Do you?
Do I use soap and a cloth?
No, I don't think so.
By the time I got him clean,
I would be very old.

Do I take him to the yard and
Squirt him with a hose?
That might work—except—
He'd think I was playing.
And squirt me with his nose!
I could take him to the lake—
I know he'd wade right in.
But
When it's deep enough for him,
It's over my head—
And I can't swim!
How do you wash an elephant?
Perhaps I could take him to a car
wash.

They'd squirt him and slosh him,
Brush him and wash him.

He'd like that so much,
He'd probably shout.
I don't have two dollars. That's out.

How can I wash that elephant?
How can I get him clean?
How can I make him shine?
He's got to be so clean and bright,
I'm proud to say he's mine.

Say, I think I've got it.

I'll get my parents' broom and pail,
Their dish detergent, too.
I'll need my parent's ladder.
I know just what I'll do.

I'll make a pile of suds in that pail
And pick them up with the broom.
I'll swish them around his legs and
tail.
I'll need plenty of room.
I'll wash his belly, back, and head.
I'll scrub him till his skin turns red.
If he's real good till the job is done,
I'll let him sleep in my bed.
When he's all covered with soapsuds,
I'll climb my parent's ladder,
With buckets and buckets of water.
I'll rinse him off so nice and clean,
I'll need sunglasses to dull the sheen.

That's how I'll wash my elephant.
I think that way will do.
I don't mind washing one elephant,
But I'm glad I don't have two.

Officer Ripplefudge

MARY ANN DISMER

Officer Ripplefudge was everybody's friend. Each morning, bright and early, he was at work directing traffic on the corner where Peanut Street ran into Main Street. It was not the busiest intersection in town, but Officer Ripplefudge didn't mind. He helped the children get safely to school in the morning, and he helped them get safely home again in the afternoon.

When little Allen Watson, who was only three years old, needed his shoe tied, Officer Ripplefudge would tie it.

"You sure tie good bows!" Allen would say.

"Of course I do," Officer Ripplefudge would reply with a big grin. "A very long time ago I used to be a shoe sales clerk. But now I help people by being a police officer right here on the corner of Peanut and Main. And I like this job the best of all."

Granny Tiddle lived just one house down from the corner. Once in a while her pet cat, Sugar Plum, got caught up in the big elm tree in the front yard. As soon as he could, Officer Ripplefudge would help to get her down.

"You climb a ladder better than anyone else!" Granny would say.

"Of course I do," Officer Ripplefudge would answer politely. "Quite a few years ago I used to be a fire fighter. I climbed lots of ladders, putting out fires. But now I help people by being a police officer right here on the corner of Peanut and Main. And I like this job the best of all!"

One wintry morning Mr. Rodgers' car would not start. He was in a terrible hurry. Officer Ripplefudge, who was on his way to work, came to the rescue.

"You started my car faster than anyone I've ever had fix it!" Mr. Rodgers remarked.

"Of course I did," said Officer Ripplefudge. "Not so very long ago I used to be a mechanic. I started lots of cars for lots of people who were in a hurry. But now I help people by being a police officer right here on the corner of Peanut and Main. And I like this job the best of all!"

Then one morning Officer Ripplefudge was not at the corner of Peanut and Main. He was in the office of the Chief of Police.

"Officer Ripplefudge," said the Police Chief, "you have been directing traffic on the corner of Peanut and Main for a long time. But you could handle a much more important job. Now I want you to come and work right here in the police station. You can be my assistant. You can have a desk of your very own and a new badge, and we will have your name painted on the door."

Officer Ripplefudge was very proud. He had never been an Assistant Chief of Police.

"But who will direct the traffic at the corner of Peanut and Main?" he asked.

"We will put in a new traffic light," explained the Police Chief.

"That would be fine!" said Officer Ripplefudge.

So it was settled. Officer Ripplefudge went to work at the police station, wearing a shiny new badge. He filled out papers and answered telephones. He held meetings with the Mayor and told younger police officers what he wanted them to do. It certainly was an important job. But Officer Ripplefudge was not happy.

One day, just as he was leaving the office to get some lunch, a call came in on the police radio. There was a traffic jam at the corner of Peanut and Main.

The Police Chief looked worried. "This has been a busy morning," he said. "I haven't one officer who isn't already doing something. Is there someone we can send?"

"I'd like to take care of this myself," volunteered Officer Ripplefudge.

"Very well," agreed the Police Chief.

Things were in an awful state of affairs when Officer Ripplefudge arrived at the corner of Peanut and Main. Horns were honking, babies were crying, and every dog in the neighborhood was barking at the noise. The people were very upset.

Poor Mr. Rodgers was more upset than anyone else. His car was stalled right in the middle of the intersection, and it would not start.

Officer Ripplefudge hurried to help him. He opened the hood. "Nothing serious," he called, connecting a loose wire.

"Thank goodness!" Mr. Rodgers shouted above all the other racket. "Thank you so much, Officer Ripplefudge. I don't know what I would have done without you." And he drove off.

Officer Ripplefudge began directing traffic. In a few moments he had cleared the traffic jam at the corner of Peanut and Main.

When Officer Ripplefudge arrived back at work that afternoon, the Police Chief's office was swarming with people. Granny Tiddle was there and Mr. Rodgers and all the other fine folks who lived near Peanut and Main. They were giving the Police Chief a very hard time.

"But you have a fine new traffic light," the Police Chief insisted.

"Yes," agreed Mr. Rodgers, "but the traffic light could not fix my car."

"Or get my cat out of a tree!" added Granny Tiddle.

"Or tie my shoe!" chimed in little Allen Watson who was sitting in the corner. Everyone laughed.

"I see what you mean," said the Police Chief. "Let me think about this for a while, and I will decide."

The next morning, bright and early, Officer Ripplefudge was at his post at the corner of Peanut and Main, still wearing his shiny new badge.

"Good morning!" Granny Tiddle called from her kitchen window. "Glad to see you back on the job!"

"Glad to be here," Officer Ripplefudge answered happily. "You know, I have been a shoe sales clerk and a fire fighter and a mechanic and even the Assistant Chief of Police. But now I help people by being a police officer right here on the corner of Peanut and Main. And I like this job best of all!"

A Song For the King

MARILYN KRATZ

King Martin should have been a very happy man. He had a beautiful kingdom and many servants. He had prime ministers to take care of the kingdom, so he never had to work. He had enough gold to buy anything he might want.

But he was not happy. And to make matters worse, he had no idea why he was so unhappy.

Then one day when King Martin was riding through the countryside, he heard a happy sound. It was the happiest sound he had ever heard.

"Stop the coach!" he called to his coachman.

"Who is singing?" he whispered to his page.

"Someone behind those bushes," said the page.

They tiptoed to the bushes and peeked over them. Hoeing a field of corn beyond the bushes was a country lad. His patched shirt and trousers flapped as he worked, and a ragged straw hat bounced atop his head in rhythm with the song he sang.

The king watched and listened until the boy finished hoeing. Then, whistling a merry new tune, the boy walked away.

"I have never seen anyone so happy," said King Martin.

All the way back to the palace he thought about the boy.

All that night the boy's happy song drifted through his dreams.

Early the next morning, King Martin sent for his messengers.

"I have decided I need a song to sing so I can be happy," he told them.

"I hereby decree that I will give half my kingdom to the person who writes a song for me that will make me happy."

The messengers carried the decree throughout the kingdom. Soon everyone was writing songs.

One after another, the people sang their songs for King Martin. Whenever he heard a song he liked, he learned to sing it. But not one of the songs could make him feel happy.

Finally he cried, "No more songs! I'm becoming sadder instead of happier."

King Martin went to his room and spent many days there alone. At last when his heart was about to break, he remembered the little country lad.

"That's the song I need!" he shouted. "Page! Have my coach brought around. We are going for a ride in the country."

When they reached the cornfield, the country lad was nowhere in sight, but they could hear him singing nearby. They followed the cheery sound of his song until they found him weeding a pansy patch beside a small cottage.

When the lad saw the king, he stood hastily and stopped singing.

"Please don't stop singing," said King Martin. "I must learn your song."

"My song?" said the boy, quite surprised. "Why, it's just an old folk song my mother taught me, but I will be honored to teach it to you."

King Martin and the country lad sat under a shady tree, and the boy taught the king his song.

Soon King Martin thought he was

beginning to feel a little happier. But after he had learned every word of the song, he began to realize it was only his voice that was singing and not his heart.

"Please, Sir," said the boy at last, "may I go back to work now? I want to have the pansy patch all weeded and neat by the time Mother returns. You see, today is her birthday."

"I'm sorry I have taken so much of your time," said King Martin sadly. "May I help you? I haven't anything else to do."

"You may use this spade to loosen the soil around each plant," said the boy when all the weeds had been pulled. "I'll water them."

The sun warmed the king's back. Perhaps it soaked all the way through to his heart. For, without realizing it, the king began to hum. At first it was only an odd tuneless hum, but by the time they were finished with the garden, the king and the country lad were singing loudly together!

Suddenly the king shouted, "Why, I'm singing! I'm so happy that I'm singing!"

"It was the work that made you happy," said the boy. "Mother says that the way to be happy is to have important work to do and to do it well."

"Of course!" exclaimed the king. "Why didn't I think of that myself? I've been so unhappy because I've done nothing to make me—or anyone else—happy. But I'm going to change. I promise!"

From that day on King Martin was so busy doing things for others, as well as caring for his own responsibilities, that there was always a song on his lips. But he found time to visit the country lad each week—just to help him weed pansies or hoe corn and to teach *him* a few new songs to sing.

Jumbled Jobs

NIL WHITTINGTON

Once a big white cat, a little tan dog, and a green-headed duck lived together in a big backyard.

The cat's job was to catch all the mice that ate the grain in the storage room, and he did his job well.

The dog's job was to chase away the strangers who walked down the alley, and he did his job well.

The duck's job was to eat the bugs that got into the garden before they ruined the vegetables, and she did her job well.

But nobody ever said thanks. So the dog and the duck and the big white cat became very unhappy.

"We're not appreciated!" cried all three.

"I'm bored with chasing strangers," said the little tan dog.

"I'm bored with chasing bugs," said the green-headed duck.

"I'm bored with chasing mice," said the big white cat.

"Let's trade jobs!" cried all three.

So the big white cat took the job of keeping away the strangers who walked through the alley.

The green-headed duck took the job of killing the mice which ate the grain in the storage room.

And the little tan dog took the job of eating the bugs that ruined the garden.

"Now we'll be happy," they said.

Soon a stranger came down the alley and, though the big white cat meowed and meowed with all his might, the stranger slipped into the house and stole the family's money.

In the night mice came, and though the duck quacked and chased, they gnawed through some sacks and ate the grain.

And try as he would, the little tan dog couldn't get a single bug into his mouth, and they ruined the plants.

So the next morning the mistress said, "You're a bad dog to let a stranger sneak into the house and steal my money!" The little tan dog felt very sad.

Going into the garden, the mistress said, "You're a bad duck to let the bugs ruin my plants!" The green-headed duck felt very sad.

And when the mistress saw the mess in the storage room, she said, "You're a bad cat to let the mice get into my grain!" The big white cat felt very sad.

All of a sudden a mouse scampered by, and without a moments thought the big white cat pounced upon him. "I like chasing the mice that eat the grain in the storage room!" he decided.

At that moment, a stranger walked down the alley, and the little tan dog raced to the fence. "Arf, arf, arf!" he barked with all his voice. Then he trotted back with a smile on his face. "I like barking at strangers who walk down the alley!"

And the green-headed duck said, "I like eating the bugs that ruin the garden!"

"Then let's go back to doing the jobs we like best," said the little tan dog.

"And do our best," said the big white cat.

"And we'll all be happier," said the green-headed duck.

"Even if we're never thanked," said all three.

So they did.

The Pig, the Cat, the Goat, and the Dishes

LILLIAN MACKEY

This story is about a pig, a cat, and a goat, who lived together in a little brown house in the forest. These three never had any quarrels over anything except dishes. You see, they all hated to wash dishes.

The pig was the cook because he knew how everything should taste. Besides, he loved to nibble at every-thing as he fixed it. Since the pig was the cook, he felt he shouldn't have to do the dishes. He thought he should take a nap after dinner, and let the cat and the goat wash the dishes.

The goat thought he should take a walk and let the pig and the cat wash the dishes. And the cat thought he should chase mice and let the goat and the pig wash the dishes. So the dishes never got done.

When it was time to get dinner again, the pig would say to himself, "I'll use some more clean dishes." Every day the same thing happened. The pig slept, the cat chased mice, and the goat went for a walk. Pretty soon, all the clean dishes were used up, so the pig went down to Billy Beaver's store and bought some more.

Finally, the sink was heaped with dirty dishes way up to the ceiling. The cupboards were full. Everything was stacked with dirty dishes, except the stove. Then dishes began piling up in the living room and the bedroom.

One night when the goat got into bed, he sat KERPLUNK on a bowl of cold porridge which the pig had put there. And the cat found a bowl of cold porridge in his bed, too. This was the last straw. They were both so disgusted that they stayed up all night and washed dishes.

Next morning when the pig got up, he found the house piled with clean dishes. He put them into his wheelbarrow and took them to Billy Beaver's store and sold them.

He saved just enough dishes for one meal. Then he took a can of paint and painted "goat" on some, and "cat" on some, and "pig" on the others.

And now each one of them washes the dishes with his name on them, and puts them away right after dinner. Then the pig goes to sleep, the cat chases mice, and the goat goes for a walk. And they never quarrel anymore.

Poems

The Mail Carrier

Walking, walking down the street
Comes the busy mail carrier.
There's no one I'd rather see
Than the busy mail carrier.
Rain may pour and sun may shine
On the busy mail carrier.
I'll be waiting at the door
For the busy mail carrier.

SUZANNE SCHULTZ, Age 8

If I were a Baker

If I were a baker,
I'd bake a cake or two.
I'd whip it, and bake it,
And frost it—for you!

BRETT McINTIRE, Age 8

My Dentist Daddy

My daddy is a dentist,
He filled my tooth for me,
He is a community helper,
He helps us all, you see.
So if you have a toothache,
Don't just mutter and moan,
'Cause my daddy's a dentist,
So just pick up the phone.

SUE WILLIAMSON, Age 12

The Hunter

If I were a famous hunter,
I wouldn't shoot a gun.
I'd be a hunter with a camera
And take pictures just for fun.

PAUL ROSANOFF, Age 8

Games and Fun

Guess Our Trade

Players are divided into two teams. These teams go to opposite sides of the room and decide among themselves some trade or occupation they will act out for the other side to guess. Each side also has a goal line, beyond which they are safe. The teams advance to the center of the area and face each other. The first team to perform chants, "Popcorn, candy, and pink lemonade, you have a chance to guess our trade." The other team responds, "Some candy is red and some is blue, show us please what you can do." Then the first team goes through the motions of the trade they have chosen. The second group must guess from their actions whether they are automobile mechanics, baseball players, movie stars, bakers, or whatever they have decided upon. When someone on the second team calls out the correct trade, the first team turns and runs back to their goal line, the second team chasing them. If any person on the first team is caught, that player joins the opposite team, and the game continues.

The Grandfather Clock

One hand is big,
the other is small.
(Hold one arm up, the other
arm bent to the side.)

I'm a grandfather clock.
I'm six feet tall.
(Stand tall, hands at sides.)

I go "tick-tock, tick-tock"
all day.
(Swing arm like a pendulum.)

"Be on time!
Don't be late!
(clap hands rhythmically, while
doing any dance step in place.)

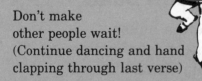

Don't make
other people wait!
(Continue dancing and hand
clapping through last verse)

And this is what
my tick-tocks say:
(continue swinging arm.)

Be on time! Don't be late!
Don't make other people wait!"

Banks

Coffee-Can Banks

Cut a slot in the plastic lid of a coffee can. Cover your coffee can with felt, fabric, or colored paper. Trim the can with scraps of material, buttons, rick-rack, lace, or anything else that you like. The bank may be trimmed to remind you of a special thing you are saving for, such as a vacation, a musical instrument, a toy, or a gift.

Banks From Tubes

Glue a piece of heavy paper to each end of a paper-towel roll. Cut a slot large enough for coins to go through.

For the clown, paint the tube white. Glue on yarn hair and features cut from paper. Feed your clown coins.

Complete the flute bank by painting the tube yellow and gluing on "finger holes" cut from black paper.

Handy Crafts

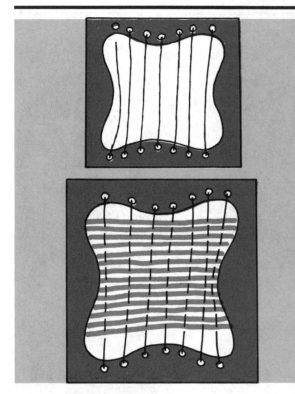

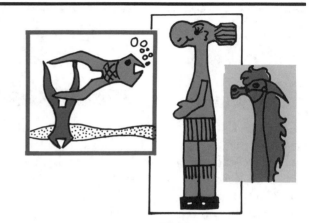

Tool People and Animals

Place a hammer, pliers, scissors, or any other tool you may have on a piece of colored paper. Trace around the tool with a pencil or marker, and cut out the shape. What does it look like? A person, a horse, a fish? What can you invent?

Paste the paper shape to a larger piece of paper. Add details such as eyes, mouth, and so on, with crayon, ink, marker, chalk, or pencil.

Weave a Design

Cut a shape from the center of a square piece of corrugated cardboard. Discard the center. Paint the cardboard frame and let dry.

Poke evenly-spaced holes in the frame along the top and bottom edges of the shape you cut out. Use a needle or a compass point for making the holes.

Tie a knot at one end of a long string. Poke the string through the upper left-hand hole. Bring the end of the string down through the bottom left-hand hole. Next bring it up through the second hole on the bottom and up to the second hole at the top. Continue in this fashion until you have all the holes filled. At the end, tie another knot to hold the string in place. You now have a loom on which you will weave your design. Tape one end of a piece of colored yarn to the back of your cardboard. Now bring the yarn through to the front and start weaving over and under the strands of string, all the way across. Keep weaving until your shape is completely filled. Different colors will make your design more interesting. When you are finished, tape the ends of the yarn securely to the cardboard at each end.

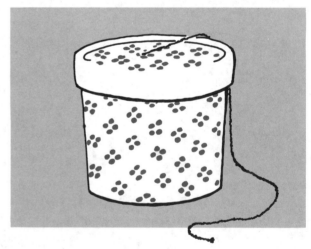

Jiffy String Holder

Wash and dry an empty one-pint ice-cream carton. Cover the sides and the flat part of the top with adhesive-backed paper. Poke a small hole in the center of the lid. Place a ball of string inside the carton and draw the end out through the hole on the top.

Point to the hat worn by a police officer.
Point to the hat worn by a construction worker.
Point to the hat worn by an astronaut.
Describe the work that each of these workers does.

Draw a circle around the pictures of the people who are working, then color.

The Carpenter's Hammer

Words by William G. Oglevee
Music by Louise M. Oglevee

Firmly, in two (♩. = 1 beat)

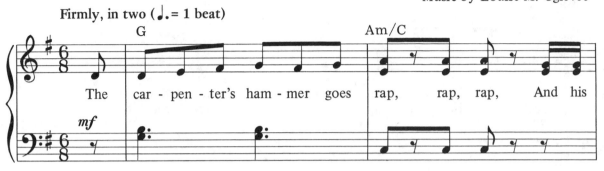

The car - pen - ter's ham - mer goes rap, rap, rap, And his

saw goes see saw see._____ He saws and meas - ures and

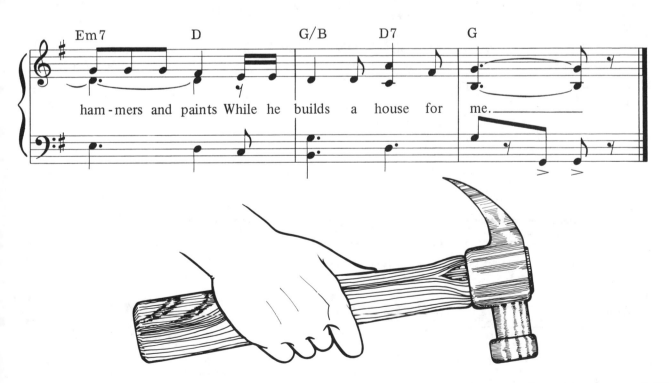

ham - mers and paints While he builds a house for me._____

Our Helpers

Words and Music by
BROOKS BAKER

Cheerfully

F   C7

1. John - ny is our help - er   all through the day,
2. Jack - ie is our help - er   all through the day,

mp

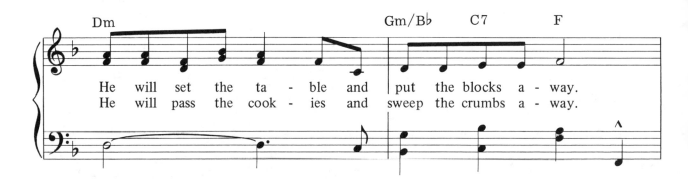

Dm   Gm/B♭ C7   F

He will set the ta - ble and put the blocks a - way.
He will pass the cook - ies and sweep the crumbs a - way.

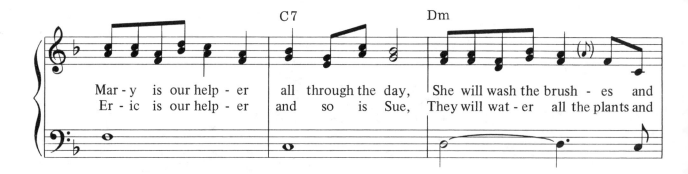

          C7   Dm

Mar - y is our help - er all through the day, She will wash the brush - es and
Er - ic is our help - er and so is Sue, They will wat - er all the plants and

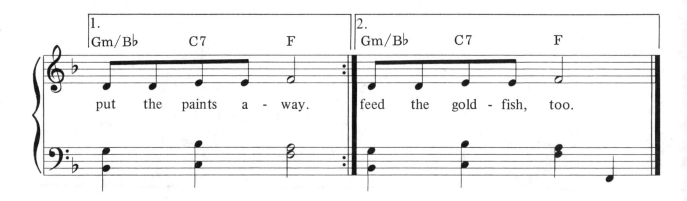

1.
Gm/B♭ C7   F   2.
              Gm/B♭ C7   F

put the paints a - way.   feed the gold - fish, too.

Fun and Play

Introduction

Play is an essential part of the young child's growing process. It is not separate from work or study; play is a major component of the work and study of young children. Through involvement in play, the child moves from isolated activity to awareness of others and participation in group activity.

This unit is designed to emphasize to the kindergarten child the pleasures and procedures involved in play. Social interaction in play activities provides a child with opportunities to develop cooperative behavior, sensitivity to others and friendship. The suggestions given in this unit are for teaching not only "what to play" but also "how to play."

Children find games universally appealing and respond to them. However, for many young children, the cooperation necessary for games is not developed behavior. Therefore, they must be introduced to the importance of sharing, of following rules, and of playing in a cooperative manner.

This unit also seeks to help the children assume responsibility for initiating play activities. Up to this point, dependency has been a major factor in the development of the young child. Learning to select and initiate independent activities will expand a child's horizons and free him or her to become an individual. The joy the child feels from playing is not its only reward. Play bestows lasting social, mental and physical benefits upon the child as well.

Concepts To Be Taught

I. The children may engage cooperatively with other children in a play activity for a short period of time.

II. When given time and a variety of play activities, the children may independently initiate a play activity.

III. The children must assume responsibility for locating play objects and returning them to the correct storage areas.

IV. Each child enjoys certain play activities.

V. The children will follow simple directions for playing a game or completing an activity described orally by a leader.

Information for Teaching Concepts

I. The children may engage cooperatively with other children in a play activity for a short period of time.

With everyone seated on the floor, roll a ball across the room, then retrieve the ball, return to a seated position and roll it again. Next, have a child sit directly across from you. Roll the ball to the child and have the child roll the ball back to you. Talk about the pleasure of sharing a play activity with another person. Also mention that it is easier for you not having to chase the ball, and more time can be spent rolling the ball. Have the children divide into pairs or small groups and roll a ball between them. Let them name other activities that are fun to do with a friend.

Play activities that require participation of the total group or small groups should be scheduled each day. Before beginning such activities, clearly describe them to the class. Have them think about the benefits gained from participating with others and the rules needed so that the activity may be enjoyed by everyone.

Place a cartoon strip under an opaque projector and outline the figures on paper (wrapping paper or butcher paper) for a class coloring project. Discuss this mural activity with the children, establishing how many children will work on the mural at one time. Make certain that each child has an assigned area for coloring and adequate time to work at the mural. When the mural is finished, talk about the cooperative effort that went into the project.

This is an excellent project to use for social modeling. Allow the children to decide on appropriate behaviors to exhibit when they work on the mural. Then, have three children demonstrate the proper way to work at the mural. Last, have each child show where she or he is to color on the mural and how she or he will work.

II. When given time and a variety of play activities, the children may independently initiate a play activity.

Select several play activities and place the materials for the activities on a table. Explain to the children that they may use one activity for a given time. When they complete an activity, they are to get a chip. Make positive comments to the children as they initiate their activities. At the end of the play period have the children show their chips. Explore with the class the concept of independence. Explain that children who choose an activity and begin to work by themselves are good workers. Have the class name the activities they can do alone or when there is no one to share play time.

III. The children must assume responsibility for locating play objects and returning them to the correct storage areas.

Ask the children what would happen if:

1) their pajamas were stored in the refrigerator
2) meat were put in a dresser drawer
3) cars were parked on the sidewalks
4) zoo animals were set loose from their cages

Read the poem, "Upside-Down Town," page 234. Talk about how easy it is to find things when they are in the right place. Play a game, "What am I?" Describe something in the class and where it is stored. Have the children name the object. At the end of the school day, have the children look around the room and make sure all the materials are placed in their proper storage areas.

Sorting activities help the children to place objects in their correct locations. A learning center activity can be established where children sort objects into the correct bins. Each bin should be labeled with a picture or color card and a basket of objects to be sorted should be located beside the bins. Examples of objects to sort are:

1) spools
2) blocks
3) pictures
4) balls
5) fabric pieces
6) envelopes

IV. Each child enjoys certain play activities.

Each day provide a few play activities for a structured play time. Children are to describe the play activity they have selected. As a new game, toy or activity is introduced to the children, be sure to demonstrate the proper procedures for using it.

Make large illustrated charts of, "Toys I Enjoy", "Games I Play With Friends", and "Activities That Are Fun." Examples for each are:

Toys I Enjoy

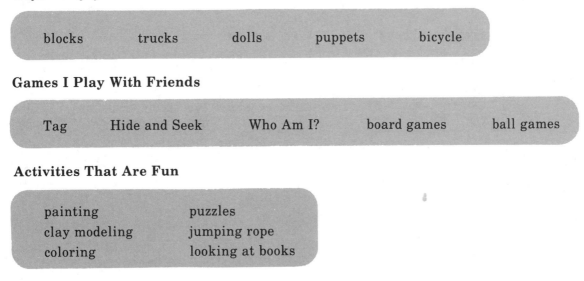

blocks   trucks   dolls   puppets   bicycle

Games I Play With Friends

Tag   Hide and Seek   Who Am I?   board games   ball games

Activities That Are Fun

painting   puzzles
clay modeling   jumping rope
coloring   looking at books

Have the children role-play their participation in an activity when you point to it on the chart.

V. The children will follow simple directions for playing a game or completing an activity described orally by a leader.

Play the game, "Where Is Headley?", page 90. After the game, ask the children how they knew what to do. Point out the importance of listening to and watching the leader. Explain to the children that they are learning to follow directions. Ask, "When is it important to follow directions?" Some answers are:

to find someone's house

to bake a pie

to make a puppet

to learn a new game

to sew a jacket

to build a birdhouse

to drive to the park

to learn how to swim

Provide many experiences where the children have to follow directions, beginning with one-step instructions, then two-steps, and increasing the number of steps as appropriate. Examples are:

1) Finger Plays (page 237)
2) Stunts (page 51)
3) Crafts (pages 241, 242, 243, 244, 245, 246, 247, 248)
4) Worksheets (pages 223, 224, 239, 240)
5) Games (pages 238, 244)

Review the classroom jobs that the children might be given. Then, assign one job to each child. Tell them they are to teach that job to a friend. Before they can teach the job, they must prepare some directions for their friend to follow. Talk about one job during a discussion time and examine the tasks involved. Have the child assigned to that job tell a friend how to perform it. Let the child learning the job demonstrate to the others how he or she performs the job based on the directions given.

Children should have extensive practice in giving, receiving and following directions. Perhaps special clothing can be worn or a special chair marked "director" used when a child is giving directions, to add interest and meaning.

Thinking and Reasoning

Ask your children these questions:

Do ice skates have wheels? Do roller skates?

Why don't we use an egg to play ball?

Do you usually swim outdoors in winter or in summer?

When do you play more, by day or by night?

When do you make more noise, when you play with another child or when you play alone? When do you run more?

Can a rabbit stand on its head? Can you?

Which is larger, a marble or a ball? Which is harder?

Which is bigger, a tricycle or a bicycle? Which has more wheels?

Which can you throw farther, a football or a baseball? Why?

Is the game of marbles played on the ground or on a table?

When a ball bounces several times, is the first bounce or the second bounce higher?

Which requires more strength, playing football or playing checkers?

Does a kite have a motor in it?

What is the difference between skating and skiing? Between skate boarding and roller skating?

Can a dog ride a bike? Why?

Can two people read a book at the same time?

If you put a ball at the bottom of a hill, will it roll up the hill?

Can you jump over your house? A car? A bike? A curb? A piece of rope?

Can a person play football alone?

Which is a better swimmer, a bird or a fish?

Is it possible to ice skate indoors?

If four children are sitting on a swing, is it heavier or lighter than if only two children sit on it?

If you are putting together a puzzle and you drop one piece, can you continue to work on the puzzle or must you first find the piece you dropped?

How many people can play tennis at one time?

Which is faster, running or walking?

Are crayons all one color, or many different colors?

Can people on the radio hear you when you laugh and talk? Can you hear them?

Are there any fish in a swimming pool? In a lake?

Can you hide under a rug?

Can you ride a sled in your house?

What kinds of games can you only play outdoors?

What kinds of sports can you only play in the summer? What sports can you only play in the winter?

Which is larger, a baseball or a basketball? Which is easier to catch?

Why does a snowman take a long time to melt?

Name some sports that you might wear a helmet to play.

Which person is working?
Which is resting?
Which is playing?
When do you work? rest? play?

Connect the picture on the left to the matching picture on the right by drawing a line.

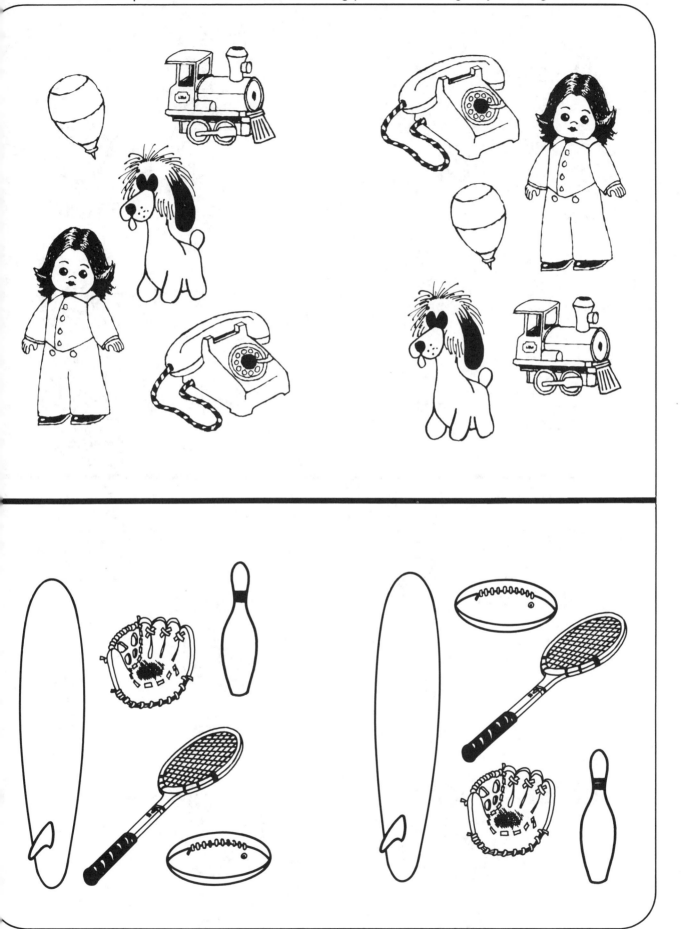

FUN AND PLAY   **223**

Connect the picture on the left to the matching picture on the right by drawing a line.

Which are having fun alone?
Which are having fun with others?
Which do you enjoy more—having fun alone
or with others?
What is your favorite fun?

FUN AND PLAY **225**

Koko, the Unfunny Clown

ELAINE CAMPBELL SMITH

Koko was the saddest clown in the world. He wasn't funny. He stopped being funny when his dog, Fifi, disappeared. She had been gone for a month.

Koko looked everywhere for Fifi. He had to find her. The circus manager told Koko that he must be funny or he would lose his job. No one wanted a clown who wasn't funny.

Koko sat beside the big circus tent. He held his head in his hands. He was very, very sad.

Joe and Melissa came around the tent. They saw Koko.

"Hi, Koko," said Joe.

"Hi, Koko," said Melissa.

Koko didn't answer. He sat with his head in his hands.

"What's the matter, Koko?" Joe asked.

Koko looked at the children. "I'm not funny anymore," he said.

Melissa and Joe were surprised. "You're a clown. Clowns are always funny," Melissa said.

"I'm not funny," Koko told her. "My dog, Fifi, is gone. I'm too sad to be funny. If I could find Fifi, I would be funny again."

"Don't worry, Koko," Joe said. "We'll help look for Fifi."

"We want you to be funny when we come to the circus tonight," Melissa added.

"If you find Fifi, I will be funny," Koko promised.

Joe and Melissa began to look for Fifi. They looked under the bleachers in the big tent. They looked in the costume tent. They looked in the animal tent. They looked for Fifi till it was time for the circus to begin. The only dog they saw was a little white poodle, hiding under a cage in the animal tent. She had four tiny puppies with her.

Joe and Melissa went to Koko.

"Is Fifi little?" Joe asked.

"Yes," Koko said.

"Is she white?" asked Melissa.

"Yes," said Koko.

"Is she a poodle?" Joe asked.

"Yes," sighed Koko.

Melissa and Joe looked at each other. They smiled.

"You had better get ready for the show," Melissa said.

Koko went to the costume tent. Joe and Melissa ran to the animal tent.

When it was time for Koko to do his act, he walked slowly into the big tent. He did a trick with an umbrella. No one laughed. Koko wasn't funny.

Then Koko heard Melissa and Joe. "Hey, Koko," they shouted.

Koko looked toward the entrance. There was Fifi, dressed in her pink, ruffled skirt. She ran toward Koko. Behind Fifi were four tiny puppies. They had pink ruffles around their necks.

The puppies romped and tumbled together. They bit at each other's ruffles. Fifi leaped into Koko's arms. The crowd cheered.

Koko was not a sad clown anymore. He was happy. He was the funniest clown in the world.

Rabbits For Timothy

JOSEPHINE BALFOUR PAYNE

Once there was a little boy named Timothy who loved rabbits. He didn't love horses and he didn't love dogs and he didn't love cats—he just loved rabbits.

Whenever he went walking by himself or with his Nanny he looked for rabbits. He looked everywhere.

"I wish I could see a rabbit," he said to Nanny. "I wish I could see two rabbits. No, three rabbits. No, hundreds and thousands of rabbits."

"Gracious!" Nanny said, "One's enough."

"Not for me," Timothy said, and he went out into the garden and sat down near the rows of carrots and lettuce waiting for a rabbit to come along.

He sat and he sat and he sat. And while he was sitting there an odd-looking man looked over the fence and saw Timothy sitting there staring at the rows of carrots and lettuce.

"Dear me, whatever are you doing?"

"I'm waiting for a rabbit to come along," Timothy said.

"You'll wait a long time, then. How can a rabbit possibly come when all the rabbits are in my hat?"

"In your hat?" said Timothy.

"Of course, I'm a magician. I take rabbits out of my hat and put them back again. All good magicians do. Haven't you ever seen a magician do that?"

"Never," Timothy said.

"Dear me," said the magician, coming into the garden and closing the gate after him. "Look."

He took off his hat and turned it upside down. He put his hand down into his hat, and when he took his hand out again—there was a rabbit!

Timothy laughed and clapped his hands.

"It's a little, little rabbit. Now may I have a medium sized rabbit, and a big, big rabbit? May I have hundreds and thousands of rabbits—all sizes?"

"Of course," said the magician obligingly, "all you want."

The magician kept reaching into his hat and bringing out rabbits of all sizes. After a while the garden was quite filled with them.

They were everywhere.

"Dear me," cried Nanny, and tried to shut the door, but there were so many rabbits she couldn't shut it at all. The rabbits hopped past Nanny.

They hopped into the house.

They hopped up the stairs.

They jumped into Timothy's bed and into the dresser drawers.

They squeezed into the chairs.

"I'm afraid we have taken out too many," said the magician.

"Can't you put them back into the hat?" asked Timothy.

"It's a great deal harder to put them back than it is to take them out," said the magician. "You have to catch them first."

"I know," said Timothy. "Let's open the garden gate wide, and then let's say—all together—'SHOO.' Then they will hop out of the house and through the gate and into the fields and meadows and woods. Then whenever I go walking by myself or with Nanny I can always find a rabbit."

"How wonderful," said the magician. "Of course."

So they opened the garden gate very wide, and Nanny and the magician and Timothy took a big breath, and they said—all together—"SHOO!"

The rabbits hopped out of the house and through the gate and into the fields and meadows and woods just as fast as they could go until there was not a one left anywhere.

"Now," said Timothy happily, "now whenever I wish, I can find a rabbit." And he always did, too.

Oh, Sarah

BETH TOBLER

Once there was a little boy named Johnny who had a baby sister named Sarah. It was not unusual to hear him cry, "Oh, Sarah."

Johnny had a problem.

When Johnny built a tower with his blocks, he stood back to admire it. He called, "Mom, Dad, come see my . . ."

But even before he finished, there was Sarah. With one swing of her baby hand, his tower tumbled into a pile of blocks at his feet. "Oh, Sarah," he sighed.

Johnny climbed up on the sofa to enjoy some of his favorite books. It wasn't long before Sarah climbed up beside him eager to see, too. Johnny started, "Once upon a time . . ."

Before he finished, Sarah was ready to turn the page. "Wait, Sarah!" But Johnny was too late. The page tore, leaving only half a page still in the book. "Oh, Sarah," moaned Johnny.

Johnny liked to work puzzles. His favorite was the raccoon puzzle Grandma gave him. Puzzle-working was not easy. He had to think where to put each piece. When he finally got near the end, he could not find the last piece. "It must be some . . ."

Then he spied Sarah. She was al-ways chewing on something, but this time it was his last puzzle piece. "Oh, Sarah," Johnny said in anger.

Johnny liked to color pictures to give to people. He was careful not to color on anything but paper, and took good care of his crayons. Johnny was busy coloring a tree one day, so he didn't notice Sarah getting into his crayon box.

When he did see her, he quickly said, "No, Sarah, they might . . ." Before he finished, there was his red crayon in two pieces. "Oh, Sarah," he said sadly.

Johnny made a ferris wheel with his Tinkertoys. He told Dad, "When you turn this handle, the ferris wheel will turn around."

"That's great, Johnny," Dad said with pride.

One day Johnny was outside playing with his friend Cindy. Mother was busy, and Sarah quietly crawled in to inspect the prized ferris wheel. After all, she had been left out. Johnny came running in with Cindy. "Look at this terrific . . ." He stopped short. There sat Sarah with just a pile of Tinkertoys and no ferris wheel. "Oh, Sarah," the children both said.

Johnny had a special orange ball

that was great for throwing, kicking, or catching. One day he was looking for the ball in his toy box. When he reached in and pulled it out, he saw a large piece missing from it. "What happened? It looks like a bite is out of it . . ." Then he knew. Oh, how he knew. "Oh, Sarah," he said weakly.

Johnny went on having problems, and Sarah was almost always the cause of them. But time passed, and Sarah began to walk and talk.

One day Johnny built a tower with his blocks. In came Sarah. Johnny said, "No, Sarah. Please don't . . ."

But before he finished, she placed a block on top of the tower carefully. "Oh, Sarah," he said in surprise. Together they built a big tower.

Johnny climbed up on the sofa, and Sarah followed, ready to read with him. As he started, he stopped to say, "Now Sarah, don't . . ."

But as he was talking, he noticed she wasn't doing anything but listening. "Oh, Sarah," he said, pleased to share his book with her. They laughed and giggled at the story together.

As Johnny started the raccoon puzzle, in walked Sarah. Quickly he warned, "Puzzle pieces don't go in . . ."

But while he was talking, Sarah put a piece in the puzzle. "Oh, Sarah," he said happily. They finished that puzzle and went on to another.

Johnny got his crayons out to color. When he saw Sarah coming, he said, "Leave the crayons . . ."

But before he finished, Sarah started coloring her own picture. "Oh, Sarah. That's good!" Together they colored pictures to give to people.

One night Johnny was building another ferris wheel with his Tinkertoys. Sarah sat down. Right away he said, "Don't take it . . ."

But before he finished, she had put some pieces correctly into the ferris wheel. "Oh, Sara," Johnny said. "I didn't know you could help." They both had a great time building.

One day Johnny spied Sarah with his orange ball. He ran quickly across the room saying, "Sarah, wait . . ."

He saw her take aim and throw the ball to him. "Oh, Sarah," Johnny said, out of breath. "Perfect throw!" Together they played catch all day.

Johnny is happy that he no longer has a problem.

Poems

Hey Diddle Diddle

Hey diddle diddle,
The cat and the fiddle,
The cow jumped over the moon.

The little dog laughed
To see such sport,
And the dish ran away with the spoon.

Jack Be Nimble

Jack be nimble, Jack be quick,
Jack jump over the candlestick.

The Too-Little Horse of the Merry-Go-Round

LILIAN LE BOIT MOORE

Toby was a little black horse on the merry-go-round in the park. He was a fine looking horse, with silky black hair on the back of his neck and a long black tail that someone had braided with bright red ribbons. All day long he rode around and around and up and down to the rollicking song of the merry-go-round.

The merry-go-round was a new one that had just been brought to the park. The children who came to the park to play had never before seen one like it. It was big. It was gay. And it was full of strange and wonderful animals. Can you imagine a large green elephant with a golden seat on his back, big enough for two to ride in at one time? Or a yellow spotted giraffe that you could sit way up on as you held fast to his long, l-o-n-g neck? Then, too, there was a big orange tiger with a wide smile painted on her face. And a seal. A fat red seal with whiskers. He balanced a ball on the tip of his nose just like a real seal in the circus. Biggest of all, I guess, was the purple lion, so large and fierce that the children sometimes quarreled to see who would ride him first.

Toby had been very proud to find himself part of this beautiful new merry-go-round. How excited and happy he had been when the children had crowded around, saying, "Oh! Oh!" and "Isn't it wonderful?" It had seemed then as if everyone was glad he had come, and as if it would be fun always to live here in the park.

But Toby was not very happy now. No, he was quite a sad little horse. Day by day he would hear the children call to each other, "Oh, look! Just see the big giraffe!" or "I want to ride that 'normous tiger." Or perhaps someone would say, "I'm going to wait for that big old lion. He's best of all!" It seemed to Toby that day by day he was growing smaller and lonelier until now it was no fun at all to be part of a wonderful new merry-go-round. Even the song to which he went around seemed to sing, "Too little! Too little! Too little!"

One day he said to the lady tiger, who rode so cheerfully beside him, "I'm tired of being on this merry-go-round. I'm tired of going up and down and around and around."

The lady tiger smiled her wide painted smile and said in a motherly voice, "You'll get used to it, Little Horse, after a time."

"No," said Toby, "it's no fun any more. Do you know what I wish? I wish I were a real horse."

The lady tiger shuddered. "Oh, not I!" she said quickly. "My, I'm glad I'm not a real tiger. I'm afraid of real tigers!"

"If only I were a real horse," said Toby with a far-away look in his eyes, "a horse that could ride down the road in the wind. Then you would see how all the children would want to ride me. Why, someone might even wish to have me for his very own horse." As he went around and around and up and down, Toby kept thinking how fine it would be to be a real horse. Sometimes he closed his eyes and tried to make believe he was real, but it didn't help.

That very afternoon a little boy in a blue sailor suit came and stood by the merry-go-round. He was quite a little boy and he held tightly to his mother's hand. Toby passed him many times. "Why doesn't he get on?" Toby wondered. The merry-go-round would stop. The other children—laughing and shouting—would hop off and hop on, and off would go the merry-go-round, singing its jolly song. But the little boy just stood there beside his mother. The next time Toby went around he took a good look at him. Then Toby knew why the little boy just stood and watched. He was afraid. He wanted very much to ride on the merry-go-round, but he was afraid.

"Look, dear," said the boy's mother, as she pointed to the big green elephant with the golden seat. The boy just shook his head. Then she showed him the tall giraffe. The boy's big brown eyes grew rounder, but still he just stood and looked. She pointed to the fierce purple lion and the friendly tiger. Still the boy shook his head.

Then, suddenly, for the first time, the little boy saw the little black horse. As the merry-go-round came to a stop he let go of his mother's hand and ran quickly to Toby. Climbing up all by himself on Toby's back, he leaned forward, put his arms around the horse's neck, and hugged him hard. "My horse," he cried. "This is my horse!" The little boy was so excited and happy that all at once Toby felt glad, too. And, as they rode off together, Toby felt exactly like a real horse riding down the road in the wind.

Things to Make

Spongy Characters

BEVERLY BLASUCCI

Find the large oval-type sponge that comes in bright colors. They are about 8 inches by 4 inches and a nice size to work with. First of all, make a cardboard base shaped like two silly feet to set your sponge on. This base can be covered with a bright fabric or painted to look like feet. Cut the bottom of the sponge flat and glue on the feet.

Use felt, buttons, and other scraps to make the faces. These can be sewed or glued in place. Antennae can be made with colored pipe cleaners. Fringe is especially good for making shaggy hair.

You may want to make a double-faced spongy character to suit the mood you are in. Just make a happy face on one side of the sponge and a sad face on the other side.

Nancy at the Zoo

SHIRLEY MARKHAM JORJORIAN

It was a sunny Saturday, and Nancy could hardly wait. She was going to the zoo. Every time she went to the zoo, she liked to see what the animals could do.

First she went to the elephant cage. The big gray elephant swayed its trunk back and forth. Nancy said, "I can do that." And she locked her hands together and swayed them back and forth. The elephant looked at Nancy. The elephant had never before seen a little girl do that.

Then Nancy went to see the ferocious lion. The lion opened its mouth big and wide. It roared loud and long. Nancy said, "I can do that." And she opened her mouth just as wide as she could and she roared with all her might. The lion looked surprised. The lion never knew that a little girl could roar so loudly.

Nancy skipped to the giraffe's cage. The tall giraffe reached to the top of a tree and smelled a leaf. "I can do that," said Nancy to the giraffe. Nancy stretched her neck just as far as she could and she smelled a leaf on a small green bush. The giraffe had never seen such a sight in his life.

Nancy went to see the shiny black seals. "Arf, arf," said one seal as it clapped its flippers, flip-flap, flip-flap. "Oh, that's easy," said Nancy. She clapped her hands, clip-clap, clip-clap, and she said, "Arf, arf." The seal looked at Nancy. How could a little girl make a sound like a seal?

Next Nancy visited the kangaroo. She watched the kangaroo hopping all around. Nancy said, "I can do that." And she hopped and hopped all over the ground. The kangaroo watched Nancy hop-hop away. The kangaroo was surprised that little girls could hop at all.

Down to the cage of the big black bear Nancy hopped. The bear stood with its paws on the cage. Then it dropped down on all four paws. Nancy said, "I can do that, Mr. Bear." And she dropped her hands to the ground and walked around like the big furry bear. The bear stared at Nancy. How funny a little girl looks on all four feet!

Nancy passed by the ostrich pen. The ostrich came running and flapping its wings. Nancy said to the ostrich, "I can do that." And she tucked her hands underneath her arms. She flapped her arms and ran like the ostrich did. The ostrich had never seen such an ostrich-looking girl.

Nancy came to a deer with great big antlers. "I can look like that," said Nancy. She put her hands to the top of her head and spread her fingers to look like the antlers on the deer. The deer started to run. Then it looked again. It was just a little girl trying to look like a deer.

Last of all, Nancy went to the monkey cage. She liked the monkey best of all. The little brown monkey jumped up and down and said, "Chee-chee." Nancy said to the monkey, "I can do that." And she jumped up and down, and she said, "Chee-chee." The monkey scratched its head. Nancy said, "I can do that, too." And she scratched her head.

"Bet you can't do this, little monkey," Nancy said as she stood on her head. But the monkey copied Nancy and stood on its head. Nancy turned a sommersault and so did the monkey. Then Nancy sat on the ground and touched her toes. "Bet you can't do that," said Nancy. But the monkey sat down and touched its toes just as Nancy did.

Nancy thought and thought. What could she do that the monkey couldn't do? Finally she said, "I know what I can do that you can't do!" She stood up straight. She put her hands at her sides. And she took a deep breath. Then she said, "A-B-C-D-E-F-G-H-I-J-K-L-M-N-O-P-Q-R-S-T-U-V-W-X-Y-Z! Now, do that if you can, monkey!"

The monkey opened its mouth and said, "Ah-bah, dab-ah, chee-chee," but it couldn't say the ABC's.

The monkey stared at Nancy for a long, long time. Never before had it seen a girl do so many different things.

Nancy said good-bye to all the animals in the zoo. She liked to see what they could do. And she was proud that she could do what she could do.

Craft

Mr. Marble Holder

KATHERINE CORLISS BARTOW

Cut a paper mouth pattern ½ inch in diameter. Draw around pattern 1½ inches from one end of a cardboard tissue tube. Cut out mouth.

Cut a piece of colored paper to fit around tube. Trace mouth pattern 1½ inches from top center of paper. Cut out. Glue paper around tube, centering mouth over tube hole.

Cover thin cardboard ears with colored paper. Glue on ears.

Eyebrows are made with a black marker; eyes can be of white paper with small black centers. The nose is red paper. Color red around the mouth.

Punch armholes. Insert pipe cleaner arms and glue in place.

Glue a cardboard circle with feet, covered with colored paper, on the bottom.

Glue short pieces of yarn hair over edge of tube.

Poems

School is over,
  Oh, what fun!
Lessons finished,
  Play begun.
Who'll run fastest,
  You or I?
Who'll laugh loudest?
  Let us try.

  KATE GREENAWAY

If

AUTHOR UNKNOWN

If I had a kite,
  With a very short tail,
And a very stout cord—
  And there came a great gale—
I'd hold fast to the string,
  And away we would fly
I and my kite
  Up, up to the sky.

I Meant To Do My Work Today

RICHARD LeGALLIENNE

I meant to do my work today—
But a brown bird sang in the apple tree,
And a butterfly flitted across the field,
And all the leaves were calling me.
And the wind went sighing over the land,
Tossing the grasses to and fro,
And a rainbow held out its shining hand—
So what could I do but laugh and go?

The Swing

ROBERT LOUIS STEVENSON

How do you like to go up in a swing,
  Up in the air so blue?
Oh, I do think it the pleasantest thing
  Ever a child can do!

Up in the air and over the wall,
  Till I can see so wide,
Rivers and trees and cattle and all
  Over the countryside—

Till I look down on the garden green,
  Down on the roof so brown—
Up in the air I go flying again,
  Up in the air and down!

A Wish

GARRY CLEVELAND MYERS

I wish I often put myself
In your place
With my imagination
So I could see
A little as you see
And think of you instead of me.

The Slide

LOLA BIKUL

Up you go,
Just so,
To the top,
Then stop,
look around
At the ground.
All clear?
No one near.
Away you go!
Feet land
In the sand
Down below.

Bubbles

Bubble soap is so much fun.
Some bubbles go high,
Some bubbles go low,
And some I can catch,
And some I let go.

STEVEN KNUDSON, Age 5

Cat-astrophe

KEVIN O'HARA

Cat is fat.
When he sat
On my hat
Hat went splat.
That was that.

The Playground

The playground is fun.
We like to run.
We slip and slide.
It's fun playing outside.

SUSAN MASON, Age 7

Merry-Go-Round

RACHEL FIELD

Purple horses with orange manes,
Elephants pink and blue,
Tigers and lions that never were seen
In circus parade or zoo!
Bring out your money and choose
your steed,
And prance to delightsome sound.
What fun if the world would turn
some day
Into a Merry-Go-Round!

Upside-Down Town

ELSIE M. FOWLER

Upside-Down is a funny town!
The folks stand on their heads.
They walk on ceilings, not on floors,
And never sleep in beds.

The children go to school at night
And stay at home by day.
They start the alphabet with Z
And end it with an A.

The Fishing-Pole

MARY CAROLYN DAVIES

A fishing-pole's a curious thing;
It's made of just a stick and string;
A boy at one end and a wish,
And on the other end a fish.

The Circus Parade

The circus parade
   Has come to town.
In the parade
   Is a big, fat clown.

The drummer is drumming
   His big bass drum,
It seems to be saying,
   "Come, children, come."

There is a man
   With a bright flashy suit,
He plays on a horn
   That gives a great toot.

The circus parade
   Has come at last.
Rush to the corner
   And watch it go past.

JOAN CAROL DAUGHERTY, Age 9

The Circus

The circus is fun
With clowns, elephants,
and
Dancing bears.
And monkeys on bicycles
Riding up stairs.
There are tigers and lions
Out of their cages.
People on tightropes,
All different ages.
But best of all,
I like the clowns,
Some dancing,
Some prancing,
and
Some with frowns.

CAROLINE WITCOFF, Age 7

Red Balloon

Red balloon,
floating high
in the sky,
saying Hi
and Good-bye
to the moon,
to the sun,
to the stars.
POP!

GUL GOKSEL, Age 9

Songs

Songs are beautiful,
Songs are fun.
Some you sing,
And some you hum.

Some are happy,
Some are sad,
And lots of them
Make me glad.

ROBBIE CATALANO, Age 8

Clowns

Clowns can be tall
Or very small.
Clowns can be thin or fat.
My favorite clown
Walks upside down
And wears a floppy hat.

THERESA LOGUE, Age 7

Finger Plays

Riding the Pony
MARGUERITE GODE

Give him yellow corn to eat,
(motion of eating)

And don't forget to say,
(shake finger)

"Thank you, little pony,
For my pleasant ride today."
(nod head)

Ride, ride, ride your pony
(hands extended;
motion of galloping up and down)

Up the hill and down.
(higher motion, lower motion slowly)

Ride him through the country.
Ride him into town.
(continue galloping motion)

Jack-in-the-Box

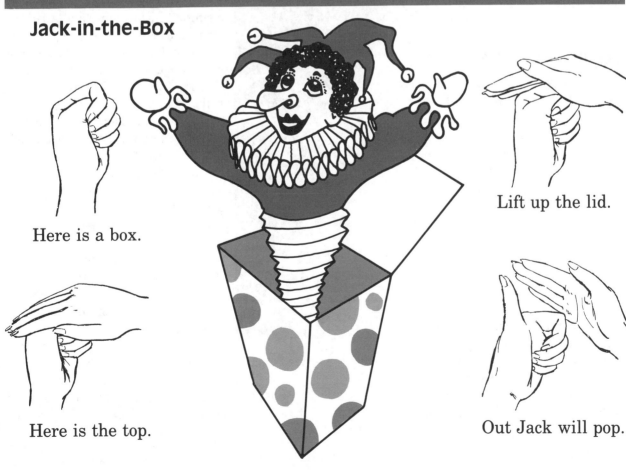

Here is a box.

Here is the top.

Lift up the lid.

Out Jack will pop.

Games

Topsy-Turvy

The holder is made by cutting bottoms from two quart-sized round plastic detergent bottles. Fasten the two bottle caps together with two-pronged paper fasteners, then screw the bottles onto the lids. Paint the numbers 1 and 2 on the holder as shown. Decorate it as desired.

The player grasps the holder in his hand with the Number 1 compartment UPRIGHT. The player tosses the ball into the air from compartment 1, then does a quick turn of the wrist and catches the ball in compartment 2. The game continues in this order.

If two or more players want to play a scoring game, each player takes a turn, continuing until one misses a catch. The player with the highest number of catches is the winner.

A Game From Jamaica

Boys and girls on the island of Jamaica, which is in the Caribbean Sea not far from Cuba, play a game that goes like this:

The players sit around a table and sing a song. Then the leader, at the head of the table, calls "bird fly" or "dog fly" or "rabbit fly." When the leader names something that really does fly—for instance, when he says "bird fly"—all the players must raise their hands quickly. When he calls something that does not fly, such as "pig fly," the players must keep their hands on the table without moving them.

Any player who puts his hand in the air at the wrong time, or who doesn't put his hands in the air quickly enough at the right time, must pay a forfeit.

Toss-and-catch Game

Cut the top section (just below handle) from a plastic bleach bottle. Cut a piece of yarn about 18 inches long. Insert one end of the yarn into a hole punched into a small piece of sponge and glue in place. Wrap the other end of the yarn around the top of the plastic bottle and screw the lid on over the yarn. Decorate the bottle with a border of yarn. The object of the game is to catch the sponge in the open end of the bottle.

Spear-The-Ring-Game

Spear-The-Ring is a game to play when bad weather keeps you indoors.

It is easy to make. A thin stick about 18 inches long, a piece of string 36 inches long, and a rubber jar ring are all you require.

The string is tied securely to the stick about an inch from one end. The ring is then tied to the other end of the string.

To play the game, the stick is held in one hand and with a quick jerk upwards the ring is thrown in the air. The game is to catch the ring as it comes down on one of the ends of the stick.

If you catch the ring on the string end of the stick (top) you score 1 point. If you are quick enough to twist your wrist while the ring is in the air and catch the rubber dodger on the lower end of the stick you score 2 points.

In 10 tries, if your total score is over 10 you will know you have a steady hand and a sharp eye.

Keep playing and try to beat your own record. After a while you will be trying for 2 points at every toss.

Imitate each of the actions shown in the picture and then connect the matching figures.

FUN AND PLAY   **239**

Cut out the pieces shown and then paste them together to make a picture. Color the picture.

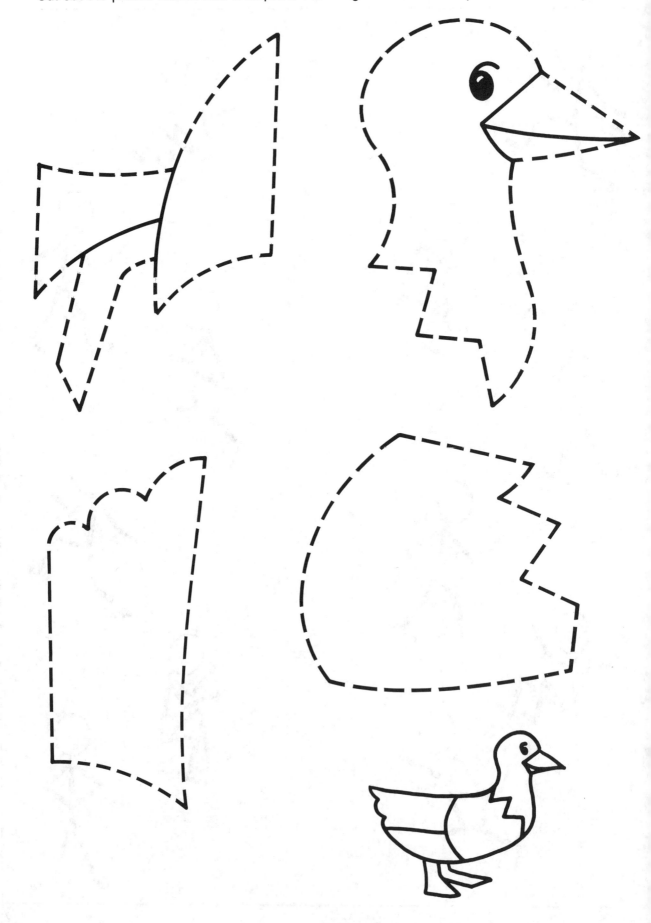

Things to Make

Doggy Mobile

Draw a half-pattern on folded paper. From opened pattern, cut two black paper heads, and one from lightweight cardboard. Cut four black paper eye circles and two cardboard circles.

Glue a thread hanging-loop to the cardboard head. Glue one end of a short white thread to each cardboard eye. Glue the other thread end in place on the head.

Glue the paper heads and eyes to each side of the cardboard pieces. Eye centers are white circles.

Easy Finger Puppets

Find an old glove and cut off the fingers. Cut little characters out of felt and glue to the fronts of the glove fingers. Put your finger into a glove finger, and have fun!

Stretch Your Imagination

Place a rubber band on a piece of colored paper. Use a pencil to doodle until you get some good ideas. If you like, cut up a rubber band to add to your design. With a mark here or a mark there and a stretch of the imagination—create your own design. Once your idea is complete, glue the rubber band to the paper and go over your pencil details with pen or felt-tip marker.

Puppets

Clown Thumb Puppet

First, make the clown from a round ball of clay, about the size of a plum. Press it down over your left thumb.

Now roll a little piece of clay into a carrot shape. Place the wider end of the clay in the middle of the round ball—for a nose. Two small round balls will make eyes. Use your fingernail to make a smily line in the eyes.

Next, roll a sausage shaped piece for the mouth. Curl the ends up for a smily face, or down for a sad face. Press a line along the mouth shape to make it look like lips.

Two wing-shaped pieces will make hair. Put them on the sides of the head and bend them back and up. With a pencil, make marks in the clay like hair blowing in the wind.

A fat carrot shape will make a high pointed hat. A small ball will make the tassel on the end.

Sock Puppets

Use a large sock that fits over your hand. Experiment—open and shut your hand with the sock over it. What kind of a face do you see? A fox, a dog, a duck?

For the ears use felt or paper or cloth that can be pasted or sewed on. Eyes may be made from felt, buttons, or beads. Hair can be made from yarn, string, cloth, straw, or any kind of material you think would be good. How will you make the nose and mouth? Experiment with various materials.

Sponge Hand Puppets

Cut a slit in the edge of a cellulose sponge large enough so your three center fingers will fit in the slit.

From felt, paper, or cloth, cut out a mouth, eyes, nose, and ears. Glue them in place. The ears should be glued into a slit on each side of the head.

Make felt puppet hands for your thumb and little finger, like the double-hand shape shown. Glue or sew around the edge, leaving the bottom open for inserting your thumb and little finger.

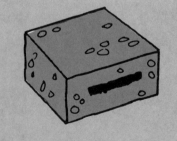

Clean-up Crafts

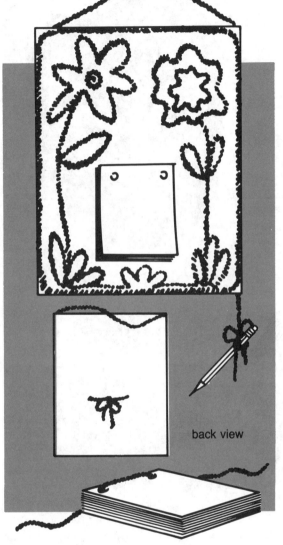

back view

Scrap Box for Rainy Days

Use a large brown paper bag or medium-sized cardboard box. Decorate outside with any scraps you may have or just color with crayons. Then ask your parents to put any empty boxes, tubes, plastic lids, containers, yarn, bits of ribbon, material, and so on into your box. Then when a rainy day comes along, or whenever you feel like making something, you can get out your scrap bag or box and let your imagination go to work!

Handy Keeper

Clean out a large can—the kind that coffee comes in. Cover it with wallpaper or construction paper. Draw a picture or design on the can, or paste on a picture cut from a greeting card or a magazine. Label the can "Tiny Toys," "Small Things," "Just Junk," or something similar. Use the can for storing your own small items or give it as a present.

Recycled Memo Pad

Cut scrap paper into uniform-sized pieces (about 4 inches square). Stack and punch two holes in the top of the stack. Run a piece of yarn or string through the holes.

Place the stack of paper on a sheet of cardboard. Draw a design around the stack, keeping the shapes rather simple. With white glue attach lengths of leftover yarn around the shapes you have drawn. When your design is complete, punch holes in the cardboard to correspond to the holes in the paper and tie the memo sheets to the cardboard.

Glue a long string of yarn on the back of the cardboard and tie a pencil to the end.

Games and Toys

Paper-plate Clown

Cut most of the rim from a paper plate, leaving some for the clown's hair. Clip the hair into a fringe effect. From another paper plate, cut a hat, ears, eyebrows, mouth, nose, and so on. Glue in place.

Use ring-shaped paper reinforcements for eyes. A sequin glued in the center will add sparkle. A piece of paper doily makes a ruffle.

Use bright-colored crayons to color the clown's features.

Tin-Can Stilts

For making these stilts you will need two empty cans—the tall kind that fruit juice comes in. Decorate the outside of the cans with colored paper, cut-out pictures, crayon designs, or whatever you like. Use a can opener to make two holes (opposite each other) in the side of each can near the top. Run a piece of rope or heavy cord through the holes in each can.

The ends of the rope are to be tied together where you will hold onto it while using the stilts. Get someone to help you as you figure out how long the rope should be. Stand on the cans, let your arms hang down at your sides, and knot the ropes so that you can hold them comfortably.

Peg in the Bucket

Get a wide-mouthed jar and clean it. Cut small circles from colored paper, and glue them to the outside of the jar.

On heavy cardboard draw the face of a person or animal, a little larger than the opening of the jar. Make a very large mouth on the person or animal you draw.

Paint the face with tempera or poster paint. When dry, cut it out. Also cut out the mouth. Glue the face to the top of the jar.

Make several three-inch long pegs from pieces of thin dowling or sticks. Paint each one a different color. Or you can make pegs from three-inch squares of colored paper, rolled tightly and fastened with tape. Write a different number on each colored peg.

To play the game, put the jar on the floor and stand with your feet close to it. From directly above, try to drop the pegs, one by one, into the mouth of the face on the jar. Shake out those that go in, and count up your score by adding the numbers on the pegs.

Give your friends a chance to play, too.

Funny People

Mixed-Up Mobile

Draw pictures of two different funny people on two pieces of light cardboard.

Paper-clip the two pictures together and cut them into five or six strips, horizontally.

Lay the strips of one picture, face down, with small spaces between the pieces. Apply glue to the backs of these strips. Lay a piece of string down the center of the pieces, leaving extra string at the top.

Attach each piece of the second picture, face up, over the pieces of the first picture, being sure to keep the pieces in the correct order.

Twisties

Take a wire twist-tie from a plastic bag. Bend it into a circle. Twist the ends together but let the tips stick up like ears. This is the head.

Take another twist-tie and make the letter U. Make two.

Turn one U upside down. Take one more twist-tie, put it inside the upside down U, and twist it around the curved part, leaving about ½ inch to stick out for a tail.

Take the other end of this last twist-tie, put it inside the other upside down U, and twist it around the curved part leaving about ½ inch to stick out for a neck. Take the head and, with the ears up, twist the neck around the base of the circle.

Adjust the legs (sides of the U) until figure stands by itself.

For short legs, bend the ends of the U's a little to look like paws.

Put a curve in the tail.

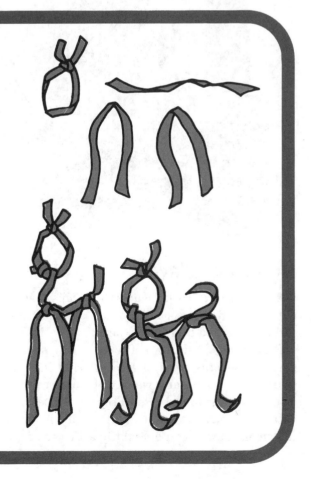

Art Crafts

Macaroni Pictures

You will need macaroni of different sizes and shapes. Put several drops of food coloring in a small paper cup. Fill it about one-third full of water. Put several pieces of macaroni in the mixture. Leave them in for about five minutes. Remove with a spoon and lay them on a paper towel to dry. Turn occasionally while drying so they will not stick to the towel. Make several different colors of macaroni.

Now, make different pictures from the macaroni. Use your imagination. Glue the macaroni on paper plates or plastic-foam meat trays. A yarn loop can be attached to the back of the picture for hanging.

Comb Designs

You will need tempera, white construction paper or newsprint, and a small comb. You can use broken pieces of combs, also.

Dip the comb in the tempera. Move it any way you want on your construction paper. You will need to dip the comb in the paint each time you move it on the paper. Let the paper dry thoroughly after your design is finished.

See how many different designs you can make.

Modeling "Clay"

Combine in a bowl: 1 cup salt, 2 cups flour, 1 cup water, 3 tablespoons cooking oil. Mix well. Put on a floured board and knead.

Poke a hole in the ball of "clay" with your finger. Put several drops of food coloring into the hole. Knead again and watch it become colored. You may want to add a few drops of peppermint extract (or any favorite extract) for an interesting smell. Store in an airtight, plastic container.

More Puppet Ideas

Envelope Puppet

Make a cut across the back of a business-size envelope one-third of the way down. Now seal the envelope above and below the cut.

Turn the envelope over. Draw a line across the front of the envelope at about the same level as the cut on the back. Above the line draw a face and hair. Below the line draw clothes for your puppet. Color as you like.

Or, instead of drawing the clothes and features, you may wish to cut them from yarn, cloth, or construction paper and glue in place.

Slide your three middle fingers into the cut in the back of the envelope. Your thumb and little finger make arms for your puppet.

Tongue Depressor Puppets

Paint a face on a tongue depressor with watercolor, tempera, or a felt-tipped marker. Ears can be made from felt, paper, or cardboard and glued in place on the tongue depressor. Whiskers can be made from toothpicks, pipe cleaners, or yarn and glued in place. To use as a puppet, glue a stiff paper ring to the back for your finger. For a mobile, make three or four of these faces and add a piece of string to the top of each. Tie these to a coat hanger and hang in a good place in your room.

Puppets from Fast-Food Restaurant Throwaways

Save the foam boxes, paper cups and lids, small coffee-creamer cups, cardboard french-fry holders, and straws you get when you eat at a fast-food restaurant.

To make a puppet from a foam box, glue the box edges together and insert a Popsicle stick at the bottom. Add features cut from colored felt and yarn.

To make a puppet from a throwaway cup and lid, cover the cup with white paper. Glue the lid in place. Insert the straw in the lid and glue in place. Glue on small coffee-creamer cups for ears and a french-fry holder for a hat. Glue on features cut from colored felt.

Stamp Pad Fun

You can have fun and make interesting designs by using a stamp pad with various little things you have about the house. Stamp pads may be bought at stationery stores. They have blue, red, green or purple ink. It is nice to have at least two colors to work with. The more you have the more variety you can get in your designs.

Do your printing on papers placed on a pad of a dozen sheets of newspapers. The handiest thing to start with is just the eraser on a pencil. Slice the tip off so it will print flat. Press it on the stamp pad then press it on the paper. Group the dots together in different combinations. Choose one combination and repeat it, evenly spaced, in rows for a border design or as an all over pattern.

You can make quite a few designs with just one eraser but by using two or more, the possibilities are multiplied. Slice other erasers off evenly, then cut them into other shapes, a triangle, a square, a half moon or a tiny star. Combine these different prints for a lot of new designs.

Now look around for other materials to make large and more intricate designs. Almost anything that will pick up the ink when pressed hard on the pad, will do. Here are some things: large erasers, spools, corks, wooden dowels, carrots, potatoes. With scissors, cut small pieces of inner-tube rubber into designs and glue them to a block.

The papers you print can be used many ways; as gift wrappings, book covers and linings, writing paper, and cards. Paper napkins take a print so well you can print enough for a party.

Some day you may want to go further and print a design with more detail than it is possible to cut in these soft materials. Use linoleum. Cut away the background as you did on the erasers. If you want letters, remember to reverse them. You will have to provide more pressure to pick up the ink. Tap the linoleum with a hammer or roll on it with a rolling pin.

To print a small linoleum block a number of times quickly, mount it, by tacking to a curved surface such as a rolling pin or a wooden disk. You can pick up the ink by rocking it back and forth. A single rolling on the paper will give good pressure for a clear print. Small greeting cards, labels, or party favors can be made by the hundreds this way.

Draw a creature that nobody has ever seen.

What Shall We Do?

Traditional

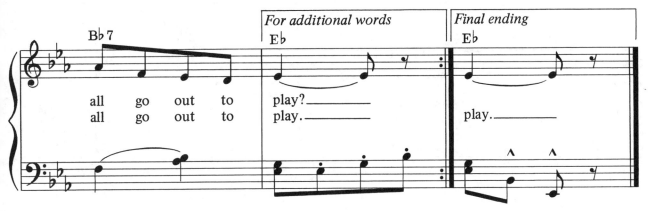

(continue similarly)
3. . . . climb a tree
4. . . . bounce a ball
5. . . . play a game

This Old Man

English Folk Song

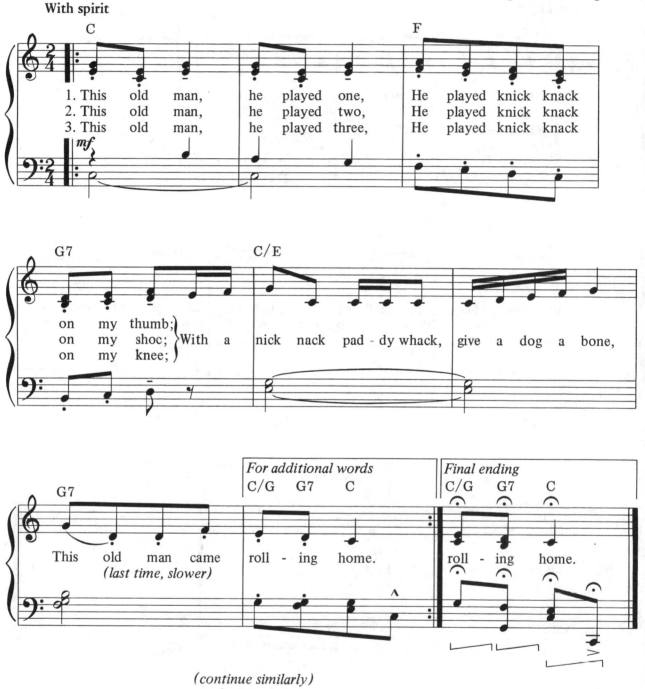

With spirit

1. This old man, he played one, He played knick knack
2. This old man, he played two, He played knick knack
3. This old man, he played three, He played knick knack

on my thumb;
on my shoc; } With a nick nack pad-dy whack, give a dog a bone,
on my knee;

For additional words

This old man came rolling home.
(last time, slower)

Final ending

rolling home.

(continue similarly)
. . . four. . . door
. . . five. . . hive
. . . six. . . sticks
. . . seven. . . this old man will go to heaven
. . . eight. . . plate
. . . nine. . . spine
. . . ten. . . this old man will start again

Section 11

Seasons

Fall

Ask your children these questions:

Can you think of a reason that this season might be called "fall"?

What happens to the leaves before they fall off the trees?

What kind of clothes do you need when the weather turns cool?

What are some games that can be played in the fall?

Would you rake leaves with a fork? Why?

Does school start or end in the fall?

Do flowers bloom in the fall?

Can you swim outdoors in the fall?

Can you think of any special holidays that happen in the fall?

What might you do with a pumpkin in the fall?

Mixed-up Story

Which was first? Next? Next? Last?

Connect the picture on the left to the matching picture on the right by drawing a line.

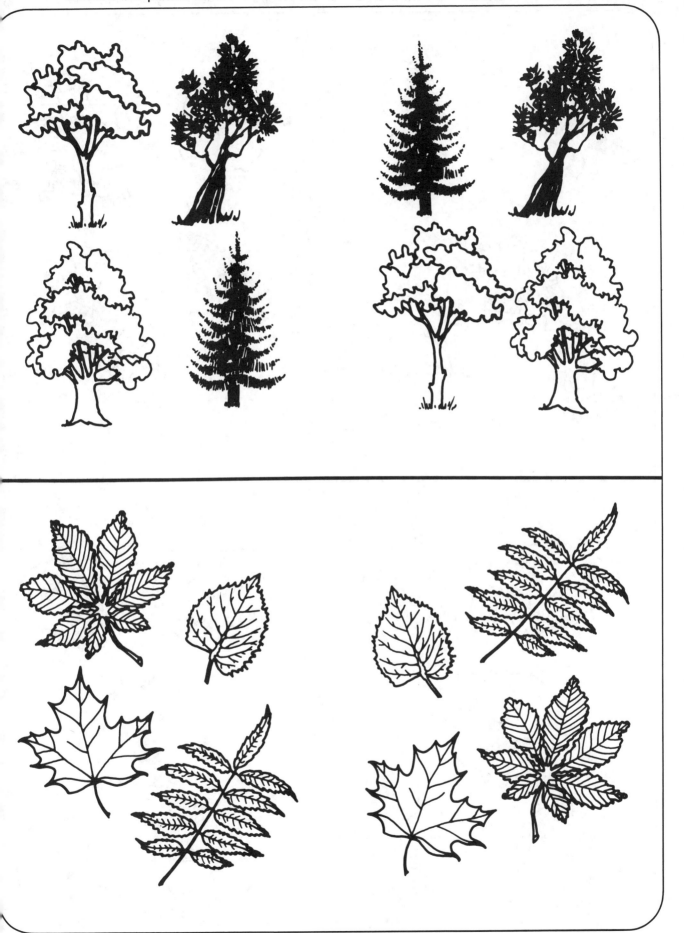

FALL   **257**

Connect the picture on the left to the matching picture on the right by drawing a line.

Poems

November

THOMAS HOOD

No shade, no shine,
No butterflies, no bees,
No fruits, no flowers,
No leaves, no birds,
November!

Spinning Wheel

IVY O. EASTWICK

Summer is over—
the leaves drift down
over the country
and over the town,
red leaves and gold leaves,
yellow and brown.

Adventure Calls

VERA RAMSDELL HARDMAN

"Come play with us," the brown leaves
called
While skipping in the sun.
"Come dance with us and sing a song,
For autumn brings such fun.

"All summer long we dressed in green
And when the sun shone bright,
We shared our coolness with the
world
And shaded it till night.

"But autumn with its golden days
Found us quite gaily dressed
In gold, maroon and crimson, for
In fall we look our best.

"But now it's time for us to go;
Adventure calls today.
So come with us," the brown leaves
called,
"Come dance with us and play."

Oh Goodness Oh Gracious

IVY O. EASTWICK

Oh goodness!
Oh gracious!
Oh mercy!
Oh my!
I saw an
old witch fly
straight up to
the sky.
She went on
a broomstick,
she went with
her cat.
Whooooooooooosh
like the wind
they went up
just like that.
Her coat swirled
about her and
scattered
the stars;
her tall
steeple hat
knocked a corner
off Mars;
her cat meeowed
with laughter
to hear Mars
exclaim:
"I'VE HAD JUST
ENOUGH OF
THAT WITCH AND
HER GAME."
But Venus called:
"Now Mars! Be
thankful,
my dear,
that Halloween
comes only
ONCE in a year."

The Big, Big Pumpkin

ANN DEVENDORF

"This Halloween I want to put a big, big jack-o'-lantern on the porch," said Mrs. Witchingham.

"Yes," said Mr. Witchingham. "The children would like to see a big, big, jack-o'-lantern when they come trick-or-treating."

"Let's go out to Farmer McDonald's today," said Mrs. Witchingham. "We can look in his pumpkin patch for a big pumpkin."

At Farmer McDonald's farm, Mrs. Witchingham asked, "Do you have a big, big pumpkin?"

"Yes," said Farmer McDonald. "On top of the hill there is a big one. It must weigh two hundred pounds!"

"Two hundred pounds!" exclaimed Mrs. Witchingham. "Two hundred pounds!" exclaimed Mr. Witchingham.

Mr. and Mrs. Witchingham and Farmer McDonald walked to the top of the hill. There was the pumpkin!

It looked as big and round as a setting sun! And it was as orange as an orange-colored crayon.

"It's the biggest pumpkin I've ever seen!" exclaimed Mrs. Witchingham. "May I buy it?"

"Yes," said Farmer McDonald.

"How will we get it into town?" asked Mr. Witchingham. "I don't think it can fit into our small car."

"I'll think of something," said Mrs. Witchingham.

"I will not hire a moving van," said Mr. Witchingham.

"I do not have a truck," said Farmer McDonald.

"How will we get it down the hill?" asked Mr. Witchingham.

"I'll get my wheelbarrow," said Farmer McDonald. "But I won't wheel it into town. That's too far."

Farmer McDonald got his wheelbarrow and wheeled the pumpkin down the hill.

They could not push the pumpkin through the door of the car. They could not fit the pumpkin into the trunk of the car.

"Can we put it on top of the car and tie it down?" asked Mrs. Witchingham.

"No," said Mr. Witchingham. "It is too heavy." "Well, then," said Mrs. Witchingham, "I will make it light!"

And she did! She cut off the top. The top fitted into the car.

She took the pulp and seeds out
of the pumpkin.
She saved some of the pulp and seeds.
Some she fed to Farmer McDonald's
chickens.

She worked and worked until there
was nothing left but a shell!
Then she carved a nose and eyes
and a smiling mouth.
"There!" she said. "I'm done!"

Farmer McDonald and
the Witchinghams

tied the pumpkin shell on the car.

The Witchinghams drove home.
Along the way, people laughed
and waved.

On Halloween the trick-or-treaters
came from near and far to see
the big, big, jack-o'-lantern.
And Mr. and Mrs. Witchingham served
roasted pumpkin seeds to all those
who came to admire the jolliest
jack-o'-lantern they had ever seen.

Fall Poems

Down!

Down! Down!
Yellow and brown!
The leaves are falling
All over the town.

KAREN GONNELLO, Age 7

Fall is Here

Summer is gone.
Wind has come.
Fall is here
For everyone.

ELYSE LEVINE, Age 5

Fall

When the once-warm air now turns
cool.
When the once-green leaves turn a
deep golden brown,
When these same leaves fall down to
the ground,
This is fall, all around.

TONY KNAPP, Age 12

Autumn

The chilling winds of autumn
Bring color to the trees.
The frost is on the pumpkin
And chilly is the breeze.

Leaves drifting downward,
Pine needles on the ground,
A full moon overhead,
Winter comes round.

LAWRENCE GEISMAR, Age 7

Trees

Trees do just as they please.
I can't throw papers on the ground,
But they throw their leaves all
around.
Trees just do as they please.

STEPHEN NEVILLE, Age 4

Poem of Seasons

Summer's over, now it's fall,
Just the nicest time of all.
As we jump, hop, and play,
Squirrels gather nuts and run away.

Maple seeds swirl around.
We try to catch them as they fall to
the ground.
We pick apples from the trees and
put them in pails.
Now you know how autumn feels.

JENNIFER LESSER, Age 7

Leaves

I like leaves,
All kinds of leaves—
Gay little red leaves,
Sad little brown leaves,
Happy little green leaves,
Sunny little yellow leaves.

DEBBIE LEWIS, Age 10

Halloween Sounds

BERTHA R. HUDELSON

I heard some steps
On our front walk
And loudly whispered
Mixed-up talk.

I heard some clicks
On our windowpane—
The softest of clicks
As gentle as rain.

I heard some taps
On our front door,
Some tiny taps
And nothing more.

I heard some laughs
Float through the air.
I opened the door—
And nothing was there!

A Halloween Poem

When witches fly
Across the sky,
And bats and cats seem to
Pass you by,
And the moaning wind
Is in your ear,
You will know that
Halloween is here.

KELLIE RAY, Age 11

Halloween is Coming

Halloween is almost here,
And everyone is full of fear,
With witches, bats, and also ghosts,
And scarecrows on big tall posts.

ANNETTE SEREVICZ, Age 12

Ready for Halloween

AILEEN FISHER

Pumpkins and all,
big ones and small,
apples and pumpkins
and cornstalks in fall . . .

Corn standing tall,
apples and all,
pumpkins to gather
and set on the wall . . .

Cornstalks to lean,
yellow and green,
bright orange pumpkins
with apples between . . .

Apples between,
shined to a sheen . . .
everything's ready
to greet Halloween!

The Witching Hour

VIRGINIA MORAN EVANS

Giants and pixies, dwarfs, and
gnomes,
    All in plainest sight,
Dance upon the purple fields
    Just before the night.

The flying steeds the fairies ride
    Wear lanterns in their tails,
Ogres stride across the hills,
    Brownies fill the vales.
You can see them, if you look
    Just before the night—
Giants, brownies, ogres, gnomes,
    All in plainest sight.

Thanksgiving Poems

When It's Thanksgiving

AILEEN FISHER

The kitchen's full of the nicest sounds:
of pans, and ladles stirring,
of bubbly pots, and kettles on,
and spoons and beaters whirring.

The kitchen's full of the finest smells:
of dinner in the making,
of turkey on, and cranberries,
and pumpkin pies a-baking.

The kitchen gives it all away
as sure as you are living—
you never have to look at all
to know when it's Thanksgiving.

Turkey Thoughts

KEVIN O'HARA

I wonder how
a turkey feels
upon Thanksgiving Day.

Is he proud
of how he looks
while on the dinner tray?

All golden brown
with stuffing filled
as if he'd like to say,

"Eat hearty, folks
and enjoy me.
I'd rather end this way."

Things I'm Thankful For

DOROTHY WALDO PHILLIPS

I'm thankful for my shaggy dog,
And for my funny speckled frog;
For candied popcorn that you munch;
For crispy crackers that you crunch;
For baseball bats and brand-new leaves;
For all those shirts that have no sleeves.

I'm thankful for electric trains,
And for the Christmas candy canes;
For roller coasters at the fairs;
For when they let me slide the stairs;
For baby robins in the spring;
For pop-up toasters going BING.

I'm thankful for my secret caves;
For bathtubs full of splashy waves;
For every rainbow, snake, and snail;
For doubly-bubbly ginger ale;
For birthday cakes and little stars;
For Saturdays and trolley cars.

I'm thankful for the sea and sand;
For teachers who can understand;
For glowworms, zoos, and jelly beans;
For pussy willows, kings, and queens;
For happy hoptoads by the lake;
For puddles, popsicles, and cake.

I'm thankful for my water wings;
For trunks all full of dress-up things;
For autumn leaves all crispy red;
For all the time I'm out of bed;
For those who cut my faults in half;
For grownups who can make me laugh.

But most of all I want to thank
The two on whom I always bank.
For sharing all my fears and fun;
For being close when day is done;
For all the thoughtful things you do;
My thanks, dear parents, go to you.

Finger Play

Five plump turkeys are we.

We sat all night in a tree.

But when cook came around
(marching motion)

We couldn't be found,
(say slowly, softly)

That's why we are here,
you see!

Halloween Games

Jack-o'-lantern

A large pumpkin with a grinning face and a medium-sized opening is placed in front of the children. Each person is allowed two throws with a bean bag. Children earn points by throwing the bean bag into the top opening of the pumpkin.

Witch and Cats

The person who is the Witch kneels on the floor with his back to the other players and pretends to stir a broth. The players arrange themselves in a line, changing their positions occasionally so Witch can't tell who they are. The Witch calls, "Number 5 tell me who you are." The player fifth in line says, in a disguised voice, "I'm a big black cat, me-ow." The Witch guesses, saying for example, "Cat Helen, come stir my broth." If correct, they change places.

A Game for Halloween

Draw the pattern of the double pumpkin, Figure 1. Cut and color one double pumpkin for each person who is to play the game. Bend a piece of wire about 2 inches long as shown in Figure 2. Push the loop through the slit in the top of the pumpkin and fasten the ends inside with Scotch tape. Draw the face. Fold the pumpkin on the dotted lines. Paste tabs together and paste to the green-paper leaf, Figure 3.

Make a fishing pole from a stick about 2 feet long with a string and a wire hook. Place all the pumpkins on a brown-paper circle and let the children fish for the pumpkins.

Black Cats and Witches

Make a number of black cats and orange pumpkins from construction paper. You should have at least five of one kind or the other for each player. Hide them in hard-to-find places around the room. Divide the players into two teams, the Black Cats and the Witches, with a leader for each team. Explain that the cats are to find only black cats and the witches are to find only pumpkins. At a signal, the players start hunting. The leader does not hunt with her team. She picks up the cats or the pumpkins that the members find. If a cat finds a black cat, she "meows" until the Black Cat leader comes and picks it up. If a witch finds a pumpkin, she lets out a witch-like shriek until her leader picks it up. Amid much meowing, shrieking, and laughter one team will finish just ahead of the other.

Games For Thanksgiving

Mayflower Game

Everyone sits in a circle. The leader (an adult) begins by saying, "When we came over on the Mayflower, we brought an ax to fell some trees." The leader starts a chopping motion with the left hand, and the players copy the motion.

All left hands continue to chop as the leader says, "When we came over on the Mayflower, we brought a broom to sweep the hearth." All right hands sweep as left hands continue to chop.

Feet move up and down for "shoes to tread the soil." Eyes dart from side to side for "a book to read." Heads rock back and forth for "a cradle to rock the baby." The actions continue throughout the game.

Corn Planting Relay

Divide the players into equal teams. Each team counts off: one—two, one—two, and so on. The "ones" are called Pilgrims and the "twos" are called Turkeys. In front of each team, place a long narrow strip of paper (masking tape will do). Mark two small circles on the strip. The first Pilgrim in each team is handed a spoon and a pie pan containing two corn kernels. At a signal, those Pilgrims begin planting corn along the row —one kernel to a circle—using only the spoon. When they finish, they hurry back to the Turkeys who are next in line. Spoon in one hand, pan in the other, the Turkeys must scoop up the corn and put it back into the pan. The only help they may have is a nudge of the nose. The Turkeys rush back to the second set of Pilgrims who must set out to replant the corn. This continues until all players have had a turn. The first team to finish wins. Their prize of corn chips should be shared with the losers in true Thanksgiving spirit.

Turkey Wishbone

For this game you will need a stool and four rubber canning-jar rings. The stool is placed upside down in the center of the room with its legs in the air. Each two legs represent a turkey wishbone. A player is given four rubber rings to try and encircle a wishbone, at the same time making a wish. If he succeeds, his wish comes true. To keep things moving, if there are more than six or seven players, use two stools or chairs and more rubber rings.

Stuff the Turkey

Make a turkey from a heavy brown grocery bag. Turn the top half down inside. Crimp and staple the folded edge to reduce the size of the opening. Push in the corners to round out the body. Stuff two small paper bags half-full with newspapers. Twist into drumsticks and add frilled paper booties—the kind a well-dressed Thanksgiving turkey wears. Glue the drumsticks upright to opposite sides of the body. For "bread stuffing" balls, wad up half-sheets of newspaper and wrap them with white tissue. The players will take turns tossing the stuffing into the turkey from a distance of four to five feet.

Crafts With Leaves

Fabric-leaf Mobile

Glue colorful and different fabrics to both sides of several pieces of heavy paper. Cut leaves from this. Tie a string on each leaf. Suspend the leaves from a small branch. Hang where the leaves will catch the breeze and flutter.

Fall Trees

Cut from brown construction paper the trunk and branches of a tree. Paste on a light-colored sheet.

Use bits of tissue of several colors for leaves on the tree.

Leaf Shapes

Bring a little fall into the classroom. Collect several well-shaped leaves and trace them on brightly colored construction paper. Cut out the paper leaves and cut each down the middle "vein." Place on black paper. Then cut two or three side "veins," and move the pieces apart just a bit to form a whole leaf, like a jigsaw puzzle. Do not cut too many parts. The black paper showing through will be the "veins." Paste down the pieces.

You can put several colors, sizes, and shapes on your black paper.

Fall Place Mat and Coaster

Stack three pieces of plastic food wrap about fifteen inches long on a piece of clean paper. Do not use newspaper. Arrange dried leaves on top of this. Stack three more layers of wrap on the leaves. Cover with a piece of clean paper and iron with a warm iron. (Do not touch the plastic wrap directly with the iron.) The wrap will melt together. Trim the edges.

Make the coaster the same way, using a small circle shape.

Puppets

Halloween Stick Puppet

From black construction paper cut a dress, arms, hat, and shoes for a witch. From pink construction paper cut hands and a head to add to the body. Add a black nose, mouth, and eyes to the head. Use small strips of yellow tissue paper for the hair. After the witch is completed, paste to a stick to make a puppet.

Scarecrow Bag Puppet

Stuff a small paper bag half-full of paper. Twist and tape the bag shut. This is the head. Cut features from paper, and glue on. Use a large bag for the body. Roll a piece of brown paper into a tube. Use this for the arms. Cut an *X* in each side of the bag and push the arms through. Glue the arms in place. Make a small cut in the bottom of the bag and push and glue the head into this. Make straw from thin strips of yellow construction paper. Glue this into the arms, around the neck and on the head as hair. Cut patches from paper and glue to the body.

Crafts

Pumpkin Mosiac From Leaves

Cut brightly colored fall leaves into small pieces. On a piece of colored paper draw the shape and face of a large pumpkin. Glue the small pieces of leaves close together on the pumpkin shape.

Cut out the pumpkin and glue it to another piece of colored paper.

Pine Cone Mouse

If you can find an unopened pine cone, one with the scales still tightly closed, you can turn it into a little mouse. Use white glue to attach two scales from another pine cone for ears. Use whole cloves for eyes and nose. A long piece of yarn or cord makes a tail.

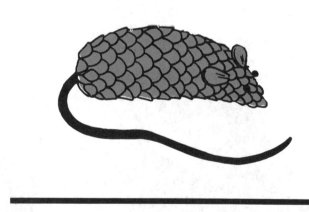

Weather Wheel

Cut paper clouds, snowflakes, raindrops, and a sun—or whatever symbols represent your climate. Arrange them around the inside edge of a paper plate and glue them to the plate. Cut an arrow from paper. Fasten it to the center of the plate with a two-pronged brass fastener.

At the plate's top, punch a hole and string a piece of yarn through it. Hang it up. You can now show the weather each day on your wheel.

Halloween Crafts

Jingle Ghost

Cut a ghost shape from the side of a plastic bottle. Punch eyes in the ghost with a paper punch. With a needle and thread, poke a hole in the bottom of the ghost, string a small bell on the thread, and tie the ends of the thread together.

Hang several ghosts on strings where people walk during the Halloween season. The wind will flutter the ghosts, and the bells will jingle.

Pumpkin-ghost House

Cut a spooky looking house with several stories from a piece of black paper. Cut several windows and a door and fold them back. Glue the house to a piece of blue paper. Add a yellow paper moon. Cut the cups from an egg carton and paint with orange tempera paint. Make faces on the pumpkins with a black marker. Add green yarn stems. Glue the pumpkins in the windows. Make a ghost from a piece of tissue and glue in the door.

On-Off Pumpkin

Fold a 1-foot strip of orange construction paper into three parts. Cut sides of paper to form a pumpkin, but do not cut folds. Open the paper out and cut eyes, nose, and mouth in the center section. Cover the inside of the top pumpkin with yellow construction paper, and the bottom one with black. Fold again, with the center section facing you. Glue on a stem made from green paper. Add lines with black felt marker to outline the pumpkin and add character. Fold so that the yellow paper shows through the features when the pumpkin is supposed to be turned "on," with the black showing when it is turned "off."

Masks

Cereal Box and Fabric Masks

Cut top and back off a cereal box. Cover the rest of box with glue. Smooth a piece of fabric onto box. The bottom of the box becomes the top of the mask. Cut out eyes, nose, and mouth. Outline features with contrasting fabrics. Glue on yarn hair. Fasten on a yarn tie at the sides of the mask.

Box Masks

Find a cardboard box that will fit nicely over your head. Mark the right places for the nose, eyes, and mouth. Cut these out very carefully.

Paint the whole box with poster paint. When dry, add details such as eyebrows, hair, ears, freckles, and whiskers. Curled paper, yarn, bits of fur, scouring pads, and steel wool all can be used for hair. Pipe cleaners can be used for antennae or feelers.

For a nose, you may use half a rubber or plastic ball. A long pointed nose can be made from a construction paper cone. A cardboard tube pasted on the box also makes a wonderful nose. Make whiskers using a few toothpicks or a few broom straws.

You may want to make an animal mask. Add an animal's nose and ears. What kind of a box mask will you make?

Newspaper Mask

Fold two sheets of newspaper about four inches from the center. Crease and glue the ends together. Cut out eyeholes. Trim with construction paper and marking pen.

Crafts

Branch Goblins

Paint a small branch a bright color. Cut a head from a double thickness of heavy paper. Cover this with one layer of pasted paper. Slip the head on the branch and glue in place. Paint the face.

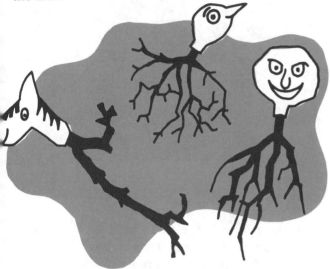

Paper-Bag Jack-o'-Lantern

Stuff a paper bag with paper. Twist and glue the top in a stem shape. Using tempera, paint the stem green and the jack-o'-lantern orange. Cut features from black paper and leaves from green paper. Glue in place.

Pumpkin Place Cards

Paint a buckeye (horse chestnut) with orange tempera. Add a small piece of yarn for a stem. Make a face on the pumpkin with a black crayon, felt-tipped pen, or paint. Glue this to a small card. Add some shredded green paper or yarn for grass around the pumpkin.

Halloween Owl

To make this owl face, cut a large circle for the head from brown construction paper. To make eyes, cut two circles from black construction paper and paste onto two larger white circles. Cut a diamond shape from orange construction paper and fold it in half, forming a triangle for the beak. Cut large eyebrows from yellow construction paper. Paste all these shapes on a piece of bright construction paper and watch your shapes turn into an owl face.

Turkey Crafts

Shape Turkey

You will need construction paper of several colors.

From different colors cut circles of about 7 inches, 6½ inches, 4 inches, and 2½ inches. Cut feet for the turkey to match the color of largest circle. Place circles as shown. Cut neck. Use one of the smallest circles for the face and cut nose and eyes. Paste to a full-sized darker sheet.

Turkey

Cut out a section of the rim of a paper plate. With cutout at bottom, draw turkey's head and body with crayons or markers. Form legs and feet from straightened-out paper clips or pipe cleaners. Tape top of each leg to back of plate. Bend legs slightly until turkey stands by itself.

An Apple Turkey

Draw patterns for turkey's head and tail. Cut from construction paper. Color the tail with bright colors. Cut a slit across the apple to hold the tail. Cut a slit for the head. Your turkey will need three toothpick legs in order to stand.

Color the cat.

Color the turkey.

Winter

Ask your children these questions:

When you get up in the morning, how can you tell whether it snowed the night before?

Carol was walking in the snow with her father. Her father said, "A man and his dog walked here before us." He did not see the man or the dog. How did he know this?

It is possible to go fishing in the winter?

What happens when you try to run on an icy sidewalk?

When snowflakes fall on you, do they hurt? What do they feel like?

Do you see any birds in the winter?

Why don't animals need coats in the winter?

Would you rather live where it never snows or gets cold, or where it snows in winter and gets very cold? Why?

Describe each object.
Tell where you might play with each.
Create stories using each object.
Role play the activities.

Connect the picture on the left to the matching picture on the right by drawing a line.

Connect the picture on the left to the matching picture on the right by drawing a line.

Circle the winter pictures.

Circle the winter pictures.

Snowflakes

YVONNE ALTMANN

A snowflake is made of tiny crystals of ice.
Go outside when it snows.
Let some snowflakes fall on your snowsuit.
Take a magnifying glass.
Look at the snowflakes.
You will find that no two will look alike.
You may find just part of a snowflake.
You will find that perfect snowflakes have six points.
You are lucky if you find one perfect snowflake.
Many snowflakes are not perfect because they are broken as they fall through the air.
Many snowflakes are not perfect because parts of the snowflake melt.

Snowflakes are formed in the clouds.
Raindrops are formed in the clouds.
Snowflakes are not frozen raindrops.
Snowflakes are water vapor changed to ice at once.
It takes cold weather to make water vapor freeze.

Water vapor is water in the air that comes from the earth.
The sun warms the water on the ground, in the ocean, or in the lake.
The water vapor goes up into the air.
The warm air which carried the water vapor up into the sky meets cold air.
The cold air turns the water vapor into tiny drops.
Many, many of these droplets make a big cloud.
When the weather is very, very cold the water vapor turns into snowflakes.

The snowflakes fall to the ground from a cloud.
They make a soft fluffy covering over the ground.
The snowflakes are so fluffy because there are many pockets of air between them.
The air caught in the layer of snow makes the snow a good blanket.
Sometimes animals bury themselves in the snow to keep warm.
Snow blankets help keep young plants from freezing.

Let some snowflakes fall into a dish.
Place the dish of snow in the sun.
The sun will melt the snow.
The snow will turn into water.
The sun will warm the water.
The water will go up into the air as water vapor.
The water vapor will freeze and come down as snowflakes.

The Three Wishes

JANE R. HOWARD

Once upon a time there were three sisters. They lived in the village of Kringle.

Maria, the youngest, was a weaver. She worked her shuttle far into the night, barely providing shelter and food for herself and her two lazy sisters.

But it had been a fortnight since her faithful loom had broken. Oh, how she yearned for a new loom, for she had promised cloth to the towns-people for the holidays.

Elsa, the oldest sister, grumbled. She loved nothing better than to eat. She swallowed the last mouthful of the porridge Maria had prepared. "Only seven days to Christmas," she whined, "and whatever shall we have for our Christmas dinner?"

Louisa, the middle sister, pouted. She dreamed only of diamonds and rubies and emeralds. "Only seven days to Christmas," she complained, "and what gift can I expect?"

Maria, the youngest, sighed and fetched a log for the fire which was dying. The moment she laid it on, a fairy appeared on the hearth. The Christmas Fairy!

At once, she placed three gold pieces before each sister, saying, "It is seven days until Christmas. Use my golden gifts with care, and I shall grant you three wishes. But, woe unto you if you use them foolishly." So saying, she vanished.

The next morning, Elsa, the oldest, heard a knock at the door. When she opened it, there stood an old man sorely in need of a warm coat. The wind blew chill, and the old man shivered.

Elsa thought of the gold pieces in her pocket, enough to buy him a coat of wool. But she sent him away.

Again she heard a knock. This time there stood a peddler loaded with Christmas pastries and goodies. Elsa's mouth began to water and, before she knew it, she had spent two of her gold pieces, one for strawberry tarts and one for frosted gingerbread. Elsa meant to save the third. But then she saw the peppermint sticks.

No sooner had she licked her tongue across the red-and-white stripes than into her right hand sprang a pudding bursting with figs and, into her left, another plump with dates. At first she was delighted and fell to eating. But the more she ate, the larger grew the puddings. And, try as she might, she could not shake them loose from her hands. They were stuck fast.

Louisa, the middle sister, had risen with the sun to set out for the village square. On her way, she came upon an old man sorely in need of a warm coat. The wind blew chill, and the old man shivered.

Louisa thought of the gold pieces in her leather pouch, enough to buy him a coat of wool. But she pushed him aside and hurried along.

She paused at the door of the jeweler's shop to gaze at the ring she had so often admired. And, before she knew it, she had lifted the latch and let herself in.

With pleasure, the shopkeeper showed her the ring.

"One gold piece?" she inquired.

"Three," he replied.

"Two, perhaps?"

"Three," he insisted.

Remembering the fairy's warning, Louisa meant to save her third coin. But the lovely blue sapphire beckoned.

"Three," she agreed.

No sooner had she slipped the ring onto her finger than there appeared upon her head a crown, encrusted with jewels. At first she was overjoyed. But her head fell to one side, for the crown was exceedingly heavy. And, try as she might, she could not remove it. It was stuck fast. Frantic, the middle sister hastened homeward.

Maria, seeing the plight of her two sisters, went out to seek help. In the drifting snow she met an old man sorely in need of a warm coat. The wind howled; the old man shivered.

Quickly, Maria placed her own cloak around the trembling shoulders. "If my loom were not broken, old man, I would weave you warm cloth for a coat."

She thought of her gold pieces. With them she planned to buy a new loom to weave cloth for the townspeople to buy.

The old man shivered and rubbed his poor hands together.

"Old man," she said, "you must have a warm coat. Come with me."

No coat could be had for less than the three gold pieces. But Maria paid them gladly. She helped the old man into his new coat and led him to the warmth of the cottage. As they entered, the Christmas Fairy appeared.

She placed a wreath of holly on Maria's head. "You used your gold pieces well," she said. "Now I shall grant you three wishes."

At this, Louisa moaned dreadfully and tugged at her crown, while Elsa leaped about, trying to be rid of the wretched puddings.

Now, despite their lazy and foolish ways, Maria still loved her two sisters dearly. So, for her first wish, she asked that Louisa be free of the heavy crown, her head once more erect. And her second wish was that Elsa be free of the monstrous puddings, her hands again useful.

No sooner had she spoken than crown and puddings disappeared. With cries of joy, the two sisters threw themselves at Maria's feet, vowing, "Never again will we be so foolish. Or selfish. Or greedy. Or lazy."

The fairy turned to Maria. "You have only one wish left, my dear. What shall it be?"

"Oh, Christmas Fairy," Maria said, "a loom, so I may weave."

And, in a twinkling, a new loom stood in place of the old. Upon this loom Maria wove cloth more splendid than anyone in Kringle had ever seen.

Christmas Day was a time of joy and sharing for the three sisters. And, ever after, they lived happily— and much more wisely.

The Ninth Reindeer

JULIET EARLE WELTON

The little man in the fur-trimmed red suit hurried on, his fur collar pulled up, his fur hat pulled down. He didn't wish to give Jack Frost a chance to do any nipping. All you could see were two twinkling eyes and a cherry-red nose framed in white fur.

The gray sky opened and out billowed swirls of snow feathers that whirled around until the little man's red suit was covered and he looked like a walking snowman. He hoped that he could find the way to Great Rock. It had been years since his last trip when he had chosen Dasher and Dancer, Prancer and Vixen, Comet and Cupid, Donner and Blitzen. And now he was about to pick another deer to help pull his sleigh.

The snowbirds had flown ahead into the heart of the forest carrying the news that

> Santa Claus is on his way
> To pick a deer
> To pull his sleigh.

The little man knew that most of the deer would be gathered at Great Rock, but he was sure that Fleetfoot would have sent several deer into the forest to watch for Santa.

As he tramped on, it became harder and harder to follow the path. Every now and then he would stop as if undecided as to which way to go. When he reached the center of the forest the road divided into two. Now he was really puzzled. He stopped, not knowing which road to take.

Out of the snow mist he caught sight of a prancing deer. His head was held proudly, and he wore a great spread of antlers on top. He ran with such swiftness that the little man watched him in admiration.

Santa—for by now you have guessed who he was—gave a shrill whistle. The deer stopped in surprise and walked over to Santa. "My friend, I seem to be lost. Can you show me the way to Great Rock?" asked the snowman.

"You just follow the road you are on," said the deer, tossing back his head. "I can't take the time to show you as I must practice my 'runs', so that when Santa comes along he will see how swift I am and choose me to be the ninth reindeer to pull his sleigh. I guess you are on your way to Great Rock to see Santa make his choice."

"Yes, I am; thank you for your directions," said the snow-covered man, and started again on his way.

The road he took wandered around and around, until he found himself going in circles. He was lost again. How would he ever reach Great Rock?

Suddenly, out of the whirling snowflakes, he spied a young deer, scampering along, rolling a snowball with his little black nose.

"Hello, there," said Santa. "May I bother you long enough to ask the way to Great Rock? I think I am lost."

The young deer stopped rolling his snowball and trotted over to the man's side.

"Yes, I'll be glad to tell you. But let me go along and show you the way, so you won't miss the road again. You must be a stranger here, not to know the way to Great Rock."

"I don't want to interfere with your snowball rolling," said the man.

"Oh, I can roll my snowball any time," said the scampering deer. "I am in the woods to show Santa the way if he should get lost, but as he hasn't come along I will take you to Great Rock and then come back to wait for him."

They started off together and as they walked along the young deer told his new friend that Santa was coming again to the forest to choose a ninth reindeer to help pull his sleigh, and that he was due to arrive that very day.

"Are there many deer waiting for him?" asked the little man.

"Yes, there is great excitement in the forest as no one knows what kind of a deer Santa is looking for this time. The last time he was here, the eight deer he chose were each chosen for something special.

Dasher for strength;
Dancer for gaiety;
Prancer for alertness;
Vixen for pertness;
Comet for speed;
Cupid for gentleness;
Donner for greatness;
Blitzen for brightness.

So we are wondering who will be chosen today."

They walked on in silence. When they reached Great Rock the young deer stopped at the edge of the clearing but his new friend walked over to Fleetfoot and patted him. Fleetfoot spoke to the snowman like an old friend.

"Well, Santa, welcome back. The herd was gathered here for you to make your choice," said Fleetfoot.

The young deer's eyes opened with surprise as he heard Fleetfoot and saw his friend brush the snow from his jacket, so that the snowman suit became a Santa Claus suit.

Why, his snow friend was Santa himself, who had been lost in the woods, and he had brought him to Great Rock.

Santa looked all the deer over. Finally, he stepped up on Great Rock and said:

"On my way to Great Rock, twice I was lost in the forest. Even with directions I couldn't find my way in the snow until a young deer gave up his game of 'roll the snowball' and was kind enough to bring me here. I might still be tramping around in the woods except for his kind thoughtfulness.

"So this scampering deer, whom I will name Scamper, is my choice. Scamper, I choose you as the ninth reindeer to pull my sleigh.

"My choice of a ninth deer is very important. When I selected my first eight reindeer, I picked them for strength, speed, brightness, and many other fine traits; but now I am to choose the one who is going to lead them, and I think kindness should lead us all.

"Scamper, I choose you to draw my sleigh.

It was your kindness that showed me the way."

A Runaway Snowball

MARION L. BARROWS

One morning in March, Tommy jumped out of his bed and ran to the window.

"Snow!" he cried.

Everything he saw, except the duckpond at the foot of the hill, sparkled in white.

Looking across white lawns, white hills, and white window sills, Tommy planned, "Today, I am going to make a giant snowman. I'll start it at the old apple tree halfway up the hill."

"Breakfast," called Tommy's mother and Tommy had to hurry.

Right after breakfast Tommy carried his dishes to the sink for his mother. "May I go out now and make a giant snowman? May I, Mother?"

"Yes, but one just your size would be nice," smiled his mother.

Once outside Tommy thought only of his plans. His big brother had taught him how to roll snowballs and a giant snowball was step one in making a giant snowman.

"Crunchie, crunchie, crunch!" the crushed snow called after him as he ran to the hill.

Tommy stopped at the foot of the old apple tree and scooped up a double handful of snow in his red mittens just as he had planned.

The mittens were special because his grandmother had made them just for him. However, they were a bit too large.

When Tommy threw the hard-pressed ball into the snow, one red mitten came off.

Tommy picked it up saying, "I'd cry if I lost you."

Then he went on with his plan to roll the snowball uphill first, then, when it got too big to push, to let it roll down by itself.

Tommy got behind the ball and pushed. He was careful to keep it round because his brother had said, "The rounder the ball, the easier it rolls."

Tommy's ball grew larger and larger. Tommy pushed and pushed. But, although the big ball of snow was nice and round, it became harder and harder to push.

Suddenly Tommy's foot slipped. A red mitten jumped off as he fell deep into the soft snow.

The big snowball stopped going up and began to come down. It rolled right over Tommy.

It captured his red mitten and rolled with it down the hill.

Tommy jumped up and chased it. All he wanted now was to get his mitten back.

Below the rolling snowball he saw the apple tree, and below the apple tree the open blue waters of the duckpond.

The runaway snowball with Tommy's mitten was headed for the pond.

"Stop that snowball, tree! Stop it!" yelled Tommy.

"Piff!" The giant snowball struck the tree and was changed like magic into a tiny snowstorm.

When the snowstorm was over, all that was left was a white pancake on the tree and a little red mitten.

Tommy picked up the red mitten and said, "Thank you," to the tree.

The Valentine's Day Hero

ANN DEVENDORF

Buster, the dog, sat under the table in the kitchen while his owners, Nan and John, ate breakfast.

"Today is Valentine's Day," said Grandmother.

"I have my valentines ready to take to school," said Nan with a happy smile. She added, "Giving and getting valentines is fun."

"Yes," said John with a grin. "I am giving a lot of funny valentines."

Buster knew it was time for John and Nan to leave for school. He knew he would have to stay in the house. He would not have any fun.

Buster watched as Nan and John put on their jackets and earmuffs and mittens. He got out from under the table. "Maybe I can sneak out with them," he thought.

"Please hold Buster," said John to Grandmother. "I think he wants to follow us. Sometimes I cannot chase him home. Sometimes he is a pest."

"Yes," said Grandmother. "He can be a pest." She took hold of Buster's collar.

Buster did not like being held. After John and Nan ran out the door, Buster lay on the floor. He put his chin on the floor.

Then Grandmother ran to the door and opened it. She called, "Nan! John! Come back! You forgot your valentines!"

Then she said, "They did not hear me. What shall I do? I cannot run and catch them and I do not have the car today."

Buster jumped to his feet. He barked.

"Buster," said Grandmother, "you could catch them. You could carry the valentines!"

Grandmother put the valentines in a bag. She tied the bag to Buster's collar. "Run," she said to Buster. "Go after Nan and John!"

Buster streaked out the door. He bounded after Nan and John. "Stop! Stop!" he barked when he was near them.

"Buster!" said John in surprise.

"What's tied to your collar?" asked Nan.

She ran to Buster and took the bag. She looked into it. "Our valentines!" she said. "We forgot our valentines and you brought them to us."

"Good dog," said John. "Good Buster. You saved the day for us. You kept Valentine's Day a happy day!"

"You are a hero!" said Nan. "A Valentine's Day hero!"

Buster wagged and wagged and wagged his tail in happiness. Then he turned and bounded for home. He was no pest. He was a hero!

The Lost Whistle of Dooly O'Day

KAY JONES

Dooly O'Day was an Irish boy who liked to whistle. Now this boy made the grandest sound that ever was heard in the whole village of Ballybankie. When Dooly started whistling, the cows gave the richest milk, the hens laid the biggest eggs, and the sheep grew the finest wool in all that green countryside. And if there happened to be a bit of an argument among the neighbors, it was: "Get Dooly O'Day, quick! His whistling will soon put an end to the quarreling."

And so it did. Nobody could listen to that sweet music for long without a smile and a dance.

Then came a day that Dooly would always remember. It started out just fine as the boy marched down the road toward the village post office to buy stamps for his mother. Soon he saw three cows in a pasture and halted to whistle them a tune. A while later, after he had passed tiny Kerry's Pond, he saw something sparkly lying in the grass.

Dooly picked the small thing up. "Tis a magic harp!" he cried. "I'll keep it to bring me good luck."

When at last he reached the post office, he saw a card in the window. Dooly read it twice: "Lost, one gold harp. If found, please leave on the tree stump beside Kerry's Pond."

Quickly drawing the harp from his pocket, Dooly stared down at it. So the owner wanted it back—the leprechaun of Kerry's Pond.

After getting the stamps, Dooly turned toward home. It seemed no time at all before he saw the tree stump. Was the leprechaun nearby? Was he hunting for his harp? Dooly thrust his hand into his pocket and fingered the small thing. He stepped into the bracken. The next minute he stepped back on the road.

"No," he said, "I'll not return the harp. Finders keepers."

A short time later he saw the cows again and pursed his lips to give them a tune—but no tune came forth. He blew and he blew, but not a sound could he make.

"Arrah, I've lost my whistle!" cried Dooly O'Day. "Whatever shall I do without it?"

And it was not only Dooly O'Day who missed his whistle. The entire village of Ballybankie missed it. The cows' milk was no longer the richest anywhere in the green countryside. The hens' eggs were no longer the biggest. And so thin was the sheep's wool, that it was not worth the taking.

As for the neighbors, they started arguing for the least bit of a reason. And much to his own amazement, Dooly suddenly found himself fighting with his best friend, Mike Muldoon. Rolling about the grass they were, in front of Dooly's house, punching and pummeling each other until Dooly's mother came running out.

"Enough is enough, boys," she shouted, pulling them apart. "Whatever's the matter that two good friends should be fighting like this? I can't think what's got into everybody lately. Folk arguing and fighting with one another all of a sudden. Come, Dooly, give us a tune to cheer us up."

Dooly shook his head. "There'll be no tunes from me. I've lost my whistle."

"Lost your whistle!" cried Mrs. O'Day. "Who ever heard of a boy losing his whistle? Mind you, find it soon, or we'll be in a sad way indeed."

Just one week later Dooly O'Day went back to the post office to mail his mother's letters. He took the long way round through Fiddler's Bog so he would not have to be passing the tree stump and maybe see the leprechaun waiting for his harp. The card was still in the window, and new words had been added.

Dooly read it again. "Lost, one gold harp. If found, please leave on the tree stump by Kerry's Pond." Then came the new words: "Tis sad I am without my harp."

"And tis sad I am without my whistle," said Dooly. "I must keep the harp to bring me luck. Maybe it will help me find my whistle."

After mailing the letters, Dooly turned his feet toward home. And so lost in thought was he that his feet took him where they pleased—straight along the road to Kerry's Pond. Halfway there, he drew the harp from his pocket. While feasting his eyes upon it, he kept thinking of those new words on the card: "Tis sad I am without my harp."

Now that he knew how it felt to lose something precious, Dooly was beginning to understand the leprechaun's feelings. A while later he had another thought. Swift and clear it was, darting at him out of the blue.

"Sure, I'd like to make the leprechaun happy again," he thought. "Then maybe I'd feel less sad myself."

And so it happened that when Dooly O'Day came to Kerry's Pond, he stepped into the bracken, marched himself over to the tree stump, and carefully laid the harp on top. Then he crouched down behind a thicket.

He had not long to wait. In three shakes of a cow's tail, he saw a figure no taller than a twig emerge from the grass. He was dressed all in green except for his cap which was flaming red. The small man climbed the stump and picked the harp up in both arms. Then he turned toward Dooly with a smile and a nod. The next moment he disappeared.

Dooly's heart was lighter when he straightened up. "I feel the better for letting the harp go," he thought. "There's one less to be sad now."

He set off down the road and soon came to the three cows, who nodded a greeting. "If it's a tune you're wanting, you'll not get it from me," he told them sadly. "My whistle's still lost."

To prove it, Dooly pursed his lips and blew. Then, greatly to his astonishment, the air was suddenly filled with lovely trilling as pure and musical as the sound of a thrush.

The lost whistle of Dooly O'Day had come back to him!

And it was no time at all before the whole village of Ballybankie knew it. Once again the cows gave the richest milk, the hens laid the biggest eggs, and the sheep grew the finest wool in all that green countryside. As for the neighbors, they were soon going about with happy smiles, for they knew Dooly O'Day was somewhere nearby, ready to whistle them a merry tune.

Winter Wind

MARGARET D. LARSON

The wind is a lion,
I hear him roar.
He rattles the window
And slams the door.

He whirls the snow
And piles it high.
He chases the clouds
Across the sky.

The trees feel him blow,
And they bend and sway
Right down to the earth,
To get out of his way.

He hurries past houses
And on down the street.
He howls with glee
If the rain turns to sleet.

And when all the people
Hurry and run,
The wild wind laughs
For he's having fun.

Furry Bear

A. A. MILNE

If I were a bear,
And a big bear, too,
I shouldn't much care
If it froze or snew;
I shouldn't much mind
If it snowed or friz—
I'd be all fur-lined
With a coat like his!

For I'd have fur boots
and a brown fur wrap,
And brown fur knickers
and a big fur cap.
I'd have a fur muffle-ruff
to cover my jaws,
And brown fur mittens
on my big brown paws.
With a big brown furry-down
up to my head,
I'd sleep all winter in a big fur bed.

Christmas

An early white Christmas with pine trees of snow,
A fragrance of roses and the wind blows.
Eight tiny reindeer circling around,
And old gray-haired Santa just left the ground.

A big bag of goodies thrown over his back,
He slides down each chimney although rather fat.
Then he flies through the sky and then over the moon,
And old gray-haired Santa arrives home 'bout noon.

MARTHA SMITH, Age 12

Winter Flowers

JEAN BERG

When winter winds begin to blow,
And winter snows begin to snow,
Then winter flowers begin to grow.

They hang from roofs and
    window sills;
And some folks call them icicles.

Snowflakes

Snowflakes, snowflakes
I'm glad you're coming down
On my roof and on the ground.
Snowflakes hurry down
Come as fast as you can
So that I can make
A nice snowman.

CAROLYN MORRIS, Age 5

My Snowman

I made a snowman big and tall.
He looked so brave and bold.
He did not fear the dark at all,
Nor did he mind the cold.

But yesterday I heard him say,
"Oh dear, here comes the sun!"
My snowman melted all away,
Before his feet could run.

EVELYN MOLARANA, Grade 4

Icicles

We are little icicles,
    Crying in the sun.
Can't you see our tiny tears
    Dropping one by one?

GERALDINE LEWIS, Age 12

Snow

Snow is puffy,
Snow is white,
Snow is crispy
And very light.

Snow is soft,
Snow is cold,
Snow is icy
And nice to hold.

DARREN BROWN, Age 12

Icicles

AILEEN FISHER

After a storm
the cold sun rouses
and ice-whiskers grow
on the chins of houses.

Poems

Winter Nap

MABEL WATTS

A bear is the funniest creature I've seen.
He's asleep for the winter before Halloween.
He snores through Thanksgiving and Christmas as well.
He's never had turkey, nor even a smell.

Little bears never see pumpkins or witches.
They never see frost on the puddles and ditches.
They've never gone zooming downhill on a sled,
For at half past September they're popped into bed.

Little bears never hear North Winds ablow.
They never see Christmas tree lights all aglow.
But the thing that to me seems to be the most shocking
Is to think that a bear never hangs up his stocking!

I know why a camel has one or two humps.
I know why a kangaroo jumps those big jumps.
I know why giraffes grow way, way up tall.
But why does a bear go to sleep in the fall?

Winter Holidays

JO MORRIS

Hanukkah and Christmas
Bring very special days
That happily remind us
Of loving, giving ways.

Here a tree is trimmed
And stockings hang in line,
While there with light undimmed
Menorah candles shine.

One child made a cradle,
The Blessed Babe to hold,
Another has a dreidel.
But the ancient tales are told

Of people of goodwill,
Of faithfulness and praise.
These things are with us still
In the winter holidays.

Christmas Lights

Sparkling Christmas lights
Brighten the dark nights
Like colored twinkling stars.
What a sight they are.

BOBBY BEAM, Age 8

Christmas Day

Christmas trees,
Chiming bells!
What's my present?
No one tells.

Christmas trees,
All gay and bright.
Decorated—
A lovely sight.

Go to bed,
Turn off the light.
It's Christmas Eve—
Just one more night.

We get out of bed,
All happy and gay.
We open each present,
For it's Christmas Day!

DENISE HOLLMAN, Age 8

December

December days are cold.
December days are gray.
But every year December brings
Our own Christmas Day.

GINGER HAMMETT, Age 8

Hanukkah

Why do lights for Hanukkah burn?
Every candle has its turn.

On the eighth night, bright and clear,
It is time for fun and cheer.

LIZZY ROSS, Age 8

Hanukkah

Eight long days,

We have a lot of fun.
Nine glowing candles,
With the Shamus the main one.

Spinning, spinning, spinning,
The dreidel goes so fast.
Oh, how I wonder
How long it will last.

Hanukkah, oh, Hanukkah—it is so near.
Hanukkah, oh, Hanukkah—my favorite time of year!

AMY and BARBARA CHERNOFF,
Ages 10 and 11

New Year

AUTHOR UNKNOWN

A year to be glad in,
And not to be sad in,
To gain in, to give in,
A happy new year.

New Year's Day

New Year's Day is a day
When everyone has time to play.
While parades are going by,
Marching bands highlight the sky
With the sound of cymbals going by.

KARLA SALMON, Age 8

The Calendar

The calendar hangs on the wall.
Page by page it will fall.
When it is done,
It's always fun
To run
To get another one.

ALAN BEREZIK, Age 9

Valentine's Day

Valentine's Day is full of hearts,
Valentine cakes, and valentine tarts.
Valentine cards and valentine candy
Make Valentine's Day very dandy.

HOWARD SMITH, Age 9

Valentines

I listen to you all the time,
So will you be my valentine?

KIM LIVESAY, Age 10

Abe Lincoln

The story begins with a wonderful
boy
Who lived in Kentucky, and then
Illinois.

He worked very hard, splitting logs
and rails,
Was given a talent of telling tales.

He proved as a clerk to be patient
and fair,
His honesty soon became known
everywhere.

Evenings would find him before a
log fire,
Studying hard, seeming never to
tire.

From simple beginnings, this man
so grand
Became a fine leader of our great
land.

SUSAN MOSSLER, Age 12

February

February is a time of giving,
Loving, and caring.
And, you know what?
It's for sharing!

MICAL PULLIAM, Age 9

| February | | | | | | |
S	M	T	W	T	F	S
	1	2	3	4	5	6
7	8	9	10	11	12	13
14	15	16	17	18	19	20
21/28	22/29	23	24	25	26	27

Fun With Fingers

And I made pine cones
With seeds hiding inside.
(hands for pine cone)

I am a Christmas tree
growing up tall,
(stretch)

The wind shakes
my branches,
(shake arms)

But when I first started,
I was this small.
(crouch)

And down those seeds fall,
(flutter fingers downward)

Then I grew bigger,
and had branches this wide,
(stand slowly, arms out)

To make new little pine trees
for tinsel and balls.
(point hands together for tree,
opening slowly to form ball shape)

Games

Valentine Jigsaw Puzzle

Prepare the puzzles by having one valentine and one envelope for every two players. Cut up each valentine like a jigsaw puzzle. Put the pieces into the envelope and seal it. When you play, players choose partners.

March of the Hearts

Make a large red heart for each player. Players line up in single file. Each is given a heart, which is put on the head. It is not to be touched afterwards. While someone plays the piano, now fast, now slow, the players march around the room with their hands folded over the chest. Object of the game is to see which player can keep the red heart on his head the longest. If a heart falls to the floor, that player leaves the game. Continue until only one player is left marching with his heart on his head.

Hit the Hearts

Make six hearts in different sizes. Make the smallest one about two inches across; the next, four inches; the next, six inches; the next, eight inches; the next, ten inches; and the largest, twelve inches across. Give each heart a number value, the smaller the heart, the bigger the value. For instance, the largest heart counts two points; the next largest, four points; and so on. Mark the value on each heart. Tie the hearts about twelve inches apart on a heavy cord. Stretch the cord between two chairs about eight feet apart. One player is appointed scorekeeper for the game and given pencil and paper. Players take turns hitting the hearts with six small rubber or ping-pong balls.

A Hearty Toss

Divide the players into two teams. Have a small box (heart-shaped, if possible) or a shoe box covered with red crepe paper for each team. Each player is given five candy hearts. Each player stands three feet away from the box and takes turns pitching candy hearts into his team's box. The team with the most hearts inside the box is the winner. If you have an especially good pitcher on each team, it is additional fun to have those two represent the two teams, to find the champion heart pitcher.

Breaking Heart

Cut a large heart from construction paper. Cut it in half vertically. Get two empty milk cartons. Paste half the heart on each carton. Set the two cartons on a stool so that the heart appears whole. The players in turn throw a beanbag at the heart, trying to knock it from the stool.

Blind Heart

Each player in turn is blindfolded and given a paper and crayon to draw a heart. After everyone has had a turn, give a small prize for the best heart.

January Make-it Fun

Sock Snowman

Stuff a white sock with cotton balls or cotton batting. Leaving 2 inches at the top, close the opening with a rubber band. Fold over the top of the sock for the hat. The heel of the sock will be the face. Make a scarf by tying a scrap of material underneath the heel, separating the head from the body.

Make facial features and buttons by pasting on scraps of black felt. Paste short pieces of yarn at the top of the hat for a pompon.

Snowman Mobile

Cut a two-inch, three-inch, and four-inch circle from heavy paper. Glue a piece of string down the center of the three circles, leaving a small space between them and a long end on top for hanging. Glue cotton on to cover the circles. Glue on yarn features. Make a hat from two pieces of heavy black paper, and glue onto the string. Hang where the wind will twirl it.

Button Art

Fasten two buttons together with glue, tape, or by putting them both on one strip of felt. The top button should be slightly smaller than the bottom one. Use yarn, sequins, beads, and felt to make little button people. They may be worn as pins, mounted on paper with a background scene, or hung as mobiles.

Ornament Crafts

Christmas Ornaments

Draw half a Christmas ornament on a piece of folded paper, starting and ending at the fold line. Cut this out. Trace around your pattern on a piece of bright-colored felt. Make two felt pieces from your pattern. Glue the two felt sections together. Let dry. Decorate both sides of the ornaments with pieces of colorful braids, rickrack, sequins, or other odds and ends.

Punch a hole in the top. Attach a hanger made out of gold cord or yarn.

Egg Cup Ornaments

Cut the cups from the bottom of a papier-mache egg carton. Cut designs into the sides of the cup. Using different colors, paint with tempera. String on yarn.

Ornaments

Cut cups from a papier-mache egg carton. Glue two or more together to make an ornament shape. Paint and decorate with tempera. You may also poke holes in the ornament and insert short pieces of drinking straw for decoration. To hang, poke a small hole at the top and glue in a piece of yarn.

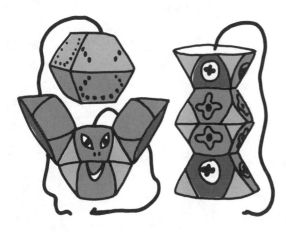

Paper-Tube Wreath

Cut the ring from the edge of a large paper plate. Paint it with tempera. Cut paper tubes into sections of various heights. Paint them contrasting colors and attach with glue.

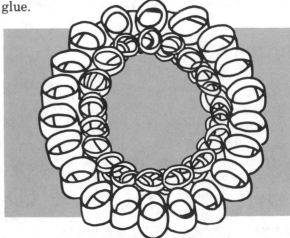

Santa Crafts

Santa Napkin Holder

To make each napkin holder, cut the Santa shape from white felt or construction paper. Next, fold a red napkin as shown. Place the Santa shape over the top side of the folded napkin and fold the extensions to the back; lap one end over the other, and glue or tape together. Add blue eyes and a red nose cut from felt or paper. Make a Santa napkin holder for each place at a Christmas party or dinner table.

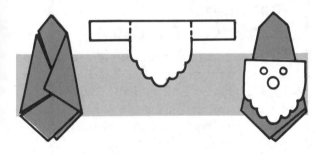

Candy-Cane Ornament

Color a red stripe one-half inch wide across the top and down one side of a white sheet of paper. Turn the paper over.

Lay a pencil across the plain white corner and roll it up in the paper toward the opposite corner. As you roll, red and white stripes will appear.

Tape down the loose corner of paper. Shake out the pencil. Roll the top of the cane around the pencil several times to form a crook. Now your candy cane is ready to go on the Christmas tree.

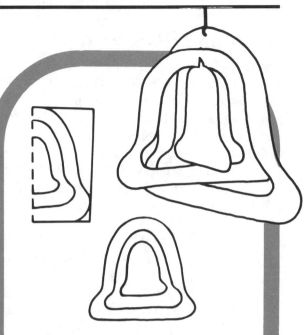

Three-in-one Bell

Glue two contrasting colors of construction paper together. Fold paper in half, and cut a bell on the fold.

Starting at the lower part of the bell, cut two additional bells, leaving one-half inch at the top not cut. Open bells. On one side of the bell cut directly to the fold. On the other side cut diagonally to the fold. Turn the bells to go in different directions.

Attach a string to the bell and hang from the ceiling, doorway, lamp, or Christmas tree.

A Santa Claus Apple

Fasten a marshmallow to the top of a big red apple with a toothpick. Use a raisin for each eye and red candy for the mouth.

Use cotton for Santa's hair, beard, and moustache. Glue them on with flour-and-water paste. Add a hat of red felt or cloth, and a black construction-paper belt.

Christmas Tree Crafts

Stand-Up Christmas Tree

Fold green construction paper in half. Draw half of a triangle-shaped tree and rectangular trunk on the fold. Cut four exactly the same size. Staple or glue at the folds. Decorate with glitter ornaments. Cut a strip of construction paper and glue or staple it into a circle. Placed in the circle, the tree will stand.

Christmas Cone Tree

Draw and cut out a large half-circle from heavy, colored construction paper, 12 inches by 18 inches. Draw four smaller half-circles on it as shown. On each of these half-circles draw a number of V-shapes about an inch apart, all pointing outward. Cut the sides of each V to form a tab.

Shape the half-circle into a cone, and staple or glue the overlap. Bend out the V-shaped tabs. Cut small paper ornaments and paste to the tabs. This tree can be made in many different sizes.

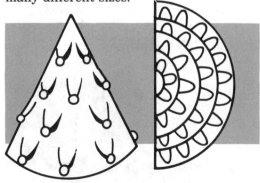

Gummed Reinforcement Cards

For each card, cut a piece of red or green construction paper 7 inches by 4½ inches. Fold in half. Stick down the reinforcements in a holiday shape. The tree is an easy one; you may want to try that first.

To each design, add the finishing touch of a star or a bow cut from a contrasting color of construction paper. Write your Christmas greeting inside.

Yarn Wreath

Cut a 2-inch wide ring from a large paper plate. Wrap the ring with bulky yarn and glue the end of the yarn in place. Glue on yarn decoration.

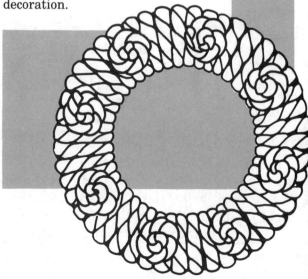

Greeting Cards

Stand-Up Greeting

Draw a bell, snowman, tree, or other seasonal figure on a piece of heavy paper. With a pencil, very lightly draw a dotted line across the middle of the paper. Starting at the middle, very carefully cut around the top half of the figure. Fold the top half back, along the dotted line, for a support. Color the card and add a greeting.

Triangle Greeting Cards

Use your imagination and a variety of colored-paper triangles to make these colorful greeting cards. Fold a piece of colored construction paper in half to make the card. Paste triangles of contrasting colors in place to form the design. Where necessary, complete the design by adding other construction-paper shapes.

Add a finishing touch by spattering white paint over the card. To spatter, dip an old toothbrush into thick white tempera, hold about 12 inches from the card, and pull the bristles of the brush against the edge of a ruler. Write your holiday greeting inside.

Holly Boy Decoration

From green construction paper, cut three large holly leaves, two medium-size holly leaves, and one small one. Also cut one large circle (for the head), two smaller circles (shoes), and nine paper-punch dots (for decorations) from red paper. Paste the leaves and circles in position as shown in the illustration to form the holly boy. Use the larger leaves for body and legs, the medium-size ones for arms, and the small one for a hat. Attach a loop of ribbon at the top for hanging the decoration.

Mr. and Mrs. Santa

Cut the cups and pillars from an egg carton. Make arms and legs from the lid of the carton. Use pillars for the heads and for Mr. Santa's hat.

Paint the faces pink and the bodies red. Add white gloves and stockings and black shoes or boots to the arms and legs. Glue movable eyes and a paper mouth to the face.

Attach all parts together with glue. The arms and legs are inserted between the two cups which form the body. Add a thread loop hanger.

Holiday Crafts

Hanukkah Mobile

Trace the outline of a small plate on a sheet of blue construction paper. Cut the circle. By cutting around and around the circle, make a spiral that is 1-inch wide.

Cut three small Stars of David from the construction paper. Punch a hole in each star. Also punch four pairs of holes through the spiral; two holes a few inches from the end of the spiral, two near the middle, two near the top, and two at the very top of the spiral.

Run a short piece of heavy black thread through each star. Attach the stars by running the thread through a pair of holes in the spiral and tying the ends together. Run a longer piece of thread through the top pair of holes in the spiral for a hanger.

Soda Straw Star of David

You need six soda straws. The plastic kind will work better and be more sturdy. You also need some strong string and a piece of thin wire to use as a needle.

First of all, you fasten a long piece of string to the wire and run it through three of the straws. Tie the string, forming a triangle with equal sides.

Now run a long piece of string through the other three straws. Before fastening them, interweave the second triangle with the first one so it forms an interwoven star. Next tie the string in the second triangle, leaving a loop to use as a hanger. A drop of white glue will hold the two triangles together.

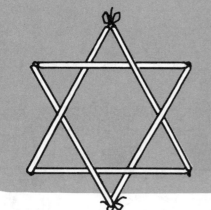

Star-of-David Mobile

Make each star from two identical triangles. Each side of the triangle must be the same length. Cut the triangles out of light cardboard. Make several stars of different sizes.

Lay one triangle on top of the other and glue or staple in place. Paint one side and sprinkle glitter on the wet paint so it will stick. When that side is dry, turn it over and paint the other side a contrasting color.

You can use coat-hanger wire for the frame of the mobile and clear fishing line to attach the stars. You will have to try several ways to balance the stars on the mobile.

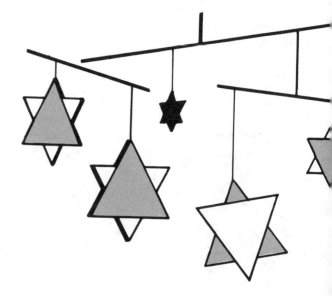

Valentines

Yarn Valentines

Fold a sheet of construction paper in half to make a card. Cut hearts from another color of paper and glue them to the front of the card. Outline the hearts with glue. Press yarn into the glue.

Write a Valentine message inside.

Apple Valentine

Cut an apple shape from red paper. Cut leaves from green paper and glue them on the apple.

Glue a black paper rectangle on the front of the apple. Glue a string border around the rectangle.

With white ink or with white liquid shoe polish applied with a toothpick, write, "An apple for my valentine."

Glue a short pipe cleaner stem on the top of the apple.

Valentine Crown

Cut a 2-inch strip of red paper long enough to fit around your head. Cut two strips of paper, 1 inch wide and 12 inches long. Fold one strip in half and make a 2-inch cut in the center of it. Glue the cut strip from one side of the headband to the other. Glue the other strip on so that the band is divided into quarters. Tuck and glue the second strip into the cut of the first. Cut a heart and glue into the center. Decorate with hearts cut from white paper.

Valentine Hat

Here is an unusual and colorful hat of hearts that you can make to wear on Valentine's Day. The only things you will need are red construction paper and a long cardboard tube from paper towels.

Starting at one end of the tube, cut ½-inch-wide strips, stopping each strip about 3 inches from the other end of the tube. Spread all the strips out slightly to make a hat which will fit your head.

Cut red construction-paper hearts and glue them all over the hat from bottom to top.

More Valentines

Stand-Up Valentines

Wrap pipe cleaners around a pencil to make springs for the bodies and legs of these animals. Twist the legs around the body. Where they join, put a spot of glue. Cut the head, eyes, ears, and feet from construction paper in heart shapes. Glue these to the pipe cleaners.

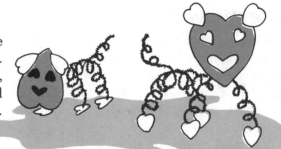

Paper Doll Valentine

Accordian-pleat a long piece of paper into folds about an inch across. With a pencil, lightly sketch half of a paper doll, being sure that the center is on a fold and that the hands come right out to the end of the paper so the dolls will be holding hands. Cut the dolls out while the paper is still folded. On the chest of each doll write a letter, for instance L-O-V-E.

If you use construction paper the dolls will stand up. Leave them partially folded and curve the end dolls toward each other.

Or cut the dolls out of white paper. Paste them on a large piece of construction paper. Print on the construction paper your message to your valentine.

Stand-Up Valentines

Make a cone from red construction paper. Glue a small plastic foam ball to the top. Decorate with pieces of paper lace doilies. Cut heart-shaped features and hair from red paper. Glue a valentine message in the doll's hand.

Punch-Dot Valentines

With a paper punch make dots from the side of a plastic bottle or heavy white paper. Trace your design on a folded piece of red paper. Glue the dots to either side of the line of the design. Write a message inside.

For February and March

Hearts and Dots

With a paper punch, punch out some dots from several colors of paper. Cut a heart from white or colored paper. Glue the paper dots on the heart in an interesting design. You could even create a picture or write a valentine message with the punched dots.

Valentine Fish Mobile

Cut four heart shapes from the sides of a plastic gallon jug. Glue other hearts cut from red construction paper to the plastic hearts so that they look like fish. Attach these with red yarn to a ring cut from the plastic jug. Also use red yarn to hang the mobile.

Fancy Shamrocks

Here is a simple way to make pretty shamrocks for St. Patrick's Day. You will need a round lid (about 3 inches across), a sheet of green paper, scraps of colored construction paper or tissue paper, and glue.

Center the lid near the top of the green paper. Hold the lid firmly and trace three-quarters of the way around it, leaving the bottom open. Move the lid so that you can trace part of another circle, connecting it to the top circle. Do the same thing on the other side of the top circle. Now draw a stem at the bottom.

Cut out your shamrock and decorate it by gluing on small squares or circles of brightly colored paper.

Your shamrock will look so nice that you will probably want to make more than one. Can you think of different ways to decorate your other shamrocks?

Drinking Straw Valentine

Cut a heart from heavy colored construction or poster paper.

With scissors cut a paper drinking straw into small ring slices. Poke a sharpened pencil through each ring to make it round again.

Rub a little glue on one edge of the straw rings and arrange them on the paper heart in an interesting design, leaving enough space to write your valentine message.

Things To Make

Wrist Valentines

Give a valentine to wear. Cut a narrow strip from the side of a plastic bottle. Staple it in a loop to fit the wrist. Decorate with red paper hearts and yarn.

St. Patrick's Day Frog Paperweight

Paint a stone green. Cut large round eyes from white paper and glue to the stone. With a felt-tipped marker and yarn, make features as shown. Glue the frog to a lily pad cut from green felt or green paper.

St. Patrick's Day Crown

Cut a band of paper long enough to fit around your head. Glue green pipe cleaners into the band. Cut shamrocks from green paper and glue to the top of the pipe cleaners. Glue green yarn to the band. On the band write "St. Patrick's Day" with a marker or crayon. Glue the ends of the band together to form the crown.

Valentine Butterfly Message

Cut a butterfly shape from red construction paper and decorate it with parts of a paper-lace doily. Glue the butterfly to a spring type clothespin painted red. The antennae are white pipe cleaners glued in place. Write a valentine greeting on a small, heart-shaped piece of paper, and glue it to the other side of the clothespin. Clip the butterfly where it will surprise the person who is to receive it.

Cut out the snowman's hat and jacket and paste them on. Then color.

Spring

Ask your children these questions:

What happens to flowers and trees in the spring?

Is the spring weather colder or warmer than winter?

Do you hear birds in the trees in the spring? What kinds of noises do they make?

What kinds of homes do birds live in?

What do you do with your winter clothes in the spring?

If your eyes were closed, how would you know that there were fresh spring flowers in the room?

What happens when you plant seeds in the ground?

Would you rather play outside or inside on a spring day?

311

Point to the pictures showing wind blowing, sunny day, rainy day.

Point to the child jumping over the fence.

Over the puddle.

Over the rock.

Over the flowers.

Connect the picture on the left to the matching picture on the right by drawing a line.

Connect the picture on the left with the picture on the right by drawing a line.

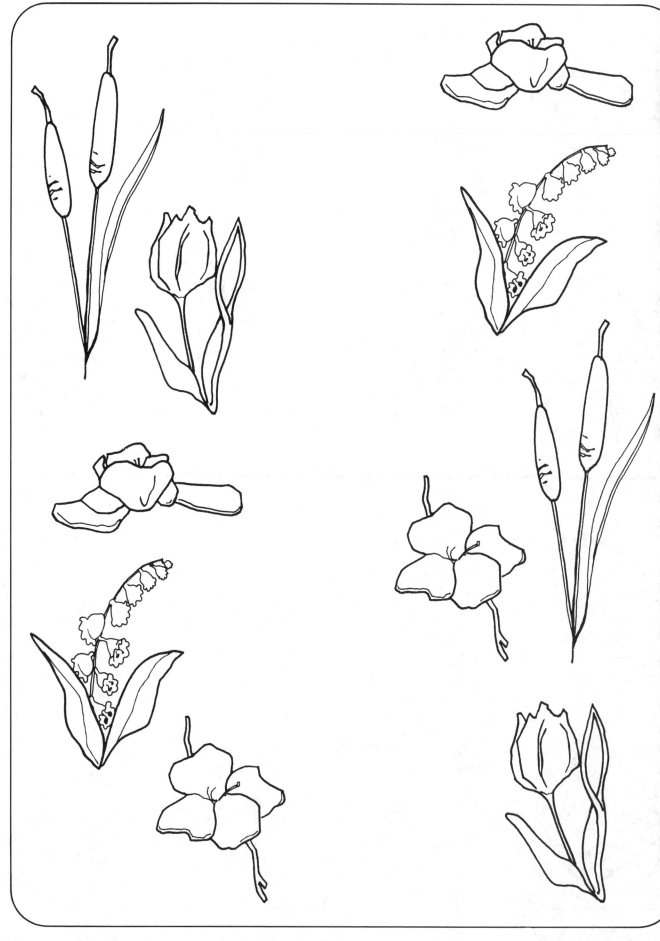

Who Got Fooled?

EDITH VESTAL

It was the first day of April.
Harry and Jack were going home from school.
Harry was in the second grade.
Jack was in the second grade.

"No one has fooled me all day," said Harry.
"But it isn't night yet," said Jack.
"I know, but I won't get fooled.
No matter what anyone says to me,
I'll say, 'April Fool, yourself.'"

They came to the corner.
Jack had to go one way.
Harry had to go another way.

Jack said. "I bet someone fools you before you go to bed."
"I bet they don't," said Harry.
Harry began to run toward home.

About five o'clock, Harry was sitting on his porch.
Jack came along.
Jack was playing with a toy plane—the very kind Harry wanted.
But Harry had spent all of his allowance.

Harry ran down to the walk.
"I wish I had a plane like that," he said.
"You can have this one for fifty cents."
"I haven't got fifty cents."
"You can have it for forty cents."

"I haven't got forty cents."
"You can have it for twenty-five cents."
"I haven't got twenty-five cents."
"You can have it for a nickel."
"All right, I've got a nickel."
And Harry ran into the house to get his nickel.

When Harry came back with his nickel,
Jack said, "April Fool,
you can have it for
nothing.
I've got two of them."

Bread-Wrapper Kite

For the tail, cut three 2½-inch wide strips from one plastic bread wrapper. Tie the ends together. Staple or tape the tail to the closed end of another wrapper. Tie a piece of string to the open end of the kite. Hold the wrapper open so the wind can blow into it. Then run into the wind. Watch the kite dip and dive.

The Funny Easter Egg Hunt

SHIRLEY MARKHAM JORJORIAN

Sandy Squirrel looked around the forest with a frown on his face. Suddenly, he said, "I've got it!" He fluffed his tail happily.

Freddy Frog hopped by just then. "You've got what?" he croaked.

"I've got a good idea, that's what!" said Sandy Squirrel. "One day I heard Ollie Owl say that two heads are better than one. If two heads are better than one, then four hands are better than two hands. Two plus two make four. Four plus four make eight. Eight plus eight make sixteen. Sixteen plus sixteen make thirty-two. Wow! That would be great," sighed Sandy Squirrel.

"What are you talking about?" Freddy Frog asked.

"You'll see," said Sandy Squirrel. "I'll make a list for everyone in the forest. You take the lists around to them. Tell them to bring the things on the list to the great oak tree near the pond this afternoon. If they bring everything, we'll have an Easter egg hunt."

"Oh, boy!" said Freddy Frog, leaping high in the air.

When Sandy Squirrel had made out all the lists, Freddy Frog hopped away through the woods to give them out.

First, he hopped to Randy Rabbit's hutch. "Here is a list of things for you to bring to the great oak tree near the pond this afternoon. Sandy Squirrel is giving an Easter egg hunt," croaked Freddy Frog.

Randy Rabbit looked at his list. Then he laughed and laughed. "What a funny Easter egg hunt! My list says: five tin cans!"

But Freddy had already hopped away to find Ollie Owl in his hollow tree. Freddy knocked on the tree trunk. Ollie Owl poked his head out. "Here," croaked Freddy Frog. "Here's a list of things for you to bring to the great oak tree this afternoon. Sandy Squirrel is giving an Easter egg hunt. See you later! I have to hurry!"

Ollie Owl took one look at his list and burst out laughing. "What a funny Easter egg hunt! My list says: ten gum wrappers!"

Freddy hopped down the lane to Charlie Chipmunk's hole in the ground. Charlie Chipmunk poked his head out of the hole. "What's that?" he cheeped as Freddy Frog handed him his list.

Freddy Frog croaked, "It's a list of things for you to bring to the great oak tree by the pond this afternoon. Sandy Squirrel is giving an Easter egg hunt." Then Freddy hopped off into the woods.

Charlie Chipmunk looked at his list. And he laughed and laughed. "What a funny Easter egg hunt! My list says: three plastic bottles!"

Freddy Frog hopped all through the forest. He gave lists to Tommy Turtle and Al Alligator and Rose Robin and Mary Mockingbird and

Denny Deer and many, many others. He saved one list for himself.

Freddy Frog looked at his own list. He laughed and laughed. "What a funny Easter egg hunt! My list says: six candy wrappers!"

In a few hours, everyone had gathered at the great oak tree, carrying bags filled with all the things on their lists.

Sandy Squirrel greeted his friends. "Put your bags by the tree, please," he said.

"What kind of an Easter egg hunt is this?" they all wanted to know.

Sandy Squirrel grinned. "Look all around you. Look at the green grass, the flowers, and the pathways. You have all done a beautiful job of cleaning up the trash. Now I'll hide the colored eggs. How pretty they'll look in the clean forest. Later we will take all the garbage to the city dump."

The animals looked at the beautiful clean forest and laughed and laughed with joy.

Things To Make

Rain Gauge

A rain gauge is easy to make and interesting to use.

You will need a cylindrical shaped plastic container such as a pill container.

Carefully measure from the bottom of the container and make a short line every ¼ inch with a marker. Apply colorless nail polish on the lines to make them waterproof. Fasten the container to a Popsicle stick with a rubber band.

When rain is expected, push the stick into the ground in an open space. Be sure it is not protected by bushes or trees. After the storm is over, you can find out how much rain fell around your house by checking the water in the gauge against the ¼-inch marks.

The next day see how close you came to the official reading of the amount of rain that fell in your city by looking at a newspaper weather report.

Caterpillar Name Cards

To make name cards for a spring party, cut a green paper leaf. Paint a "packing worm" (plastic foam piece used in packing fragile items) yellow and give it some bright spots and a face so that it looks like a caterpillar. Make a caterpillar for each leaf. Write a name on each leaf, and glue a yellow caterpillar beside each name.

Wind

ROBERT LOUIS STEVENSON

I saw you toss the kites on high
And blow the birds about the sky;
And all around I heard you pass,
Like ladies' skirts across the grass—

    O wind, a-blowing all day long,
    O wind, that sings so loud a song!

I saw the different things you did,
But always you yourself you hid.
I felt you push, I heard you call,
I could not see yourself at all—
    O wind, a-blowing all day long.
    O wind, that sings so loud a song!

O you that are so strong and cold,
O blower, are you young or old?
Are you a beast of field and tree,
Or just a stronger child than me?
    O wind, a-blowing all day long,
    O wind, that sings so loud a song!

Poems

March Wind

Rattling windows, shaking trees,
Swishing skirts and stirring leaves—
Pushing me along the street,
Blowing dust around my feet.
March wind whispers in my ear,
Won't be long till spring is here.

ANDREA HOPKINS, Age 7

Mothers

There's something nice about mothers.
Maybe it's the smile they wear
Or maybe, or maybe,
The hugs and kisses they share.

LAURA NASRALLAH, Age 7

How do you know, little seed, little
seed,
When the time has come to grow?
"Something whispers that skies are
clear,
That the sun shines bright and spring
is here,
So I lift my head and grow."

EVA MARCH TAPPAN

First Day of Spring

It's the first day of spring,
That's a very funny thing—
It is so very cold.
I guess no one has told
The wind
It's spring!

JEANNE ARBUSO, Age 7

Spring Song

April showers
Are friends to flowers.

MELINDA HIGGINS, Age 4

Spring Is Here

Look, there's a flower over here;
That's a sign that spring is near.
Look, there's a tadpole over there.
Can't you smell spring in the air?
There's a robin in that tree;
Can't you hear the melody?
Come on! Let's go spread the cheer!
Now I'm sure that spring is here.

PETER WOOD, Age 9

Spring

I like spring
and the fun it brings,
like helping my father
plant summer corn,
wearing jeans
that are old and torn,
riding a bike down a quiet road,
suddenly finding a new spring toad.

"Welcome," I say
as he looks my way,
but he hops away.
I wish he would stay,
this nice spring day,
but he still hops away . . .

MARY ANN SKWIOT, Age 12

The Rain

Mist, moist, soggy, and wet!
I'm going to get my feet wet.
Mist, moist, soggy, and wet!
I'll put on my boots
And fasten my rain suit.
Mist, moist, soggy, and wet!
I'll put on my hood
And fasten it good.
Splish, splash, splosh I go.
Mist, moist, soggy, and wet!

KAREN MORONEY, Age 9

Poems

Spring

Little spring flower,
How do you grow,
When last winter
You were dead in the snow?

Little spring birds,
In fall you went away,
And now you are back again
And I saw you today.

                    PAUL HESS, Age 8

Rain

Open the window,
Look out your doors.
Look at the clouds,
See how it pours.

                    GREG O'NEILL, Age 9

Spring Begins

When showers fall in the night,
And make flowers grow big and
bright,
And the birds begin to sing,
Then we know it is spring.

                    WILMER GIBSON, Age 10

My Mother

My mother is nice.
My mother is sweet,
Especially to
Her son named Pete.

She makes us all happy.
She makes us all kind,
And once in awhile
She makes us all mind.

                    PETER ROOT, Age 10

The Fat Little Robin

MARIAN KENNEDY

There's a fat little robin
In the apple tree.
I think he is saying
Hello to me.

It must be fun
To sing and sing,
And tell everyone
That it is spring.

Spring Is Here

What a nice day!
Today we all cheer,
Isn't it wonderful?
Spring is here.

Listen to the parade,
Listen to the band,
Listen to the music.
Isn't it just grand?

Spring is here, spring is here,
Doesn't time go fast?
Isn't it just wonderful?
Spring is here at last.

                    DOUGLAS MAO, Age 6

Far and High

BERTHA WILCOX SMITH

My kite is bobbing in the sky;
It flew up far and high.
What fun the kite is having there,
Romping in the windy air!
I'd go to join its frolicking
If I could fly upon a string.

Easter Fun

Here is the bunny
With ears so funny.

And here is his
Hole in the ground.

Each noise that he hears
He pricks up his ears,

And leaps in his
Hole with a bound.

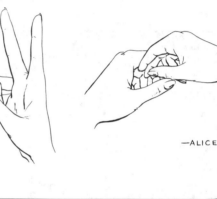

—ALICE

An Easter Egg Hunt

VIDA WIMBERLY

A jolly game for young children to play at Easter time is the game of TOUCH.

Place five hard-boiled eggs, which have been colored green, red, purple, blue, yellow, and one uncolored egg, in a nest of green paper. Leave a little space between the eggs.

One of the children will be blindfolded and given a small stick. When he or she touches a green egg, he or she receives five counters. Red gives four; purple gives three, blue gives two; the uncolored egg means no counters; the yellow egg counts for ten. Each player is blindfolded in turn and the game can end when a player gets ten counters. The eggs should be changed for each new player so he will not know where each color is.

Spring Animals

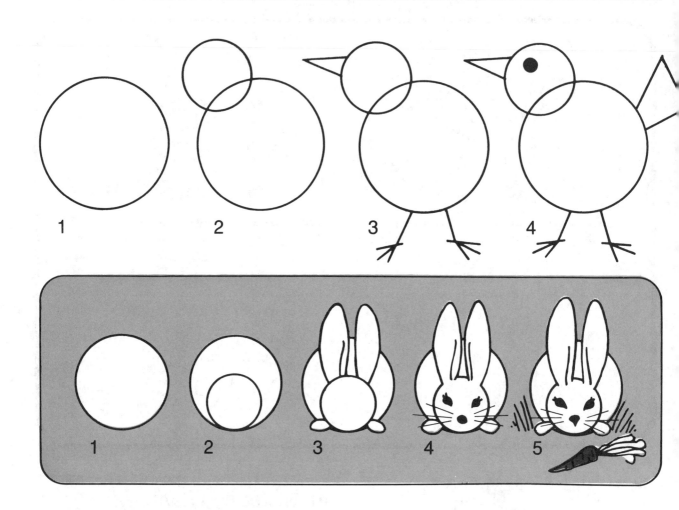

Paper-plate Caterpillar

Cut three small paper plates in half. Then cut a small semicircle out of the middle of one of the half-plates. Trace this onto the five other half-plates, and cut them out. Gather the half-plates in three groups of two each, with the insides of the plates facing one another. Fasten the plates and groups with pieces of pipe cleaner. The three sections of the body should overlap. Use left-over paper for the head and the tail. Paint features on the head, and decorate the rest of the caterpillar with black spots.

Easter Crafts

Egg Faces

All you need to turn hard-boiled eggs into these funny faces are some egg dye, colored construction paper, glue, and crayons or markers.

Make a stand for each egg face from a piece of construction paper about 2 inches wide. Fold the paper into a 1-inch-wide strip and form into a circle that fits your egg. Staple or glue the ends of the strip.

Make hats and features from different colors of construction paper. Add details with colored marker or crayon. The girl's braids are made from thin strips of colored paper.

Egg Headband

Start with a strip of lightweight cardboard about 1 inch wide, and long enough to go around your head and overlap a little. Glue the ends together. From more of the same cardboard, cut enough egg-shaped pieces to decorate the band. Paint the eggs a variety of gay colors, and when dry, decorate with contrasting colors. Glue the eggs evenly around the band.

Paper Birds

Materials: paper of various colors for head, body, tail; orange cardboard for feet, black paper for eyes.

Cut strips as follows:
1 inch by 4 inches for body
1 inch by 2½ inches for head
1 inch by 2 inches for tail
½ inch by ½ inch for bill

Feet must be of cardboard or heavy paper to make the bird stand up. Color the feet yellow.

For eyes, make two black circles with small tabs for pasting to the head circle.

An Easter Egg to Hatch

Draw an egg shape on construction paper and cut it out. Draw decorations on the egg with crayon or felt-tipped marker. Then cut the egg in half along a jagged line. Draw and cut out a chick from yellow paper. Glue the chick to the back of the bottom half of the eggshell so that it seems to be sitting in the shell. Attach the top half of the egg to the bottom half with a brass fastener. The egg can then be opened and closed.

Rabbit Crafts

Easter Table Decorations

Draw a rabbit in the center of a sheet of construction paper, making sure that it touches along the bottom. Draw extensions on both sides of the bottom as shown.

Cut out the bunny, including the extensions. Glue on yarn whiskers. Bring the extensions around to the back, overlap the ends, and staple or glue.

Fluffy Rabbit

This rabbit is made from a cardboard tube. If you have a long one, such as from aluminum foil, cut it down to about 5 or 6 inches in length. Cover the roll with fluffy white cotton, attaching it with glue. Make a ball of cotton and glue to the back for a tail. Cut two leg shapes, as shown in the picture, from cardboard. Cover the outside of these with cotton and glue to the body. Ears, eyes, whiskers, nose, and mouth are cut from colored paper and glued in place. Notice that the ears are glued to the inside of the roll at the back.

Peter Cottontail

This bunny's head is a Styrofoam ball; his body is a paper or plastic cup turned upside down. Attach the ball to the cup with white glue. Use the same glue to attach a ribbon band at the base and a bow at the neck. Cut a slit across the back of the head, near the top. Cut out two cardboard ears, paste contrasting color shapes to the centers, and slip the ears into the slit. The rabbit's features are cut from colored paper and glued to the head. Make a tail from a wad of cotton and glue at the back of the cup.

Rabbit With Built-in Ears

Look carefully at an empty tissue roll. You will see that at each end the cardboard ends in a point. Pry the points up and peel back to form ears. Mix 2 teaspoons of pink tempera with ½ teaspoon of white glue. Paint the roll inside and out. Dry with the ears propped up. Now cut fringes around the roll ends, one inch deep. Bend fringes out. For rabbit's face use felt scraps or felt-tip markers. Glue gift-wrap paper on its ears. Make a neck-hole in the bottom of the roll about the size of a dime.

Find a cardboard egg carton with cone-shaped dividers. Cut around four cups so that a cone is standing in the middle. Trim cup rims neatly. Paint everything pink with tempera. Rub glue around cone-top and push into neck-hole. Push a Popsicle stick painted pink through cone-shaped divider for arms. Glue on a cotton tail, feet, and top-knot. Tie a pink ribbon around the rabbit's neck.

Rabbit can hold Easter eggs, trinkets, or party candies.

More Bunnies

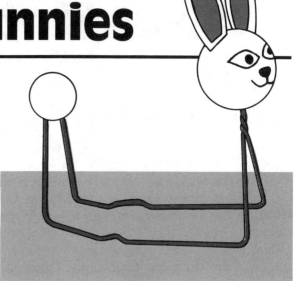

Bunny Bookholder

Hold the top and bottom of a wire coat hanger and pull. Bend up about 7 inches of the top and 5 inches of the bottom to form the shape for the base. Cover a large and a small plastic-foam ball with a layer of pasted paper. Cut two ears from cardboard and cover with a layer of pasted paper. When dry, make slits in the balls to stick on the ends of the coat hanger and also slits in the large ball for the ears. Paint with white tempera. Add features cut from paper. Stick the head and tail on the base. Stack your books in the bunny bookholder.

Bunny Card

Draw a bunny on white paper. Cut the bunny out, then cut it in half. Glue the halves to the inside of a piece of folded, bright-colored construction paper, so that half is on one side of the fold and half is on the other side. Make a paper spring and glue it so that it connects the two halves. Add pink ears and a cotton a tail.

Bunny Necklace

Cover a spool with cotton. Cut two ears from the side of a plastic milk carton. Tack the ears in place. Cut features from construction paper and glue on. Make a loop from yarn and push and glue into the hole in the top of the spool. Thread yarn through the loop for the necklace.

Rabbit-head Puppet

Use one cup-shaped part from a molded-paper egg carton. This forms the face of your puppet. Glue the ends of a 2-inch-long strip of bendable cardboard to the back of the face to help hold it on your fingers.

Paint the rabbit face with tempera paint. The eyes, nose, and mouth can be made from felt, colored paper, or scraps of cloth. Make the whiskers from pieces of tempera-painted toothpicks. These details can be glued to your rabbit head.

Stick your index and middle fingers through the loop on the back of the head. Your two fingers form the ears of your rabbit puppet.

For Mother's Day

Carnation Mother's Day Card

Fold a sheet of lightweight colored paper into fourths. You can use construction paper if you wish, but it's not as easy to cut. Draw a circle on the top layer. Staple the paper together at the center so that you can cut all four layers at the same time.

Cut out the circle. Make long slashes all around from the edge toward the center as shown.

Separate the top layer from the rest of the circles. It won't come completely off, as the staple is holding it in the center. With your fingers, cut it up to the center so it stands up. Repeat this with the other three circles to form a three-dimensional carnation. Glue it to a folded card made of construction paper. Paint the stem and leaves.

For a full carnation, simply use more layers in the beginning.

Mother's Day Card

Select small pieces of fabric scraps. For the butterfly's wings, cut eight triangles of cloth, rounded at the wide ends. Cut a black cloth body.

Fold white or light-colored construction paper for a card. Glue the body to the front center of the card. On each side, glue two triangles for the upper wings and two for the lower wings. Add antennas with pen or marker.

Write your message inside.

Mother's Day Card

Fold a piece of paper in half. Without cutting along the fold, cut out the shape of a cake. Using felt-tipped pens or crayons, decorate the cake. At the top of the cake write: "Happy Mother's Day." On the bottom write: "When it comes to mothers. . . ." Open the card and inside add: "You take the cake!"

Necklace for Mother's Day

Join paper clips together to make two chains, each large enough to go over your head. Slip one paper clip through one of the clips on each chain to join them. Attach six clips to this joining clip and slip two clips through each of the six. This makes the decorative dangle. Now cut adhesive-backed paper into pieces approximately 1-inch square. Take the backing from one square and wrap the adhesive paper around one of the paper clips. Continue until all the clips in the chains and the dangle are covered.

Color, then cut out the flower and the shoe. Fold the shoe along the dotted line.
Paste the flower inside the shoe.

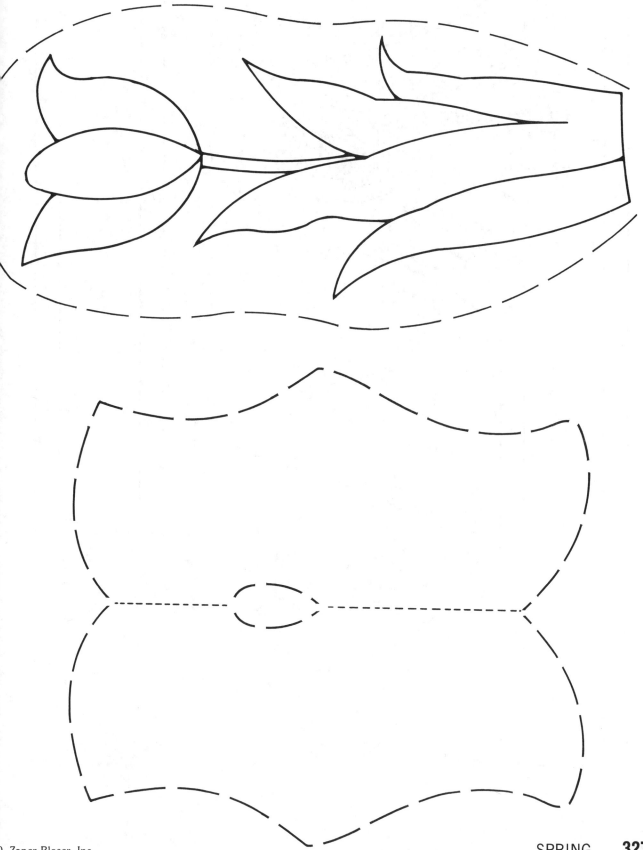

Cut out. Color as you like. Paste strip around
a glass. Fill the glass with flowers.

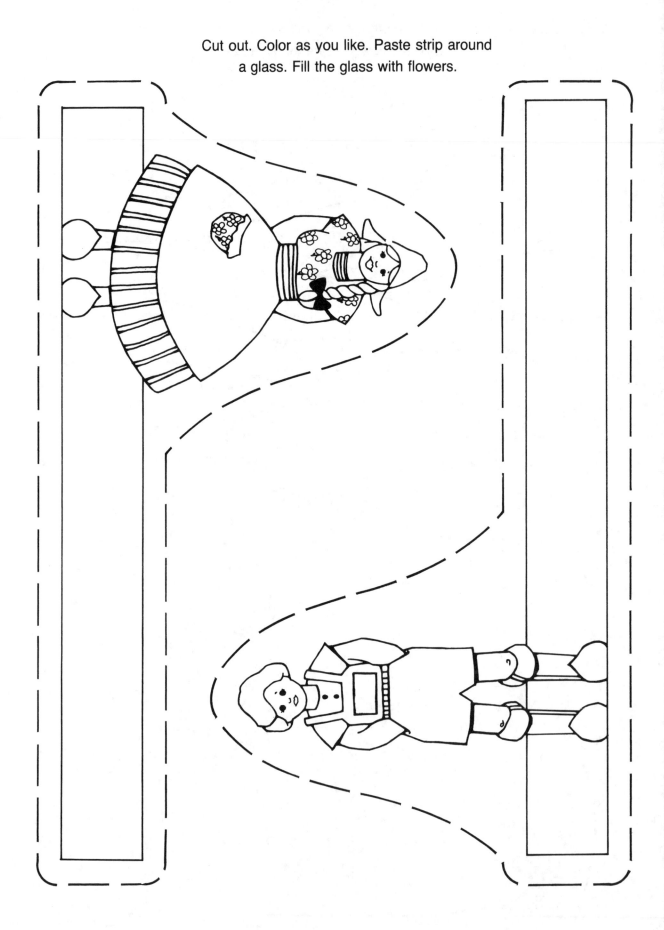

Summer

Ask your children these questions:

Would you want to wear a heavy coat on a hot summer day? Why?

On a very hot day, would you rather drink something cold or something hot?

Can you take an ice cube to school in the morning and have it with your lunch at noon?

Would you rather be in an air-conditioned room or a heated room on a summer day?

Can you swim in a glass of water? Why?

If your mother's car sits outside on a summer day with its windows closed, how will it feel when you get into the car?

What are some things you might do if you went on vacation in the summer?

If two people row a boat, will it go faster or slower than if one person rows?

Is it easier to ride your bike up a hill or down a hill?

Would you rather swim in hot water or cool water on a summer day? Why?

Why do more people wish for rain in summer than in winter?

Why is wool usually clipped from sheep late in the spring rather than in midwinter?

Why isn't football played in summer and baseball in winter?

Why do more people go on vacation in summer than in winter?

Why do more people go ice-skating in winter than in summer?

Why do we see more birds in summer than in winter?

Why do we have the longest vacation from school in summer?

Why do we have screens on the doors and windows in summer and not in winter?

Tell the Story

Look at the pictures. Discuss how you know it is summer. Describe what is happening and what you think will happen next.

Look at each thing at the left. Find the one like it at the right.

Point to the boy carrying the flag.
The girl beating the drum.
The girl playing the flute.
The boy with the hat.

Can you find the hidden bucket, rabbit, chicken, sailboat, bird, and flower in this picture?

JERI SIMKUS

Vacation Is Here

EDITH VESTAL

For weeks Sue had been asking,
"Mother, when is vacation?"
And Mother would say,
"In just a few weeks, Sue."

The next time Sue asked, Mother said,
"In just a few days now."

And Sue said,
"Oh dear, oh dear,
School is almost out."

Finally one day Sue said,
"School is out tomorrow, isn't it, Mother?"
And Mother said,
"Yes, only one more day."

Sue looked as if she wanted to cry.
"Oh, Mother, whatever will I do all day?"

Next day Sue came running into the house.
"School's over, Mother.
School's over.
Vacation is here.
You can't guess what we're going to do."

In a few minutes, Sue was out in the yard.
And so were Jane, David, and Sally.

Suddenly Sue ran into the house again.
"We're going to have lots of fun, Mother."

Mother said,
"Are you going wading?"
"Oh, no, Mother."
"Are you going to skate?"
"Oh, no."
"Are you going to jump rope?"
"Oh, Mother, you're so funny.
We haven't any jumping ropes."

And Sue ran out again.

Mother went to the door.

The children were very busy.
They were moving a bench by the garage.
They had carried a chair from the porch.
They had some books.
They had a chalkboard.

Mother said,
"Oh, you're going to practice your drawing."

But Sue said,
"Why, no, Mother.
We're going to have lots more fun than that.
We're going to play school."

The Runaway Balloons

JULIET EARLE WELTON

The balloon man tightly held the bunch of strings that were tied to his gay-colored balloons. They blew back and forth, bobbed up and down like children playing tag or hopscotch. They were getting their long strings in the most wonderful tangle.

It was their first day out. It had been very exciting to hear the balloon man say: "All right; give her the gas," and to feel themselves getting bigger and bigger, and lighter and lighter, until they were floating up in the air. It was only the strings that the balloon man had tied to their necks which kept them from sailing away among the clouds like bubbles.

This was their first peek at the world, and what an exciting world they looked down on. The circus was spread out below them.

The red-and-white canvas tent looked like a plate with scalloped edges. The animal cages around the tent looked so small they resembled toy wagons with toy animals inside. The tents where the side shows were held looked like little colored matchboxes dropped on the ground. The merry-go-round was like a bright-colored top spinning to its own music.

The balloons bobbed back and forth, the breeze tossed them here and there. A great puff of wind swirled the dust around the balloon man. He threw back his head and sneezed, "Katchoo! KATCHOO!" The last time, he sneezed so hard he let go of the balloons, and the next puff of breeze carried them up in the air out of reach.

"My balloons, LOOK, they go, there they go, help, HELP!" cried the balloon man.

The man on stilts ran out of his tent. He grabbed at the balloons but they sailed over his head.

"Let me try," said the acrobat, "maybe I can catch them."

He swung out on his trapeze and turned a triple somersault in the air, but he sailed over the balloons.

"Alas," said the circus manager. "There go all of the balloons; where will they end up?"

"Hello," said the wind. "I guess I'm the one who has caught you. I've always wanted a bunch of balloons of my own and now I have one."

"Where shall we go and what shall we do?" asked the wind.

"I wish to see the country," said the blue balloon.

"I wish to see the city," said the yellow one.

"I wish to see some children," said the red balloon.

"We'll do a little bit of each," said the wind. "First, I'll blow you out to the country."

The wind blew them over a field where woolly sheep grazed. They looked down on a creek where cows waded in the shallow water. The wind blew them over to have a look at a farm where they saw many other animals.

"Now we'll blow over the city," said the wind. "Then the yellow balloon can have her wish."

As they blew into the city the buildings grew larger and larger, and the noise became louder and louder. They looked down on trolley cars, buses, autos, and many people on the streets. As they danced over the city they noticed twinkling lights here and there, as night was falling.

"Have you had enough?" asked the wind. "It's getting dark."

"Oh, yes," said the balloons, "and we're getting tired, too."

"Now I have a surprise for you," whistled the wind. "You have all had a good time. How would you like to give someone else a little pleasure?"

"We'd like to," said the balloons.

The wind puffed out his cheeks and gave the balloons a great puff, and blew them towards a large red building. He blew them all around the building until he found a window at one end which was open. With a huge puff he blew the balloons through the window into a long room lined with little beds. The wind had blown them through the window of a children's hospital.

"Look," said the red balloon, "here are the children I asked to see."

At just that minute the door opened and a nurse in a crisp blue-and-white uniform came in. She went to each little bed to see if the child in it was asleep. Suddenly she saw the bunch of balloons bumping their heads on the ceiling. She gathered the strings together and carried the balloons into the hall.

"Look, Jane, what I found in the children's ward—a bunch of balloons. Let us tie one at the foot of each bed. What a happy surprise for the children when they awake in the morning." The nurses went up and down the rows of beds until each had a gay-colored balloon tied to it.

After the nurses left, the balloons whispered to each other.

"Red balloon, we like your wish. Seeing the country was nice; seeing the city was fun; but the best sight of all will be the joy in the children's eyes when they find us peeking at them over the foot of their beds."

Desk Organizer

KENT DOUGLAS

This might be a good Father's Day present. Cut cardboard tubes into sections of various lengths. Paint each tube a different color. Arrange them on a piece of painted cardboard and glue in place. Use the desk organizer to hold pencils, rulers, and so on.

Balloons

ANN DEVENDORF

"Balloons for sale!"
called the man.
"Pink balloons!
Brown balloons!
White balloons!
Yellow balloons!
Red balloons!
Black balloons!
And balloons with
dots, dots, dots!"

Mike looked up at the balloons.
He needed a balloon
that could fly over a mountain.
It would have to be a balloon
that could soar with the birds,
that could bump a cloud
and get close to the stars.

"What balloon shall I buy?"
thought Mike.
"Which color will go the highest?
Will the brown go highest?
Or the black or the pink or the white?
Will the red go highest?
Or the yellow? Or the dotted?"

Mike didn't know.
He asked the balloon man.

"Sir," he said,
"which color will go the highest?"

The balloon man answered,
"Sometimes the black
will go the highest, and
sometimes the brown.
Sometimes the pink.
Sometimes the white.
Sometimes the red.
Sometimes the yellow.
Sometimes the dotted."

Mike frowned and said, "Then
the color doesn't matter at all."

"Right," said the man. "Color doesn't
matter at all."

"I guess it's what's inside the balloon
that matters," said Mike.

"Yes," said the balloon man.
"Here's a balloon with lots inside."

"Thanks," said Mike
as he paid his dime.

He ran home.
He tied a note to his balloon.
On the note was his name and
address.
He let go of the balloon.
The balloon wanted to fly, to go high!
Soon it was only a dot in the blue
sky.

One day a letter came to Mike.
"Dear Mike," said the letter.
"I found your balloon and your note.
Your balloon came over
a very high mountain!"

"I thought it would," smiled Mike.
"It had a lot inside!"

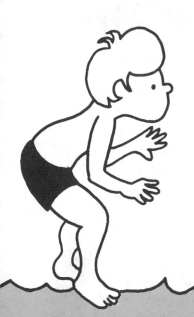

Summertime Verse

IVY O. EASTWICK

Ice Cream in Summer

It's not easy
eating ice cream
in the sun—
'tisn't easy
at all but—
it's fun!
It's a sort of
a race between
me and the sun—
we don't know
which will win—
so it's fun!

The Jellyfish

The jellyfish
is jellified—
he could not be
brave if he tried;
he shakes, he shivers,
and he quakes
from the first moment
that he wakes
until he's tucked up
tight in bed
with seaweed sheets
around his head.

When Isabel Goes to the Seashore

When Isabel goes
to the seashore,
she tiptoes
niminy-neat,
past the sea
and the spray
which dance her way
but scarcely touch
her feet.

When Jonathan goes
to the seashore,
he walks on the edge
of the sands,
till the sea and the spray
they caper his way
and splash him on feet
and hands.

When I go down
to the seashore
I run and jump
right in,
and the sea and the spray
they leap my way
and splash me up
to the chin.

Without Me!

WILMA YEO

I saw the funniest thing I ever did see—
My shoes were walking without me!
Walking, walking, walking, without me!

I saw the funniest thing I ever did see—
My sleeve was waving without me!
Waving, waving, waving, without me!

I saw the funniest thing I ever did see—
My pants were sitting without me!
Sitting, sitting, sitting, without me!

I was thinking, thinking, thinking,
That this could not be! But . . .
My shoes were walking,
My pants were sitting
My sleeve was waving,
Without me!

June

My Mother says that she likes June
Because it makes her flowers bloom.

And Dad says he thinks June is fine
Because it's golf and fishing time.

What about June do I like best?
Vacation time! My brain's at rest!

JACK HUBER, Age 11

Summer Fun

Summer is here.
Oh, what fun!
Water so clear,
Glistening in the sun.
What fun it is
To swim and play
In the warmth
Of a summer day.

MIKE BABCOCK, Age 11

Summer

Summer is happy,
Summer is bright,
Look out your window,
A beautiful sight.
Flowers are blooming,
And the sky is so blue.
What does summer mean to you?

MATT EMLEN, Age 7

My Garden

I made a garden,
I planted seeds,
I kept it watered,
I pulled the weeds.
And when it blossomed,
bright colors gay,
I gave my mother
the first bouquet.

GIDGET DEREGO, Age 8

Little Picnic

The meadow hill
Is gay with June;
The bees are humming
A bumbly tune.

The lambs are skipping,
And so are we;
We're having a picnic
Under the tree.

That's our basket
Up in the shade;
(Two cups—four cookies—
And lemonade.)

Summer

I love summer,
It's real neat.
We get to go swimming
And get sand on our feet.

KRISTEN BRINKLEY, Age 9

Games

Picture Puzzles

Cut out pictures of various historic or scenic areas of the United States. Glue them to cardboard. Cut each picture into pieces and place in an envelope. Make one for each guest. Let each person choose an envelope. At a signal they begin putting the puzzles together. The first to complete a puzzle is the winner.

Drum Race

Cover two empty salt boxes with a layer of pasted paper. When dry, paint with white paint. Glue blue yarn to the sides for the strings. Wrap about an inch on either end of the drum with red yarn. Tie pieces of white cloth padded with a tissue to two pencils for drum sticks.

Divide the players into two groups. At a signal one person from each group runs across the room, beats the drum five times, then runs back to his team, taps the next player, and so on. The team that finishes first wins.

Flagpole Toss

Fill a potato-chip can with sand or stones to keep it from tipping over. Cover the can with one layer of pasted paper. Paint with white paint. Glue a circle of blue paper and a foam ball to the lid. Glue on red and blue stripes cut from construction paper. Staple strips of cardboard into rings. Have the players take turns trying to "ring the flagpole." Keep score of the number of rings each person gets over the flagpole. The winner is the player with the highest score.

Wild Animal Shooting Galley

Draw animal pictures on posterboard, cut them out, and attach a jingle bell to the bottom of each one. With clothespins, hang the animals on a clothesline strung between two trees or poles set in the ground. Supply each player with a Ping-Pong ball. In turn, have them shoot at the animals from a line marked about 10 feet away. Each time a bell jingles, score a point.

Treasure Chest

The children sit in a circle. The player who starts says, "If I found the treasure chest I would buy—" And the player describes the article he would buy. The first one to guess what it is, is It for the next game. Continue until everyone has had a chance.

Shere Khan, the Tiger Game

Mark off two goal lines about 30 feet from each other. All the players except one stand on one of the goal lines. The extra player is the Tiger who stands in the middle, facing the rest of the players.

When the Tiger asks, "Who's afraid of Shere Khan?" the other players answer, "No one!" and then run as fast as they can to the opposite goal. The Tiger tries to tag as many players as he can. Those who are tagged join him in the middle and help catch the others. The last player to be caught is the Tiger next.

Circus Party

CHRISTINE MABRY

Clown Walk

Give each contestant two paper bags and two pieces of string. He ties the bags on his feet. Choose a starting point and a goal. At a signal, players walk (do not run) to the goal and return. The one who does it first, without breaking his bags, is the winner. For additional fun, suggest a Clown Walk in a Three-legged Race. Each pair of players is given three paper bags, one much larger than the others. The left foot of one player and the right foot of his partner are put into the large bag. The string is wrapped around the ankles of both players to hold the bag on securely. The players' other feet are put into the smaller bags and also tied. Then the fun begins! The partners who first walk to the goal and back without splitting the bags win.

Balloon Antics

Each player is given a soda straw and a blown-up balloon. At a signal, the players blow their balloons along the ground through the straws to the goal and back. Have a few extra balloons on hand. They do pop!

Stretch a string between two chairs or trees. Divide the players into two teams, with the stretched string between them. Appoint a scorekeeper for each team. Toss two or three balloons into the air. Let each team try to hit a balloon over the opposing side, winning one point.

Give each player a balloon; then see who can be the first to blow the balloon until it bursts.

Blow up a balloon, put in a small handful of navy beans, tie it tight; then let each player guess the number of beans. You know, of course.

Feed the Elephant

On a piece of an old sheet, draw an elephant with his trunk up so the mouth is open. Cut out a large mouth. Then stretch the sheet between two chairs and fasten securely at the corners with heavy string. Players stand about four feet away and are each given five peanuts to feed the elephant. If your class is large, make a clown head also, with a large mouth cut out in which to toss small rubber balls or bean bags. One half of the players can be feeding the elephant while the rest toss balls into the clown's mouth.

Tightrope Capers

Everybody loves tightrope walking! Stretch a white string about thirty feet long on the ground. Each player takes his turn with two saucers filled with peanuts. He balances the saucers on his outstretched palms, as he walks the tightrope, with the heel of the front foot against the toe of the back one all of the way. No stepping off the rope. The player who spills the fewest peanuts is declared the Champion Tightrope Walker.

Section 111

Pre-academic Skills

Matching/Classifying

Point to the picture at the left of the line. Find another picture like it at the right of the line. Name the picture at the right of the line that is not at the left.

How is the frog like the grasshopper? How is it different? Which would you find in the water?

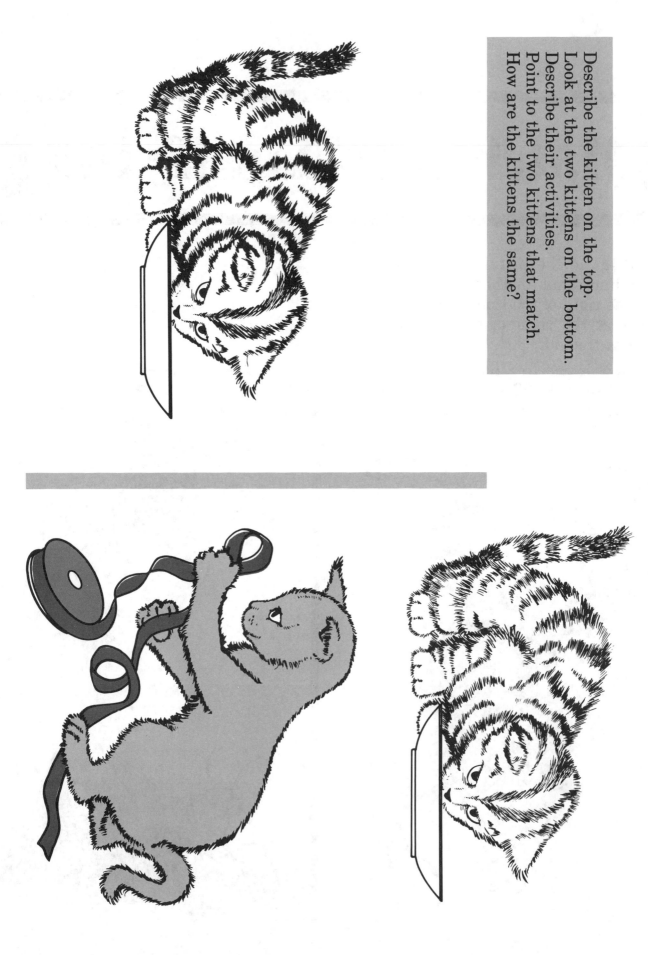

Describe the kitten on the top.
Look at the two kittens on the bottom.
Describe their activities.
Point to the two kittens that match.
How are the kittens the same?

Connect the picture on the left to the matching picture on the right by drawing a line.

MATCHING AND CLASSIFYING **347**

Look at each animal on the left. Draw a line to its shadow on the right.

Matching Activities

Matching Shapes

Look at each shape at the left.
Find another shape like it at the right.

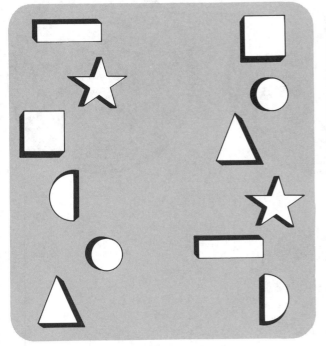

Matching Numbers

Look at each number at the left.
Find another letter like it at the right.

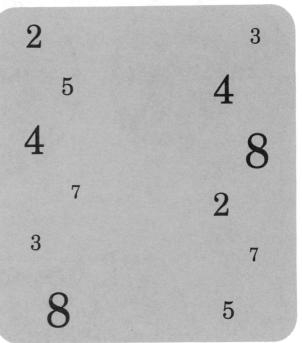

Matching Letters

Look at each letter at the left.
Find another letter like it at the right.

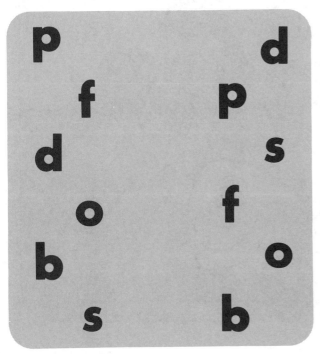

Matching Fruit

Look at each piece of fruit at the left.
Find the piece of fruit like it at the right.

MATCHING AND CLASSIFYING **349**

Name the animals.
Describe each animal's tail and match it to the animal.
How does the fish use its tail?
How does the squirrel use its tail?

Connect the picture on the left to the matching picture on the right by drawing a line.

Connect the picture on the left to the matching picture on the right by drawing a line.

Wheels

Name each of the things on the top and tell where you might find it.
Look at the wheels. How are they alike? How are they different?
Where does each wheel belong?

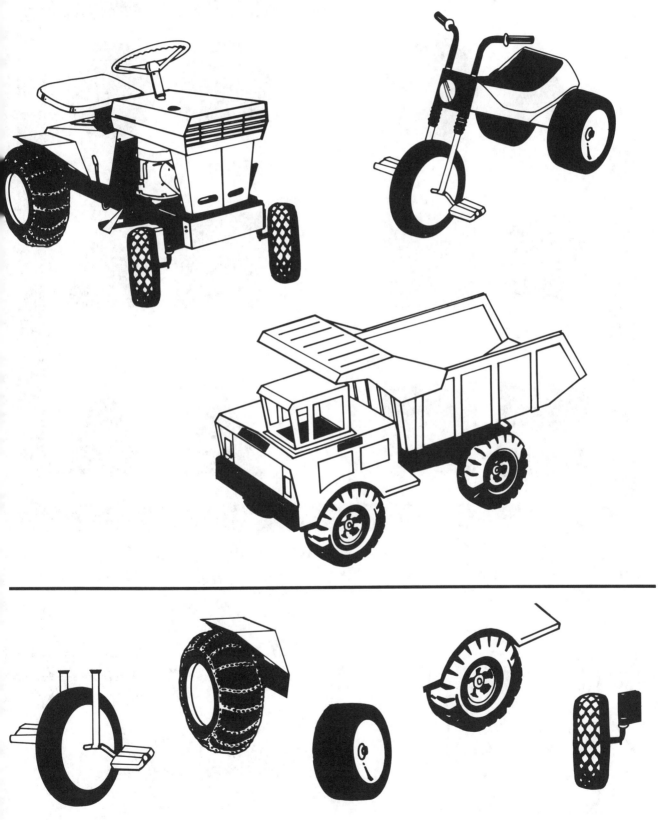

MATCHING AND CLASSIFYING   **353**

Alike or Different?

Which pairs have shapes that are the same?

In each pair which letters are the same? Which are not?

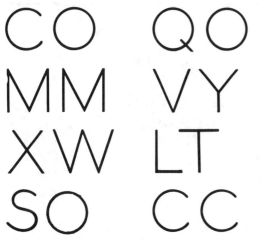

CO   QO

MM   VY

XW   LT

SO   CC

Which pair is not alike?

Animals

Which would you like for a pet?
Which do you see at the circus?
Which gives us milk?
Which gives us eggs?
Which gives us wool for clothes?
Which does not belong on a farm?

Which can fly?
Which are good runners?
Which have four feet?
Can you think of anything that has four feet but
can not run fast?

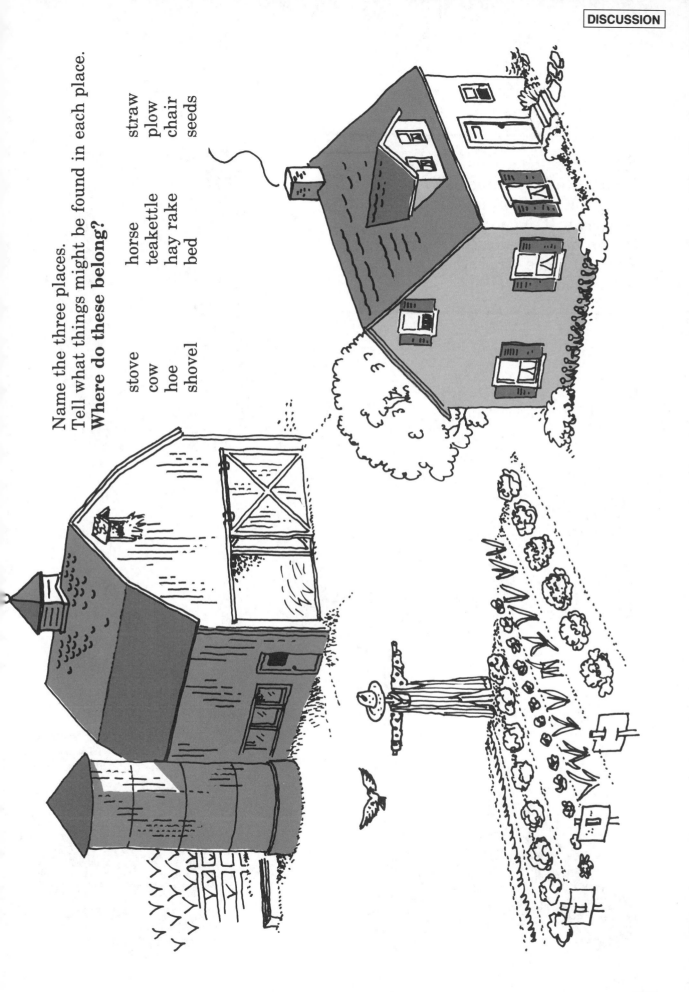

Name the three places.
Tell what things might be found in each place.
Where do these belong?

stove	horse	straw
cow	teakettle	plow
hoe	hay rake	chair
shovel	bed	seeds

Which of these are used indoors?
Which are used outdoors?
Can you think of anything that can
be used both indoors and outdoors?
Which have handles?
Can you name some other things that
have handles?

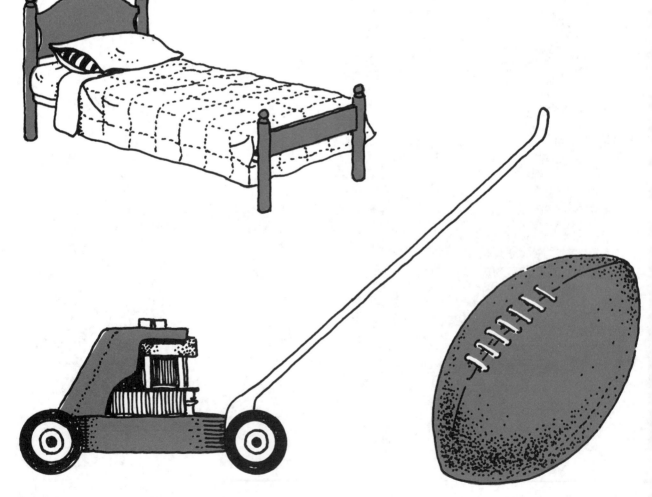

Name the mother animals. Name the baby animals.
Match the baby with the mother animal.
How are the animals alike? How are they different?
Which of the following do animal children do?

cry	get sick
play	talk
run	draw pictures
learn manners	sleep
go to school	eat
quarrel	read

MATCHING AND CLASSIFYING   **359**

How are these alike?
How are they different?
Which can be folded?
Which would you wear in cold weather?
What other things can we do to keep warm in cold weather?

Draw a line from each baby animal to its mother.

Connect the picture on the left to the matching picture on the right by drawing a line.

MATCHING AND CLASSIFYING **361**

Connect the picture on the left to the matching picture on the right by drawing a line.

Look at the picture on the left. What is it?
Which of the other objects does it go with? Why?

Name an object that often goes with:

a hammer   a needle
salt   a stamp
a coat   a knife

Thinking Questions

Which do you wear on your head?
Which do you wear on your feet?
Which do you wear on your hands?

cap, socks, mittens, slippers, earmuffs, glove

Which of these makes music?
Which do you wear on your feet?

corn, violin, shoe, guitar, drum, slip-
per, piano

Which are tools?
Which do you sit on?

hammer, chair, screwdriver, pliers,
bench, window

Which are flowers?
Which could you write with?

rose, pencil, violet, elephant, crayon,
lily, chalk

Which do you eat?
Which could you play with?

apple, peach, table, grapes, doll, banana, game

Could you hide a penny in your hand?

Could you run faster on your hands and feet, or just on your feet?

Does a baby cry when it is hungry?

Can you hop on one foot?

Do you make a fist with your hand or with your foot?

How many heels have you? How many toes?

What can you do that a fly can't do?

Which hurts more, to pull a hair from your head or to have the barber cut it with scissors?

Why do we wear shoes?

A baby creeps. Why don't you?

When you are standing up, can you kick with both feet at once?

Why do you see your fingers more often than your toes?

Does your tongue have bones in it?

Can you wear your left glove on your right hand?

Can you talk while swallowing water?

Can you touch your right elbow with your right hand?

Do you like it when someone tickles you?

Can you hear a person breathe when he is asleep?

Which are farther apart, your eyes or your ears?

Does your hair bleed when it is cut? Do your fingernails?

Cindy's mother was holding a needle. "If you are brave and hold your hand still, Cindy, I will soon get it out," said her mother. What was Cindy's mother doing?

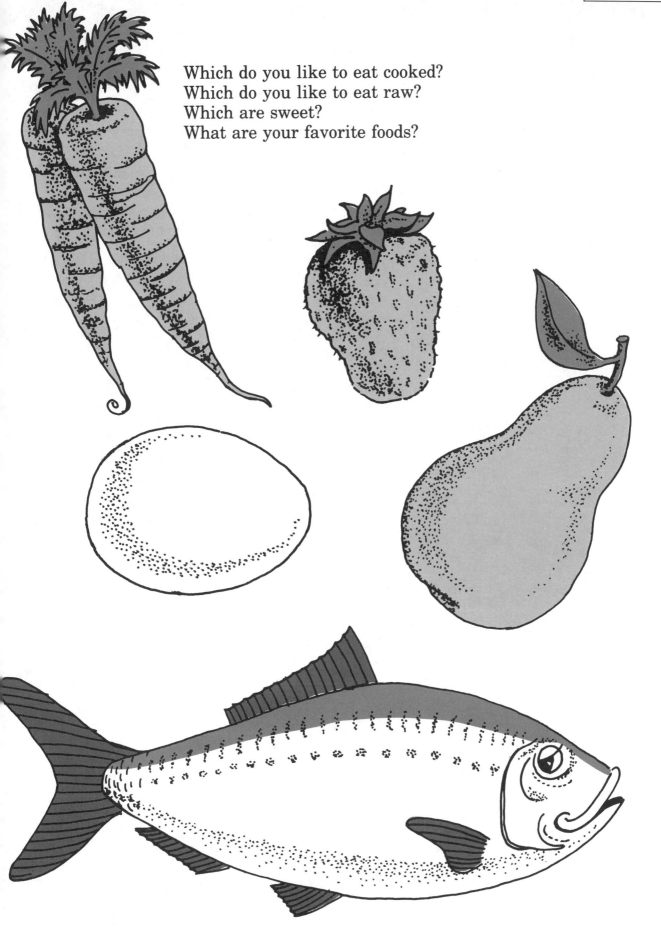

Which do you like to eat cooked?
Which do you like to eat raw?
Which are sweet?
What are your favorite foods?

MATCHING AND CLASSIFYING **365**

Directionality/Relationships

Would the girl have to reach up or bend down
to open the trunk? Hang up her coat?
Pick up the ball? Get her cap?
What is over the bed? Under the bed?
Which bunk would you like, top or bottom?
Is it harder to make the top bunk than the bottom bunk? Why?

367

Where is the bird going?
Where is the fish going?
Where is the dog going?
Move your hand in the same direction that these animals are going.
What other things can you do from left to right?

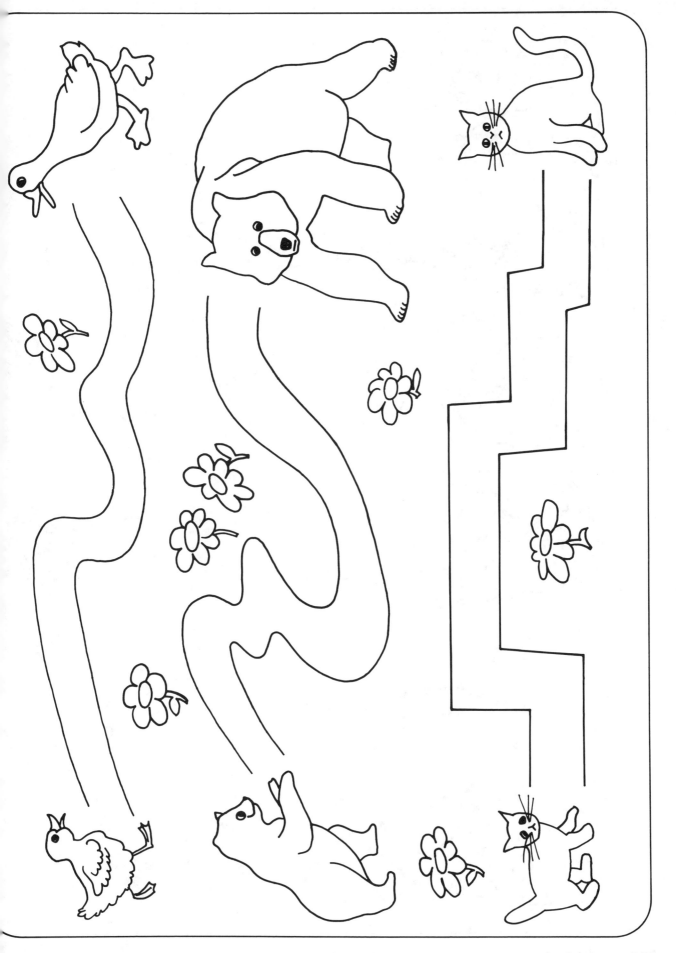

DIRECTIONALITY AND RELATIONSHIPS   **369**

Draw a line from the pictures on the left to the pictures on the right.

Draw a line from the rabbit to the lettuce.

lettuce

rabbit

Draw a line from the ax, over the kite, to the tree.

ax

kite

tree

Draw a line from the girl, under the bush, to the flower.

bush

girl

flower

Draw a line from the car, over the wagon, under the bicycle, to the horse.

car

bicycle

wagon

horse

Draw a line from the table, under the light, over the chair, to the cat.

cat

light

chair

table

Draw a line from the frog to the grasshopper.

frog

grasshopper

Draw a line from the duck, over the bush, to the hen.

duck

bush

hen

Draw a line from the cat, under the table, over the basket, to the yarn.

cat

table

basket

yarn

Draw a line from the dog, under the flower, over the box, to the bone.

dog

flower

box

bone

Point to the children on the ends.
Point to the child in the middle of the group.
Point to each child between two other children.
Point to each child beside another child.
Point to each child to the left of a child.
Point to each child to the right of a child.
Does a bench go from left to right?
What other things go from left to right?

Which child is going up?
Which is going down?
Which is going over?
Which is crawling through?
Which is under?

The Family on the Ceiling

Once there was a family by the name of Rightsideup. They always did everything in a most proper manner. They walked with their feet on the ground, they ate their food with knives and forks, and always acted like normal people.

One day the youngest member of the family, a little girl by the name of Standupstraight, came down with a fever. The doctor was called and couldn't figure out any reason for this strange fever. Standupstraight wasn't sick from the fever but she suddenly started doing everything upside down. Soon each person in the Rightsideup family caught this mysterious fever and they did everything upside down,

too. They began to walk on the ceiling, they wore shoes on their heads and hats on their feet, and went to sleep under their beds. Did you ever hear of a family who dried themselves with a towel and then took a shower? Or who turned off the TV and then sat down to watch it? Well, these are just some of the crazy things the Rightsideup family did. People came from miles around just to see this funny family. The strange fever never left the Rightsideup family so from then on they were known to their friends and neighbors as the Wrongsidedown family.

TERI FENTON, Age 8

An Old Fable

A little Frog was playing at the edge of a pool when an ox came down to the water to drink. "Wow!" said the little Frog as he hopped away home to tell his mother what he had seen. "An e-NOR-mous creature on four legs," he said. "How big is e-NOR-mous? As big as this?" asked the mother Frog, puffing herself out to look as big as possible. "Oh, yes, much bigger!" said the little Frog. The mother Frog puffed and puffed. "As big as THIS?" she asked. "Oh, yes, yes, Mother, MUCH bigger!" replied the little Frog. Then the mother Frog puffed and puffed until she was round as a ball. "As big as - -?" she began - - - - -. But then she burst.

If I Were Otherwise

JOYCE L. BRISLEY

If I were very, very tall, as tall as I could be,
I'd play with all the little birds up in the topmost tree;
I'd jump right over houses and think nothing of a wall,
If I were very, very, very, very, very tall!

If I were very, very small, as small as I could be,
I'd run among the blades of grass where you could scarcely see,
I'd play with ants and beetles and I know I'd love them all,
If I were very, very, very, very, very small!

Classroom Activities

Arrange an obstacle course in the classroom. Use chairs, blocks, rulers, and other objects. Ask the children to go *under, over, around,* and *through* the objects.

Look for the tallest object in the classroom. Look for the smallest, widest, narrowest objects in the classroom. Have the children name an object near to you, then name an object far away. Name a place in the classroom. Ask a child to demonstrate the shortest path from your desk to that place and a longer path.

Ask the children:
Which animal in each pair has shorter legs?

mouse or cat

hen or crane

cow or pig

horse or dog

Which get larger?

pencil

girl

snowman

corn

calf

haystack

Draw a line from the smallest dog to the dog with spots.

Draw a line from the smaller dog to the largest rabbit.

Draw a line from the shortest person to the taller tree.

Draw a line from the largest cow to the smallest calf.

Draw a line over the shortest way a child could go from his home to the school.

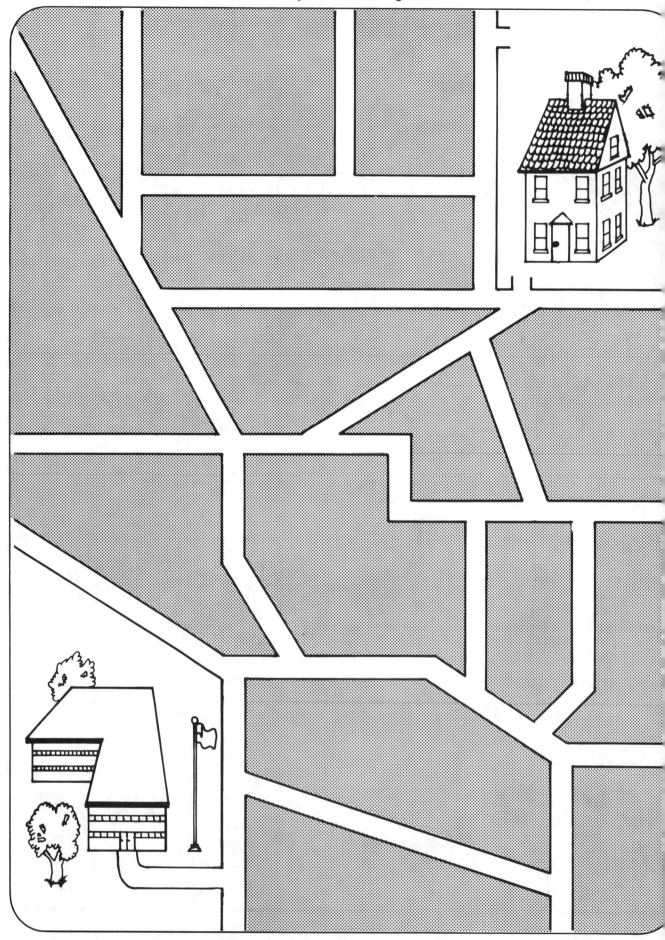

Chalkboard Activities

Draw the fish on the chalkboard.
Ask the children to:
point to the fish at the left.
find a fish that is larger.
find a fish that is smaller.
find one that is the same size.

Draw these figures on the chalkboard.

Ask the children:

Which man is taller?

Which kite is higher?

Which tree is taller?

Which boy is higher
in the tree?

Which boy is lower
in the tree?

Draw the balloons on the chalkboard.
Have the children:
point to the largest balloon.
point to the next smallest balloon.
point to the smallest balloon.
point to the balloon that is highest.
point to the balloon that is lowest.

DIRECTIONALITY AND RELATIONSHIPS   **379**

Which building is tallest?
Which is widest?
Point to the narrowest building.

Which might be oldest?
In which buildings might more
than one family live?

Shapes and Strokes

Point to all the circles.
Point to all the squares.
Point to all the rectangles.
Point to all the triangles.
Can you think of some other things
that have these shapes?

CIRCLE   SQUARE   RECTANGLE   TRIANGLE

0, Zaner-Bloser, Inc.

381

Name each missing part.
What shape is the missing part?
Make the shape in the air
with your hand.
What do you think happens
to each of these things
when a part is missing?

Which of these are left to right?
Which of these are top to bottom?

SHAPES AND STROKES   **383**

Chalkboard Ideas

Verticals and Horizontals Draw on the chalkboard models of figures made from vertical and horizontal lines. Encourage the children to make similar drawings.

Write horizontal lines.

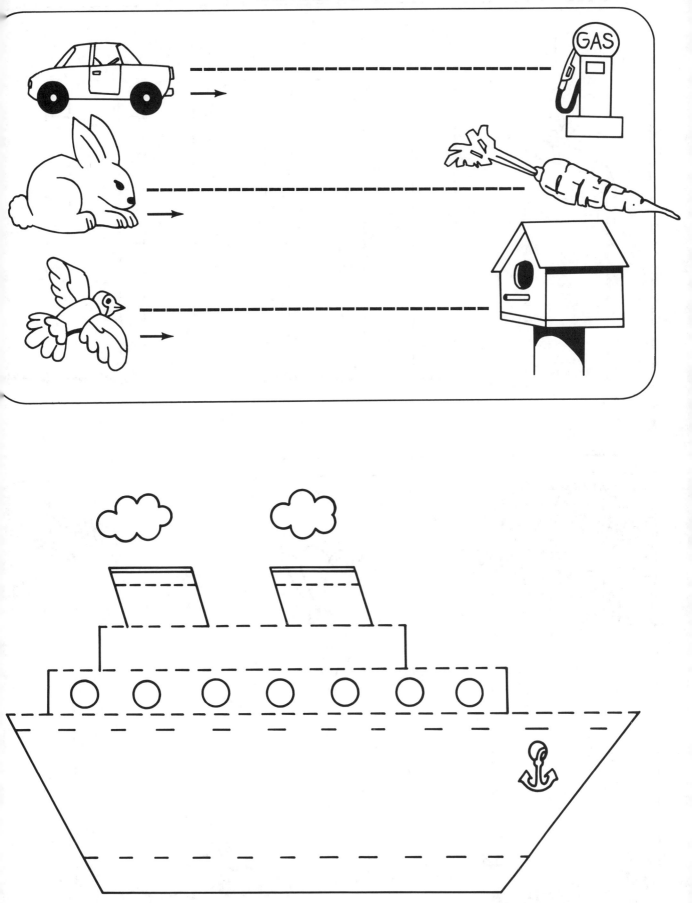

SHAPES AND STROKES   **385**

Write vertical lines.

Write backward circles.

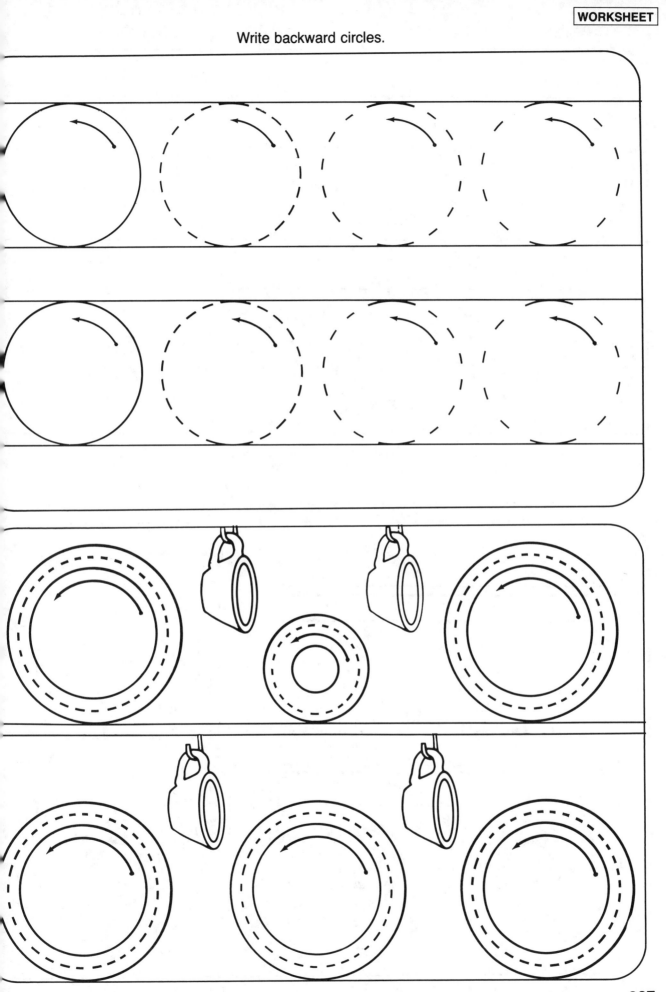

SHAPES AND STROKES **387**

Write forward circles.

Chalkboard Shapes

Parts of Circles

Draw on the chalkboard some large overcurves and undercurves. Have children come to the chalkboard and make the overcurves and under-curves into animals by adding lines and coloring in the picture.

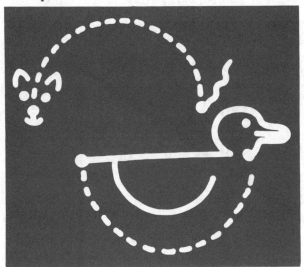

Triangles

Draw on the chalkboard models of figures made from triangles. Encourage the children to make similar drawings.

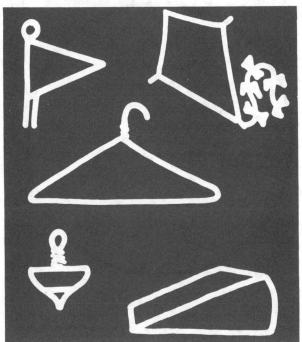

Circle Drawings

Draw on the chalkboard some models of fig-ures made from circles. Encourage the children to make similar drawings.

Which of these shapes have corners?
Which have no corners?
Which has the most corners?
Which has only one corner?
Which of these shapes has straight sides? Which does not?
Which has one straight side?
Which has three straight sides?
Which has four straight sides?
Can you draw these shapes?

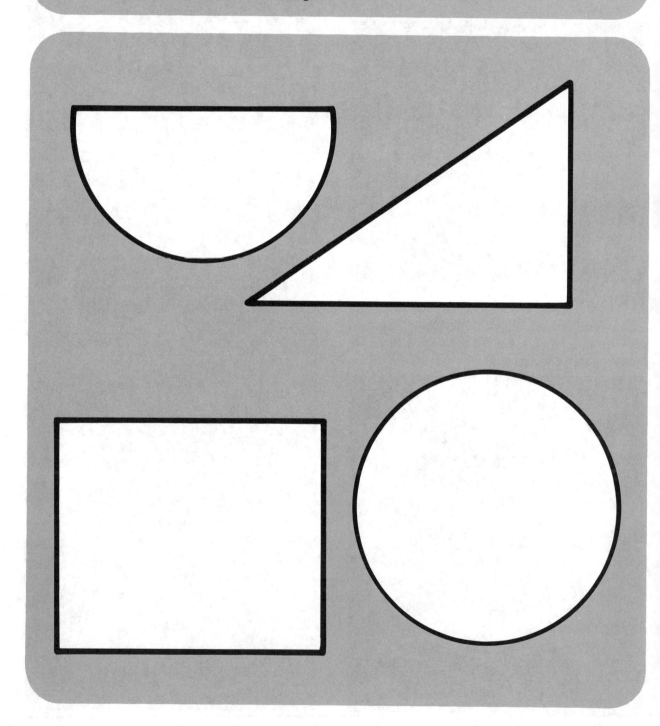

Write slant lines.

SHAPES AND STROKES **391**

Draw the objects.

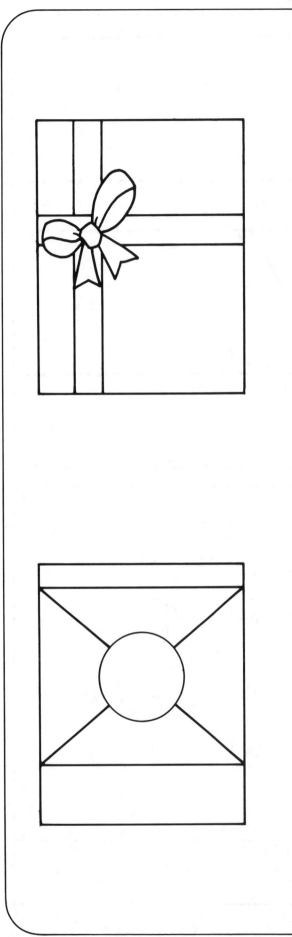

Point to the largest triangle, the next largest, the next, and then the smallest triangle.
Point to the largest circle, the next largest, the next, and then the smallest circle.
Point to the largest square, the next largest, the next, and then the smallest square.

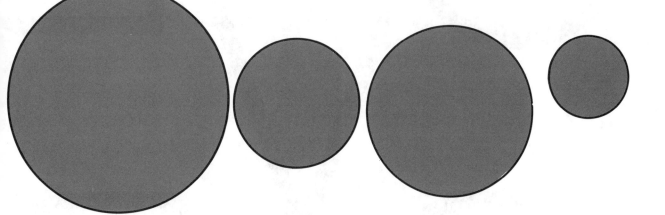

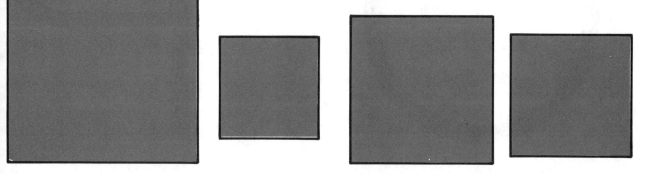

DISCUSSION

Point to the letter made only with straight lines.
Point to letters made only with a curved line.
Point to the letter made with a straight line and a curved line.
Point to the letter made with slant lines.
Say the letter names.
What other letter names do you know?

C V L

O P

Connect the matching shapes.

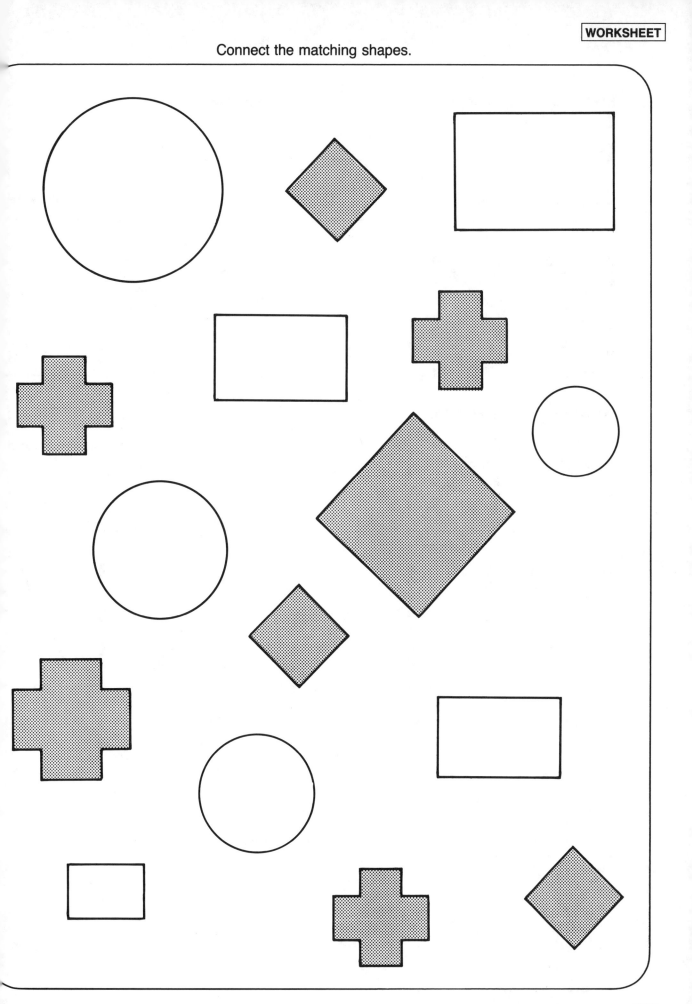

Circle the missing part.

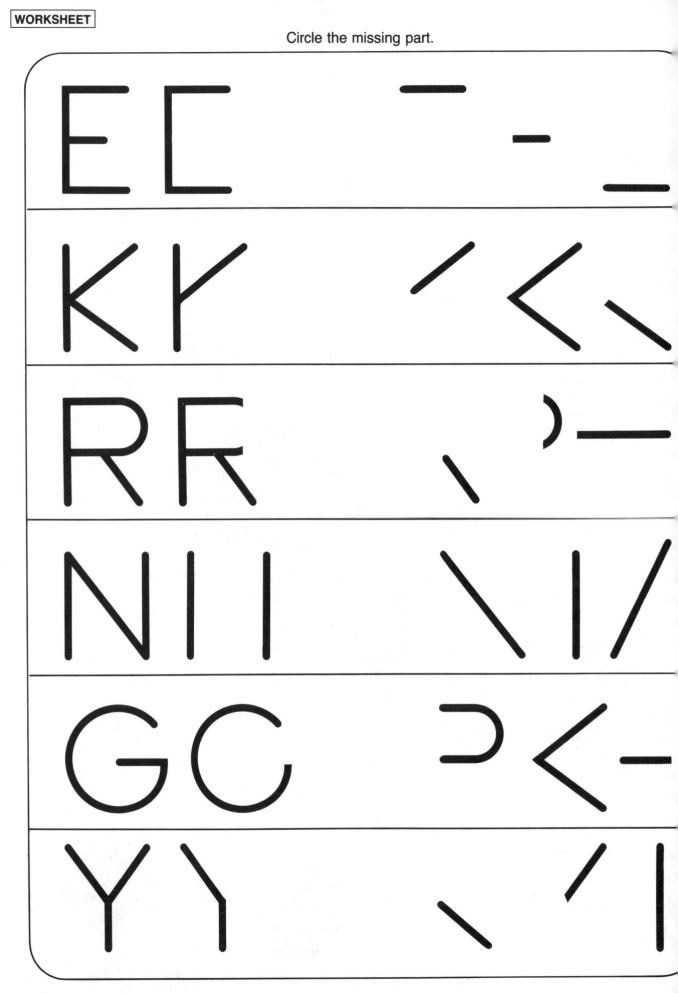

Fun Shapes With Paper

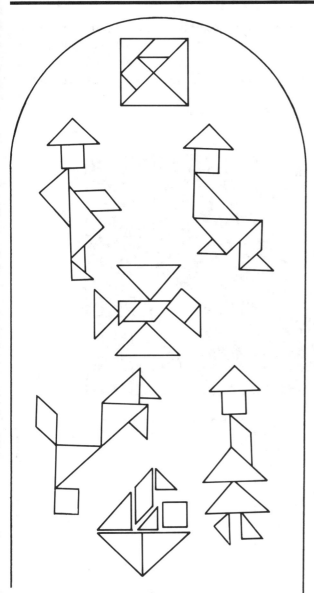

Your Own Design Puzzle

Cut out several different shapes from colored paper and place them on a piece of plain white paper. Use dry markers or crayons to draw around the shapes. You can also decorate the background if you like with lines drawn with the same crayon or marker.

To do the puzzle, mix up the cut-out shapes. See how quickly you can put them in the correct places.

Baby Owl

Cut a moon shape from construction paper to make a baby owl. Cut two black circles and paste them in the center of two larger white circles to make eyes. Cut a diamond from construction paper, fold in half to form a triangle for the beak, and paste in place. Cut two orange feet. Paste all shapes on a piece of colored construction paper.

An Old Chinese Puzzle

A 1-inch square of cardboard or heavy paper is used to make the figures shown in the illustration. Suppose you make the same figures using a 3-inch square. First mark out your square, then draw a line from one corner to the other, dividing the square in half. Then draw the other lines shown in the illustration. Cut out.

You can make better pictures if both sides of your square are the same color. If you use white paper for your pictures you will want colored paper on which to paste them. You must use every piece in each picture you make.

Bird House

On a sheet of paper draw the patterns for the birdhouse and the birds.

From colored construction paper, cut a piece like each pattern given for the birdhouse. Cut three pieces for each of the patterns for the birds. On a sheet of brightly colored construction paper mount the three birds and the birdhouse. You will notice that some of the half circles which are used for wings are folded and that a fold is made in the piece used for the tail before it is pasted on the paper. See what else you can make from these patterns.

Circle the different one in each group.

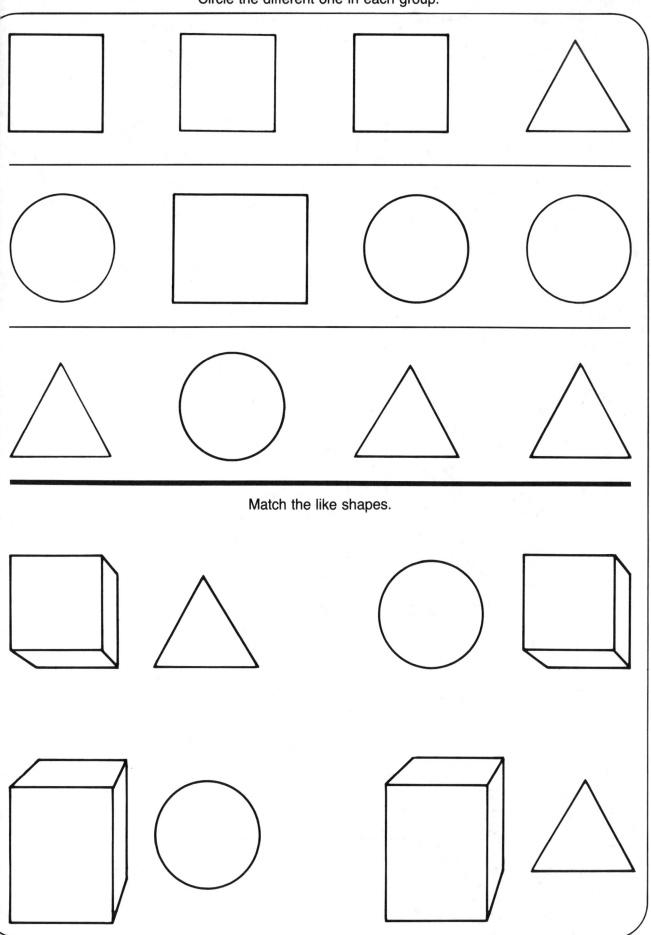

Match the like shapes.

SHAPES AND STROKES **399**

Color.

Fun With Shapes

Scissorettes

Using these shapes, see how many interesting things you can make.

From black and white paper, cut shapes like those below. For the circular pieces, use a compass or draw around objects such as a quarter or a paper cup. Make several sets. Keep each in a separate envelope. These are the ONLY shapes you will use.

You need not use all the pieces in any one creation, but you should use each piece ONLY ONCE. When you have arranged the pieces to make a picture you like, glue the pieces onto colored paper and give it a title.

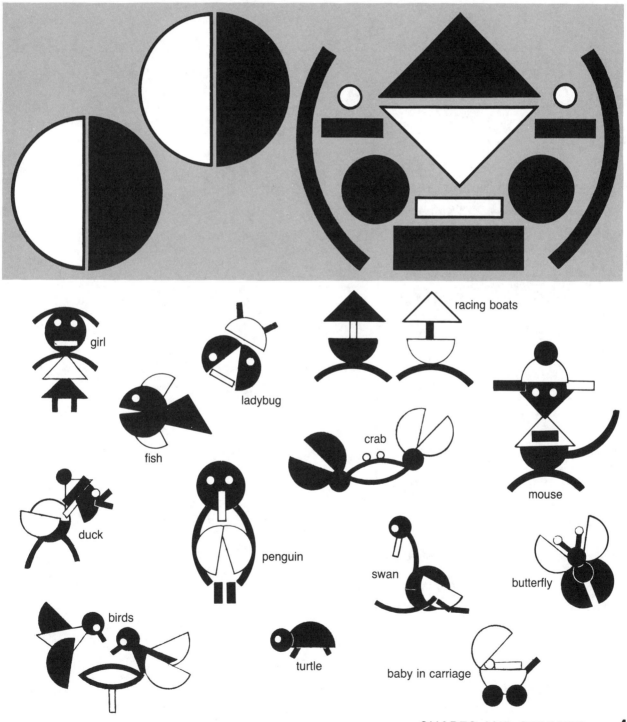

girl

ladybug

racing boats

fish

crab

mouse

duck

penguin

swan

butterfly

birds

turtle

baby in carriage

Colors

Ask your children these questions:

Some apples are red. Were they painted? What other colors can apples be?

What is the color of a banana? Of spinach?

What color is salt?

What color is the sky when there are no clouds?

What is the color of a lemon? Of a crow?

Is most paper white or black?

When you are painting a picture with watercolors and have different colors of paint to use, how can you make more colors as you paint?

What is the color of an apple after it is peeled?

Is chocolate candy white?

Is grass always green? Are bananas always yellow?

Name as many colors as you can. Which color do you like best?

What are the two colors of a hard-boiled egg?

What two colors do you most often see on Christmas packages?

What color do you get when you mix blue and yellow?

What color do you most often see on valentines?

What color is your house?

Is black a dark color or a light color?

Does a rainbow have one color or more than one?

If you came home from school one day, and the outside of your house was painted a different color, would you still be able to find your house? What things might help you find it?

If grapes and bananas were both blue, how would you be able to tell them apart?

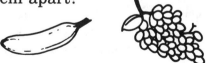

Would it be easy to find a white rabbit in the snow? Why?

Can you smell a color? Can you hear it?

Name some colors that birds can be.

What color is a strawberry? A cherry? How can you tell them apart?

403

Color Card Activities

Cut out 32 color cards, containing four each of red, green, yellow, blue, orange, white, purple, and black.

1. Distribute a color card to each child. Name a color by asking, "Where is Mr. Red Card?" Those children who have red cards hold them up and respond, "Here is Mr. Red Card."

2. Construct small game boards with eight colored squares. Each board should be different. Give each child a board. Place the 32 color cards in a box. Have a child be a leader, drawing out a color card and telling the color. The children cover the square that matches that color. The child who covers his or her board first wins.

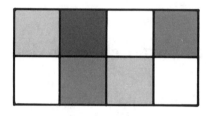

3. Give a child the 32 color squares in a bag. Place eight envelopes, coded by colors, in front of a child. The child is to sort the colors into correct envelopes.

4. Give each child a color card. Ask her or him to locate an object in the classroom that is the same color and stand by it. The children take turns saying the color and the object located.

5. Collect an assortment of buttons that are the eight basic colors. Place all the buttons in a box. Give a child eight basic color cards. The child is to sort buttons by color, placing each button on the card that it matches.

6. Lay color cards on the floor in random order. Ask a child to walk from red to yellow, using as few steps as possible. Continue by giving a variety of directions, for example, "Place your left hand on green and your right foot on red."

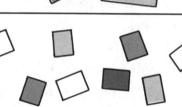

7. Construct a color wheel by dividing a pizza board into eight sections. Color each section, using the eight basic colors. Paint eight clip clothespins the eight basic colors. Have children match colors by clipping the clothespin in the matching pie section.

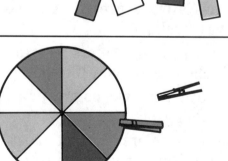
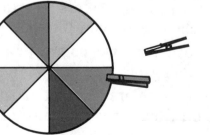

Color each thing the proper color.

COLORS   **405**

Color the boxes in the color indicated, then color the scarecrow by number.

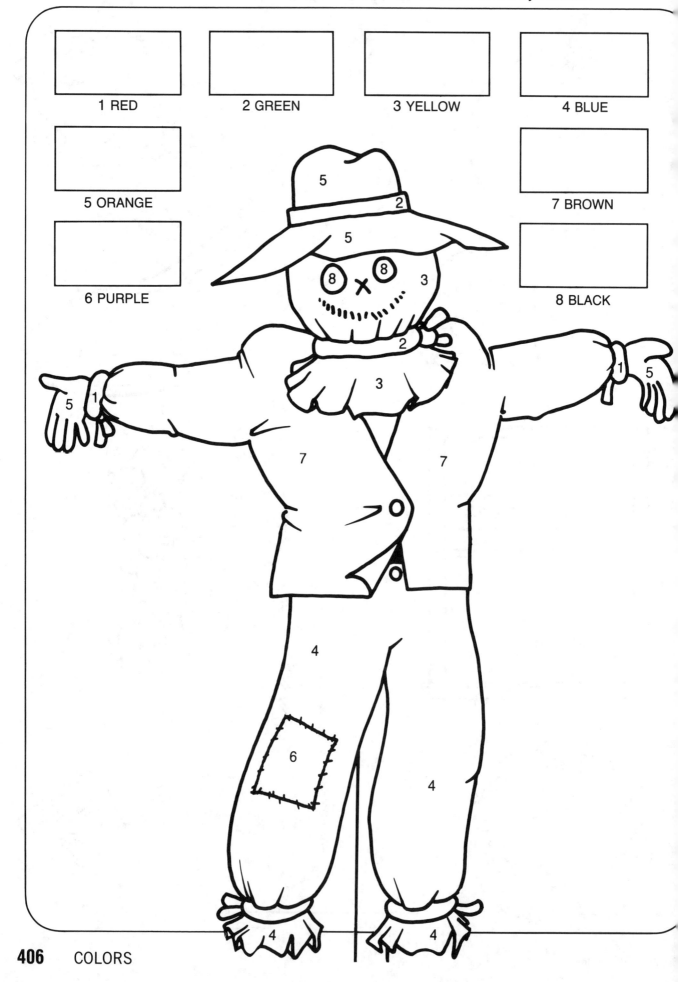

1 RED

2 GREEN

3 YELLOW

4 BLUE

5 ORANGE

7 BROWN

6 PURPLE

8 BLACK

Things To Do

Following Directions

Say to the child, "Watch me. Wait until I have finished, then with this pencil tap the blocks as I did."

Tap the yellow block two times. Tap the yellow block once and the green block three times. Tap the blue block three times, the yellow block twice, and the green block once. Tap the green block four times, the yellow block three times, and the blue block twice. Tap each block once, then each block twice, then each block three times.

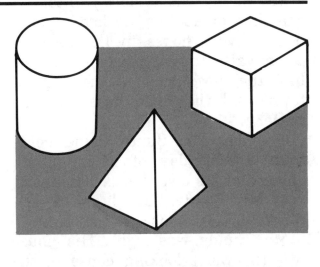

A Rainbow Treasure Hunt

It is surprising and exciting to find color in so many things we usually look at casually: bits of rock, stems, feathers, and the like.

Sometime, when you and the children are going for a walk look for Rainbow Treasure. In other words, suggest that they look for and bring back things with many colors. Each child should match each of the colors of the rainbow with something he or she finds on the hike. There will be six things in all.

If you want to make the game more difficult let each child find rainbow colors in the following order: red, orange, yellow, green, blue, and purple. This will mean that each child must find red before picking up any of the others. If a child should first find something blue he or she would have to leave it until he or she had found objects which are red, orange, yellow, and green.

This can be played at any season of the year. The winner will be the one who first finds objects of the rainbow colors in the order named.

Fireworks Picture

On black construction paper, draw lines with white glue in a design that fireworks might make. While the glue is still wet, sprinkle it with glitter. Carefully shake any glitter that does not stick to the glue back into the glitter container so that it can be used again. If you would like to make more than one fireworks design on a page, a different color of glitter may be used for each design. The fireworks that you make will be enjoyed long after real fireworks are just a memory.

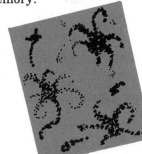

Crayon Creations

Peel the paper off a crayon. Then, with your fingernail or the point of a pair of scissors, carefully make narrow notches in the crayon. All the notches should be on one side of the crayon, but they may be spaced any way you wish.

Rub the notched edge along a piece of paper. Experiment with straight or wavy strokes. Add details with pencil, pen, or crayon.

The Painter's House

MARY RADLOFF

Mr. Bundy was a house painter. At one time or another he had painted nearly every house in the town of Sunnyvale—the big old house on the hill, the new house at the edge of town, and the little house on the corner.

One day Mr. Bundy came home from a long day of painting. He glanced at his own house. "Oh dear!" said Mr. Bundy. "My house is the worst looking house in the town!"

Mr. Bundy was right. His house was the worst looking house in the town of Sunnyvale. Mr. Bundy had been so busy painting all the other houses he had forgotten all about painting his own. There was no paint left anywhere on Mr. Bundy's house. He couldn't even remember what color it used to be. It just looked old and dull.

"Oh dear!" thought Mr. Bundy. "What color shall I paint my house?"

All that evening Mr. Bundy thought about what color to paint his house.

All that night Mr. Bundy dreamed about what color to paint his house.

The next morning at breakfast Mr. Bundy thought about what color to paint his house. He just could not decide what color to choose.

After breakfast Mr. Bundy went out to his paint shed. He looked at all his cans of paint. Some were full, some were half-full, and some had just a bit of paint left in the bottom. Suddenly Mr. Bundy had an idea.

"I know!" said Mr. Bundy. "I will try a little paint on my house. I will try several colors until I find one I like."

Mr. Bundy tried a little red paint on his front door. It looked friendly.

Mr. Bundy tried a little blue paint on the front porch. It looked bright and pleasant.

Mr. Bundy tried all the different colors of paint on his house. He painted the back door white and the back steps gray. He made one side of his house pink, one side yellow, one side purple and one side orange.

All day long Mr. Bundy painted his house. All the time he was painting he tried to decide which of all those colors he liked best.

All at once Mr. Bundy stopped painting. He saw that he had painted every single inch of his house. But he still couldn't decide what color to choose. He felt very sad and worried.

Just then the school bus stopped at the corner, and the children got off the bus.

"You have painted your house all colors!" said Ellen.

"Yes," said Mr. Bundy sadly.

"That is just the right way for a painter's house to look!" cried Barby.

Mr. Bundy looked at his newly painted house. He liked his bright, shining all-color house. Mr. Bundy smiled a bright, shining smile.

"Yes," said Mr. Bundy with great joy. "You are right. That is just the right way for a painter's house to look."

And to this day Mr. Bundy, the painter, lives in the best looking house in Sunnyvale. People come from all over to see it. Mr. Bundy is happy because he never did have to decide what color to paint his house.

Color the painter's house.

Color.

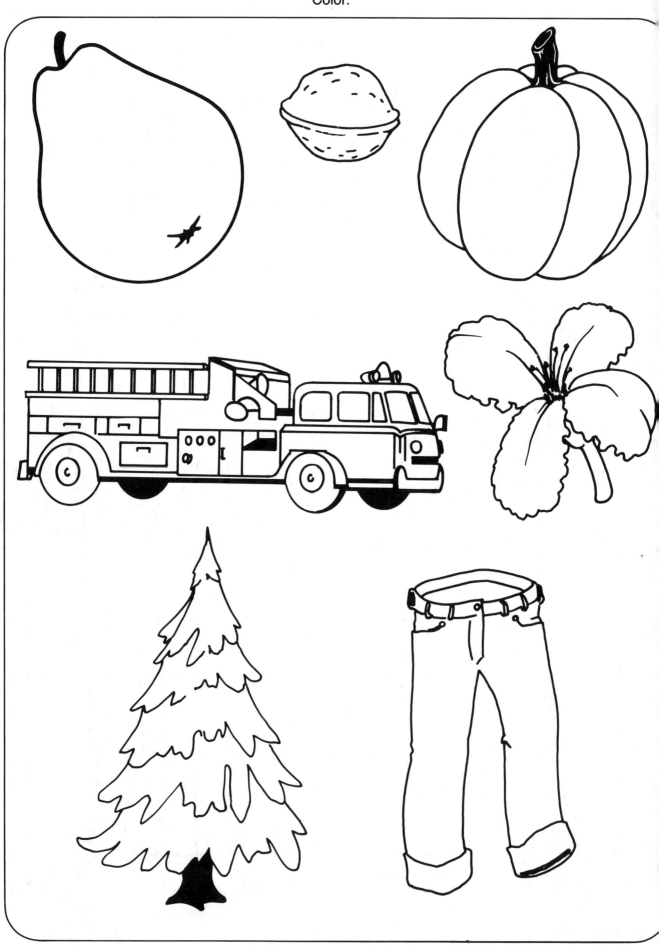

How Butterflies Got Their Colors

It was a beautiful day and all the animals were happy as the warm sun beat down on their backs. Everybody was happy except the butterflies. The butterflies were unhappy because they had no colors. It had never occurred to them that they were ugly until today when the magpie had said, "Oh brother, will you look at all those ugly butterflies."

The butterflies had been so hurt that they all went back to their den to talk about it.

The leader was flying back and forth in the den trying to think of something to do. He kept coming up with ideas but nobody liked them.

"Maybe I shouldn't be the leader if I can't think of a way to make us butterflies beautiful. Oh dear, I wish I had a good idea."

The leader couldn't think of anything, so he went outside to sit in the sun. While he was sitting in the sun, a beautiful rainbow came out to make the day prettier. The rainbow was so tempting that he forgot about his color and flew right into it.

When he came out the other end he had beautiful colors on his wings. He was so happy he did somersaults in the air.

"Oh boy, I better tell the others before the rainbow goes away."

So the leader called all the butterflies into the den. The butterflies were so amazed at all the colors the leader had that they couldn't sit still. The leader told them about the rainbow and showed them where it was.

All the butterflies got in a line and flew into the rainbow. One by one the butterflies went in the rainbow and when they came out they hardly had the same pattern on their wings. Now the other animals couldn't tell them they were ugly!

WENDY WEITZNER, Age 11

The Strawberry Frog

Once upon a time in a valley, a beautiful strawberry frog lived in a pond filled with strawberry soda.

All day he silently sat on a vanilla lily pad catching chocolate covered mosquitoes, and munching on cherry flavored ladybugs.

He was a lucky frog because he had a friend who was a beautiful princess, and never failed to come to the pond every day to play with her golden Yo-Yo. The frog liked the Yo-Yo. He was amazed at how it went up and down. But one day she lost it in the pond. She asked the frog to go and get it for her. He dived down into the water and little did the frog know that the princess was really an enchanted frog.

When he came up from the bottom of the pond he had the Yo-Yo.

She kissed him, and she turned into a beautiful frog and they were married and lived happily ever after in the strawberry pond.

KIM LEWIS, Age 10

Color Poems

Paints

ILO ORLEANS

When I put YELLOW
Paint on RED,
The colours change
To ORANGE instead.

And, mixing BLUE
And RED, I get
A pretty shade
Of VIOLET.

Another trick
That I have seen:
YELLOW and BLUE
Turn into GREEN.

There's magic when
My colours mix.
It's fun to watch them
Doing tricks.

A Poem for Colors

CHRISTINA GEORGINA ROSSETTI

What is pink? a rose is pink
By the fountain's brink.
What is red? a poppy's red
In its barley bed.
What is blue? the sky is blue
Where the clouds float thro'.
What is white? a swan is white
Sailing in the light.
What is yellow? pears are yellow,
Rich and ripe and mellow.
What is green? the grass is green,
With small flowers between.
What is violet? clouds are violet
In the summer twilight.
What is orange? why, an orange,
Just an orange!

World of Many Colors

Green for the grass,
Blue for the sky,
Brown for the dirt,
And red apples for pie.
Colors of the rainbow
Everywhere you look.
The world is much prettier,
Than any picture book.

DONNA SMITH, Age 10

Stoplight

Red on top,
Green below.
Red says, "Stop!"
Green says, "Go!"
Yellow says, "Wait!
Even if you're late."

JACKIE NASON, Age 10

The Purple Cow

GELETT BURGESS

I never saw a Purple Cow,
 I never hope to see one;
But I can tell you, anyhow,
 I'd rather see than be one.

Nature's Paints

KEVIN O'HARA

Night is black and sky is blue,
Apples are red or green in hue,
Sun is yellow, earth is brown,
Colors give the world its crown.

Color Crafts

Mixing Colors

Make a circle by drawing around a saucer on cardboard (1). On one half the circle on each side paste bright yellow paper or color it with bright yellow crayon. Color the other half blue. About one-fourth inch on either side of the center of the circle, make a hole with a darning needle (2) and through these two holes draw a long string, joining the two ends.

Take hold of both ends of the string and throw the disc around until the string is twisted (3).

As you pull the string back and forth the circle will revolve rapidly. What color does it seem to be?

Red, White, and Blue Weaving

You will need a 9-inch by 14-inch piece of onion sack and 9-inch pieces of red, white, and blue yarn to weave a placemat. Use the piece of onion sack as a base. Weave the red, white, and blue strips through it. Trim the edges. Squeeze some white glue on the back of the mat along the edges of the onion sack to hold the yarn in place. You may want to make a set of these placemats.

Colored Sawdust

Fun with sawdust! Who doesn't enjoy feeling it, playing with it? Now we can make pictures with it in any colors we choose.

The picture here used three colors: yellow for the chickens, red for tulip, and green for tulip leaves and grass.

Color the sawdust as follows: In each of three cups place respectively a few brushfuls of tempera yellow, red, and green. Watercolor may be used but it will need to be thick. Add a couple of spoonfuls of water. Then stir in a few "pinches" of sawdust. No particular rule can be given, but

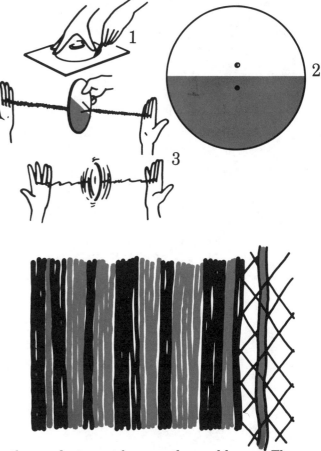

the sawdust must be very thoroughly wet. Then spread on papers to dry. This may take overnight. You will know when it is dry. Put a portion of the colored sawdust in an envelope marked for safekeeping.

On drawing paper, draw a picture. If you use one like the illustration, first make the chickens. Pour a little glue on each, one at a time, and paint it in carefully with a small brush. Sift yellow sawdust on it, and shake back all extra sawdust into your envelope. Let dry. Repeat same process for tulip flower, using red. Lastly do leaves and grass.

Numbers

Give each member of the group two cards each of red, green, yellow and blue. (The cards may be cut from construction paper.) In the front of the room have four boxes, each marked with a color: red, green, yellow and blue.

Tell the class, "I am about to hold up some cards, either one or two at a time. When you can match exactly the cards I am holding up, you hold up your matching cards. Then come to the front of the room and put your cards in the matching color box."

Hold up two yellow cards. The class drops two yellow cards into the box. Hold up one green card. The class drops one green card into the box. Hold up one blue card. The class drops one blue card into the box. Hold up two red cards. The class drops two red cards into the box. Hold up two green cards. The class should say, "That's impossible," or "It can't be done." Ask the class why they cannot put two green cards into the box. They should answer that they only have one green card.

Ask the class if they can put two blue cards into the box. They should answer that they cannot because they only have one blue card. Tell the class, "I want to put two cards in boxes. How can I do this when I only have one green and one blue?" Let the class work out the problem and explain their answers.

Set up two stuffed toys on a board that is resting between two chairs. Divide the class into two teams. Teams alternate turns.

A child lines up about five feet from the animals. She or he picks a number from a box. If the child picks a *1*, she or he gets one toss of a bean bag to knock the animals off the board. If she or he picks a *2*, she or he gets two throws.

The team that knocks the most animals off the board in a specified time limit is the winner.

Draw or mark out on the floor, two sets of six boxes parallel to each other.

Also make a spinner with *1*'s and *2*'s on it. (Or use a die with one and two spots on it.)

(Or you may use a box with cards of *1* and *2*.) In a large box, place six cards, five with the word *forward* written and illustrated on them, and one with the word *backward* written and illustrated on it.

Divide the class into teams of two. One member from each team (A) lines up at the starting line, while the other (B) spins the spinner and picks from the box. The two teams alternate turns.

B spins and picks from the *forward–backward* box. A moves that many spaces forward or backward. The other team does likewise.

When team member A makes it to the end of the boxes, he or she switches places with team member B. The first team where both members finish wins the game.

Activities for *3* and *4*

Call three children at a time to the front of the room. Give a bell to one child, a wood block and striker to the second child, and a drum to the third child. Hold up a number card with *2, 3,* or *4* written on it, or two, three or four fingers.

When you hold up two fingers (or a *2* number card), the child who has the bell should ring it two times.

When you hold up three fingers (or a *3* number card), the child who has the wood block should strike it three times.

When you hold up four fingers (or a *4* number card), the child who has the drum beats it four times.

As the children make these sounds, the rest of the class may count along.

Pick six children to come to the front of the class. Give each of the six children from one to four pictures of a single animal. There should be, for example, one lion picture, two pigs, three cows, three cats, four ducks, and four sheep.

A child makes the sound of the animal whose picture she or he holds, one time for each picture. (If he or she has three cats, the child would meow three times.) The class then tells how many of each animal the group has, after each member's turn.

Continue picking other children to come to the front of the class, until each child has had a turn.

On each of two desks or tables in the front of the room place one hat, one scarf, and two mittens. Also, place on each table a box with the following number cards inside: one *1,* two *2*'s, three *3*'s, and four *4*'s.

Divide the class into two teams. The teams line up about five feet from the tables. The first child on each team runs to that team's table, picks a number from the box, puts on that many items of clothing, then removes the clothing and returns the number card to the box. The player should then run back and touch the second player of his or her team. The second player fol-

lows the same procedure. The first team to finish is the winner.

Give each child in the class four bottle caps.

In turn, each child tries to toss her or his bottle caps into a pail about five feet away. The child counts each of her or his tries. The rest of the class counts the number of tosses that go into the pail.

Give each child a sheet of paper with several series of dots, varying each line from one to four dots.

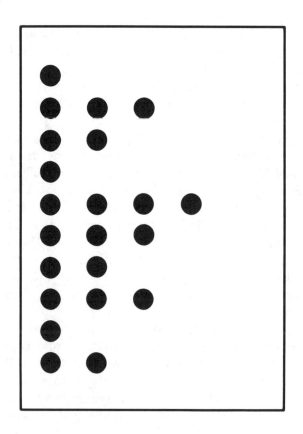

Each child is to add enough dots so that there are four on each line. Tell the children that if there are four dots already on a line they do not have to add any more to that line.

If you prefer, this exercise can be done at the chalkboard.

Match the numbers to the right amount of objects by drawing a line.

How many birds are there? How many cats?
How many people? How many fish?

NUMBERS **417**

Match the number of objects on the left to the same number of objects on the right by drawing a line.

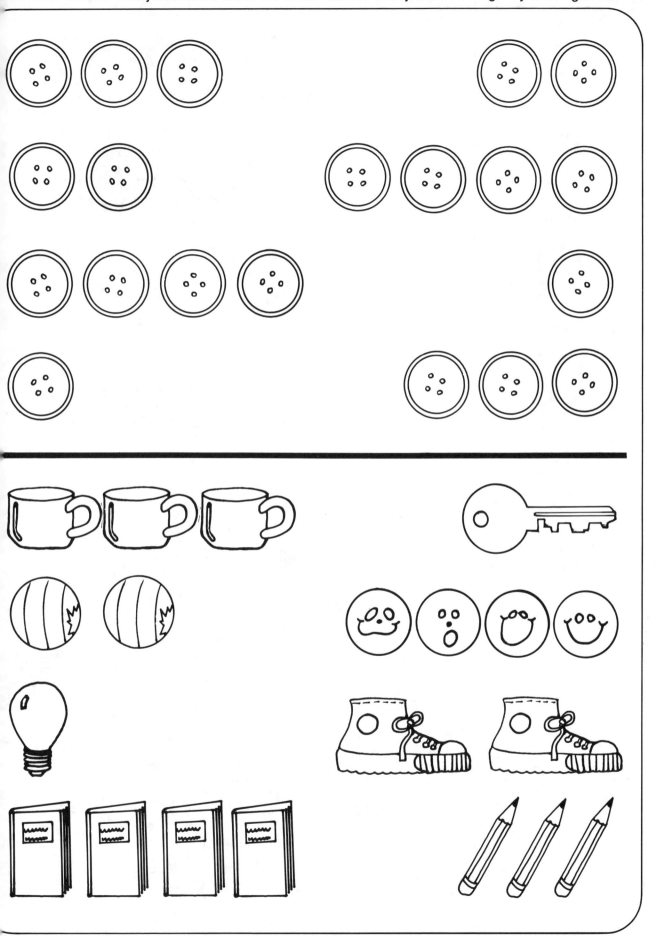

Match the numbers to the right amount of objects by drawing a line.

1
2
3
4

How many pumpkins are there?
How many birds?
How many rails in the fence?
How many scarecrows?

Match the number of objects on the left to the same number of objects on the right by drawing a line.

Match the numbers to the right amount of objects by drawing a line.

3
4
5
6

How many birds are there on the bush?
How many on the ground?
How many on the clothesline?
How many on the fence?

Activities for 5 and 6

Face the class and tell them, "I am going to clap my hands now. If I clap 3 times, you are to sit down. If I clap 4 times, raise your arms. If I clap 5 times, stand up. If I clap 6 times, you clap 6 times."

Start slowly, and increase speed as children become familiar with the directions.

Divide the class into groups of six and give each group a color name.

A member of the first group calls a number to the second group, for example, "Blue group— five." Five children from the Blue group stand up. The caller counts them. If they are correct, Blue gets one point. A member of the Blue team then gets to call the Green team and the Green team calls the Red team (if three groups are used).

Play until each one in the class gets a chance to call a number and check the answer. The team with the most correct tries is the winner. (The numbers are restricted to 1 to 6.)

Make up cards with pictures of three, four or five like animals, one card for each member of the class. In addition, make up many cards with only one of the same animal. You need not use more than three or four different animals if you wish.

Each member of the class picks a card from a bag or box, and goes back and studies it. When called again, he or she comes to the front of the room and takes enough like single-animal cards to total six when added to his or her card. If the child is correct, he or she drops his or her cards back into the box. If wrong, he or she studies the cards again and then has another chance. If still wrong, child can call a classmate to help.

Divide the class into groups of five and six.

In front of the class hold up cards with groups of five or six items on them.

If the card has five items on it, each member of the 5 group hops on one foot five times, counting as he or she does so.

If the card has six items on it, each member of the 6 group hops on both feet six times, counting as he or she does so.

Five Nickels

EDITH VESTAL

Yesterday Danny was a little boy.
Next day he was a big boy.
It was his birthday.
He was five years old.

Daddy had given Danny a ball.
Mother was going to make him some cookies with pink frosting.

Just then Mother called.
She needed some milk.
She asked Danny to go to the store.

Mother gave him five nickels.
"Five nickels because you are five years old.
Don't lose them, Danny.
Count them."
Danny counted:
"One, two, three, four, five."

Danny shut his hand tight.
They would never fall out with his hand shut tight.

In the next block were some workmen.
They had made a big, big pile of dirt.
Danny stopped.

Some boys were sliding.
Up to the top they would climb.
Then down they would slide.
Danny wanted to slide.
He ran to the dirt.

Then he remembered.
This was his birthday.

He had on his new pants.
Besides, he had the milk money.
He might lose it.

He opened his hand.
He counted:
"One, two, three, four, five."
All the nickels were there.
He shut his hand tight.

He began to skip.

There was the bridge.
It was fun to look into the water.
He saw hundreds of minnows.

He began to count minnows.

"One, two, three, four, five, six, seven, eight, nine, ten."
He counted again:
"One two, three, four, five, six, seven, eight, nine, ten."
But there were too many.

There was one more thing to do.
It was the most fun of all.
There was a low railing by the store.
He could walk on it.

He climbed up.
But something happened.
He slipped.
He threw out his hand.

Then he heard—
Clink—clink—clink—clink—clink.
His hand had opened.
Every nickel had fallen out.
They were rolling down the walk.
Then down through a grating,
Down, down, down they fell.
One, two, three, four, five.
All went through the grating.

Danny got down on his knees.
There they were.
He counted:
"One, two, three, four, five."

But he couldn't reach them.
No one could reach them.
Not even a giant with long arms.

Suddenly Danny heard a voice:
"Hello, young fellow. What's the matter with you?"

It was Uncle Mike.
Danny showed Uncle Mike the nickels.
"Can you get them?"

Uncle Mike found a long stick.

He bought some gum.
"Chew this, Danny.
Then you can get your nickels."

Danny chewed the gum.
Then Uncle Mike put it on the end of the stick.
"Now put the gum down on top of a nickel and pull it up."

Danny did.
He pulled up one nickel.
He pulled up another nickel.
He put the stick down five times.
He pulled up five nickels.

Now Danny was smiling again—
"Oh, Uncle Mike, come over to my house. I'll give you half of my cookies."

Fun With Fingers

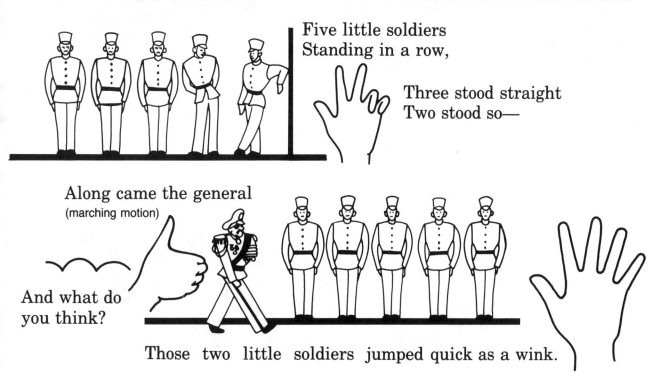

Five little soldiers
Standing in a row,

Three stood straight
Two stood so—

Along came the general
(marching motion)

And what do you think?

Those two little soldiers jumped quick as a wink.

Activities for 7 and 8

Using a piano, triangle or some other means of making distinct musical sounds, play notes to the class. Tell the children, "I am about to play musical notes to you. If I play six notes, you clap six times. If I play seven notes, you clap seven times. If I play eight notes, you clap eight times."

Tell the class to stand up. Tell them, "Santa Claus has eight reindeer. I am sure you know their names—Dasher, Dancer, Prancer, Vixen, Comet, Cupid, Donner and Blitzen. I am now going to call some of them by name. If I call all eight of them, you take eight steps forward. If I only call seven of them, you take seven steps backward."

Call the names, mixing their order so the class has to count them. You can have the class count aloud if you like, either while you are calling reindeer or while they are stepping.

Divide the class into groups of two. Have one member of the group turn his or her back and close his or her eyes.

Hold up number cards (either numerals or dots). The second member of each group touches the one with his or her back turned that many times on the shoulder. The one touched tells how many times he or she was touched. The partners then switch roles.

Make up cards in sets of eight, at least one card for each child in your class. On seven of the cards draw a picture of a dwarf, numbering each dwarf card from 1 to 7. (Either numerals or dots may be used.) The eighth card has a picture of Snow White, with an 8 or eight dots on it.

Mix up the cards and then give one card, placed face down to each member of the class. The children turn their cards over and try to form groups of eight—Snow White and the Seven Dwarves (in order).

If you like, the first group formed could be declared the winner.

Make up a skiing course with eight sets of "gates."

The "gates" can be two chairs back-to-back, marked with a number from one to eight.

The class pretends to be skiers and maneuvers between the "gates", counting each one as they go through.

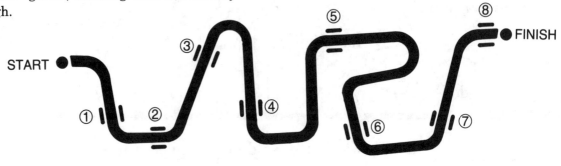

Match the number of objects on the left to the same number of objects on the right by drawing a line.

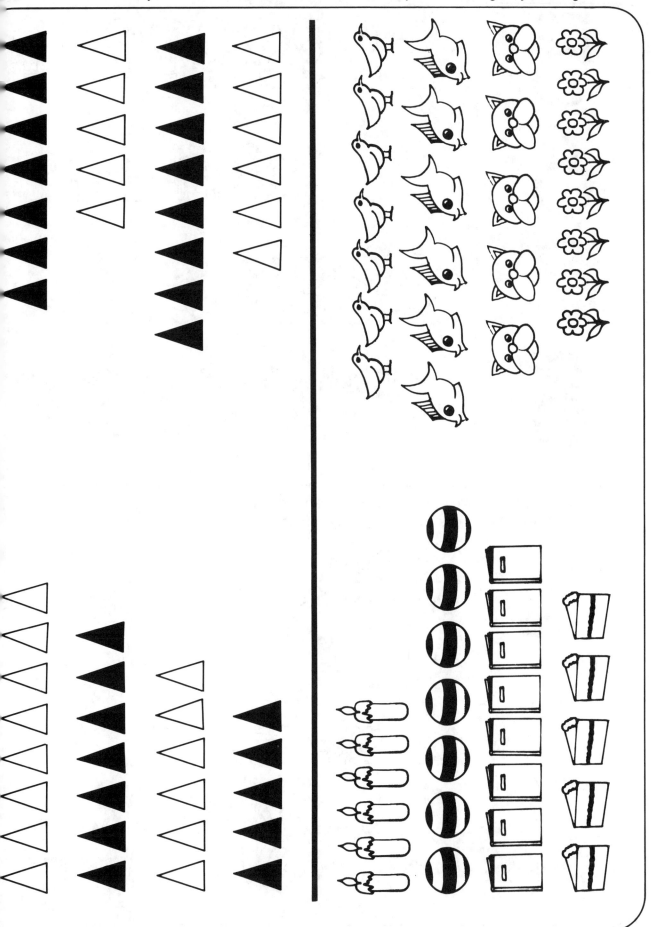

Match the numbers to the right amount of objects by drawing a line.

5
6
7
8

How many apples are there? How many children?
How many baskets? How many rays of the sun?

NUMBERS **429**

Match the numbers to the right amount of objects by drawing a line.

7

8

9

10

How many feet do you see? How many boards are in the fence?
How many eyes and ears altogether? How many peanuts?

giraffe

elephant

flamingo

Activities for 9 and 10

Gather together a variety of means of making musical sounds, such as a bell, a wood block, a drum, a triangle.

Tell the class to stand. Play notes in sets of nine and ten, sometimes all with one instrument, sometimes one note at a time on each instrument.

When you play nine notes, the class claps their hands over their heads one time.

When you play ten notes, the class squats down and taps the floor one time.

Later, have the class count the notes as you play them.

Show the class either a picture of a cat or a picture of a dog. Explain to the class that if you hold up the picture of the dog, they are to bark nine times.

If you hold up the picture of the cat, they are to meow ten times.

If you hold up both pictures, they are to clap their hands ten times.

Set up five boxes around the room with pictures or drawings on them of a bird's nest, a dog house, a barn, a bee hive, and a pond.

Next to each home, place a pile of appropriate animal cards: bird, dog, horses, bees, and fish.

Attach a card to the front of each home with either nine or ten dots on it.

The children go to each home, count the dots on the outside, and then put the correct number of birds, dogs, horses, bees, or fish in it. Each child visits all five homes.

The number of dots on the homes may be changed during the game. Empty the boxes every few rounds, or whenever the pile of animal cards outside the home runs out.

Prepare a group of cards that are plain on one side but have a red or green circle on the other side. Place a pail in the front of the room, together with a pile of clothespins.

Each child draws a card from the pile. If the card is red, the child takes nine clothespins from the pile. If the card is green, the child takes ten clothespins from the pile.

The child then drops the clothespins, one at a time into the pail, counting them as they fall.

Have the children trace both of their hands on a piece of paper and number the fingers from *1* to *10*.

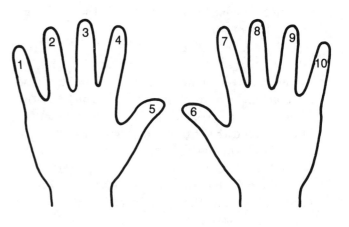

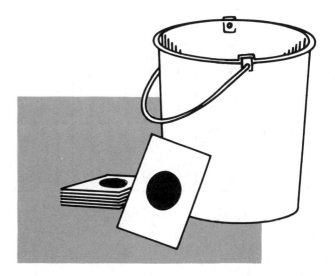

Activities for *0*

Face the class, holding a harmonica or flute. Play one, two, three, or zero short notes on the instrument. (For zero notes, put the instrument up to your mouth, but do not play a note.) The class stamps their feet or claps their hands the number of times that corresponds to the number of notes played. For zero notes, the children must sit very still.

Four children come to the front of the room. Each of the four children is given a plastic or tin container and two, four, six, or zero pennies. Stand behind the children and say, "Ready, go", then knock on the desk two, four, six, or zero times. The child with the number of pennies corresponding to the number of knocks drops his or her pennies into the container one at a time, while the class counts aloud. The child with zero pennies turns his or her container upside down, when no taps are heard, to show the class that there is nothing in his or her container.

Give each child a wooden stick or pencil. Stand in front of the class and say, "one," "three," "five," or "zero." The children tap the wooden stick on their desks or tables that number of times. When you say, "zero," the children must hide the wooden sticks behind their backs.

Place number cards *0* through *9* face down in a box in the front of the room. Also in the front of the room, have a large bag of peanuts and one empty bag. Each child goes to the front of the room, picks a card out of the box, shows it to the class, then takes that many peanuts out of the bag and puts them into the empty bag, while the class counts. After every child has had a turn, the children may eat the peanuts.

Construct a board game with two rows of thirty squares each. (The chalkboard may be used instead of a board.) Also, make a spinner with the numbers *1* through *9*, and several *0*'s.

Divide the class into two teams. Each team has a marker, which they place on their side of the board. Each member of the team gets a chance to spin the spinner and move the marker according to the number he or she spins. When a child spins a *0*, he or she does not move at all. The first team to move their marker across the finish line wins the game.

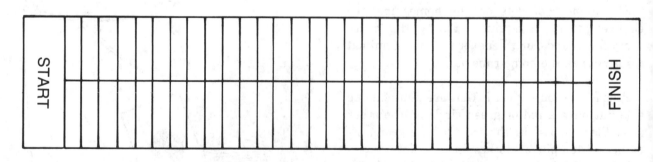

Connect the numeral on the left to the correct picture on the right by drawing a line.

0　2

5

4　3

Match the number of objects on the left to the same number of objects on the right by drawing a line.

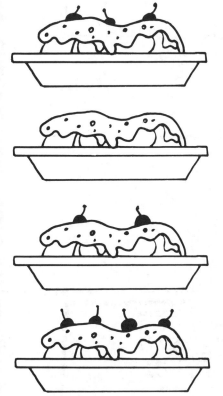

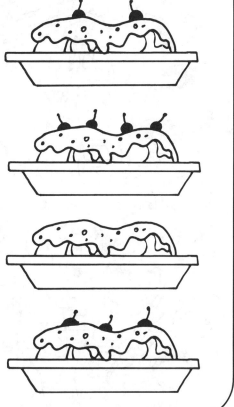

Can you find 1 kiddie car, 3 bears, 5 candles, 6 dolls, and 7 balls in this picture?

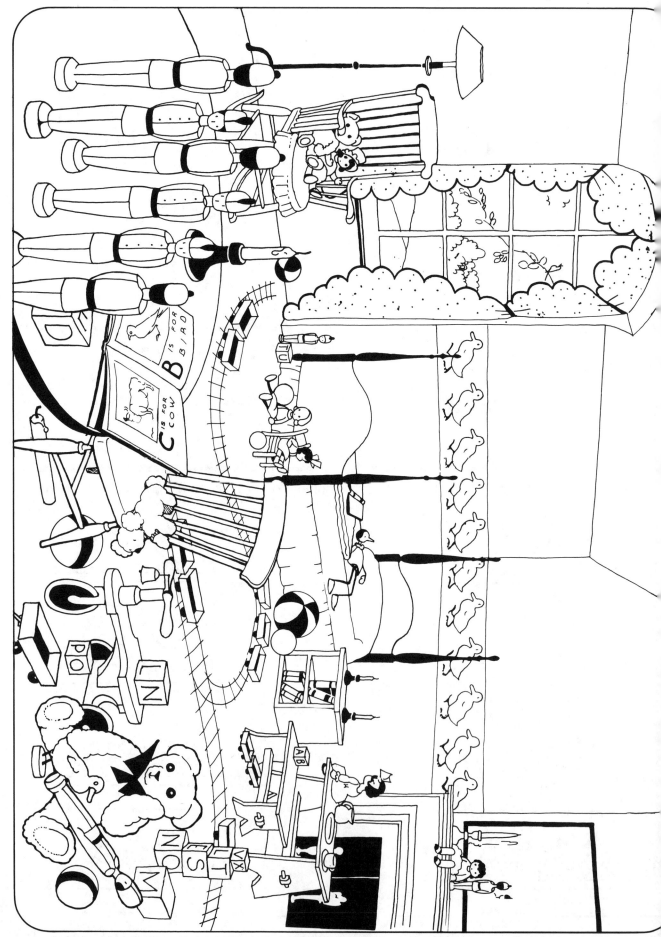

Thinking and Reasoning ▬▬▬▬▬

Ask your children these questions:

If you have two sisters and one brother, how many children are in your family?

If you have eight blocks, is this more or less than six blocks?

If you went to a farm and saw one cow, one horse, one pig, and one sheep, how many animals would you see?

Do you have one arm or more than one?

Which do you have more of, toes or heads?

Would you rather walk up and down your street one time or nine times? Why?

How many wheels are on a car? How many wheels are on a tree?

What are the numbers that are less than *4?*

If you have six apples and four oranges, which do you have more of, apples or oranges?

How many pets do you have?

How many cars does your family have?

How many days a week do you go to school? How many days a week do you not have to go to school?

If you wore a ring on every finger of your right hand, how many rings would that be?

Do you have four ears?

Can you think of anything that has more legs than you do?

Could you eat breakfast eight times in one day?

How many times do you wake up in one morning?

Which do you have more of, hands or noses?

How many birthdays do you have in one year?

How many teachers do you have?

How many legs does a chair have?

How many teeth does a crayon have?

Which do you have more of, friends or parents?

How many years old are you?

If you have three red crayons and one yellow crayon, which color do you have more of?

How many beds do you have?

How many windows are in your classroom?

How many floors are in your classroom?

How many doors are in your classroom?

How many corners are in your classroom?

How many shoes can you wear at one time?

If you have two mittens, and you lose one of them, how many are left?

If you have six white hats and two brown hats, which do you have more of, white hats or brown hats?

Can two people eat one apple? How do you think they could do it?

How many fingers are on one of your hands?

How many brothers do you have?

One, two,
Buckle my shoe;
Three, four,
Knock at the door;
Five, six
Pick up sticks;
Seven, eight,
Lay them straight;
Nine, ten,
A good, fat hen.

MOTHER GOOSE

A Counting Tongue-Twister Story

RUTH E. LIBBEY

One old owl observed
two tan turtles toddling toward
three tall thorny thistles.
Four funny fish find
five fat flies.
Six sheep sleeping soundly.
Seven ships sailing slowly.
Eight eels exercising.
Nine noisy nuthatches nibbling nuts near
ten tumbling toads.

A Halloween Counting Poem

MARY ANN GEORGE

ONE scary witch
is coming down the street;
She's tapping at doors and calling,
"Trick or Treat."

TWO black cats
appear at the gate;
With arched-up backs, they watch
and wait.

THREE jack-o'-lanterns
sit grinning in a row;
Their candles flicker an eerie glow.

FOUR bats awake
and begin to fly,
Swishing and swooping across the sky.

FIVE tree stumps
in the shadows deep
Crouch like monsters ready to leap.

SIX orange leaves
float down through the air;
They rustle and whisper, "Beware,
beware!"

SEVEN gray clouds
slide the moon from sight.
They stop; they hover; they darken
the night.

EIGHT white objects
twist and twine.
Are they ghosts or sheets on a line?

NINE little field mice
scatter and run.
Spooky nights are not much fun.

TEN owls
smile—they know, you see,
It's Halloween, and the witch is ME!

Fun With Fingers

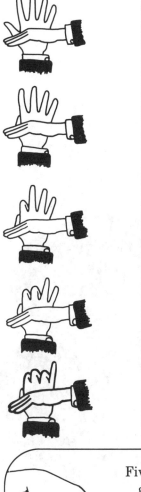

Five little birds sitting on a door.
One jumped off. Then there were four.

Four little birds happy as can be.
One flew away. Then there were three

Three little birds with nothing to do.
One fell off. Then there were two.

Two little birds chirping in the sun.
A bird flew away. Then there was one.

One little bird sitting in the sun.
Away he flew. Then there were none.

Five little kittens
    going out the door,
(walking motion with fingers)
One saw a mouse,
Then there were four.

Four little kittens
climbing up a tree.
One scampered down again,
Then there were three.

Three little kittens
purring as they do,
One chased a butterfly,
Then there were two.

Two little kittens
miaowing just for fun,
One chased a chipmunk,
Then there was one.

One little kitten
sleeping in the sun,
Thought he heard a dog bark,
Then there were none.

Point to the number that tells how many wheels a tricycle has.
The number of legs a puppy has.
The number which tells how old you were on your first birthday.
The number of fingers on one hand.
The number of ears you have.
The number which tells how many wings you have.

Cut out the pictures and paste them in correct order by numbers so they will tell a story.

Connect the dots in proper order to make a picture.

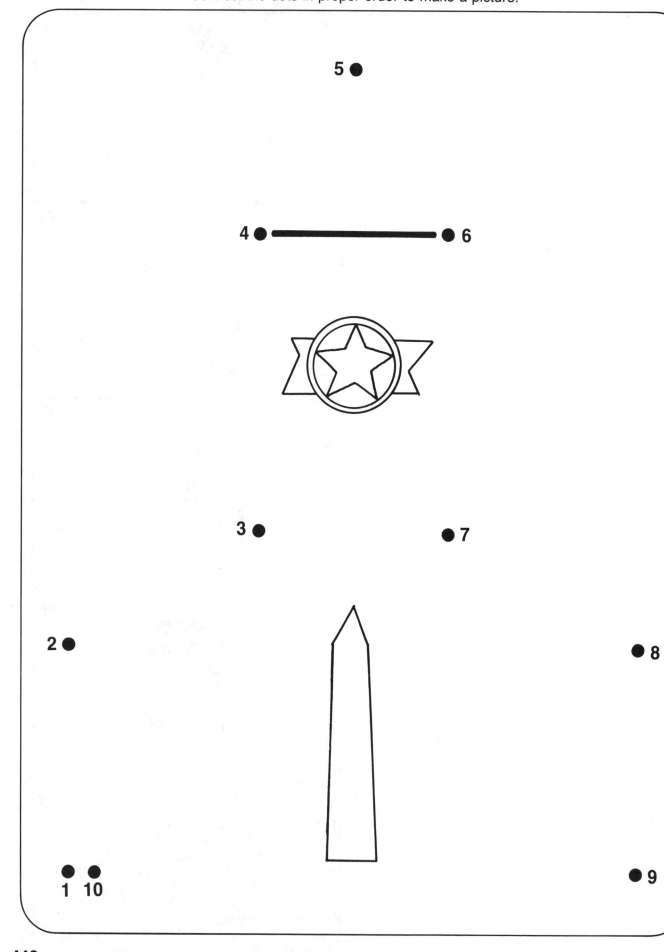

5 ●

4 ●━━━━━━━━━● 6

3 ●   ● 7

2 ●   ● 8

1 ● 10 ●   ● 9

A x

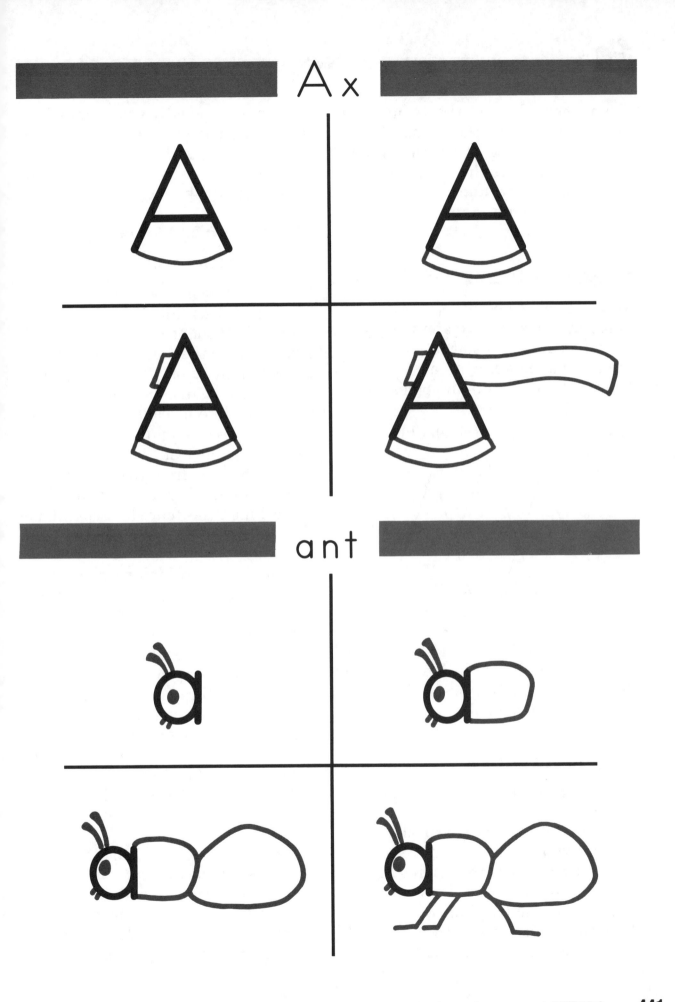

ant

Show the children how to draw these figures, beginning with the letter forms.

The names of three things in each group of four have the sound of ă in them. Pick out the one in each group that does not have the sound of ă.

deer, magic, cat, back
flat, hanger, frog, bag
lamp, bike, ham, glass

Tongue Twisters

Alice Adams is absent.
Applesauce makes alligators angry.
Andy has ants in his attic.
Aunt Anna answered an ad.
Actors admire arrows in apples.

Draw this figure on the chalkboard.

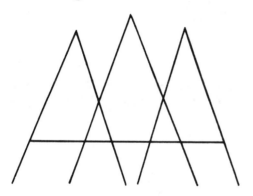

Ask the class how many letter *A*'s they can find. Have children come to the chalkboard and trace each *A* in a different colored chalk.

Beginning with *a*

For each clue, say a word that beings with ă.
1. A tool with a very sharp edge that you swing to chop down trees.
2. A kind of car with flashing lights and a siren. It is used to bring sick people to the hospital.
3. A long, thin stick with a point at one end and feathers at the other end. It is usually shot from a bow.
4. An animal with a long head and tail, big mouth and thick, rough skin. It lives on land and water and looks like a crocodile.

The Lion and the Alligator

Retold by GLENNDA SHERMAN

One day Lion was sitting by the river, admiring his reflection in the water. He thought himself quite good-looking. No other animal in the jungle could boast of a mane as golden and fluffy as his. No other animal could roar like he could.

"I am truly magnificent. I deserve to be king," he said.

Just then, up from the muddy river came Alligator. "Did I hear you claim to be king?" he roared. "Look at my fine teeth. Surely these are the teeth of a king!"

"Humph," said Lion with scorn. "A king needs strong legs to carry him swiftly through the jungle; yours are very short. I do not think they would carry you very fast."

"Aargh," snapped Alligator. "Why should I run through the jungle when I can swim the river, for I am a powerful swimmer. I should be king."

Lion sat very still and considered what Alligator had said. "Very well," he said at last. "You, Alligator, will be king of the river, and I, Lion, will be king of the jungle."

"Seems fair to me," said Alligator, and he swam away.

Lion was very proud of himself. After all, a true king must not only be strong and fair to look upon; he must also be very, very wise.

Connect the picture on the left to the matching picture in the center by drawing a line, and then connect the line to the matching word.

arrow   ambulance

ant

anchor

ambulance

ant

anchor

apple

apple

arrow

Connect the picture on the left to the matching picture in the center by drawing a line, and then connect the line to the matching word.

book

boat

boat

ball

book

ball

Find as many things as you can in this picture that begin with the sound of *b*.

b

The names of three things in each group of four begin with the same sound of *b*.

Pick out the one in each group that begins with a different sound.

box, bat, telephone, bed
kite, bell, banana, bus
bear, bag, bubble, apple

Tongue Twisters

Bob Boggs bought brown bread.
Bill blew a big blue bubble.
Better beat the batter better.
The black back brake broke.
A big black bug bit a big brown bear.

Beginning With *b*

For each clue, give a word that begins with the sound of *b*.

1. where you sleep
2. what you hit a baseball with
3. day you were born
4. a yellow fruit
5. cook in an oven
6. what you put on a cut
7. a toy that bounces
8. place where you save money
9. person who cuts hair
10. a very young child
11. what you are with your shoes and socks off
12. house for cows
13. place where you can swim
14. very pretty
15. hair on a man's chin
16. animal that chews down trees
17. two-wheeler
18. creature that flies
19. keeps you warm at night
20. what you make toast out of
21. first meal of the day

An animal whose name begins with *b* is the **bee.**

Bees live in burrows which they dig in the ground.

Bees are attracted to flowers with unusual shapes and colors.

When a bee finds a source of nectar, he does a "bee dance" to let the other bees know where it is.

Honeybees are important for the honey and beeswax they produce.

Honeybees use scent to mark their hives and to alert other bees to danger.

Me a Bee

I am a bee,
So look at me.
My stripes are yellow and black—
They're on my legs,
And on my head,
And also on my back.

STEVEN HARVELL, Age 8

Bees

Buzzy bees,
Busy bees
Work busily
On their nest.

ERIC ANDERSON, Age 6

Birdies

Two little birdies,
Sitting in a tree,
Flying around their nest,
Keeping their babies company.

KRISTEN LAWREY, Age 6

Belt

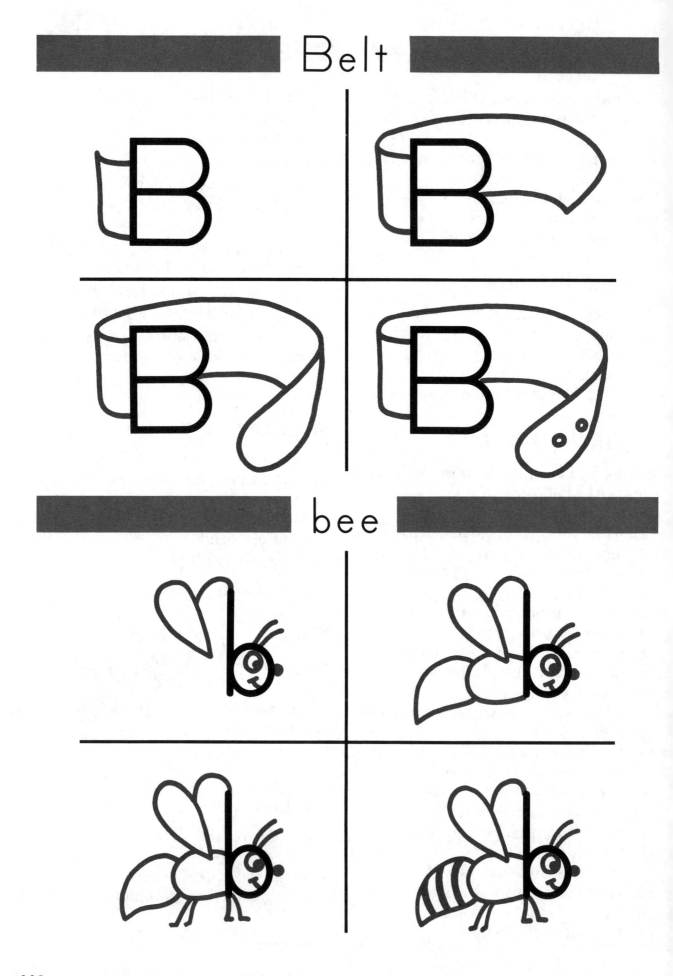

bee

Show the children how to draw these figures, beginning with the letter forms.

Canoe

clown

The names of three things in each group of four begin with the same sound of *c*. Pick out the one in each group that begins with a different sound.

cat, cane, book, collar
cookies, ant, camel, cave
girl, cow, cap, can

Beginning with *c*

For each clue, say a word that begins with *c*.

1. The opposite of *hot*.
2. The thing with which you take photographs.
3. The person at the circus who tries to make you laugh.
4. The person who rides a horse and tends herds of cattle.
5. The food that has candles on it, that you eat at your birthday party.
6. The bed with sides where a baby sleeps.

An animal whose name begins with *c* is the **cow.**

Cows are important for meat and milk.

In India, cows may not be killed because they are sacred.

Cows have four stomachs to help digest their food.

Most cows are milked by machines, on dairy farms.

In this country there are four times as many beef cows as there are dairy cows.

Tongue Twisters

The cold camel carried a coat.
The cows cried in the cave.
A copper coffee can can't cook cookies.
The clown crushed the cat's cap.
The carrot cake and cookies came.

The Moo-Cow-Moo

EDMUND VANCE COOKE

My pa held me up to the Moo-Cow-Moo
So close I could almost touch,
En I fed him a couple of times, or two,
En I wasn't a 'fraid-cat much.

But if my papa goes into the house
And mama, she goes in, too,
I just keep still, like a little mouse,
For the Moo-Cow-Moo might moo.

The Moo-Cow-Moo's got a tail like a rope
And it's raveled down where it grows,
And it's just like feeling a piece of soap
All over the Moo-Cow's nose.

And the Moo-Cow-Moo has lots of fun
Just swinging his tail about;
And he opens his mouth and then I run—
Cause that's where the moo comes out.

Connect the picture on the left to the matching picture in the center by drawing a line, and then connect the line to the matching word.

cookie

crib

cake

can

crib

car

can

cookie

car

cake

Connect the picture on the left to the matching picture in the center by drawing a line, and then connect the line to the matching word.

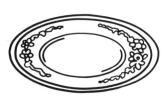

desk

drum

dog

dish

dish

dress

dress

desk

drum

dog

The names of three things in each group of four begin with the same sound of *d*. Pick out the one in each group that begins with a different sound.

dog, cup, duck, door
dart, deer, dream, man
elephant, doctor, daughter, dentist

Tongue Twisters

Deer dream of ducks.
The doll's dress dried.
Dinosaurs and dragons do dance.
Daddy dropped the dripping dish.
The doctor and dentist drove.

My Dog Caesar

I have a dog, Caesar,
And a great dog is he.
He turns over the trash
And who picks it up? Me!
He pulls all the clothes
Off the line.
He may not be much,
But at least he's mine!

CRAIG HILL, Age 8

The Dog

A dog came walking
Down our street.
He wasn't pretty
Or very neat.
He had no collar
And just one eye.
But I just loved
That cute little guy.

DANNY HEYDER, Age 9

Draw a group of large and small dishes on the chalkboard and sets of large and small glasses with drinks in them. Mark the large ones with an upper-case *D* and the small ones with a lower-case *d*. Also, draw a bunch of large daisies with an upper-case *D* and some small diamonds with a lower-case *d*.
Tell this story:

The Dinosaur and The Dwarf

Long ago, a dinosaur and a dwarf decided to have dinner together. Because of their different sizes, everything for the big dinosaur was marked with an upper-case *D* and everything for the little dwarf was marked with a lower-case *d*.

Which dishes were the dinosaur's and which were the dwarf's?

Which drinks were the dinosaur's and which were the dwarf's?

What did the dinosaur eat for dinner?

What did the dwarf eat for dinner?

After a delicious dinner and dessert, they danced until dark.

An animal whose name begins with *d* is the **dog.**

A newborn dog is called a puppy.

A puppy cannot hear or see when it is born because its ears and eyes are sealed for about two weeks.

Dogs can be helpful in hunting.

Dogs have been tamed by people for 10,000 years.

Dogs can hear sounds that people can not hear.

Dogs are color-blind.

Dart

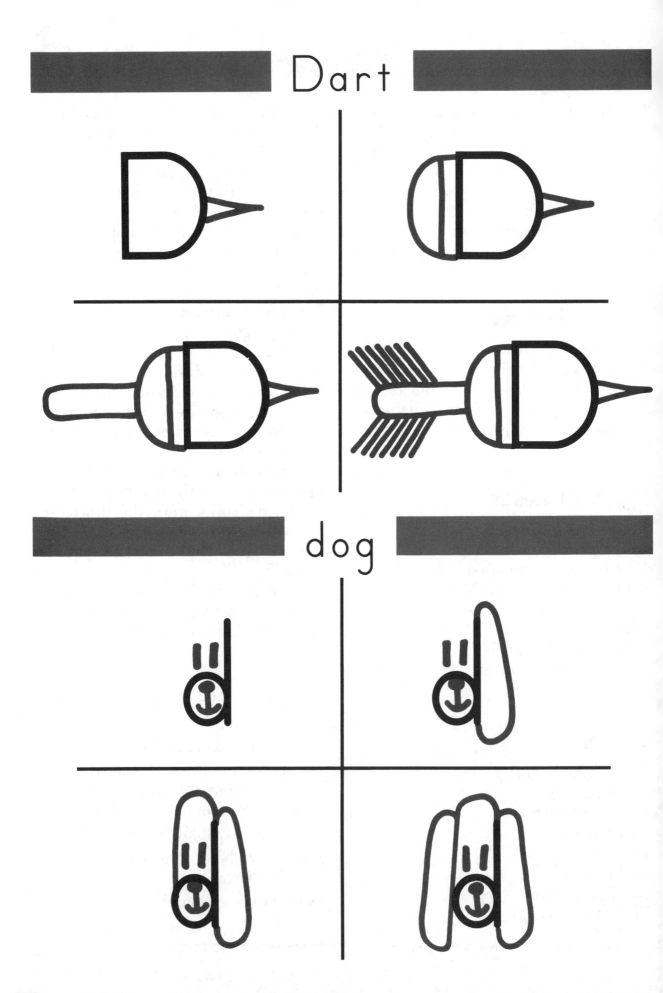

dog

Show the children how to draw these figures, beginning with the letter forms.

Eagle

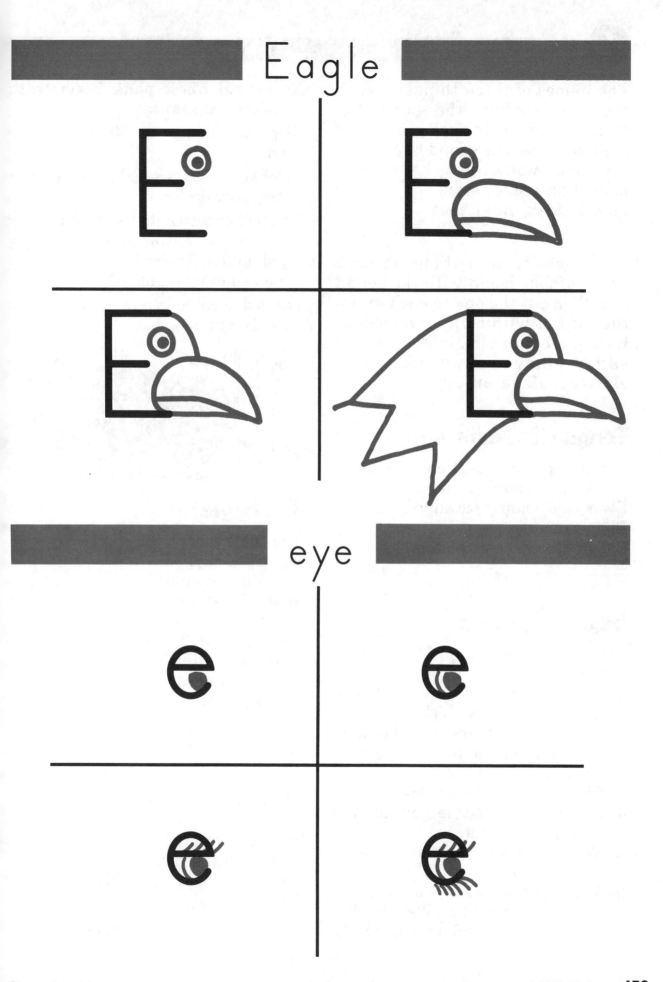

eye

e

The names of three things in each group of four have the sound of ĕ. Pick out the one in each group that does not have the sound of ĕ.

red, pen, met, cup
cent, boat, sled, stem
mend, desk, pool, rest

The names of three things in each group of four begin with the sound of ĕ. Pick out the one in each group that begins with a different sound.

banana, echo, elm, edge
editor, elbow, puppy, elk
elf, tree, elevator, egg

Tongue Twisters

The educated elephant entered.
Every elk escaped Eddie.
Elves enjoy empty elevators.
Ellen examines eggs.
Egbert elbows on escalators.

Beginning with ĕ

For each clue, say a word that begins with ĕ.

1. What a chicken lays that can hatch into a baby chick.
2. The moving stairs in a building that carry people from one floor to another.
3. The opposite of beginning.
4. A very big, four-legged animal with a long trunk.
5. The part of the car that makes it go; the motor.
6. The paper container we put a letter in for mailing. We put the name, address, and a stamp on it.

An animal whose name begins with ĕ is the **elephant.**

Elephants live to be 60 or 70 years old.

Elephant tusks are valuable because they provide ivory.

An elephant uses its trunk the way a person uses her arms—for carrying and pulling. It also breathes through the end of its trunk.

Trained elephants are very popular circus animals.

The Eagle

The eagle soars
Up in the sky,
Viewing the land
With his keen eye.

He can hardly breathe
In the smog-filled air.
He sighs and says,
"They just don't care."

The crystal lakes
He once knew
Are no longer
The color blue.

He seems to say
As he looks at me,
"Why have they done this
To my country?"

JENNIFER PERA, Age 12

Connect the picture on the left to the matching picture in the center by drawing a line, and then connect the line to the matching word.

engine

envelope

egg

bell

engine

egg

shell

envelope

shell

bell

Connect the picture on the left to the matching picture in the center by drawing a line, and then connect the line to the matching word.

foot

fork

fork

fireman

fireman

foo

Find as many things as you can in this picture that begin with the sound of f.

The names of three things in each group of four begin with the sound of *f*. Pick out the one in each group that begins with a different sound.

fire, grapes, fan, finger
fence, fish, duck, faucet
foot, feather, flower, book

Tongue Twisters

Frances Fox finds fresh fruit.
Five funny fellows fixed fudge.
Freddy found a friend in the fog.
The freckled frog flew from faraway France.
Freida fried fat fish on a flat farm.

An animal whose name begins with *f* is the **frog.**

Frogs are members of the amphibian family.

Although frogs have no ears on the outside, they can hear very well with their inner ears.

Frogs breathe through their skin and their mouths.

In the winter, frogs gather together in large numbers in rotten logs or mud banks.

The frog sometimes sheds its skin and grows a new one.

Who Likes the Rain?

SOLVEIG PAULSON RUSSELL

Who in the world likes rain the best?
Who loves the mud where the rain has pressed?
Who sits squatting where raindrops fall?
Who loves the raintime most of all?
Who sings a chorus in praise of rain
Down by the pool at the foot of the lane?
Who loves the spatter and feel of each drop,
And wishes the rain would never stop?

Who loves the rain? The happy frogs,
Awash with wetness in rain-soaked bogs.
Awash with joy—pelted with rain,
They chortle and gurgle a deep refrain;
They drum out *churug's* in a steady beat,
Churug and *churug*—repeat and repeat.
If I were a rain cloud I'd travel far
To splash down drops where the gay frogs are.

Fish

If I had a wish
That was all mine,
I'd wish for a fish
To take my line.
I'd reel and reel
Until my hands could feel
The fish that I wish for
Is really real.

BRYAN OSSOLINSKI, Age 8

Fork

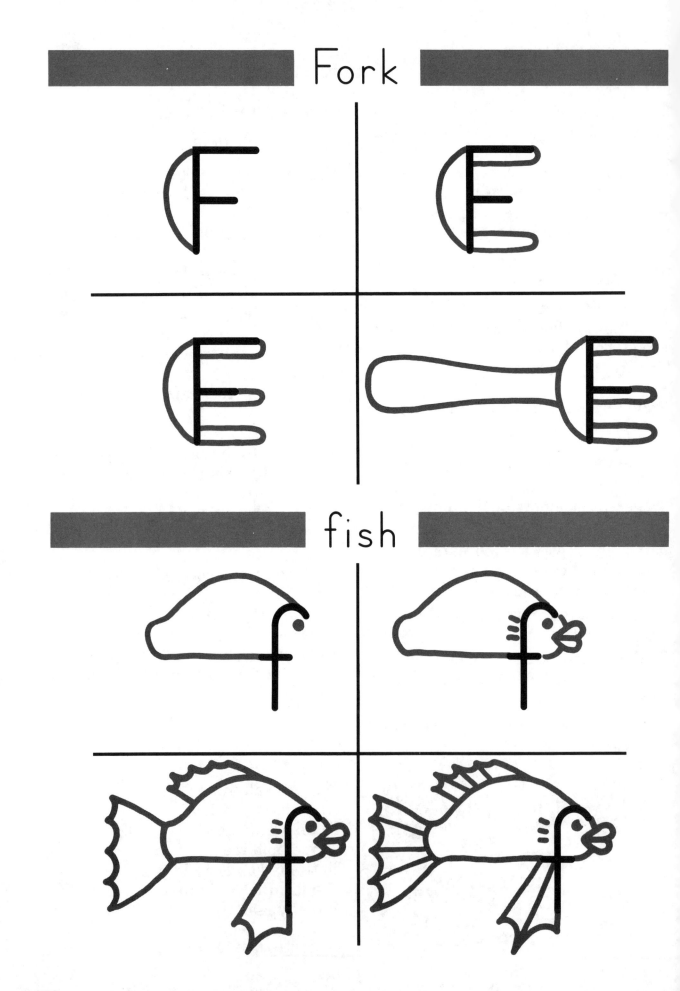

fish

Show the children how to draw these figures, beginning with the letter forms.

Guitar

gift

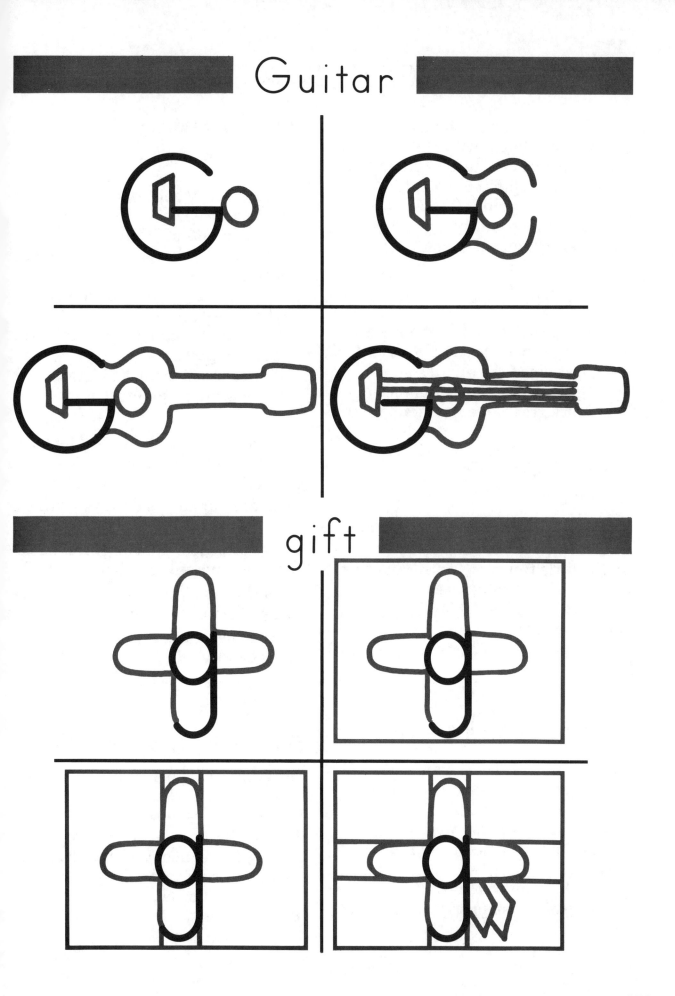

Show the children how to draw these figures, beginning with the letter forms. LETTERS **459**

g

The names of three things in each group of four begin with the sound of g. Pick out the one in each group that begins with a different sound.

grin, garden, gold, friend
turtle, game, good-bye, go
green, snow, gang, grass

Tongue Twisters

The gray geese grazed in the grass.
Girls get gravy on green gloves.
The ghost glued the guard's gun.
Goats grin at grasshopper games.
Grandma's great green garden grows.

Grasshopper Green

AUTHOR UNKNOWN

Grasshopper Green is a comical chap;
He lives on the best of fare.
Bright little trousers, jacket, and cap,
These are his summer wear.
Out in the meadow he loves to go,
Playing away in the sun;
It's hopperty, skipperty, high and low,
Summer's the time for fun.

Grasshopper Green has a quaint little house;
It's under the hedge so gay.
Grandmother Spider, as still as a mouse,
Watches him over the way.
Gladly he's calling the children, I know,
Out in the beautiful sun;
It's hopperty, skipperty, high and low,
Summer's the time for fun.

Beginning with g

For each clue, say a word that begins with g.
1. The place where you grow grass and plant flowers and vegetables.
2. The opposite of "Hello."
3. The noise a dog sometimes makes if it is angry.
4. The clothes you put on your hands when they are cold.
5. The sticky liquid you use to paste things together.
6. The color of frogs and grass and many growing plants.

An animal whose name begins with g is the **grasshopper.**

A grasshopper has five eyes so that it can see up and sideways without moving its head.

As a grasshopper gets bigger, it sheds its skin and grows a new one.

Grasshoppers smell with the two long antennas on their heads.

Grasshoppers are green or gray, so they can hide in the grass.

Grasshoppers have two pairs of wings and six legs.

The Glippy Glopper

The Glippy Glopper is a very colorful creature that nobody has ever seen. The Glippy Glopper has antennas that shoot out a beam of sun. It has two big horns about 23 feet long. Its teeth are about 2 feet long. Its tail is so sharp that when it touches a rock it splits open.

DEAN ADLER, Age 8

Connect the picture on the left to the matching picture in the center by drawing a line, and then connect the line to the matching word.

hat

hammer

wagon

bag

hammer

rabbit

bag

hat

rabbit

wagon

Connect the picture on the left to the matching picture in the center by drawing a line, and then connect the line to the matching word.

hand

house

heart

hear

hand

house

Find as many things as you can in this picture that begin with the sound of *h*.

462   LETTERS

The names of three things in each group of four begin with the sound of *h*. Pick out the one in each group that begins with a different sound.

girl, hamster, hen, hog
home, hall, truck, hose
hair, owl, head, heel

Tongue Twisters

He hurried home to a hot house.
The hammer hit the handle hard.
The hero hummed while he hunted horses.
The hen hid her head as she hopped up the hill.

Beginning with *h*

For each clue, give a word that begins with the sound of *h*.
1. A cooked patty of meat served on a bun.
2. The animal that a cowboy rides.
3. What you wear on your head on a cold day.
4. The sweet food that bees make.
5. The opposite of *soft*.

Harvey and the High Hat

VERA L. WIMBERLY

Harvey was a very unhappy hippopotamus. He was the unhappiest animal in the whole zoo where he lived.

Now, Harvey had always wanted to be important, not just an animal that lolled around all day. A high hat, he thought, would make him the most important animal in his zoo. Perhaps one day he could be Mayor.

But where was he going to get a high hat? It wasn't as if he could go into a store and buy one. Hippopotamuses are not allowed in stores.

Harvey pondered on this all the time until one day a group of young people came to the zoo. One of the boys made fun of how fat he was and how dumb he looked.

The boy wore a funny cap. It had buttons that sparkled like jewels. The turned-up brim was cut in points, which made it look like a crown.

"I think I'll put my cap on this silly looking hippo," the boy said. He leaned way over the rail and put the cap on Harvey's head. The children laughed and clapped their hands in glee.

Harvey was so upset he moved to the back of his cage.

The boy leaned over the rail again, but he couldn't reach Harvey. "My cap. Come back here," he called.

"Come, children," their mother said. "Here's the bus. We have to leave."

"But my cap. My cap is on the hippo's head," the boy cried.

"I'm sorry. You shouldn't have put it there. Come on," she said.

Harvey watched them go. He tilted his head back and forth, but the cap wouldn't slide off.

Jerry, the giraffe, stuck his long neck over the fence and said, "Harvey, you look distinguished in your crown hat."

Harvey hesitated a minute, then he said, "Does it really make me look distinguished? And important?"

"It does," the giraffe said. "Anybody with a crown hat could be Mayor of any zoo."

Harvey wasn't unhappy any longer. After all, a crown hat with jewels was better than a high hat any time.

House

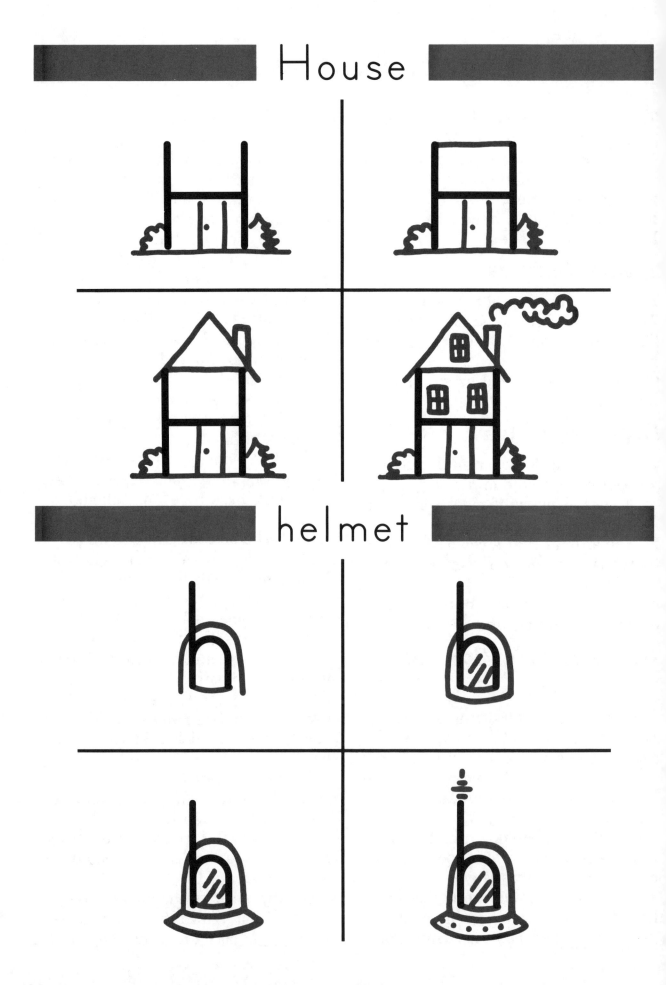

helmet

Show the children how to draw these figures, beginning with the letter forms.

Insect

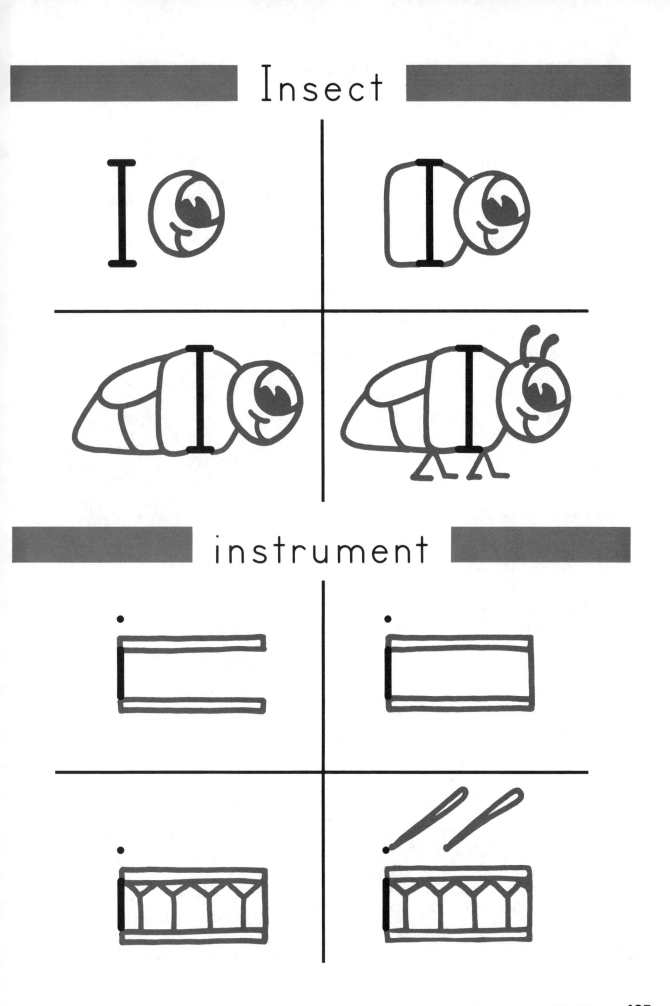

instrument

Show the children how to draw these figures, beginning with the letter forms.

i

The names of three things in each group of four have the sound of ĭ in them. Pick out the ones that do not have the sound of ĭ.

robe, hit, pig, witch
ring, late, kick, swim
win, dish, pill, wheel

The names of the three things in each group of four begin with the sound of ĭ. Pick out the one in each group that begins with a different sound.

if, ill, hat, imagine
zebra, imp, inch, indoors
it, invent, is, candy

Tongue Twisters

It is itchy in igloos.
Is the insect ill?
Instructing imps is impossible.
Imagine insects imitating ink.
Invite invisible infants and inventors.

Beginning with ĭ

For each clue, say a word that begins with ĭ.
1. A colored liquid used in a pen for writing or drawing.
2. The opposite of outside.
3. A tickly feeling on your skin; it makes you want to scratch.
4. A house built of blocks of snow.
5. Sick; not healthy

For each clue, say a word that has a short ĭ in the middle.
1. A large pinkish animal with a curly tail.
2. The sound a bell makes.
3. Large; huge.
4. The number that comes after five.
5. An animal that swims well and lives in water.

The Insect

ERMA CARR LOAR

I saw a little insect
   A-crawling on the ground.
He was so fat, I do declare,
   That he was nearly round.

He had a little chubby nose
   That turned up at the end,
And little eyes that popped way out
   And then popped back again.

He was as fuzzy as could be.
   He looked much like a bear.
I think I'd like to have a coat
   Made from his fuzzy hair.

Connect the picture on the left to the matching picture in the center by drawing a line, and then connect the line to the matching word.

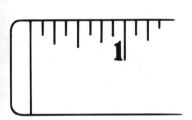  insects

igloo

  ink

insects

 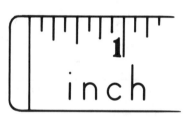 inch

infant

  igloo

ink

  infant

inch

Connect the picture on the left to the matching picture in the center by drawing a line, and then connect the line to the matching word.

jug

jewelry

jacket

jug

jewelry

jacket

Find as many things as you can in this picture that begin with the sound of *j.*

The names of three things in each group of four begin with the sound of *j*. Pick out the one in each group that begins with a different sound.

jar, box, jam, jelly
jail, juice, water, jeep
jump, jet, lion, jacks

Tongue Twisters

John makes jam, jelly, and juice.
Jean judged the jolly jokes.
The jockey jogged joyfully.
Joan juggles jugs and jars.
Jack jumped on the jackrabbit's jacket.

An animal whose name begins with *j* is the **jaguar.**

Jaguars live in swamps, jungles and other wooded regions.

A jaguar is the largest member of the cat family.

A jaguar's food consists of deer and other animals, and birds and fish.

Jaguars are good swimmers.

Most jaguars are tan with black spots.

The High Jump

Two big rabbits were showing off. "I can jump higher than you can," said Joanie Rabbit.

"Oh, no you can't," Jackie Rabbit told her. "I can jump much higher." Little Susie Rabbit sat and thought. "Let's have a high jump contest," Susie said. "We can ask our friends to come."

All the rabbits came to the high jump contest. First, Joanie Rabbit jumped. She jumped very high. Everyone clapped. Then Jackie Rabbit jumped even higher. Everyone clapped. Just then little Susie Rabbit sat on a bee and jumped highest of all!

ANGELA PERELLA, Age 8

Beginning with *j*

For each clue, give a word that begins with the sound of *j*.
1. The liquid that comes from an orange.
2. The funny stories you tell to make people laugh.
3. To hop or leap off the ground.
4. An airplane that moves very fast and leaves smoke in the sky behind it.
5. The names of the two children who went up the hill to fetch a pail of water.
6. The grape food that goes well with peanut butter.
7. The first month of the year.
8. The glass container that holds jam and jelly.
9. A short coat.
10. A toy that pops out of a box when you turn the handle.
11. The tool that props up the car when it has a flat tire.

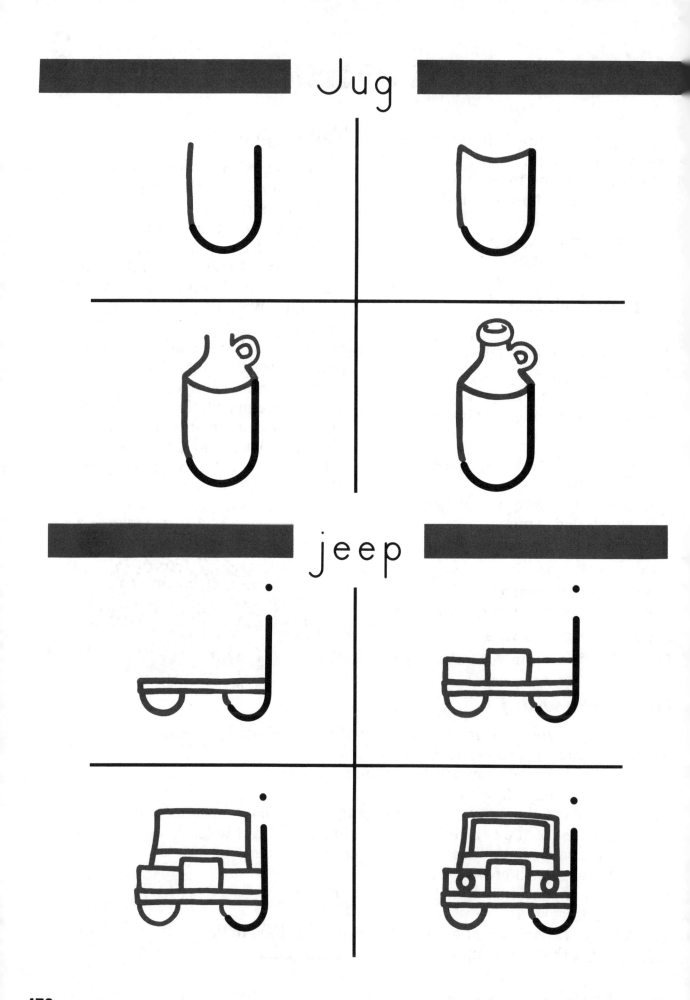

Jug

jeep

Kites

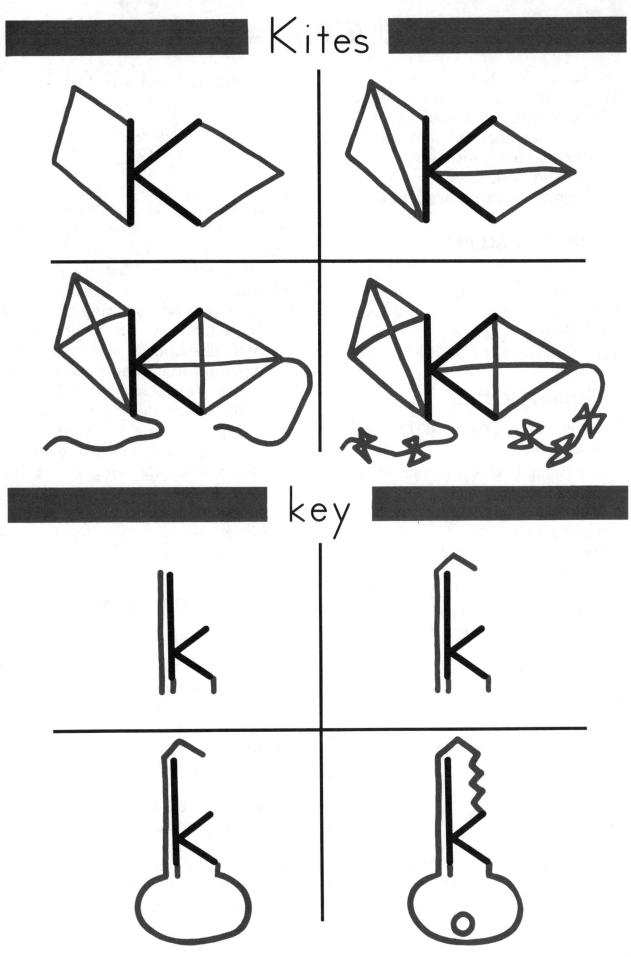

key

Show the children how to draw these figures, beginning with the letter forms. LETTERS **471**

k

The names of three things in each group of four begin with the sound of *k*. Pick out the one in each group that begins with a different sound.

kangaroo, band, kite, king
jam, kitten, kid, kiss
kindergarten, kind, key, wall

Tongue Twisters

Ken keeps keys.
Kangaroos kick kettles.
Kindergarten kitchens kept kites.
Kind kings keep kittens.
Karl from Kansas kissed Karen.

Beginning with *k*

For each clue, say a word that begins with *k*.

1. The small piece of metal that opens a door or lock.
2. The school grade that you are in right now.
3. To touch with your lips to show your love.
4. The room in your house where food is cooked.
5. A red tomato sauce that you put on hamburgers.
6. A baby cat.

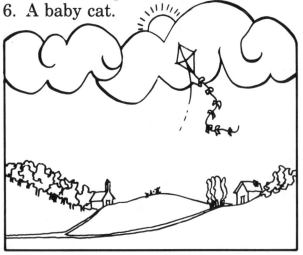

How Many k's Can You Find?

Once upon a time there was a king who had a pet kangaroo. But instead of a baby kangaroo in her pouch, there was a kitten. The kitten was always getting into trouble. She hid the king's keys, let the bottom of the kettle burn, and, most terrible of all, broke the king's favorite kite. The kangaroo finally got fed up with her and put the kitten on her knee and gave her a good spanking. But the kitten didn't care. She made more mischief. The king was so upset that he began to hiccup and couldn't stop. The kitten was so sad she asked the king what she could do for him so he could stop hiccuping. He said, "Stop your trouble," and the kitten promised she would. The king got better and the kitten was so proud she stayed out of trouble for the rest of her life.

BETSY KEIFFER, Age 9

The Adventurous Kite

HELEN HOWLAND PROMMEL

A kite once went,
On adventure bent,
    To sail in the misty sky.
He looked quite frail
But his great long tail
    Helped him to learn to fly.

He reached the blue
Where the sun came through
    And clouds looked round and fat.
Then the winds all stopped
And the poor kite flopped
    To the ground, and lay there flat.

Connect the picture on the left to the matching picture in the center by drawing a line, and then connect the line to the matching word.

kettle

kite

king

kettle

king

kick

kite

key

key

kick

Connect the picture on the left to the matching picture in the center by drawing a line, and then connect the line to the matching word.

leg

lion

log

leg

lion

lamp

lamp

lightning

lightning

log

The names of three things in each group of four begin with the sound of *l*. Pick out the one in each group that begins with a different sound.

lemon, lollipop, turkey, lunch
leopard, land, light, king
luck, rose, lark, letter

Tongue Twisters

The lamb licked a long leaf.
Lemons and limes look lovely.
Linda likes liver and lettuce.
Lucy Leopard leaps a large log.
Leo Lion loves little lollipops.

Beginning with *l*

For each clue, say a word that begins with *l*.

1. The two outside edges of your mouth that you kiss with.
2. What do you do when you hear a funny joke.
3. The opposite of *high*.
4. A tool used for climbing. It has steps or rungs between two long sides.
5. A message that you write and send through the mail.

An animal whose name begins with *l* is the **lion.**

Male lions usually have a mane, or fur, on their heads and necks.

Lions roar loudly in the evening before they go out hunting, and again at dawn.

A group of lions is called a pride.

Many times the hunting is done by the female lion, or lioness.

Wild lions live about eight or ten years, but lions in zoos may live up to twenty-five years or longer.

Shoe-box Lion

JUNE ROSE MOBLY

To make this ferocious lion you need a shoe box (complete with lid), paints, glue, and a piece of lightweight cardboard.

Cut a shoe box and its lid in half. Glue one of the lid halves to each end of one of the shoe-box halves to form the lion's body and legs.

Cut slits all around the three sides of the other shoe-box half and bend them out for the lion's mane. Glue this box half to one end of the lion's body-legs section. From lightweight cardboard, cut a tail shape and glue it to the lion's body.

Paint the entire lion and add features with paint or felt marker.

Letter

leaf

Show the children how to draw these figures, beginning with the letter forms.

Mushroom

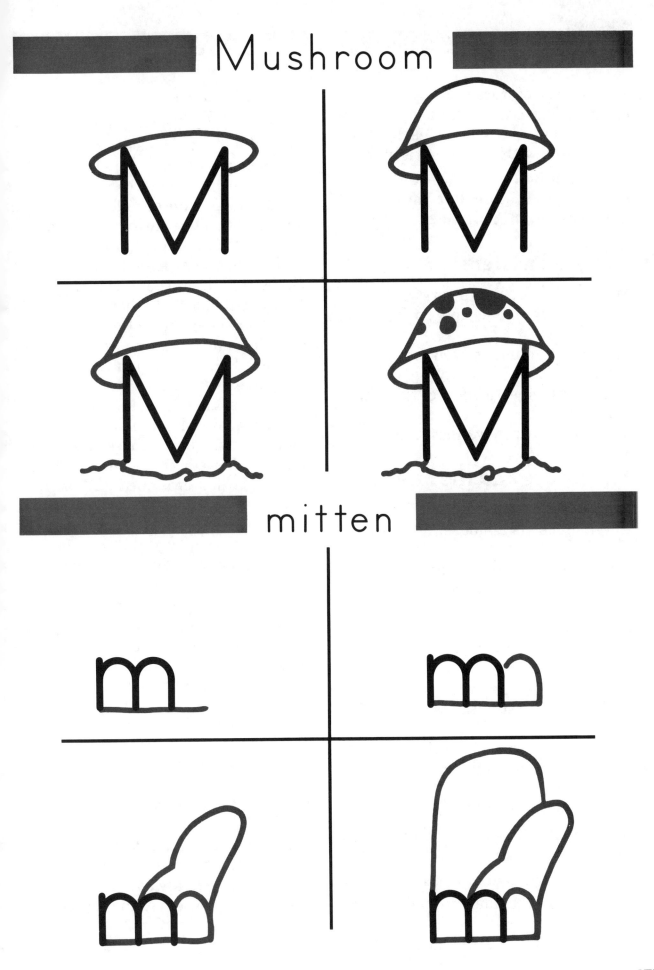

mitten

The names of three things in each group of four begin with the sound of *m*. Pick out the one in each group that begins with a different sound.

mitten, moon, monkey, duck
milk, magician, basket, man
mouse, leaf, medal, map

Tongue Twisters

My mask makes me merry.
My mommy made me many mud pies.
The mean man mixed milk and mustard.
Mr. Martin met a mob of marching monkeys.
Machines must move most mornings.

The House and the Mouse

A house is a house,
And a mouse is a mouse.

Some houses have mouses,
And mouses have houses.

If I had a mouse,
I would keep it in the house.

I would feed it cheese
And make a nest out of weeds.

It would play and have fun—
On the wheel it would run.

BRIAN JERD, Age 8

An animal whose name begins with *m* is the **monkey.**
Most monkeys live in trees.
Monkeys are popular animals in the zoo.

An Old Fable

Once upon a time a Country Mouse invited a Town Mouse to come to see her at her home in the fields.

The Town Mouse came and they sat down to a dinner of corn kernels and roots. The Town Mouse didn't like the food and presently she said:

"My poor, dear friend, you live here no better than the bugs and ants. You should just see how I fare! My larder is always full of good things to eat. You must come to see me, and I promise I shall give you the best food you have ever eaten."

So when the Town Mouse returned to her home she took the Country Mouse with her. There the Town Mouse showed the Country Mouse into a larder crammed full of flour and meal and figs and cookies and honey and dates. The Country Mouse had never seen anything like it.

Soon they sat down to dinner. But before they had well begun, the door of the larder opened and in walked a person. The two mice scampered off and hid themselves in a narrow, uncomfortable hole. The Country Mouse was terribly frightened.

Presently, when all was quiet, the mice ventured out again; but after they had taken a few nibbles, some one else came in. They ran to the dark hole again.

This was too much for the visitor. "I'm going back to my home in the field," she said, all out of breath with fright. "You have wonderful things to eat but you are always in danger. At my home I can enjoy my simple dinner in peace. Goodbye!"

Connect the picture on the left to the matching picture in the center by drawing a line, and then connect the line to the matching word.

mitten

moon

mask

Find as many things as you can in this picture that begin with the sound of *m.*

Connect the picture on the left to the matching picture in the center by drawing a line, and then connect the line to the matching word.

necklace

noteboo

NOTES

newspaper

necklac

NOTES

notebook   newspape

Make up a story, using four of these words.

nickel

napkin

nuts

note

needle

net

nail

nest

nurse

The names of three things in each group of four begin with the sound of *n*. Pick out the one in each group that begins with a different sound.

new, night, road, nest
near, water, no, nod
baby, noise, number, nurse

Tongue Twisters

A new needle is now necessary.
Neat nurses need necklaces.
Nine nieces nibbled nuts.
Never nudge a noisy navy.
Nancy is nice to nasty neighbors.

Bird's Nest

JUNE ROSE MOBLY

Form a piece of plastic mesh bag into the shape of a nest. (You will find that such bags are used to package oranges or onions at the supermarket.) Fasten the ends together by twisting a bit of pipe cleaner around them.

Cut Mother Bird and a row of babies from lighweight cardboard. Paint with tempera. Attach a piece of pipe cleaner to the bottom of the large bird and at the sides of the baby-bird row. Use these pipe cleaners to attach the birds to the nest.

Beginning with *n*

For each clue, say a word that begins with *n*.

1. The time when it is dark; the opposite of day.
2. A place built by a bird for laying its eggs.
3. To sleep for a short time.
4. The part of the body that is just below your head.
5. The person who helps a doctor to take care of a sick person.
6. What you hit with a hammer.
7. The opposite of *yes*.
8. What you are called.
9. The number that comes after *eight*.
10. The tiny piece of metal that you use with thread to sew.
11. The opposite of *old*.
12. The people who live next door to you.

An animal whose name begins with *n* is the **nightingale.**

Nightingales are songbirds; they sing a beautiful song during the day and the night.

Songbirds learn their song from other birds around them.

Songbirds do not sing until they are about two years old, even though they have learned their song a long time before that.

Nightingales usually eat insects.

The nightingale is the best singer of all the songbirds.

LETTERS   **481**

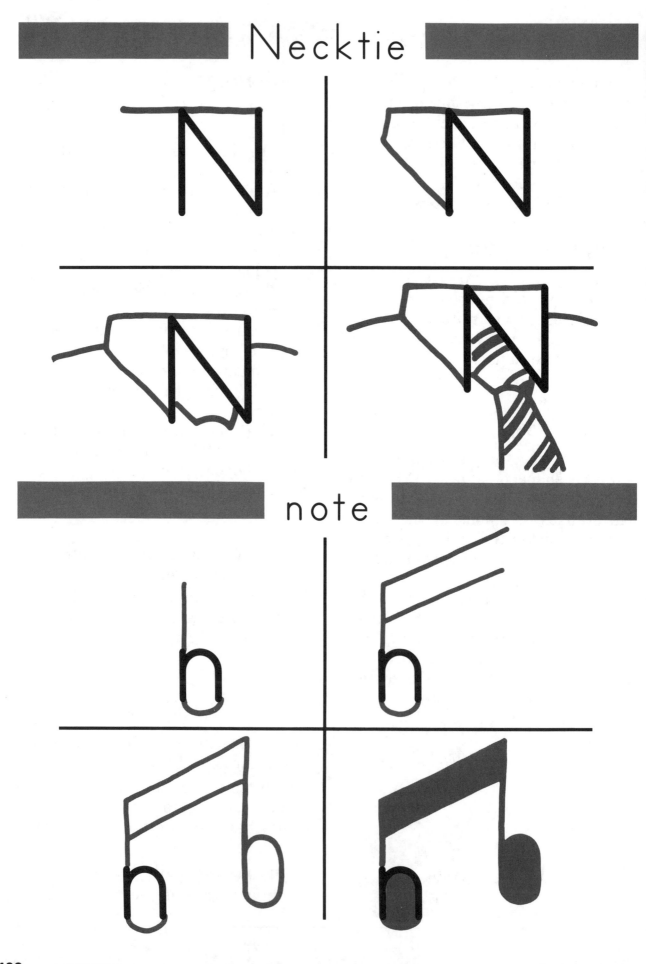

note

LETTERS   Show the children how to draw these figures, beginning with the letter forms.

Octopus

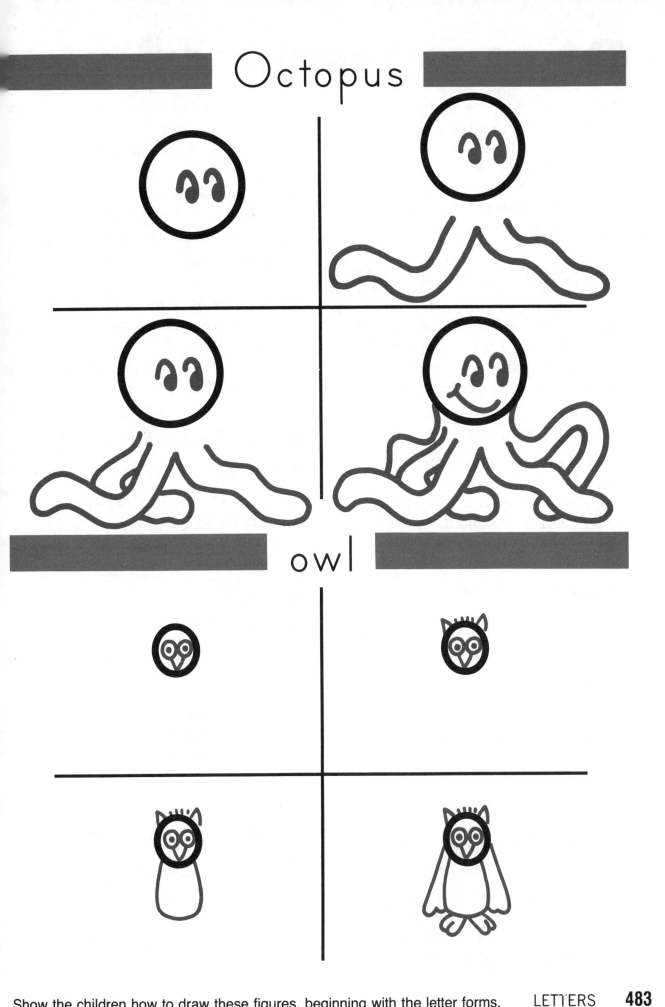

owl

Show the children how to draw these figures, beginning with the letter forms.   LETTERS   **483**

O

The names of three things in each group of four have the sound of ŏ in them. Pick out the ones that do not have the sound of ŏ.

knock, break, mop, shot
time, hot, copper, pop
cob, lock, baby, rocket

The names of three things in each group of four begin with the sound of ŏ. Pick out the one in each group that begins with a different sound.

otter, object, night, octopus
omelet, opposite, ox, house
October, step, operate, odd

Tongue Twisters

Odd Ollie operates on autos.
Oscar is an odd octopus.
Otto the otter operated on an owl.
Ogden eats olives and omelets.
The ox went to the opera in October.

Beginning with ŏ

For each clue, say a word that begins with ŏ.
1. The surgery done by a doctor in a hospital.
2. A kind of fish with eight arms.
3. The opposite of *on*.
4. The person who would answer the telephone if you dialed *0*.
5. Something unusual or strange.

An animal whose name begins with ŏ is the **octopus.**

The octopus has eight arms which help it crawl.

When an octopus is in danger, it squirts an inky liquid. This helps hide the octopus so it can escape.

An octopus can also hide by changing color.

An octopus is very big, but it can squeeze through an opening that is very small.

Most of the time, an octopus is afraid of people.

Winky The Owl

MIRIAM CLARK POTTER

Here comes a queer thing—
A big barn owl
With a flapping wing;
Run! Skedaddle!
Do not stay;
You'd better hide
Till she flaps away!

The Owl

Big and brown it has to be,
A great big owl flying free.
It flies so nice, smooth and gay,
It never hunts throughout the day.

Its claws so sharp, beak the same,
Rats and mice you could hardly blame
For running back to their home
When the big owl starts to roam.

ROBERT BROWN, Age 10

Connect the picture on the left to the matching picture in the center by drawing a line, and then connect the line to the matching word.

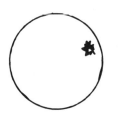

ostrich

olive

octopus

owl

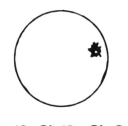

orange

ostrich

olive

orange

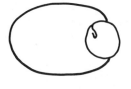

owl

octopus

Connect the picture on the left to the matching picture in the center by drawing a line, and then connect the line to the matching word.

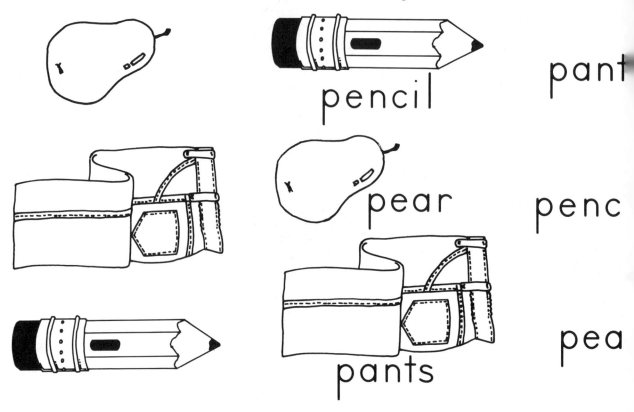

pencil

pant

pear

penc

pants

pea

Find as many things as you can in this picture that begin with the sound of *p*.

MEAT and P

'ABLES

The names of three things in each group of four begin with the sound of p. Pick out the one in each group that begins with a different sound.

pony, saw, pot, pump
plane, puppy, horse, pancake
wheel, parade, pearl, pet

Tongue Twisters

Please place the party plates on papers.
Please pedal Pearl to the palace.
Patty patched pots and pans.
Paul's parents peeled pears and peaches.
Peter Piper picked a peck of pickled peppers.

A Party-Going Gentleman

IRMA V. SANDERSON

I'd like to meet a penguin
All dressed in black and white.
I'd say, "How do you do?" to him—
At least I think I might.
And perhaps he'd wave a flipper
In a friendly sort of way
And dive into the water
To swim. Or else he'd say,
"I'm invited out to dinner,"
And he'd waddle on his feet
Like a party-going gentleman
In his evening clothes so neat.

I'd like to meet a penguin;
We'd be good friends, he and I,
For we'd have one thing in common:
We can neither of us fly.

The Pelican And His Pouch

OSMOND P. BRELAND

The pelican is a very strange looking bird. It has a long bill or beak, and a large pouch under its lower jaw. There are several different kinds of pelicans. Some are white and others are gray, but they all look very much alike. They are often seen along seacoasts. Pelicans use their pouches as nets to catch fish. When a pelican sees a group of fish, it puts its lower jaw into the water and opens its mouth. Then it swims among the fish, using the pouch like a scoop net. When some fish are caught in the pouch, the bird closes its mouth. The water runs out and the fish are caught in the pouch for the pelican to eat. The pouch is also used as a serving bowl to feed the young pelicans. When Mamma Pelican comes to the nest, the young ones start jumping up and down and squawking hungrily. Mamma Pelican then opens her mouth, and the youngsters stick their heads into the pouch and eat the pieces of fish they find in it.

The Penguin

I am a penguin,
Black and white.
My wings won't lift me
To any height.

But my wings will help me
Swim and play
And let me have fun
In every way.

MIKE WEAVER, Age 8

Pencil

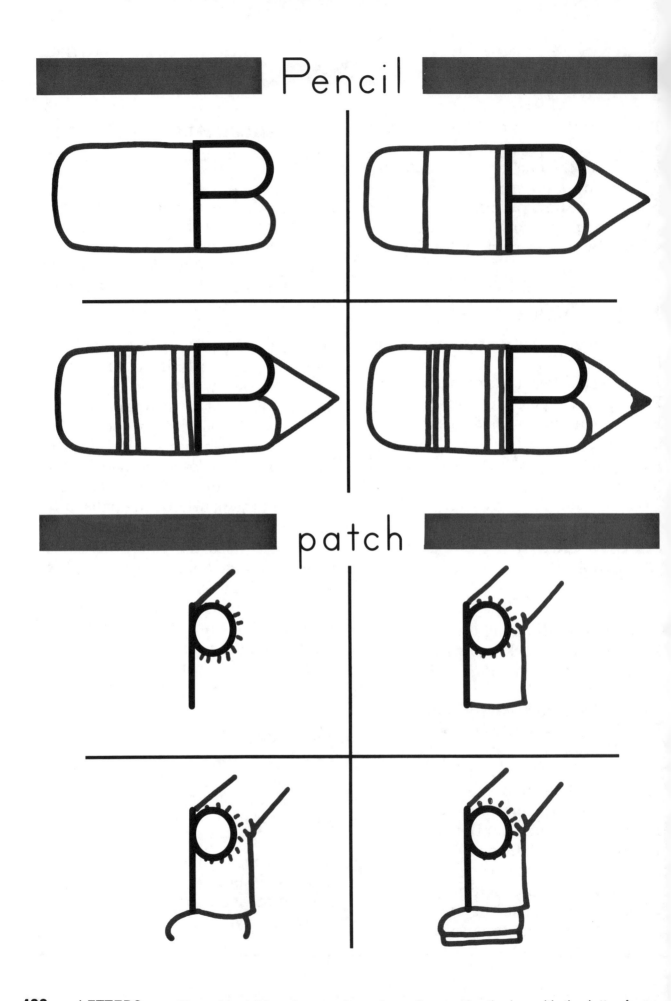

patch

Queen

queen

Show the children how to draw these figures, beginning with the letter forms. LETTERS **489**

q

The names of three things in each group of four begin with the sound of *q*. Pick out the one in each group that begins with a different sound.

quarrel, quick, quart, puppet
quake, queer, face, quarter
window, quail, quiet, queen

Tongue Twisters

"Quickly," quacked the quacker.
The quilt was quite queer.
The quail quaked in quicksand.
Quinn quit quickly.
The queen questioned the quarrelers.

Beginning with *q*

For each clue, say a word that begins with *q*.
1. The sound that a duck makes.
2. An angry argument.
3. What you ask to get an answer.
4. Twenty-five cents.
5. When there is no noise.
6. Something that is fast.
7. The wife of a king.
8. A kind of blanket made of patches.
9. The kind of sand you would not want to fall into.
10. To stop doing something, or to leave your job.

An animal whose name begins with *q* is the **quail.**

A quail is a small game bird which lives on seeds and berries.

One kind of quail, the singing quail, has a musical call.

Most quail live in the open country areas.

Quail eggs and meat are good to eat.

The Queen's Magic Rice Pudding

Mary was the queen in the palace in the Kingdom of Oshkub.

Everyone said the food she made was perfect. "But why don't you sometimes make rice pudding?" they asked.

Today she was rummaging through rice pudding recipes and deciding which one to make.

Soon she started making the pudding. But at that moment the king called her and she left her work.

But then the princess was passing by and she said, "One shake of magic powder in this pudding will make it taste better."

Then the prince passed by saying, "One shake of magic powder will improve its flavor."

Many people passed by, giving the pudding shakes of magic powder.

The queen came back. She gave the pudding a shake, too. But the pan of pudding started rising. It flew out the door and never came back.

"Too much powder, I guess!" said the queen.

KATHERINE SOBOLEV, Age 8

Connect the picture on the left to the matching picture in the center by drawing a line, and then connect the line to the matching word.

quarrel

quarter

quarter

quarrel

quilt

quilt

quail

queen

queen

quail

80, Zaner-Bloser, Inc.

LETTERS **491**

Connect the picture on the left to the matching picture in the center by drawing a line, and then connect the line to the matching word.

record

robo

roof

recorc

robot

roof

Find as many things as you can in this picture that begin with the sound of *r*.

The names of three things in each group of four begin with the sound of *r*. Pick out the one in each group that begins with a different sound.

red, queen, race, ring
apple, rake, rest, row
ruler, right, tail, reach

Tongue Twisters

The red radio roared rock and roll.
The resting rabbit ran from the reckless racoon.
Ralph raked ripe raw raspberries.
Roberta rents rockets to rodents.
The ragged rascal ran around the rugged rock.

Betsy's Garden

DONALD BRUCE NAUGHTON

Bunny Rabbit loved to go to Betsy's garden. Each morning when the sun came up, Bunny Rabbit would creep under the fence and nibble the tender carrot tops. This made Betsy sad because when the tops of the carrots were gone, she could not find the carrots which were growing under the ground. So every time Betsy saw Bunny Rabbit in the garden, she would chase him home to his hollow tree. One day Betsy came to the place where Bunny Rabbit lived and knocked on the hollow tree. "Bunny Rabbit," Betsy said, "you are making me sad. You eat the tops off my carrots and then I cannot find the carrots to eat." Bunny Rabbit poked his head out of the hole in the hollow tree. "You make me sad, too," he told Betsy. "I do not like you to chase me away from your garden." Then Betsy told Bunny Rabbit her idea. "When the sun comes up each morning, I will pick some carrots from my garden. I will leave the tops for you." Bunny Rabbit liked that idea. Now he and Betsy could share the good things of the earth.

Roberta Rabbit

Roberta Rabbit hopped and hopped.
She came to a fence.
She saw a hole in the fence.

She went through the fence.
She went into the garden.
Roberta Rabbit saw some lettuce.

She hopped to the carrots.
She nibbled at the carrot leaves.

She sat on her tail.

She scratched her left ear.
She scratched her right ear.
She scratched her tummy.

Roberta Rabbit heard a mouse.
A dog came running.
Roberta Rabbit ran.
She jumped over the basket.
She ran through the fence.
The dog jumped against the fence.
Roberta Rabbit ran home.

Rabbit

robot

LETTERS   Show the children how to draw these figures, beginning with the letter forms.

Snowman

smoke

Show the children how to draw these figures, beginning with the letter forms.   LETTERS   **495**

The names of three things in each group of four begin with the sound of s. Pick out the one in each group that begins with a different sound.

rooster, splash, sun, stage
saw, split, table, stop
soap, fan, seal, sleep

Tongue Twisters

Susan sells shoes and socks.
Seven suffering skunks sipped soup.
The sun shines on stop signs.
The snack shop sells sandwiches and salad.
Sammy saw six spaceships sailing smoothly.

Beginning with s

For each clue, say a word that begins with s.
1. The opposite of happy.
2. What you do with your eyes.
3. The number that comes after five.
4. An animal who eats nuts and has a very bushy tail.
5. What you do with a needle and thread.
6. Two pieces of bread with peanut butter and jelly between them.
7. The season of the year when all the flowers bloom.
8. The bright spots of light that you see in the sky at night.

Sun and Stars

String a clothesline across part of the classroom, low enough to be reached by the children. Have enough clothespins for all the children. Cut several sun shapes from yellow construction paper, and several star shapes from foil. Have these shapes near the clothesline.

Make up cards for the entire class, half with upper-case S on them, and half with lower-case s on them. Place these cards in a box.

Each child picks a card out of the box. If the child picks an upper-case S, he or she takes a sun shape, marks it with upper-case S, and hangs it on the clothesline. If the child picks a lower-case s, he or she takes a star shape, marks it with a lower-case s and hangs it on the clothesline.

Otha, the Nut Collector

Otha, the nut collector, was a little fat squirrel. He was always collecting nuts and that's why he was fat. He would scramble around under the leaves as fast as he could so he could get all the nuts before the other squirrels.

Every other day Otha would go deep down into the forest and he would bring with him the best nut he found in two days. When he got there, there were already a lot of squirrels. They were all seated in front of a big tree stump. Guess what! Otha was going to auction off his nuts. He got up on top of the stump and started chattering away!

ELYESE McNAIR, Age 10

Connect the picture on the left to the matching picture in the center by drawing a line, and then connect the line to the matching word.

shoe

star

snake

shoe

star

snake

Find as many things as you can in this picture that begin with the sound of *s*.

LETTERS **497**

Connect the picture on the left to the matching picture in the center by drawing a line, and then connect the line to the matching word.

truck

telephone

telephone

tree

tree

truck

Find as many things as you can in this picture that begin with the sound of *t*.

Beginning with *t*

For each clue, say a word that begins with the sound of *t*.

1. Very, very small.
2. To speak to someone.
3. A living thing that has branches and leaves.
4. The big bird that we usually eat on Thanksgiving Day.
5. The number after *one*.
6. The piece of furniture where we put the food for dinner.
7. An animal that carries its shell on its back.
8. What you use to call your friends up and talk with them.
9. What a dog wags when it is happy.
10. The very front parts of your feet.

The names of three things in each group of four begin with the sound of *t*. Pick out the one in each group that begins with a different sound.

turtle, tomato, sell, toe
target, rabbit, tent, turkey
bear, taxi, tail, ticket

Tongue Twisters

Tongue twisters twist tongues.
Tina Tinker taught twenty tots.
Twelve tired tailors tied twine.
Two toads tried to trot to Texas.
The turtle thanked the turkey for the ticket.

Terrence The Turtle

KENNY HINDS

Once upon a time there lived in the great woods a turtle called Terrence. Any time he was alarmed about anything, all he had to do was pull his neck, legs, and tail inside his shell and his worries were over.

But one day he encountered Freddy Fox, who happened to be in a very mischievous mood. Terrence stopped as soon as he saw the fox and waited to see what was going to happen. Freddy ran right over to him, barking playfully. Terrence withdrew quickly into his shell. Freddy put his forepaw under Terrence and flipped him over on his back. Terrence fell between two rocks, lodging there. After Freddy pawed him a few times, Freddy went away through the bushes, never dreaming Terrence was stuck. Poor little Terrence lay there on his back for a little while, then pushed his head out for a look. There was no room to turn over. He stuck his legs out and pushed with all his might, but just couldn't help himself.

A day and night passed. Terrence was getting weak and hungry. Fritzy Fieldmouse stepped from behind one of the rocks to look the situation over. She was sorry to find Terrence in such a helpless situation. So she crawled underneath him, putting her back against his and began pushing with all her strength. She was pretty strong for her size. Soon Terrence began to move backwards. Fritzy pushed harder. All of a sudden Terrence slid out from between the rocks, lighting on his side with a thud. With a quick push of his legs he turned over, right side up.

"Thank you very much, Fritzy. That was certainly a good deed," he said gratefully.

Television

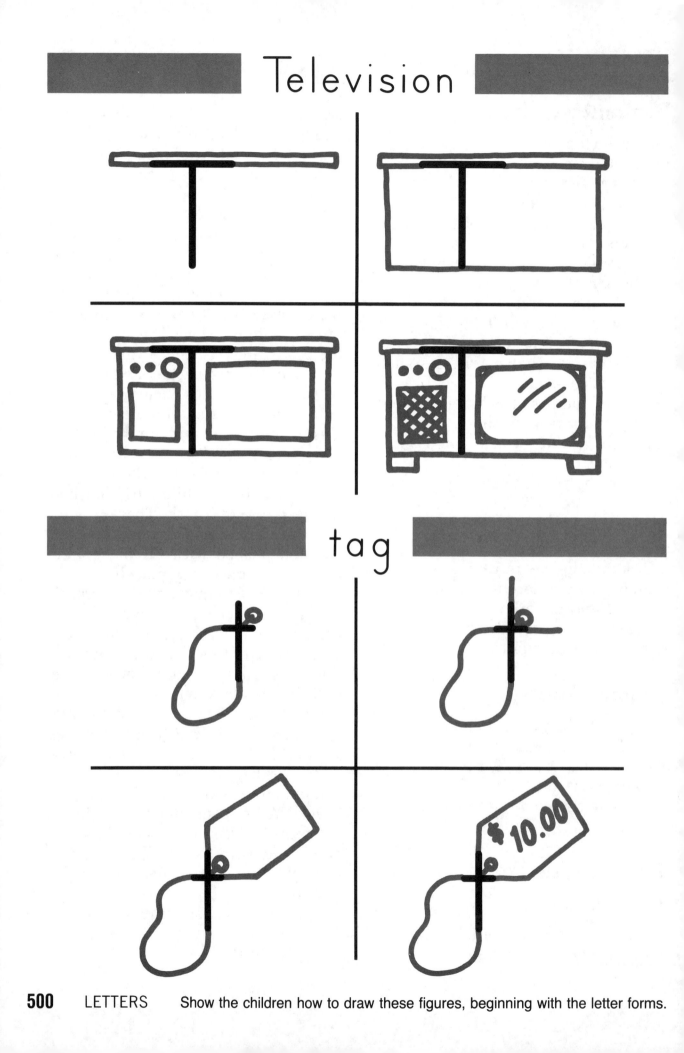

tag

Show the children how to draw these figures, beginning with the letter forms.

Underwater

umbrella

The names of three things in each group of four have the sound of ŭ in them. Pick out the one that does not have the sound of ŭ.

dust, bone, truck, bug
luck, fun, bucket, sad
tiger, mud, crust, nut

The names of three things in each group of four begin with the sound of ŭ. Pick out the one that does not begin with the sound of ŭ.

uncle, ugly, usher, rose
unload, up, tree, us
untie, uncover, under, girl

Tongue Twisters

Unfold ugly umbrellas.
Unhappy umpires are unusual.
Uncle Gus untied the umpire upstairs.
Ursula uncovered the unbroken urn.
We understand he was underground and undercover.

Beginning with ŭ

For each clue, say a word that begins with ŭ.

1. Beneath or below the water.
2. Not pretty or handsome.
3. The man who married your aunt.
4. What helps keep you dry in the rain.
5. How things look when you stand on your head.

Which of the following pairs of words rhyme?

sun—fun	**dust—crust**
rust—glad	**pup—cup**
west—tug	**bus—sad**

Umbrellas

ROWENA BENNETT

When the rain is raining
  And April days are cool
All the big umbrellas
  Go bumping home from school.
They bump the blowing cloudburst,
  They push the pushing storm.
They leap a muddy puddle
Or get into a huddle
  To keep each other warm.

But who is underneath them
  You really cannot tell
Unless you know the overshoes
  Or rubbers very well
Or the flippy-flop galoshes
With their swishes and their swashes
Or the running rubber boots
With their scampers and their scoots.

Oh, when the rain is raining
  And April days are cool
I like to watch umbrellas
  Come bumping home from school
I like to watch and wonder
Who's hiding halfway under . . .

In The Bathtub

DOROTHY LANDIS

There's something living down the drain
But what it is, I can't explain.
As soon as I take out the plug
It starts to snort and go, "Ug-glugg."
I hear it saying, "Gup-gup-gup,"
As it drinks the dirty water up.
It's so silly is what I'm thinking,
'Cause bath water's not so good for drinking.

Connect the picture on the left to the matching picture in the center by drawing a line, and then connect the line to the matching word.

unbutton

unhappy

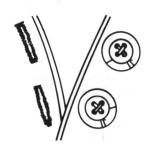

upstairs

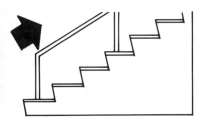

umpire

umbrella

umpire

Connect the picture on the left to the matching picture in the center by drawing a line, and then connect the line to the matching word.

violin

vest

vest

valentine

valentine

violin

Find as many things as you can in this picture that begin with the sound of *v*.

The names of three things in each group of four begin with the sound of *v*. Pick out the one in each group that begins with a different sound.

umbrella, valley, video, vat
vote, view, gate, vase
vein, king, visit, voyage

Tongue Twisters

The veal and vegetables vanished.
The vice-president viewed the veterans.
Valerie values vim and vigor.
The visitor viewed the village in the valley.
The violet violin is very valuable.

Beginning with *v*

For each clue, give a word that begins with the sound of *v*.

1. The time when you take a trip for fun and rest.
2. A machine used in the house to clean the rugs.
3. To disappear.
4. A pretty jar used to hold flowers.
5. The sound that comes from your mouth when you talk or sing.
6. The name you give to peas, carrots, green beans, spinach, corn, and celery.
7. A purple flower.
8. A very small town.
9. A small musical instrument with strings.

Fresh Vegetables for Sally

ANNE ROLL

"Mother," said Sally, "the sun is shining. May we plant my garden now?"

"Yes, Sally," answered her mother. "The flowers are in bloom. The cold weather is over. Spring is here, and it is time to plant your garden."

Sally found her shovel and rake and dug the ground. A bird hopped here and there, and every once in a while it pulled a worm from the loose soil.

"Now, Sally," said Mother, "we must plant your garden so that the sun will shine on the short plants as well as on the tall ones. Green beans and yellow corn both grow tall. We can plant them along the fence."

"Now we should plant the potatoes," said Sally. "But we have no seeds for them."

Mother showed Sally some cut-up pieces of potato. "When we plant these, they will grow into new potato plants."

Sally laughed. "Let's plant carrots, too. I like them."

Sally and her mother worked hard planting all the vegetables. Then Sally said, "Mother, we have planted beans, corn, potatoes, and carrots. Now we must water them."

So Sally watered her garden with her very own watering can. Each day she waited and watched. And finally one day, Sally ate fresh vegetables from her very own garden.

Vest

valentine

Show the children how to draw these figures, beginning with the letter forms.

Worm

win

Show the children how to draw these figures, beginning with the letter forms. LETTERS **507**

The names of three things in each group of four begin with the sound of *w*. Pick out the one in each group that begins with a different sound.

was, walk, vest, water
white, sky, where, what
work, woman, wolf, bat

Tongue Twisters

Wanda wishes for warm weather.
Window washing was wonderful work.
The white wagon had a worn wooden wheel.
The wind weakened the west wall.
We wondered whether wool was washable.

An animal whose name begins with *w* is the **whale.**

Whales can be many different sizes, from five feet to sixty feet long.

Smaller whales are called dolphins or porpoises.

Whales are important for their oil, which we use for soaps.

Whales breathe through holes in the tops of their heads.

Whales move through the water by moving their tails up and down.

Place pictures or drawings of these eight animals in the front of the room: whale, wolf, worm, wildcat, woodchuck, wasp, walrus, and wood-pecker. Make up eight large cards, four with upper-case *W* on them and four with lower-case *w* on them. Then, tell the class this story.

A whale, a wolf, a worm, a wildcat, a woodchuck, a wasp, a walrus and a woodpecker were wandering one winter. They discovered a pile of *W*'s. Four were upper-case *W*'s and four were lower-case *w*'s. They wanted to share the *W*'s among themselves by giving each large animal an upper-case *W* and each smaller animal a lower-case *w*. Which *W* did each animal get? The whale? The wolf? The worm? The wildcat? The woodchuck? The wasp? The walrus? The woodpecker?

As the children match the *w*'s and *W*'s to the animals, place the cards next to the picture of the appropriate animal.

Wind

Wind has a whistling sound
That hits low on the ground.
You can't see wind
But you know it's there
Because wind is everywhere.

Wind can blow high
Wind can blow low.
But you know that wind is there.
If wind went away,
I couldn't fly my kite
Or I couldn't play.

LARRY McCLUNG, Age 8

Connect the picture on the left to the matching picture in the center by drawing a line, and then connect the line to the matching word.

watch

window

wheel

wheel

watch

window

Find as many things as you can in this picture that begin with the sound of *w*.

Connect the picture on the left to the matching picture in the center by drawing a line, and then connect the line to the matching word.

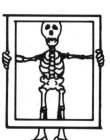

exercise

excavate

X-ray

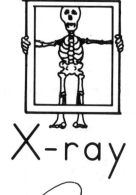

excavate

X-ray

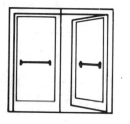

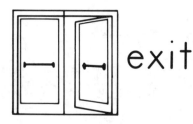

exit

exercise

exit

explode

510   LETTERS

Ending With *x*

For each clue, say a word that ends with sound of *x*.
1. A square container for cereal.
2. A big heavy animal that can pull a plow.
3. A sharp cutting instrument that could be used to split a log.
4. The liquid that makes a clean floor shiny.
5. An animal that is like a wolf.

The names of three things in each group of four end with the sound of *x*. Pick out the one in each group that ends with a different sound.

wax, red, box, tax
top, fix, ox, mix
fox, ax, pin, six

Percival The Ox

FLORENCE M. CHASE

Percival was a great dumb ox. He was always discontented because he felt that he was much smarter than other oxen.

"Why should I spend my time plowing furrows for Farmer Boss?" he said. "I am much too smart for that."

It was plain to see that he did not mean to budge, so Farmer Boss put another ox in his place.

Percival sat there. For five days he sat there THINKING.

Finally, he began to walk down the lane.

Percival walked through the long rows of corn. The corn tassels tickled his ears but he paid no attention because he was THINKING.

Soon he came to the meadow, where the cows were busy eating grass to make rich milk for Farmer Boss.

"Good afternoon," said Bell Cow, "and how is it that you are not plowing for Farmer Boss?"

"I'm much too smart for that."

Bell Cow shook her head sadly. Percival walked on.

He walked and walked until he was too tired to walk any more.

He sat down.

His stomach felt empty, but as far as Percival could see there was nothing but gravel and rocks.

Pretty soon he felt very, very thirsty. He looked around for a brook or spring but there was none.

Percival sat down and wept! Over onto the hard pebbly ground he fell. After a long, long time, he heard a crunching sound on the gravel.

The sound got louder and louder. At last, it stopped close by Percival.

"Ho there!" shouted a familiar voice, "why, here he is! Help me get him into the cart. He is too weak to walk."

It was Farmer Boss. Was Percival glad! All the way home, riding in the cart, he sat—THINKING.

When an ox pulled the plow for Farmer Boss he had nice green grass to eat; sweet grain, too—and when he was thirsty, good cool water.

At last, safe in his stall back in Big Barn, Percival smiled in his sleep.

Never again would he refuse to do his share of the work for Farmer Boss.

Ever after, so it has been said, Percival plowed the straightest furrow in all the country.

X marks the spot

fox

Yo-yo

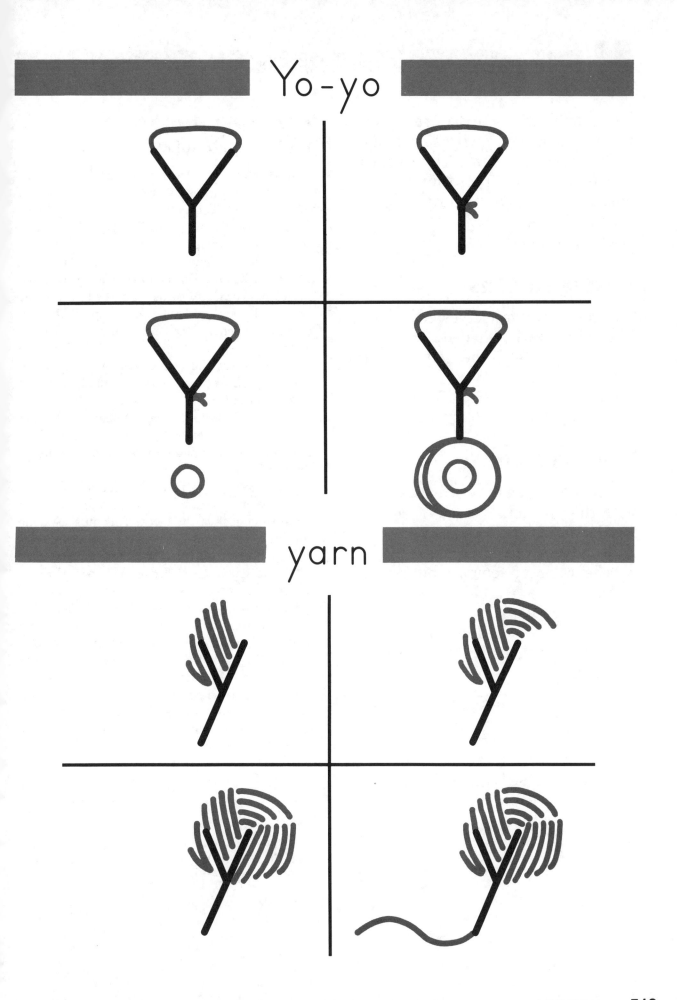

yarn

Show the children how to draw these figures, beginning with the letter forms.   LETTERS   **513**

y

The names of three things in each group of four begin with the sound of *y*. Pick out the one in each group that begins with a different sound.

truck, yellow, yard, yoke
yeast, yak, sandwich, yo-yo
yes, candy, yell, year

Tongue Twisters

The youngster yelled yesterday.
The yellow yacht yielded.
The yak yanked the yams in the yard.
Yankees yawn yearly.
Yes, the yellow yo-yo is yours.

Beginning with y

For each clue, say a word that begins with the *y* sound.
1. The day before today.
2. It is twelve months long.
3. The color of lemons, butter, and the sun.
4. The opposite of *no*.
5. The yellow part of an egg.
6. A toy that goes up and down on a string.

Make Your Own Yo-Yo

ELLA L. LANGENBERG

Materials: two blocks of wood ⅜ to ½ inch thick and 2½ inches square, one ⅝-inch piece of ¼-inch dowel, about a yard of strong string; coping saw, file, sandpaper, drill, glue, ruler, pencil, compass, vise, tempera paint, clear shellac.

First measure and saw the two blocks of wood, 2½ inches square. On the top of each block draw lines from corner to corner. This will locate the center. Measure and set your compass at a radius of 1¼ inches. Place the point of the compass at the center where the lines cross, and draw a circle. Now set the compass at a radius of ¾ inch, and draw a second circle inside the first. Do this on both blocks.

Fasten the blocks in the vise and saw around the outer circle. Remember to saw outside of the line; that is, so that the drawn line remains on the wood.

With the blocks still in the vise, file the surface of each in a curve from the smaller circle to the bottom edge of the block. This must be done smoothly and evenly all the way around. Sandpaper the surface to a satin-smooth finish.

On the flat side, or bottom of piece of wood, drill a ¼-inch hole, using a ¼ inch bit.

Put a little glue in the holes and insert the piece of dowel rod. Put a touch of glue on one end of the string and wind it around the dowel. Allow the glue to dry on this small end of the string before winding the remainder of the string around the dowel.

Paint the yo-yo in any bright combination of colors and finish with two or three coats of clear shellac.

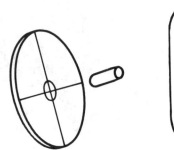

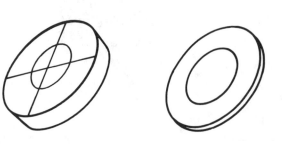

Connect the picture on the left to the matching picture in the center by drawing a line, and then connect the line to the matching word.

yacht

yolk

yo-yo

yarn

yolk

yo-yo

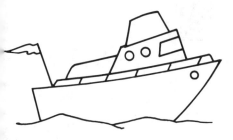

yarn

yawn

yawn

yacht

Connect the picture on the left to the matching picture in the center by drawing a line, and then connect the line to the matching word.

zipper

zebra

O

zero

zip code

zebra

zoo

zip code

zero

O

zoo

zipper

The names of three things in each group of four begin with the sound of z. Pick out the one that begins with a different sound.

zebra, zip, yo-yo, zoo
zoom, zither, zig-zag, bank
rabbit, zero, zone, zipper

Beginning with z

For each clue, say a word that begins with the z sound.

1. An animal that looks like a horse with black and white stripes.
2. One way to fasten your clothes.
3. A place where animals are kept for people to see them.
4. The number you use to show where there is nothing.
5. The noise a car might make if it went very fast.

Zip the Zebra

JULIET EARLE WELTON

The circus train wound its way up the track and stopped. Zip poked his head out of the boxcar to look at the town where the circus was to perform. Looking around, he thought he saw another zebra, out of the corner of his eye. He turned his head to have a better look, but it wasn't a zebra at all. There, level with the window, was a long board that had black and white stripes painted on it. The board was across the road like a gate to keep anyone from crossing the railroad tracks while the trains were passing.

When Zip was taken out of the boxcar he walked over to the board zebra who guarded the tracks.

"Are you a new kind of zebra?" asked Zip.

"Oh, no," said the gate. "I guard the children who cross my tracks on their way to school. I am painted black and white so they will be sure to see me and STOP. They wait while the train goes by."

"I think you have a fine job," said Zip. "Now, I must go with the other zebras or I will be left behind."

"Please come and see me again," said the gate.

"I will," said Zip.

One day Zip found the gate in serious trouble. It was smashed to pieces and there were bits of black and white board all over the road.

"What happened to you?" asked Zip.

"A runaway car coasted down the hill, crashed into me and smashed me to bits," said the gate. "Who will guard the children now when the trains are due?"

"Look at me," said Zip. "I have black and white stripes. I will stand in your place."

Zip took his place by the railroad crossing. The children were so surprised to find a zebra there that they were more careful than ever before.

The boys and girls were so grateful to Zip that they built him a little house with black and white stripes. Over the door they put a large sign which said:

STOP—LOOK—LISTEN

Between trains, when he does not guard the children, you will zee Zip sitting in front of his black and white house, reading his black and white newspaper.

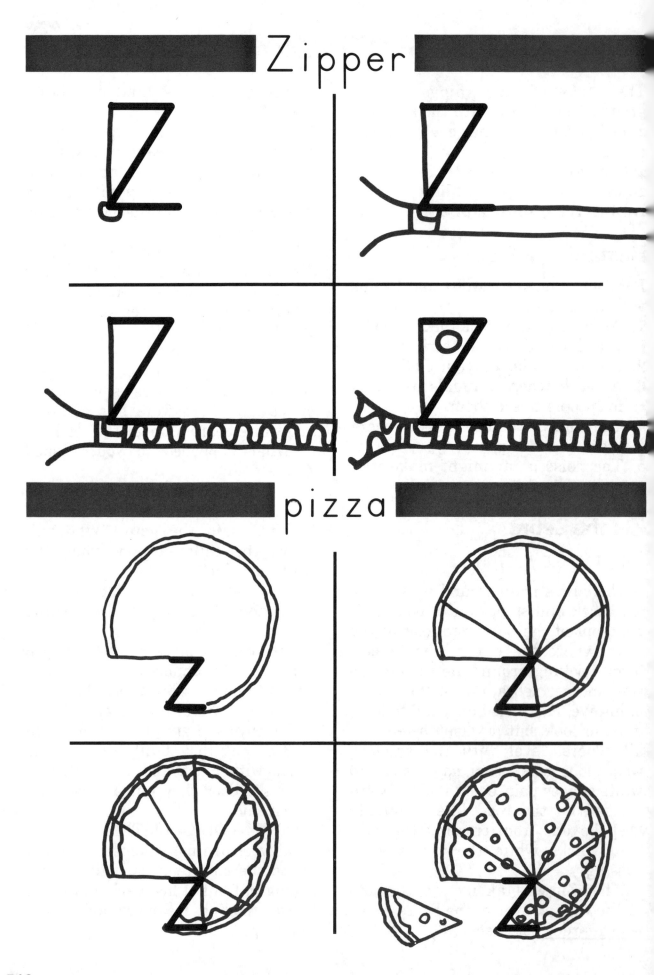

Zipper

pizza

Show the children how to draw these figures, beginning with the letter forms.

Look at each child's name below.
Find something that begins with
the same letter.

Manuel
David
Heather
Bob
Lisa

ball

motorcycle

dog

ladder

hamburger

It's picnic time, and scattered among the goodies
are all the letters of the alphabet, except four.
Find the missing letters.

Can you find the three letters
of the alphabet *not* in this
drawing?

Connect the letters of the alphabet in order from *a* to *z* to draw a picture.

v

w •————————————• u

•t

x•

h   •e   •d

i•

y•

s

520   LETTERS

BASIC SOURCES FOR THE KINDERGARTEN TEACHER

Adams, Ruth J. THE KINDERGARTEN HOW-TO-DO-IT BOOK. Minneapolis: Dennison, 1962.

Brown, Re Mona. KINDERGARTEN BULLETIN BOARD IDEAS. Minneapolis: Dennison, 1971.

Brown, Re Mona. KINDERGARTEN CALENDAR. Minneapolis: Dennison, 1970.

Foster, Josephine C. and Headley, Neith E. EDUCATION IN THE KINDERGARTEN. New York: American Book, 1948.

413 MORE KINDERGARTEN-PRIMARY TIPS. Dansville: Owen, 1957.

Fox, Helen Young. PRACTICAL PROJECT UNITS FOR KINDERGARTEN. Minneapolis: Dennison, 1970.

Gore, Lillian L. and Kaury, Rose. EDUCATING CHILDREN IN NURSERY SCHOOLS AND KINDERGARTENS. Washington: U.S. Department of Health, Education and Welfare, 1964.

Green, Arthur S. THE KINDERGARTEN ARTS AND CRAFTS BOOK. Minneapolis: Dennison, 1962.

Headley, Neith. THE KINDERGARTEN: ITS PLACE IN THE PROGRAM OF EDUCATION. New York: The Center for Applied Research in Education, 1965.

Heffernan, Helen and Todd, Vivian. THE KINDERGARTEN TEACHER. Lexington: Heath, 1960.

Holland, Bernice C. HOW TO INDIVIDUALIZE KINDERGARTEN TEACHING: NEW APPROACHES LEARNING THE KEY SENSORY MODES. Englewood Cliffs: Prentice-Hall, 1974.

Hurd, Helen Bartlet. TEACHING IN THE KINDERGARTEN, Minneapolis: Burgess, 1965.

Lee, Carvel and Lee, Lorita. KINDERGARTEN BULLETIN BOARD GUIDE. Minneapolis: Dennison, 1964.

Miller, Mabel Evelyn. A PRACTICAL GUIDE FOR KINDERGARTEN TEACHERS. Englewood Cliffs: Prentice-Hall, 1970.

Miller, Mabel Evelyn. KINDERGARTEN TEACHER'S ACTIVITIES DESK BOOK. Englewood Cliffs: Prentice-Hall, 1974.

Moore, Joan C. HANDBOOK OF KINDERGARTEN ACTIVITIES FOR EVERY DAY OF THE YEAR. Darien: Teachers, 1970.

Northrup, Anne Holmes. CHILD DEVELOPMENT PRINCIPLES IN KINDERGARTEN EDUCATION. Greenfield: Mitchell, 1954.

Ollila, Lloyd O. THE KINDERGARTEN CHILD AND READING. Newark: International Reading Association, 1977.

Robison, Helen. NEW DIRECTIONS IN THE KINDERGARTEN. New York: Teachers College Press, 1967.

Rudolph, Marguerita and Cohen, Dorothy. KINDERGARTEN: A YEAR OF LEARNING. New York: Appleton-Century-Crofts, 1964.

Schickedanz et al. STRATEGIES FOR TEACHING YOUNG CHILDREN. Englewood Cliffs: Prentice-Hall, 1977.

Smith, Mary F. A YEAR IN KINDERGARTEN. Minneapolis: Dennison, 1968.

Stendler, Celia Burns and Martin, William E. INTERGROUP EDUCATION IN KINDERGARTEN-PRIMARY GRADES. New York: Macmillan, 1953.

Swift, Mildred and Rather, Lois. KINDERGARTEN LEARNING GAMES. Minneapolis: Dennison, 1971.

Taylor, James L. and Gore, Lillian L. FUNCTIONAL SCHOOLS FOR YOUNG CHILDREN. Washington: U.S. Department of Health, Education and Welfare, 1961.

Weber, Evelyn. THE KINDERGARTEN: ITS ENCOUNTER WITH EDUCATIONAL THOUGHT IN AMERICA. New York: Teachers College Press, 1969.

Wills, Clarice Dechent and Stegman, William H. LIVING IN THE KINDERGARTEN: A HANDBOOK FOR KINDERGARTEN TEACHERS. Chicago: Follett, 1956.

STORYTELLING

Anderson, Paul S. STORYTELLING WITH THE FLANNEL BOARD. Minneapolis: Dennison. 1971.

Arbuthnot, May Hill. ARBUTHNOT ANTHOLOGY OF CHILDREN'S LITERATURE. New York: Lothrop, Lee & Shephard, 1971.

Arbuthnot, May Hill. TIME FOR FAIRY TALES, OLD AND NEW. New York: Lothrop, Lee & Shephard, 1961.

Baker, Augusta and Green, Ellin. STORYTELLING: ART AND TECHNIQUE. New York: Bowker, 1977.

Baver, Caroline Feiler. HANDBOOK FOR STORYTELLERS. Chicago: American Library Association, 1977.

Carlson, Bernice. LISTEN! AND HELP TELL THE STORY. Nashville: Abingdon Press, 1965.

Colwell, Eileen. A SECOND STORYTELLER'S CHOICE; A SELECTION OF STORIES, WITH NOTES ON HOW TO TELL THEM. New York: Walck, 1965.

Colwell, Eileen. A STORYTELLER'S CHOICE; A SELECTION OF STORIES, WITH NOTES ON HOW TO TELL THEM. New York: Walck, 1964.

Cook, Elizabeth. THE ORDINARY AND THE FABULOUS. New York: Cambridge University Press, 1969.

Cundiff, Ruby Ethel and Webb, Barbara. STORYTELLING FOR YOU: A HANDBOOK OF HELP FOR STORYTELLERS EVERYWHERE. Yellow Springs: Antioch Press, 1957.

Fitz-Gerald, Carolyn and Gunter, Dolores. CREA-

TIVE STORYTELLING FOR LIBRARY AND TEACHER AIDES. Dallas: Leslie Press, 1971.

Gruenberg, Sidonie. FAVORITE STORIES OLD AND NEW. New York: Doubleday, 1955.

Hardendorff, Jeanne B. JUST ONE MORE. Philadelphia: Lippincott, 1969.

Mitchell, Lucy Sprague. HERE AND NOW STORY BOOK. New York: Dutton, 1948.

Moore, Vardine. PRE-SCHOOL STORY HOUR. Metuchen: Scarecrow Press, 1972.

Sawyer, Ruth. THE WAY OF THE STORYTELLER. New York: Viking Press, 1962.

Shedlock, Marie. THE ART OF THE STORY-TELLER. New York: Dover, 1951.

Tashjian, Virginia. JUBA THIS AND JUBA THAT. Boston: Little, Brown, 1969.

Tooze, Ruth. STORYTELLING. Englewood Cliffs: Prentice-Hall, 1959.

Wagner, Joseph Anthony and Smith, Robert W. TEACHER'S GUIDE TO STORYTELLING. Dubuque: Brown, 1958.

Ziskind, Sylvia. TELLING STORIES TO CHILDREN. New York: Wilson, 1976.

MUSIC

Boardman, E. and Landis, B. EXPLORING MUSIC: KINDERGARTEN. New York: Holt, Rinehart & Winston, 1969.

Choate, Robert. MUSIC FOR EARLY CHILDHOOD. New York: American Book, 1970.

Jaye, Mary. MAKING MUSIC YOUR OWN. Morristown: Silver Burdett, 1971.

McCall, Adeline. THIS IS MUSIC FOR KINDERGARTEN AND NURSERY SCHOOL. Boston: Allyn & Bacon, 1966.

Nelson, M. and Tipton, G. MUSIC IN EARLY CHILDHOOD. Morristown: Silver Burdett, 1952.

Nye, Vernice. MUSIC FOR YOUNG CHILDREN. New York: Brown, 1974.

Pitts, Lilla Belle. SINGING AND RHYMING. Boston: Ginn, 1950.

Seeger, Ruth C. AMERICAN FOLK SONGS FOR CHILDREN. New York: Doubleday, 1977.

Smith, Robert. DISCOVERING MUSIC TOGETHER. Chicago: Follett Educational, 1968.

Wilson, Harry. GROWING WITH THE MUSIC. Englewood Cliffs: Prentice-Hall, 1966.

TITLE INDEX

STORIES ABOUT ME AND THOSE AROUND ME

ALEXANDER AND THE TERRIBLE, HORRIBLE, NO GOOD, VERY BAD DAY. Viorst, Judith. New York: Atheneum, 1972. From the time Alexander got up in the morning until he went to bed, *everything* went wrong.

BLUEBERRIES FOR SAL. McCloskey, Robert, New York: Viking Press, 1948. The story of Sal and her mother who discover they aren't the only ones who are berry picking.

BOY, WAS I MAD. Hitte, Kathryn. New York: Parents' Magazine Press, 1969. Story tells how many things can happen to keep a boy from being mad and running away from home.

CARROT SEED, THE. Krauss, Ruth. New York: Harper & Row, 1945. The simple story of a child planting a seed which no one else believes will come up.

CATFISH. Hurd, Edith Thacher. New York: Viking Press. 1970. Catfish grows up as the town rascal, but is accepted when he performs a deed of honor.

DADDY. Caines, Jeannette. New York: Harper & Row, 1977. A little girl whose parents are separated finds special joy in the activities she and her father share on Saturdays.

DAY THE GANG GOT RICH, THE. Katzwinkle, William. New York: Viking Press, 1970. When George comes into a windfall of five dollars, he unselfishly shares his riches.

DEAD BIRD. Brown, Margaret Wise. Reading: Addison-Wesley, 1958. Children in this story encounter death.

EMILY AND THE KLUNKY BABY AND THE NEXT DOOR DOG. Lexau, Joan M. New York: Dial Press, 1972. Story of a girl whose parents are divorced, who runs away from home.

EVAN'S CORNER. Hill, Elizabeth Starr. New York: Holt, Rinehart & Winston, 1967. A small boy finds his pleasure in having a place of his own is increased by sharing it with his brother.

FIND OUT BY TOUCHING. Showers, Paul. New York: Crowell, 1961. Gamelike spirit of this book sharpens the child's curiosity and extends his knowledge through the sense of touching.

GO AND HUSH THE BABY. Byars, Betsy. New York: Viking Press, 1971. An affectionately humorous account of how a boy attempted to quiet his crying baby brother.

GOGGLES. Keats, Ezra Jack. New York: Macmillan, 1969. Daschund Willie outmaneuvers some bullies trying to take the old goggles found by Peter.

GRANDPA. Borack, Barbara. New York: Harper & Row, 1967. A story of the fun a little girl has with her grandfather.

HERE COMES TAGALONG. Mallett, Anne. New York: Parents' Magazine Press, 1971. Universal theme of the younger child who tags along with older children.

HI, CAT. Keats, Ezra Jack. New York: Macmillan, 1970. The story of Archie, who loves to pretend, and his tag-along cat.

IZZIE. Pearson, Susan. New York: Dial Press, 1975. A gentle story of a cloth cat doll who suffers numerous disfigurements while accompanying its owner.

JANE'S BLANKET. Miller, Arthur. New York: Viking Press, 1972. Children can identify with Jane who loved her blanket for so long only shreds remained.

LITTLEST LEAGUER, THE. Hoff, Syd. New York: Dutton, 1976. The story of a boy who uses his size to best advantage.

MINE! Mayer, Mercer and Marianna. New York: Simon &

Schuster, 1970. A book whose hero makes a definite statement of property rights.

MY AUNT ROSIE. Hoff, Syd. New York: Harper & Row, 1972. The story of the warm relationship between a special aunt and her favorite nephew.

MY FIVE SENSES. Aliki. New York: Crowell, 1962. Alerts the child to his senses and ways he can learn through them.

NOBODY ASKED ME IF I WANTED A BABY SISTER. Alexander, Martha. New York: Dial Press, 1971. A story of a brother's jealousy with his baby sister.

NOTHING EVER HAPPENS ON MY BLOCK. Raskin, Ellen. New York: Atheneum, 1966. While the hero of this story sits on the curbstone complaining of the lack of excitement, incredible things are happening all around him.

ONE MORNING IN MAINE. McCloskey, Robert. New York: Viking Press, 1952. The story of Sal on the day she loses her first tooth.

POCKETFUL OF CRICKET, A. Caudill, Rebecca. New York: Holt, Rinehart & Winston, 1964. When a boy takes his cricket with him on the first day of school, his teacher accepts it as a bridge between home and school.

SAM. Scott, N.H. New York: McGraw-Hill, 1967. A sensitive story of a boy whose family is too busy to notice him.

SAM, BANGS, AND MOONSHINE. Ness, Evaline. New York: Holt, Rinehart & Winston, 1966. A small girl learns to distinguish between truth and "moonshine" after her flights of fancy almost bring disaster.

SHE COME BRINGING ME THAT LITTLE BABY GIRL. Greenfield, Eloise. Philadelphia: Lippincott, 1974. The story of a small boy's reaction to his new baby sister when he realizes she isn't a boy.

SNOWY DAY, THE. Keats, Ezra Jack. New York: Viking Press, 1962. The story of a little boy enjoying the snow.

SUNFLOWERS FOR TINA. Baldwin, Ann Norris. New York: Four Winds Press, 1970. Story of a young black girl of the ghetto who longs to grow something pretty.

THAT PEST JONATHAN, Cole, William. New York: Harper & Row, 1970. This book explains Jonathan's behavior by contending that "all small boys are pests."

THEODORE. Ormondroyd, Edward. Berkeley: Parnassus Press, 1966. A much-loved smudgy Teddy bear is not recognized by his owner after he is accidentally washed.

UMBRELLA. Yashima, Taro. New York: Viking Press, 1958. The story of a small girl's enjoyment of her new umbrella on dry and wet days.

WHAT DO YOU SAY, DEAR?. Joslin, Sesyle. Reading: Addison-Wesley, 1958. A question and answer book that is an excellent introduction to manners.

WHAT MARY JO SHARED. Udry, Janice May. Chicago: Whitman, 1966. A story of Mary Jo, a little black girl, and what she had to share.

WHAT'S GOOD FOR A FIVE-YEAR-OLD? Cole, William. New York: Holt, Rinehart & Winston, 1969. In this amusing story, the author asks what five-year-olds really like.

WHISTLE FOR WILLIE. Keats, Ezra Jack. New York: Viking Press, 1964. Peter tries to learn to whistle and finally succeeds.

YOUR SKIN AND MINE. Showers, Paul. New York: Crowell, 1965. An explanation of the many functions of our skin and other related information.

STORIES ABOUT THE WORLD WHERE I LIVE

CHICKEN AND THE EGG, THE. Mari, Iela and Enzo. New York: Pantheon Books, 1970. Without text, the book shows the reproduction and growth cycle.

DAY OF SUMMER, A. Miles, Betty. New York: Knopf, 1960. Text describes the effects of weather and time of year on nature and the activities of people.

FROG, FROG, FROG. Welber, Robert. New York: Pantheon Books, 1971. The story of a boy who wants to find a frog.

GROWING STORY. Krauss, Ruth. New York: Harper & Row, 1946. A little boy watches things grow but doesn't realize until fall that he, too, has grown.

I HAVE A TREE. Chaffin, Lillie D. New York: White, 1969. A little boy tells all the uses he can find for a tree throughout the year.

IF I FLEW A PLANE. Young, Miriam. New York: Lothrop, Lee & Shephard, 1960. A child, hoping to be a skywriter and astronaut, dreams about all the kinds of planes he will fly when he grows up.

LADY BIRD, QUICKLY. Kepes, Juliet. Boston: Little, Brown, 1964. Story based on the old rhyme, "Lady bird, fly away home. . ." with a surprise ending.

LITTLE HOUSE, THE. Burton, Virginia Lee. Boston: Houghton-Mifflin, 1942. The little house is shown as it changes from a well-loved country home, to a shabby, empty house in the city, and back again to a respected country dwelling.

LITTLE ISLAND, THE. MacDonald, Golden. New York: Doubleday, 1946. Changes of the season and night and day are shown in this story of a kitten who visits an island.

LITTLE TIM AND THE BRAVE SEA CAPTAIN. Ardizzone, Edward. New York: Walck, 1955. Beautifully illustrated; shows an understanding of sea and ships.

LITTLE TRAIN, THE. Lenski, Lois. New York: Walck, 1940. Engineer Small and his shiny black engine provide information that children would like to know about trains.

MAKE WAY FOR DUCKLINGS. McCloskey, Robert. New York: Viking Press, 1941. The story of Mrs. Mallard and her ducklings who march through Boston traffic to reach the pond in the Public Garden.

PLAY WITH ME. Ets, Marie Hall. New York: Viking Press, 1955. Story of a little girl who tries to play with the wild creatures of the meadow.

RAIN DROP SPLASH. Tresselt, Alvin. New York: Lothrop, Lee & Shephard, 1946. The rhythm of the falling rain is caught in the brief text telling what happens on a rainy day.

TREE IS NICE, A. Udry, Janice May. New York: Harper & Row, 1956. Rhythmic text and colorful pictures combine to tell why trees are nice.

WHERE DOES THE BUTTERFLY GO WHEN IT RAINS? Garelick, May. Reading: Addison-Wesley, 1961. Book that discusses the profound question raised in the title.

WHITE SNOW, BRIGHT SNOW. Tresselt, Alvin. New York: Lothrop, Lee & Shephard, 1947. Conveys the beauty of the first snowfall, the activities of winter, and the approach of spring.

WINTER BEAR, THE. Craft, Ruth. New York: Atheneum, 1975. A rhyming account of a winter walk.

WINTER CAT, THE. Knotts, Howard. New York: Harper &

Row, 1972. This story is illustrated with fine lines and soft shapes, giving it a mood of winter.

STORIES FROM OTHER LANDS

BELL FOR URSLI, A. Chonz, Selina. New York: Walck, 1953. Ursli searches for the biggest bell so he can lead the procession during the spring festival.

FISH IN THE AIR. Wiese, Kurt, New York: Viking Press, 1948. Little Fish and his kite are carred off by a big wind.

JOSEFINA FEBRUARY. Ness, Evaline. New York: Scribner's, 1963. A little Haitian girl must choose between a burro which she loves and a pair of leather shoes for her grandfather.

MADELINE. Bemelmans, Ludwig. New York: Viking Press, 1939. The story of a child in a boarding school in Paris.

PELLE'S NEW SUIT. Beskow, Elsa. New York: Harper & Row, 1929. Pelle, a farm boy of Sweden, earns a new suit and follows each step in the process of its making.

SALT BOY. Perrine, Mary. Boston: Houghton Mifflin, 1968. A Navaho Indian boy saves the littlest lamb in the flock from drowning.

SONG OF THE SWALLOWS, THE. Politi, Leo. New York: Scribner's, 1949. A tender story of a boy and how he helped ring the bells at the Capistrano Mission to welcome back the swallows.

THY FRIEND, OBADIAH. Turkle, Brinton. New York: Viking Press, 1969. Story about an engaging Quaker boy.

TIKKI TIKKI TEMBO. Mosel, Arlene. New York: Holt, Rinehart & Winston, 1968. This tale tells why the Chinese started giving their sons short names.

STORIES OF FOLK AND FAIRY TALES

CHANTICLEER AND THE FOX. Cooney, Barbara. New York: Crowell, 1958. The old favorite of the fox who almost flattered the vain cock into becoming his dinner.

EMPEROR AND THE KITE, THE. Yolen, Jane. Cleveland, 1967. Chinese legend of the unshakable loyalty of the emperor's smallest daughter.

FOX WENT OUT ON A CHILLY NIGHT, THE. Spier, Peter. New York: Doubleday, 1961. An old song transformed into a beautiful picture book.

FROG WENT A-COURTIN'. Langstaff, John and Rojankovsky, Feodor. New York: Harcourt Brace Jovanovich, 1955. The old tale is beautifully illustrated by Feodor Rojankovsky.

GREAT, BIG, ENORMOUS TURNIP, THE. Tolstoy, Alexei. New York: Watts, Franklin, 1969. This version of an old cumulative folktale is developed with humor and visual appeal.

HARE AND THE TORTOISE, THE. La Fontaine, Jean de. New York: Watts, Franklin, 1967. This fable is beautifully illustrated by Brian Wildsmith.

HOW THE WORLD GOTS ITS COLOR. Hirsh, Marilyn. New York: Crown, 1972. Oriental legend of how color came to the world.

JOHNNY CROW'S GARDEN. Brooke, L. Leslie. New York: Warne, 1903. A delightful picture book that has become an old favorite due to the irresistable humor of the drawings.

JOURNEY CAKE, HO!. Sawyer, Ruth. New York: Viking Press, 1953. The exciting version of a long-time favorite tale.

JUST SO STORIES. Kipling, Rudyard, Gleeson, J.M. (illus.). New York: Doubleday, 1912. A collection that includes stories telling how the whale got his throat, the camel is hump, and the leopard his spots.

LITTLE RED HEN, THE. Holdsworth, William Curtis. New York: Farrar, Straus & Giroux, 1969. Humorous interpretation of the classic nursery story.

MOMMY, BUY ME A CHINA DOLL. Zemach, Harve. New York: Farrar, Straus & Giroux, 1975. A little girl suggests a ridiculous swapping of sleeping places (taken from an Ozark children's song).

STORIES OF FUN AND FANTASY

AMELIA BEDELIA. Parish, Peggy. New York: Harper & Row, 1973. The disastrous effects of the several meanings of the same word provide hilarious situations.

ANATOLE. Titus, Eve. New York: McGraw-Hill, 1956. Anatole, the most contented mouse in France, reveals his secret for happiness.

AND TO THINK THAT I SAW IT ON MULBERRY STREET. Seuss, Dr. New York: Vanguard Press, 1937. A small boy's imagination peoples a street with strange and marvelous creations.

ANDY AND THE LION. Daugherty, James. New York: Viking Press, 1938. A modern version of "Androcles and the Lion," about Andy who meets a lion with a thorn in his paw while on his way to school.

ANGUS AND THE DUCKS. Flack, Marjorie. New York: Doubleday, 1939. An inquisitive Scottie dog finds adventure when he escapes his leash.

ANIMALS SHOULD DEFINITELY NOT WEAR CLOTHING. Barrett, Judith. New York: Atheneum, 1970. Humorous story of how absurd and bothersome clothes are for animals.

ASK MISTER BEAR. Flack, Marjorie. New York: Macmillan, 1958. A small boy tries, with the help of the farm animals, to find just the right present for his mother's birthday.

BEAR CIRCUS. DuBois, William Pene. New York: Viking Press, 1971. The story of true friendship between koala bears and kangaroos.

BEDTIME FOR FRANCIS, Hoban, Russell. New York: Harper & Row, 1960. Francis, the badger, spends her time thinking up reasons for not going to sleep.

CAPS FOR SALE. Slobodkina, Esphyr. Reading: Addison-Wesley, 1947. While a tired peddler sleeps, some mischievous monkeys take all his caps.

CORDUROY. Freeman, Don. New York: Viking Press, 1968. An engaging teddy bear, unsold in a department store because one of his overall buttons is missing, has an exciting adventure and finds a home.

CURIOUS GEORGE. Rey, H.A. Boston: Houghton Mifflin,

1941. The story of a small monkey and his difficulty in getting used to the city.

DANDELION. Freeman, Don. New York: Viking Press, 1964. The story of a vain lion who goes to a tea party so overdressed no one recognizes him.

DUCHESS BAKES A CAKE, THE. Kahl, Virginia. New York: Scribner's, 1955. A story with a rollicking rhythm that catches and holds young listeners.

FINDERS KEEPERS. Lipking, William and Mordinoff, Nicolas. New York: Harcourt Brace Jovanovich, 1951. The story of the dilemma of two dogs with one home.

FIND THE CAT. Livermore, Elaine. Boston: Houghton Mifflin, 1973. Children have to search each page to locate the cat.

500 HATS OF BARTHOLOMEW CUBBINS, THE. Seuss, Dr. New York: Vanguard Press, 1938. Bartholomew is nearly executed as magical hats keep appearing when he is ordered to take off his hat to the king.

FREDERICK. Lionni, Leo. New York: Pantheon Books, 1966. In the summer, while other field mice gather food, Frederick gathers words and colors to share with his family in the winter.

FROG AND TOAD ARE FRIENDS. Lobel, Arnold. New York: Harper & Row, 1970. A collection of five amusing stories about a green frog and a brown toad.

GEORGE AND MARTHA. Marshall, James. Boston: Houghton Mifflin, 1972. Humorous and sensitive portrayal of what it means to get along with one another.

GUARD MOUSE, THE. Freeman, Don. New York: Viking Press, 1967. Story of Clyde, the guard mouse at Buckingham Palace.

HAPPY LION, THE. Fatio, Louise. New York: McGraw-Hill, 1954. The story of the friendly lion who escapes the zoo to return visits with the townspeople.

HAPPY OWLS, THE. Piatti, Celestino. New York: Atheneum, 1964. The quarreling barnyard folk ask the owls why they are so happy.

HAROLD AND THE PURPLE CRAYON. Johnson, Crockett. New York: Harper & Row, 1958. Harold uses a purple crayon in order to "draw" himself into and out of adventures.

HARRY THE DIRTY DOG. Zion, Gene. New York: Harper & Row, 1956. Harry buries the scrubbing brush and spends a glorious day getting dirty, but finds soap does have its uses after all.

IMPOSSIBLE POSSUM. Confor, Ellen. Boston: Little, Brown, 1971. Story of Randolph who, because of a lack of confidence, has difficulty sleeping by hanging from his tail.

INCH BY INCH. Lionni, Leo. Stamford: Astor-Honor, 1962. An inchworm saves himself from becoming dinner by proving his usefulness as a measurer.

KEEP YOUR MOUTH CLOSED, DEAR. Aliki. New York: Dial Press, 1966. Humorous account of a crocodile family that accidentally solves the problems of their son who swallows everything in sight.

LAZY BEAR, THE. Wildsmith, Brian. New York: Watts, Franklin, 1974. The lazy little bear learns to share work as well as fun.

LEO THE LATE BLOOMER. Kraus, Robert and Arvego, Jose. New York: Windmill Books, 1971. All the animals can read, write, draw, and eat neatly but Leo, the tiger cub.

LITTLE BEAR. Minarik, Else Holmelund. New York: Harper & Row, 1957. Easy text and interesting pictures tell of four events in the life of Little Bear.

LITTLE RABBIT'S LOOSE TOOTH. Bate, Lucy. New York: Crown, 1975. A story of what to do after losing a first tooth.

LITTLE TOOT, Gramatky, Hardie. New York: Putnam's, 1939. Little Toot, the tug boat, had no ambition until he became a hero during a storm.

LOVABLE LYLE. Waber, Bernard. Boston: Houghton Mifflin, 1969. Lyle, a crocodile who loves everyone, is confused when he receives hate notes.

LYLE, LYLE, CROCODILE. Waber, Bernard. Boston: Houghton Mifflin, 1965. Adventures of Lyle the pet crocodile.

MAY I BRING A FRIEND? De Regniers, Beatrice Schenk. New York: Atheneum, 1964. All kinds of animals appear when the King and Queen extend an invitation to "my friends."

MIKE MULLIGAN AND HIS STEAM SHOVEL. Burton, Virginia Lee. Boston: Houghton Mifflin, 1939. Mike and his red steam shovel dig all kinds of holes until one day they dig themselves into a cellar and can't get out.

MILLIONS OF CATS. Gag, Wanda. New York: Coward, McCann & Geohegan, 1938. Folklore quality story of a very old man who goes out to look for a cat and returns with millions.

MISTER RABBIT AND THE LOVELY PRESENT. Zolotow, Charlotte. New York: Harper & Row, 1962. A little girl meets Mr. Rabbit and asks him to help find a birthday gift for her mother.

MORRIS AND BORIS. Wiseman, Bernard. New York: Dodd, Mead, 1974. The hilarious stories of Boris the Bear and Morris the Moose.

MR. GUMPY'S OUTING. Burningham, John. New York: Holt, Rinehart & Winston, 1971. A beautifully illustrated story with a pastoral background.

MUSHROOM IN THE RAIN. Suteyev, A. New York: MacMillan, 1974. Huddling under a mushroom in the rain, first an ant, then others come crowding, always finding room for the newcomers.

NO ROSES FOR HARRY. Zion, Bene. New York: Harper & Row, 1958. Another Harry the dog story.

OH, WERE THEY EVER HAPPY! Spier, Peter. New York: Doubleday, 1978. While their parents are away, three children decide to paint their house.

PETUNIA. Duvoisin, Roger. New York: Knopf, 1950. Petunia, a silly goose, believes carrying a book can make her wise.

PITSCHI. Fischer, Hans, New York: Harcourt Brace Jovanovich, 1953. The story of a foolish kitten who always wants to be something else.

RAIN MAKES APPLESAUCE. Scheer, Julian. New York: Holiday House, 1964. Nonsense tale whose sequence does prove that rain does make applesauce.

ROSIE'S WALK. Hutchins, Pat. New York: MacMillan, 1968. Fine illustrations display the pursuit of an oblivious hen by an unfortunate fox.

SECRET HIDING PLACE, THE. Bennett, Rainey. Cleveland: World, 1960. A story of a little hippo who wanted to be alone, but not too alone.

SNAIL, WHERE ARE YOU? Ungerer, Tomi. New York:

Harper & Row, 1962. Children have fun finding the spiral pattern of the snail in this picture book.

STORY OF BABAR, THE LITTLE ELEPHANT, THE. De Brunhoff, Jean. New York: Random House, 1937. A favorite about the little elephant who ran away from the jungle to the city, and returned to be crowned King of the Elephants.

SURPRISE PARTY, THE. Hutchins, Pat. New York: Macmillan, 1969. Various animals misinterpret what they hear, making a surprise party almost a disaster.

SWIMMY. Lionel, Leo. New York: Pantheon Books, 1963. After Swimmy's companions have been swallowed by a hungry tuna, he explores the ocean's depths alone.

THEODORE TURTLE. MacGregor, Ellen. New York: McGraw-Hill, 1955. A funny picture book telling of the forgetful turtle who mislays his possessions.

THORNTON THE WORRIER. Sharmat, Marjorie, New York: Holiday House, 1978. Until he meets an elderly gentleman, Thornton Rabbit worries about everything.

TOPSY-TURVIES: PICTURES TO STRETCH THE IMAGI-NATION. Anno, Mitsumasa. New York: Weatherhill, 1970. A book filled with figures moving up, down, and around the pages.

VERONICA. Duvoisin, Roger. New York: Knopf, 1961. Veronica the hippopotamus, wanting to be famous, goes to the city.

WHERE THE WILD THINGS ARE. Sendak, Maurice. New York: Harper & Row, 1963. A small unruly boy sent to bed supperless dreams he sails to a land where the wild things are.

WINNIE-THE-POOH. Milne, A.A. New York: Dutton, 1961. The well-loved story of the funny little bear and his companions.

WHOSE MOUSE ARE YOU? Kraus, Robert. New York: Macmillan, 1970. A small mouse saves his family from peril only to find that he has an additional family member.

ZOO FOR MISTER MUSTER, A. Loberl, Arnold. New York: Harper & Row, 1962. An exciting adventure with an understanding and endearing character.